ENGLISH SYNTAX

A Grammar for English Language Professionals

ENGLISH SYNTAX

A Grammar for English Language Professionals

Roderick A. Jacobs
University of Hawai'i at Mānoa

Oxford University Press

Oxford University Press

200 Madison Avenue
New York, NY 10016

Great Clarendon Street
Oxford OX2 6DP England

OXFORD is a trademark of Oxford University Press.

Library of Congress Cataloging-in-Publication Data
Jacobs, Roderick A.
    English syntax: a grammar for English language professionals / Roderick A.
Jacobs.
      p. cm.
      Includes index
      ISBN 0-19-434277-8
      1. English language — Syntax — Outline, syllabi, etc.   2. English language —
Grammar — Outlines, syllabi, etc. I. Title.
      PE 1365.J33   1993   93-25121
      428.2 — dc20   CIP

ISBN 0-19-434277-8

Editors: Randee Falk, Amy Cooper
Associate Editor: Edward Mansour
Designer: M. Chandler Martylewski
Production Manager: Abram Hall

Cover Design by M. Chandler Martylewski

Diagrams by Stephan Van Litsenborg

Printing (last digit): 10 9 8 7 6 5 4 3 2

Printed in the United States.

CONTENTS

TO THE INSTRUCTOR

This is an ambitious book. It is presently the only text for English language professionals that incorporates the results of the most recent linguistic research. However, much of the work in both theoretical and applied linguistics is very hard to read and to adapt for teaching. I have worked to make the material accessible and practicable for the classroom.

The book has been tried out with classes under both the semester and quarter systems. The book's 25 chapters contain enough material for a semester class, but it is not necessary that all chapters be covered. For example, an instructor can use chapters 1–12, 16–20, and 25, which together provide a solid account of the major constructions in English. A mixed class of undergraduates and graduates comfortably completed these 18 chapters in a quarter; a lower-level undergraduate course completed them in a semester, with time to spare for group discussion of pedagogy. A class of undergraduates and graduates under the semester system completed those chapters and chapters 13–15, which deal with information structure. In short, the book is flexible enough to be used in a range of courses.

Because some instructors find constituent structure trees useful for the development of an understanding of sentence structure and meaning, I have included numerous illustrations of them and exercises asking students to produce them. However, a high level of skill in this area may not be necessary for all students and courses. Where this is the case, have the students work actively with constituent structure trees up through Chapter 7, and subsequently require only a passive understanding of the illustrative trees in each chapter, omitting the tree exercises. Since an answer key has been provided, instructors can use the trees in it for further illustration. This strategy provides more time for instructors wanting to explore other topics or to cover additional chapters.

Each chapter ends in a summary. Several instructors who field-tested the book found these summaries were helpful not only to students but also as an aid in planning their classes. I would welcome any further suggestions for making this more useful to students and instructors.

PREFACE

This is a sentence-grammar of English. Its intended readers are language professionals needing to understand the major principles underlying English sentence structure. Such an understanding helps English language teachers to sequence language material for presentation and evaluate the language development of their students. It helps speech therapists determine more accurately grammatical differences characterizing the language of aphasics and others suffering from language disorders. The literary critic should be able to pinpoint more precisely the syntactic features of an author's prose style. Researchers investigating the replication of natural language by computers benefit from a more detailed knowledge of how sentences are constructed in English.

This grammar describes the basic units and processes of sentence formation in English. Although its author happens to be British, this is *not* a grammar devoted to British English. Nor is it restricted to American English. I have drawn upon the linguistic intuitions of speakers of most of the major geographical dialects of English. As I note in the first chapter, despite the existence of grammatical differences among the major dialects of English, they share a significant core of grammatical units and relations, a core which enables us to speak of a single language English and which constitutes the subject matter of this English grammar. An important goal of this grammar is to explain, wherever possible and practical, how sentences that native speakers accept as grammatical for English differ from those they reject as ungrammatical, whether the English is American, Australian, British, Canadian, New Zealand, or South African. This is not to say that speakers of these varieties of English can accurately describe for us the units, processes, or principles they employ. But the sentences they produce and understand conform quite closely to the kinds of principles and processes described in this grammar.

For example, English speakers make frequent use of verb sequences such as these:

might have been talking
is being painted

These sequences consist of one or more auxiliary verbs followed by a main verb expressing a core notion. The auxiliary verbs in each sequence are lined up in a particular order. Other orderings, although logically possible, are unacceptable. Thus the first sequence could not be reordered this way:

*have talking been might

Few English-speakers could explain what the ordering principles are that underlie the grammatical versions; yet speakers must have *internalized* such principles early in their acquisition of English. Particular auxiliaries can be omitted from a sequence, but the relative order always remains the same.

This grammar provides the kind of information any English language professional must start with. Books that go further tend to be rather technical linguistic discussions.[1] The present book starts on a more general, basic level, and should help readers wanting to pursue their study further to follow the grammatical dimensions of the more specialized works. There is one feature of this book that requires mention here. The exercise set at the end of each chapter typically includes one or two questions with an applied focus. These questions deal with topics such as first and second language acquisition, classroom matters, computers, and language.

Obviously, English language professionals will benefit from an understanding of

English grammar. But what about students developing English language skills? Do they need to study English grammar? Perhaps, but language professionals themselves, supported by a considerable body of experimental work, are at odds over whether the study of grammatical rules is an efficient and effective way to develop the English language capabilities of either native or non-native students. It is clear both that students vary considerably in learning styles and that traditional rote-learning approaches to grammar are seriously defective.[2] Still, the systematic study of the major constructions of English should make students, whether native or non-native speakers, aware of the range of grammatical options available to them and of the special syntactic and semantic characteristics of the rich resources of the language.

Underlying all the specific claims for the value of the study of English syntax is a more basic assumption: There is intrinsic value in the study of the workings of language as revealed in particular languages. The properties of language must reflect basic properties of human perception and intelligence. Otherwise, how could infants acquire their native language so rapidly and efficiently, uttering and understanding not only the strings of words they've already encountered but also infinite numbers of new well-formed combinations? Chimpanzees, even when extensively and systematically exposed to language, have no such competence.

Language acquisition results from the interaction of two key factors: the innate biological structure with which humans are endowed, and human life experience, including exposure to language. The amount of language exposure we undergo in our first five or six years of life is very small in proportion to the richness and flexibility of the language systems we master during those years. Learning about language is a way of learning about ourselves.

NOTES

1. ESL/EFL teachers and materials writers may find helpful the papers in A. Urquhart and J. C. Alderson, eds., *Linguistic Competence of Practised and Unpractised Non-native Readers of English* (London: Longman, 1985). For what is still the best study of scientific English, see Rodney M. Huddleston, *The Sentence in Written English: A Syntactic Study Based on an Analysis of Scientific English* (Cambridge: Cambridge University Press, 1971).

2. For an insightful discussion of these issues for second language teaching, see Michael Canale and Merrill Swain, "Theoretical bases of communicative approaches to second language teaching and testing," *Applied Linguistics* 1 (Spring 1980): 1–47, and P. Dickins and E. Woods, "Some criteria for the development of communicative grammar tasks," *TESOL Quarterly* 22 (1988): 623–46. For mother-tongue instruction, see Janice Neuleib and Irene Brosnahan, "Teaching Grammar to Writers," *Journal of Basic Writing* 6 (Spring 1987): 28–35; this is a very useful article with an excellent bibliography.

A NOTE ON THEORY

A word about the theoretical assumptions drawn on in this book. This is not a textbook on syntactic theory, but it does draw on major insights from more recent developments in linguistic theory, most notably the considerable body of research that has followed Noam Chomsky's seminal work, *Lectures on Government and Binding* (1981). The Case Theory developed in this framework turns out to be very useful as a pedagogical tool for explaining the distribution of noun phrases and complements. I have tried to provide the necessary background in the text and have simplified or omitted some dimensions, most notably the interdependence of Case Theory and thematic role assignment. A second core component of this framework, X-bar grammar, is an important and interesting attempt to account for the parallel behavior of major categories across languages. Researchers in second-language acquisition as well as such typologists as Hawkins have been testing and applying X-bar concepts.[1]

It is important to note, however, that this book is not an attempt to demonstrate the validity of this framework, referred to either as the Principles-and-Parameters approach or as the Government-and-Binding framework, by applying it to English syntax. Though it has provided important and useful insights into English syntax, it is far from ideal. When the details of the Principles-and-Parameters approach are examined from a theoretical perspective, it appears clumsy and uneconomical. As a way of pairing forms with meanings, it is unnecessarily complex and powerful. Processes such as *wh* movement and constraints having to do with pronominal and anaphoric binding, case, and thematic role assignment apply at the levels of D-structure and S-structure. But they look too much like other processes and constraints needed for the level of Logical Form, processes and constraints like Quantifier Raising and the major binding constraints. At Logical Form, these are especially important for languages like Chinese, Japanese, and Korean, which lack any syntactic counterpart to *wh* movement. Case Theory makes an awkward distinction between nominative case assignment for finite clause subjects and accusative case assignment elsewhere. If the specifier-head relation central to X-bar grammar is exploited more consistently, it may be possible to unify these two kinds of case assignment. A simpler model is needed, one which requires fewer levels. Chomsky and others are presently working on such a model, an effort that will go well into the second half of this decade.[2]

The theoretical simplicity achieved by generalizing over previously distinct domains, however, comes at the cost of much greater abstractness. Since this book is aimed directly at a fairly concrete account of English syntax, the levels presented in the Principles-and-Parameters approach and the more concrete kind of generalizations achieved appear far more useful. Analysis of D-structure forces us to explore more thoroughly the semantic relations less obviously manifested at S-structure. The simplified version of Binding Theory presented herein provides an understanding of the major processes and constraints that English language professionals should be aware of. The more abstract theoretical framework now under development will certainly employ versions of the binding constraints later discussed.

The Principles-and-Parameters approach and its still very programmatic successor were not the only frameworks considered. I have adapted material from the Generalized Phrase Structure approach of Gazdar, Klein, Pullum, and Sag and the Lexical-Functional Grammar of Bresnan and Kaplan.[3] Forthcoming works by Peter Fries and others within the Hallidayan functional grammar tradition deal in some depth with English from a fresh and insightful perspective.

I have also drawn from the typologically oriented research of Comrie, Greenberg, Hawkins, Keenan, Thompson, and many others,[4] who have provided important insights into what is involved for the learner in the acquisition of English as a second or foreign language.

The approach of this grammar, then, might better be thought of as *compatible with* current frameworks, but without their technical apparatus and with as little as seemed reasonable of their terminology. Indeed, I have redefined certain terms in an effort to present the major features of English grammar as clearly as possible.

NOTES

1. For example, J. Hawkins, *Word Order Universals* (New York: Academic Press, 1983) and Suzanne Flynn and I. Espinal, "Head-initial/head-final parameter in adult Chinese L2 acquisition of English," *Second Language Research* 1 (1985): 93–117. A brief introduction to this component is presented in Appendix D of the journal.

2. It may turn out to be theoretically more elegant and economical to assign many functions now assigned to D-structure and S-structure, such as, for example, thematic role assignment and the verification of case assignment, to some other level, perhaps the semantic level known as Logical Form. For an important but highly technical discussion, see N. Chomsky, "A Minimalist Program for Linguistic Theory," *M.I.T. Working Papers in Linguistics:* Monograph 1 (1992).

3. For a useful introduction to Chomsky's Principles-and-Parameters approach, see "Government-Binding Theory," in Peter Sells, *Lectures on Contemporary Syntactic Theories* (Stanford, CA: Center for the Study of Language and Information, 1985). The chapters on the rival theories are equally useful. Another more current account is provided in R. Freidin, *Foundations of Generative Syntax* (Cambridge, MA: M.I.T. Press, 1992).

4. For an extremely useful compilation of typological research, see Timothy Shopen, ed., *Language Typology and Syntactic Description*, vols. 1–3 (Cambridge, UK: Cambridge University Press, 1985).

ACKNOWLEDGMENTS

This book was intended to be readable for nonlinguists. For help on this, as well as on content, I thank the following:

Stephanie Amedeo, Robert Bley-Vroman, Jeff Carroll, Iovanna Condax, Jeanne Gibson, Lena Jacobs, Suzanne Jacobs, Marilyn Kim, Edith Moravcsik, Judy Van Zile, Roger Whitlock, and, especially, my editor, Randee Falk.

I am also grateful to the many students in both my ESL and linguistics syntax courses who helped shape this book. I owe much to Peter Rosenbaum, the then fellow student, who in the mid nineteen-sixties wrote with me *English Transformational Grammar*, a product of the intoxicating early days of generative-transformational grammar.

Although the thrust of this book is not a theoretical one, the influence of my first teacher of linguistics, Noam Chomsky, should be apparent.

SOME BASIC NOTIONS

1

Grammar and Types of Grammars

For most aspects of their work, English teachers need firmly based knowledge of the ways English sentences are organized to construct meaning. This grammar seeks to provide for such knowledge.

English consists of many dialects, each of which has its own special features; but the major principles of sentence organization described in this grammar are shared by most, if not all, dialects.

Obviously, some background in English phonetics and phonology is necessary also, and many other kinds of knowledge are important because sentences do not occur in a vacuum. Units of language larger than sentences are studied in *discourse analysis*, while the ways our real world knowledge and beliefs affect language use and structure are explored in the discipline known as *pragmatics*. References to these other fields occur in some chapters, but this book deals primarily with English grammar.

Even here, some further clarification is needed, because the term *grammar* is used in a number of sometimes confusing ways. For example, in the sentence:

It's not good grammar to say "ain't."

the term is used to criticize the language behavior of speakers of less prestigious dialects of English. The kind of grammatical study we are interested in is quite different. It will be defined here in terms of its goals and its major components.

LANGUAGE ANALYSIS

Grammarians examine a language to find out what kinds of language units speakers are organizing into utterances; they try to work out how the units are combined or structured, and how these units and their combinations correspond to the content—the basic meaning—of the utterances. The units may be combinations of words or they may be properties of specific words of the lexicon (or vocabulary) of the language.

Grammarians consider the relations of the different kinds of units to each other and seek to determine the general grammatical principles that govern the structures and processes of the language, that enable language to be produced and understood.

Grammar thus deals with language forms and meanings and the ways they are inter-connected.

Three major components of grammar are considered in this book:

1. Syntax: the grammatical principles, units, and relations involved in sentence structure

2. Lexicon: the set of individual words, suffixes, and prefixes

3. Semantics: the meanings associated with the lexicon of a language and with the units and relations in sentence structures.

These three components necessarily interact. The grammatical principles determine the kinds of units the language can have, the orders in which these units can be arranged, and the kinds of relations (or functions) they participate in. From the lexicon come the actual words, suffixes, and prefixes that fit into the slots provided by the syntax, while the semantic component determines the range of interpretations associated with each lexically filled syntactic structure. Other components affect the workings of language, most notably pragmatics. Nevertheless, the grammatical properties of English sentences can profitably (though not comprehensively) be studied without a detailed study of pragmatics, important as context is to language comprehension. The situation is different for languages like Japanese, Korean, and Chinese, in which situational factors have more direct effects on the grammar.

ENGLISH

Can we really say there is a single, uniform language, English, rather than a cluster of languages, each with its own special properties? If uniformity is the criterion, the answer is no. Factors like age, sex, social status, regional origin, and the context of the utterance influence grammatical forms, vocabulary, and pronunciation.[1] So to hear a cloth-weaver from the north of Scotland, a country lawyer from Alabama, and a sheep rancher from Australia, can cause a non-native speaker of English to wonder about any so-called uniformity of English.

However, English speakers, whatever their age, regional origin, and so forth, display very consistent intuitions about sentence grammar. Their intuitions regarding which word combinations are well formed for English are generally consistent. An utterance like this one:

She is liking very much of her staying in this country.

would be identified by any English speaker as a non-native utterance. Though there may be some grammatical differences among dialects of English, they share a significant central core of grammatical units and relations, which enables us to speak of a single language English and which constitutes the subject matter of this English grammar.

KINDS OF GRAMMARS

The term *grammar* is used in a number of different senses. Here it is of interest to distinguish three senses, or three kinds of grammars.

Grammar is used to refer to the rules and principles native speakers use in producing and understanding their language. These rules and principles are almost all acquired in childhood and are "in the heads" of native speakers. Such a grammar might be called a *mental grammar*. No one knows the precise form a mental grammar takes because it cannot be directly observed. What can be observed is the *output* of a mental grammar—the utterances that speakers use and recognize as sentences of their language.

The term *grammar* is also used to refer to the set of generalizations (and exceptions to them) formulated by grammarians, who examine grammatical utterances, perhaps compare them with other logically possible strings of words, and then try to determine the properties that differentiate the well-formed strings of words (or sentences) from those that speakers reject as ill formed. This kind of account of the language is referred to as a *descriptive grammar*. Descriptive grammars are attempts by grammarians to provide visible analogs to the invisible mental grammars of native speakers.

In a third sense, the term *grammar* refers to certain kinds of language rules not necessarily based on usage by the ordinary native speaker but on the kind of English believed characteristic of the most educated speakers of the language. Sometimes these rules have less to do with English usage than with the grammar of Latin, notions of logic, or even irrational feelings as to how we should speak and write. This kind of grammar is known as *prescriptive grammar*, because the grammarian is attempting to *prescribe* certain ways of speaking and writing. Prescriptive grammars have their uses, especially in education, where they are often referred to as school grammars. School grammars, if based on accurate observation of contemporary educated usage, can be helpful in guiding writers toward clearer expression. Textbooks for non-native speakers and grammars for computers processing a particular human language require a prescriptive approach. They are really telling us what the learners or computers ought to say if they are to use English as a well-educated native speaker would.

But this prescriptive approach to grammar can be abused by those who seek to impose outdated conventions or what the prescriber thinks a form ought to mean rather than the meaning understood in general usage.

How might a prescriptive grammarian set about imposing a convention? Suppose he or she, perhaps biased by Latin grammar, disapproves of the use of *me* in this sentence:

> *It's me!*

preferring instead this version:

> *It is I!*

The grammarian might formalize this preference—and this notion of what "good" English should be—as a grammatical rule such as the following, which excludes the *me* sentence and similar forms:

> When personal pronouns occur after forms of the copula verb *be*, the nominative forms *I, he, she, we, they* should be used instead of the objective forms *me, him, her, us, them.*

Our second example of a prescriptive rule is one in which a grammarian prescribes what she thinks a form ought to mean rather than the meaning understood in general usage. This example comes from a grammar text addressed to native speakers of English. The author, discussing this sentence:

> *I'm going to try to help the victim.*

makes the following comment:

> A variation that is common in colloquial English substitutes *and* for *to*, the sign of the infinitive: I'm going to try *and* help the victim. In this case *and* is simply inaccurate; the usage is inappropriate in Standard Written English.[2]

The author has in mind some semantic distinction between *to* and *and* constructions that doesn't really apply to this idiom with *try*. The rule itself, but not the explanation, does in fact capture one minor characteristic of a formal dialect of *written* English. Note that both this prescriptive rule and the one requiring *It is I* go against current spoken usage by educated speakers of English.

The prescriptive approach can be seriously abused when the rules are based on the spoken English of the privileged and powerful. Those who speak dialects of English more common among minorities or the poor are too often not hired if they have not also acquired a prestige dialect. The problems, as we have seen, are not *inherent* in prescriptive grammar, but arise rather from its abuse.

Since prescriptive grammars are really grammars for learning and teaching some version of a language, they serve *pedagogical* or teaching function, and are often referred to by grammarians as *pedagogical grammars*. The better grammars of this type provide an understanding of English language principles and processes and are based on research in the descriptive, scientific tradition; but, for good pedagogical reasons, they do not offer comprehensive coverage of the grammar of the language. Furthermore, because such a grammar has to be selective and easily understood, its generalizations are often "tidied up" and abbreviated.

GRAMMAR, MEANING, AND PRAGMATICS

Speakers of a language associate meanings with its forms. The core meaning of a sentence is usually referred to as the *propositional content,* which is the most literal meaning dimension of language. It depends crucially on the interaction of the three components discussed earlier: syntax, the lexicon, and semantics. But meaning has other dimensions, too. This is where we briefly take up the function of the fourth component, pragmatics.

What do you notice about the reference of *he* in the following pair of sentences? Who does the *he* stand for?

The inspector refused the arrested man's request because he had suspected an escape attempt.

The inspector refused the arrested man's request because he had made an escape attempt.

In the first sentence, *he* almost certainly refers to the inspector, while in the second sentence, *he* equally obviously refers to the arrested man. Yet the two sentences are structurally identical. Our judgments as to the reference of *he* are based not on grammatical knowledge but on pragmatic knowledge, in this case, knowledge of police arrest situations.

Here is another example. Consider the following sentence spoken to a worker by his supervisor:

Your desk is a mess.

The speaker attributes a certain property to the worker's desk. This is the propositional content of the sentence. But the sentence almost certainly communicates much more. In the context of a business office and a supervisor-worker relationship, the sentence probably communicates the message that the worker should clean up the desk. Context, which is not part of the propositional content, may radically modify what is being communicated.

Speakers use their nonlinguistic knowledge to make inferences. The propositional content of the following response to a dinner invitation consists of an expression signifying regret and a claim concerning the activity schedule of the persons referred to as *we:*

Sorry, we're busy all week.

Yet the person being addressed might infer from this utterance the speaker's unwillingness to be friends with him or her. Of course, this interpretation is speculative, since too little context has been provided. Single sentence examples rarely provide enough evidence. But note that the additional evidence needed is not grammatical evidence; the interpretation depends on situational, rather than grammatical, factors. This kind of study is part of pragmatics rather than grammar.[3]

Important as situational factors are, they are not core subject matter of grammatical study in the way that the propositional content of sentences is. As indicated already, propositional content, the core semantics of a sentence, arises fairly directly from the syntactic and lexical features of the sentence. In the next chapter, we consider the nature of this connection between syntax and the lexicon on one hand and semantics on the other. We'll be discussing the kinds of grammatical forms and relations needed to account for propositional content.

SUMMARY

English teachers and other language professionals need to be familiar with the grammar of English, grammar being understood as the analysis of the properties characterizing well-formed sentences of the language. The three crucial components of this grammar are syntax, the lexicon, and semantics. Other factors such as pragmatic knowledge influence language structure, but for English it is useful to start by considering sentence structure and meaning independently of situations in which the sentences might be uttered. The propositional content of a sentence is the core meaning that it has independent of context. The major principles and properties noted are shared by the family of dialects we refer to as English.

EXERCISE SET I

1. State whether each of the following rules is prescriptive and/or descriptive.
   a. The single-word form *maybe* is an adverb meaning "perhaps." The two-word combination *may be* consists of an auxiliary verb followed by the copula verb, *be*.
   b. The possessive forms for *everyone* are *his* and *her*. So do not say, "Everyone brought *their* own lunch," but rather "Everyone brought *his* (or *her*) lunch."
   c. The infinitive form of a verb is always uninflected. It should follow immediately after the infinitive marker *to*. No word should intervene between *to* and its verb. So this sentence:

   The Fourth Armored Division tried to totally destroy the hideout.

   should really be:

   The Fourth Armored Division tried to destroy the hideout totally.

   d. Present tense verbs with a third-person singular subject take the suffix *-s*; e.g., *Fred understands*.

2. It is said that native speakers of a language *know* the rules of their language. How is this kind of knowing different from the knowing needed to pass the written part of a driver's license test?

3. Read the dialogue below and answer the questions.

a. What generalizations about grammar does the child appear to have worked out?
b. What is the adult trying to do, and how effective is it? What does this dialogue suggest to you about first language acquisition?

Child: *My teacher holded the baby rabbits and we petted them.*
Adult: *Did you say your teacher held the baby rabbits?*
Child: *Yes.*
Adult: *What did you say she did?*
Child: *She holded the rabbits and we petted them.*
Adult: *Did you say she held them tightly?*
Child: *No, she holded them loosely.*[4]

4. How, in your opinion, should English *grammar* instruction for students planning to study literature in English in their own country differ from instruction for students who will later be working in their own country for an Australian company selling computers?

NOTES

1. For example, take regional differences. Most dialects of American English do not require the definite article before *church* and *school* in sentences such as, *She's in church now.* However, they do require the article with *hospital: She's in the hospital now.* Most speakers of British, Australian, and New Zealand English (can) omit the article: *She's in hospital now.*

2. Martha Kolln, *Understanding English Grammar*, 2nd. ed. (New York: Macmillan, 1986), 343.

3. A useful introduction to such matters is G. Brown and G. Yule, *Discourse Analysis* (Cambridge: Cambridge University Press, 1983).

4. The dialogue is from Courtney Cazden, *Child Language and Education* (New York: Holt, Rinehart and Winston, 1972).

2

Propositional Content

Learners of English have to know what English utterances *mean*. Although the social context of any speech situation may radically influence the interpretation of a sentence, the sentence nevertheless has a propositional content or meaning independent of context. Thus, while the following sentence:

Those plums look good.

may have one interpretation when spoken by a child looking longingly at a bowl of fruit and another when spoken by a produce manager buying fruit for a store, its propositional content is always the same. The propositional content of a sentence is that sentence's core meaning.

VERBS AND MEANING

For most English sentences a crucial part of the meaning resides in the verb; the concept expressed by the verb is typically the heart of the propositional content of a sentence.

Semantics, the study of meaning, includes both the study of the meaning contained within a single word (*word-internal* semantics) and the study of the meaning relationships that a word or phrase has with other parts of a sentence (*external* semantics). Let's consider word-internal semantics first.

Not all verbs express simple meanings. The verb *die* seems relatively simple, meaning something like BECOME NO LONGER ALIVE. Clearly the meaning of *die* is simpler than that of *kill*, which not only includes the notion BECOME NO LONGER ALIVE but also specifies an event requiring an additional participant, someone or something that brings about the death; in other words, *kill* means something like CAUSE TO BECOME NO LONGER ALIVE.

But *killing* need not involve any violation of law. A soldier may kill in an appropriate military situation. The verb *murder*, however, adds a dimension of criminality; that is, it means something like CRIMINALLY CAUSE TO BECOME NO LONGER ALIVE.

We go one stage further with the verb *assassinate*, which is semantically even more complex. In addition to including the complex notion CRIMINALLY CAUSE TO BECOME NO LONGER ALIVE, it further imposes two requirements: that the victim be someone politically prominent, and that the assassin's motive be a political one; its meaning is something like CRIMINALLY CAUSE POLITICALLY PROMINENT INDI-VIDUAL(S) TO BECOME NO LONGER ALIVE. A great deal of meaning is packaged up in that one verb. This explains the oddness of a sentence like the following:

A thief assassinated a dental technician last night.

The sentence is odd because the role of dental technician is not normally viewed as a politically prominent one.

This kind of word-internal semantic analysis is an important part of the study known as *lexical semantics*. However, just as important as word-internal semantics are the external semantic relationships of a verb with other parts of its sentence.

If the verb is seen as the semantic core or nucleus of a sentence, then the other parts can be viewed as participants in the situation represented. Some of the participants may be *required,* others are *optional.* If you know the meaning of a verb, you also know its required participants. For example, you know that *die* requires only one participant, the one that dies, and that *kill* requires two participants, a killer and a victim. Verbs express a relationship between the entities that the required participants stand for. In this sentence:

The Philistines feared Samson.

the verb *feared* expresses a relation between Philistines, the people who experience the emotion, and Samson, the person who arouses it.

The most common kinds of participants that verbs require are forms like *the trees, they, a bushy-tailed fox* , which consist of either a noun (*fox*), often accompanied by articles (*a, the*), adjectives (*bushy-tailed*), and other forms, or a pronoun (*they*). Such participants are known as *noun phrases* since their most characteristic form includes a *noun* as the *head word.* (We will see later in this chapter that participants are not always expressed as noun phrases.)

We can usefully define the head word (or just *head*) of a phrase as the word in the phrase that determines how the phrase can be used. Single nouns (or pronouns) can often function alone as subjects and objects; articles, on the other hand, cannot. Hereafter, we will be using the term *noun phrase* even when the participant is expressed as just a single word. This is because single-word noun phrases and multi-word noun phrases function linguistically in the same way within a sentence.

Verbs differ as to the number of noun phrases they require. In the following example with the verb *die,* there is just one obligatory noun phrase:

The cockroaches died.

As noted earlier, the verb *kill* requires two noun phrases:

The gas killed the cockroaches.

while *give* requires three noun phrases:

The inspector gave the man his sunglasses.

No verb requires more than three noun phrases. Some require one, some require two, and some require three. The number of noun phrases that a verb requires is known as its *valency.*

It is, of course, possible for a verb to occur without a noun phrase, even though its normal valency might be one or two noun phrases. This happens in *imperative sentences* like the following:

Scram!

However, for the sentence to have any meaning, a participant, the one told to scram, is necessarily understood to be involved in the action. Except for such imperative sentences, some question forms, and abbreviated constructions in special contexts, English sentences require at least one noun phrase, its subject, and this subject precedes the verb. Any other required noun phrases, of course, follow the verb, as shown in our example about the inspector—*The inspector lent the man his sunglasses.*

REQUIRED NOUN PHRASES AND VERB MEANING

There is a clear connection between the number of noun phrases that a verb requires and the sense of the verb. Think again about the concepts expressed by the verbs *die*, *kill*, and *give*. *Dying* is a process requiring only one participant. *Killing* involves at least two participants. There must be someone or something that kills and something that dies. *Giving* involves three participants—a giver, a receiver, and the gift itself.

This way of thinking about meaning is based on an approach common in the study of logic. The verb and its noun phrases constitute not only a syntactic unit but a semantic unit, one referred to as a *proposition*. A proposition is not the semantic equivalent of a sentence, because a sentence may express more than one proposition. The grammatical unit closest to the proposition is probably that of the *clause*, which we'll define for the time being as the grammatical combination of the verb, its required noun phrases, and any optional phrases. The core meaning of the clause is the content of the proposition it expresses, that is, its *propositional content.*

When we are analyzing the *propositional content* rather than the *form* of a clause, we can adapt from logic a useful convention of semantic representation. The *concept* represented by the verb is shown in uppercase letters—for example, DIE, KILL, SEE, WALK—while lowercase symbols—*x, y, z*—stand for each noun phrase that must occur with the verb. So, since *die* and *walk* require only one noun phrase as participant, the concepts they express can be shown this way:

x DIE

where *x* might be the noun phrase *the dog* in this sentence

The dog died.

and

x WALK

where *x* might be the noun phrase *that teddy bear*, as in this next sentence:

That teddy bear walks.

The two-participant relations expressed by *kill* and *meet* could be shown this way:

x KILL y

as in this example:

A renegade soldier (x) killed the dog (y).

and this way:

x MEET y

as in

> The ambassador (x) met King Faisal (y) last week.

The relations expressed by *award* require three noun phrases:

> x AWARD y, z

as in this sentence:

> The inspector (x) awarded the restaurant (y) a gold medal (z).

The same is true for *give:*

> x GIVE y, z

as in

> That kind of behavior (x) gives our school (y) a bad reputation (z).

PREDICATES

We have so far been treating verbs as the nucleus of any clause and have taken verbs and noun phrases to be the grammatical units basic to propositional content. The notation used had the verb concepts in upper case (e.g., SEE) and showed each required noun phrase slot as a lowercase symbol (*x, y, z*). But the assumption that verbs and noun phrases are the only such basic units is justified. To understand why, consider two semantically crucial properties of verbs, properties that characterize the verb as the nucleus of its clause.

The first property is valency—verbs differ in the number of noun phrases they require. The second property of verbs—or more precisely of the concepts they represent—is that they place certain restrictions on the noun phrases that must occur with them. The verb *quarrel,* for instance, requires that its subject refer to a mind-possessing creature. So *the cupboard* would be ruled out as a subject for *quarrel:*

> *The cupboard always quarreled.

The asterisk in this last example shows that the sentence is not a well-formed one. (We will continue to mark such sentences with asterisks.) The sentence could sound right only in a fairy tale. Except in fantasies, cupboards are not capable of quarreling. Human beings, of course, are quite capable of quarreling. They can fill the role of quarreler:

> The brothers always quarreled.

The verbs *enjoy* and *please* place very different requirements on their subjects and objects. In its most common usage, *enjoy* has to have as its subject a noun phrase designating human beings or other creatures capable of experiencing enjoyment. It is all right to say this:

> The critics enjoyed the show.

but not this:

> *The turnips enjoyed the show.

The semantic role of the subject noun phrase of *enjoyed* is the role called *experiencer.* We could not determine this role only from looking at the subject. It is the verb that assigns the subject its semantic role. But, unlike the subject, the object of *enjoy* need not be an entity capable of experiencing joy. It could be *the show, apples,* or even a phrase like *peeling potatoes.* The verb assigns a more general role to its object, that of *theme,* a role discussed later in this chapter.

However, if we substitute *pleased* for *enjoyed* in one example just cited:

*The critics **pleased** the show.*

the sentence fails to make sense since, although *please* also requires an experiencer, it requires the experiencer to be the object rather than the subject. Even verbs with very similar meanings can thus differ as to the roles they assign noun phrases and the specific slots in which the noun phrases must occur.

This property of verbs, the assignment of specific semantic roles to the right kinds of noun phrase, will be called *role assignment.* Verbs *assign* particular semantic *roles* to their noun phrases. If the subject has to stand for a "doer," then the noun phrase *the brothers* could fill it, but not *the cupboard.* Of course, additional noun phrases can also appear with *quarreled:*

The brothers always quarreled with Trudy about the car.

Although *Trudy* and *the car* are noun phrases, their occurrence is not required by the verb. They are optional noun phrases. Those noun phrases actually required by the verb are called *arguments* of that verb. So the valency of a verb is the number of arguments that it requires.

We've noted that *valency* and *role assignment* characterize the verb as the nucleus of its clause. But do only *verbs* possess these properties?

Compare this next sentence with the earlier example:

The brothers were always quarrelsome.

Clearly the word *quarrelsome* is an adjective, not a verb. Like other adjectives, it does not take past tense inflection (*quarrelsomed*) nor can it take the *-ing* suffix (*quarrelsoming*). Note, however, that it is like the verb *quarrel* in two significant respects: it requires just one argument, and it assigns exactly the same semantic role to the subject as did the verb in the previous example—the subject noun phrase must refer to mind-possessing creatures capable of quarreling. Quarreling is an action and thus must involve someone to carry out the action, a role referred to as the *agent* role. There is, of course, a verb preceding *quarrelsome* in this sentence, *was.* But this verb is obviously not the core semantic relation in the sentence; little meaning is associated with the word *was.* Its main function is to carry the past tense marking, since *quarrelsome,* an adjective, cannot do this. The major propositional content of *was quarrelsome* is carried by the adjective *quarrelsome.*

Our conclusion? The close semantic parallels between the sentence with *quarreled* and the sentence with *quarrelsome* demonstrate that this adjective plays the same kind of nucleus role as the verb *quarrel* did in its clause. So it is clear that both verbs and adjectives can express the major propositional relation in a clause.

Two other categories can also be used to express this relation. In the following sentence about the brothers, the noun phrase *big quarrelers* occurs instead of the verb *quarrel:*

The brothers were always big quarrelers.

Notice that this noun phrase imposes the same requirements as do the verb *quarreled* and the adjective *quarrelsome.* It too is the semantic nucleus of its clause, and it also assigns a semantic role, that is, it requires the subject of its clause to refer to a mind-possessor. In short, valency and role assignment properties cannot be said to arise from membership in the grammatical category *verb*. The adjective *quarrelsome* and the noun phrase *big quarrelers* also have these properties and are thus the semantic nuclei of their clauses. In fact our analysis could be extended to prepositional phrases like *in a quarrelsome mood*.

These special properties shared by verbs, adjectives, noun phrases, and prepositional phrases actually arise from their semantic relation to the rest of their clause, a relation known as the *predicate* relation. Unfortunately, the term *predicate* is also used for the grammatical unit made up of the verb plus other constituents following it. To avoid confusion without departing too far from conventional usage, we will be calling this grammatical unit the *predicate phrase*. For us, then, a predicate is a semantic concept, a property specified (or *predicated*) of some entity or entities. Thus the predicate in the sentence, *The brothers were always big quarrelers,* is *big quarrelers.* The need for a special term like *predicate* arises from the fact that there are semantic units which do not correspond on a one-to-one basis to grammatical categories. Forms functioning as predicates need not be verbs.

ARGUMENTS

Now that we have seen that the core predicate of a proposition can be expressed as a verb, adjective, noun phrase, or prepositional phrase, it is time to see whether the forms referred to as *arguments* in the proposition must be noun phrases. Just as the predicate of a proposition need not be a verb, so an argument need not be expressed as a noun phrase. Clauses can serve as arguments.

The argument positions (the *x, y,* and *z* slots) in a proposition are sometimes filled by clauses instead of noun phrases. We'll define a clause more precisely here as a construction that:

1. contains a verb that is (a) in the past or present tense, or (b) follows a modal verb like *will* or *may,* or (c) is an infinitive introduced by *to,* e.g., *to dance.*

2. contains the required units functioning as arguments and any optional phrases.[1]

The predicate SHOW, for example, is associated with three argument slots:

x SHOW y, z

These slots can be filled by three noun phrases:

Her friends (x) **showed** *the inspector (y) her letters (z).*

Let's list the correspondences between the semantic units and the grammatical forms this way:

PRED: showed
ARG X: her friends
ARG Y: the inspector
ARG Z: her letters

But note now that two of the argument slots could be filled with clauses instead of noun phrases. We'll replace the noun phrase *her friends* with the clause *for her to arrive late again* and replace *her letters* with the clause *that she was unreliable:*

For her to arrive late again *(x) showed the inspector (y)* **that she was unreliable** *(z).*

The subject in this example is not the noun phrase *her friends* but the clause *for her to arrive late again*. Moreover, the object noun phrase *her letters* has been replaced by the clause *that she was unreliable*. Let's list the parts of this second sentence:

PRED: showed
ARG X: for her to arrive late again
ARG Y: the inspector
ARG Z: that she was unreliable

The arguments of predicates thus need not belong to the category noun phrase. Both clauses and noun phrases can be arguments.

A proposition, then, must have a predicate and one or more arguments. We've seen that some predicates have just one required argument slot (e.g., x DIE), others have two (e.g., x KISS y), and yet others have three (e.g., x TELL y z). Propositions are the semantic counterparts of clauses. Presumably, when a speaker utters a series of clauses, hearers who have understood the clauses have matched them up with the appropriate propositions; they have identified which arguments go with which predicates.

ARGUMENT ROLES AND GRAMMATICAL RELATIONS

Think about the meaning of these next two sentences:

The Duke of Wellington attacked Napoleon Bonaparte.
Napoleon Bonaparte attacked the Duke of Wellington.

We know that the predicate *attack* requires two arguments, one standing for the attacker, the other for whatever is attacked:

x ATTACK y

In the example sentences, the arguments *the Duke of Wellington* and *Napoleon Bonaparte* are both noun phrases referring to specific people. Each fills a position required by the verb. But it is not enough to understand a sentence as referring to an action of attacking involving two participants, the Duke and Napoleon. If the sentence is well formed, it should also be clear who attacked whom. We'll consider notions like attacker and victim to be semantic roles. These are crucial roles, the role of the attacker and the role of the victim. How, then, is this information made clear in the sentence?

It might seem that we could determine the semantic role from the grammatical relation of a noun phrase (that is, its subject or object status). A noun phrase in the subject position might always correspond to a specific semantic role, while one in the object slot would have a single different role. In both sentences, the subject argument is a noun phrase referring to the attacker, while the object argument is a noun phrase referring to the victim. So the semantic roles of *the Duke of Wellington* and *Napoleon Bonaparte* seem to depend on their grammatical relation. The subject is always the "doer" of the action and the object is always the "undergoer," the entity the action is done to; that is, the subject and object arguments have different semantic roles.

We have already seen that this cannot be so from our comparison of *enjoy* and *please*. In English, although word order is closely connected to the grammatical relations of arguments, it is more loosely connected to their semantic roles. The subject relation is an essential grammatical relation rather than a semantic one. A subject is marked not only by its special position before the verb, but also by its characteristic of requiring a present tense verb to take the singular suffix *-s* if it is itself singular. No other argument in a clause can do this. (The process is known as *number agreement*.) As we've already noted, for each element functioning as a predicate, native speakers know not only how many arguments it requires but also which role is assigned to the subject and which to the object, if there is one. They determine this from their knowledge of the predicate. Also, they know that predicates taking two objects assign semantic roles to each of them. We'll look at an example of this because it brings up a further issue.

For convenience in the following example, the second object of the predicate is abbreviated as OBJ2.

> *The president offered* **the rebels** (OBJ) **military supplies** (OBJ2).

An alternative order is available in which *the rebels* is the object of the preposition *to*. In that case, *the rebels* is the object of a preposition. Yet it still bears a special semantic relation to the verb. We will call such objects *oblique objects*. Only those objects of prepositions that bear this kind of semantic relation to the verb are oblique objects. We will mark these objects with the abbreviation OBL and indicate their introducing preposition:

> *The president offered* **military supplies** (OBJ) *to* **the rebels** (OBL-to).

Here are oblique objects with different prepositions:

> *Dora demanded from/of* **the company** (OBL-from) *a new contract* (OBJ).
> *Oberon brought* **a wand** (OBJ) *for Puck* (OBL-for).

Thus the grammatical relations subject and object do not in themselves specify the semantic role of the argument. It is the predicate that does the specifying. Now consider two other examples. What grammatical relation does the argument *her clothes* bear in each?

> *Her clothes dried on the line.*
> *Chester dried her clothes on the line.*

In the first sentence, the noun phrase *her clothes* is the subject, whereas in the second it is the object. Yet, despite this difference in grammatical relations, it is clear that *her clothes* has the same semantic role in both sentences. Both sentences assert that drying takes place and that the drying is undergone by the clothes. If we look at the sentence from the point of view of grammatical relations, the two subjects have very different semantic functions. The subject of the first sentence, *her clothes*, is an "undergoer," whereas *Chester*, the subject of the second sentence, is a "doer," not an "undergoer." To capture these differences, the grammar must specify a set of semantic roles separate from the set of grammatical relations. These semantic roles, though hard to define precisely, are crucial to understanding sentences. Moreover, the issue of *how* semantic roles are assigned is important for an understanding of what is involved in language comprehension.

SUMMARY

The propositional content of a sentence is the meaning that it has independent of context. A sentence contains one or more propositions. A proposition consists of a predicate, which forms the heart of the proposition, and one or more arguments, that is, participants, living or nonliving, in the situation expressed as a proposition. Verbs are not the only grammatical category that can function as predicates in the propositional content. Noun phrases, adjectives, and prepositional phrases can also be predicates. Similarly, not only noun phrases but also clauses can serve as arguments for a predicate. The number of arguments each predicate requires is known as its *valency*.

Predicates assign semantic roles to their arguments. But there is a mismatch between the semantics and the syntax. A particular semantic role (e.g., *doer* or *undergoer*) does not always correspond to the same grammatical relation (e.g., *subject* or *object*). So a grammar must specify semantic roles separately from grammatical relations. Native speakers identify not only the semantic role of each argument but also the predicate that assigns the role. Such identification of the assigner of the semantic role is an important part of the comprehension process.

EXERCISE SET 2

1. In the chapter, we discussed certain properties of the following sentences:

Her clothes dried on the line.
Chester dried her clothes on the line.

The following sentences have similar properties. Discuss the differences in meaning between the verbs in each pair of sentences.

A1. *The cheeses age slowly in the cellars.*
A2. *Home Dairies ages the cheeses slowly in the cellars.*
B1. *The jewels are in her safe.*
B2. *Dolly put the jewels into her safe.*
C1. *Jerrold walked to the station.*
C2. *Marsha walked Jerrold to the station.*

2. The meaning of the second of the two sentences below includes the meaning of the first sentence. But the main verb *accused* adds extra meaning. Describe what meaning it adds.

a. *Neilsen said that Gloria Mowat wrote that letter.*
b. *Neilsen accused Gloria Mowat of writing that letter.*

3. A vocabulary assignment given to an intermediate level ESL class in Malaysia required students to check in their classroom dictionaries the meanings of the following adjectives and verbs:

ADJECTIVES: *soft, hard, short, dark, quick*
VERBS: *soften, harden, shorten, darken, quicken*

In a subsequent class the teacher tried, with only partial success, to get the students to formulate some grammatical and semantic generalizations about the data they had obtained. What organizing principle do you think the teacher was trying to exploit?

4. Use the logical notation introduced in this chapter to represent the concepts expressed by the following verbs. Show only the arguments typically required. Include an example sentence for each.

lend, know, smile, find, elapse, offer

5. What is the valency of the predicates listed below?

EXAMPLE: *terrify:*   x TERRIFY y   valency = 2
a. *(be) hungry*   b. *(be) a scientist*   c. *examine*   d. *tell*

6. List the arguments for the boldfaced predicates below:

    a. *Doctor Tam **told** Leonard that he would prescribe erythromycin.*
    b. *To make a false confession would have been **easy.***
    c. *Captain Sullivan **believed** her daughter to be a liar.*
    d. *Whoever robbed that house must have been **an acrobat**.*

7. What do you think might be the relevance of propositional analysis to providing instruction in comprehension?

NOTES

1. We therefore include infinitive clauses in our definition of clause, contrary to the practice of some traditional grammarians. Gerundive constructions, such as *Trotwood's disturbing the pigeons,* might also be included in a definition of clause, but there are some problems associated with this, which we'll discuss in a later chapter.

3

Thematic Roles and Levels of Structure

Language learners need various kinds of strategies for interpreting what they hear or read. They need strategies for interpreting contextual clues, which can provide them with information about the likely content of the language to which they are being exposed.[1] Just as important, if not more, are strategies for determining and interpreting the grammatical units and relations that make up what they hear and read. An English sentence, like sentences in any language, is made up of units that combine to contribute to an overall semantic interpretation. Each unit of the sentence bears a grammatical relation to some other unit or combination. Noun phrases and sometimes clauses can bear a subject or object relation within the larger structure. These noun phrases and clauses also function as arguments of their predicate, and their semantic roles, roles such as "doer," are essentially semantic relations within the larger language structure. These two types of relations, grammatical relations and semantic roles, do not exactly match each other. We will explore this lack of correspondence between grammatical relations and semantic roles in some detail here. First a revision of terminology: Because the term *semantic role* suggests a semantic concept broader than the set of roles assigned to arguments, we instead use the term *thematic role*, the term used in most technical discussions (along with an abbreviated form *theta role*).

SEMANTIC AND GRAMMATICAL RELATIONS

Suppose each grammatical relation did, in fact, correspond to a distinct thematic role. What would this suggest about how sentences are interpreted? The process of understanding who does what to whom in a clause would then require three major steps:

1. identifying the predicate and the argument slots required;
2. identifying the noun phrase or clause arguments filling the slots;
3. identifying the grammatical relations these arguments bear (e.g., subject or object) in order to identify their thematic roles (e.g., "doer," "undergoer").

In other words, the grammatical relations would correspond directly to the thematic roles, which would just be the semantic translation of the grammatical relations. Indeed, this claim seems valid for many sentences:

Lady Macbeth painted her nails.
Gomer Pyle shampooed the poodle.
Ahmed will carry the passports.
She is selling her Mercedes.

The noun phrase before each verb is the grammatical subject. The noun phrase after each verb is the grammatical object.

From the semantic point of view, the subjects (*Lady Macbeth, Gomer Pyle, Ahmed,* and *she*) refer to the participants who do the actions, while the grammatical objects (*her nails, the poodle, the passports,* and *her Mercedes*) refer to the entities that undergo the actions. So, if the subject were always the "doer" and the object always the "undergoer," learners of English would face a straightforward task. Since the grammatical relations would correspond directly to thematic roles, to understand the thematic role of each argument in a sentence, the learner would just have to be able to pick out the subject and any objects. The thematic role of each argument would then become obvious.

In fact, it is likely that, at one early stage, second or foreign language learners do employ this strategy of matching up the noun phrase before the verb with the "doer" and the noun phrase after the verb with the "undergoer." Children acquiring English as their first language also follow this strategy in their sentence production. In their early sentences, the units that seem to be their subjects and objects have been observed to correspond closely to "doers" and "undergoers."[2]

Such a strategy works well for a sizable proportion of the clauses encountered, especially those in which the main verb is one of physical action (*bring, take, paint, destroy*). The subject is the "doer," the role we shall now refer to as *agent*, and the object is the "undergoer," the role we shall refer to as *theme*. The theme is the entity to which the action happens. In the next example, *a bewildered young woman* has the agent role and *the red button* has the theme role:

A bewildered young woman was about to push the red button.

This is as we would expect. The sentence is about a "doer," an "undergoer," and the action undergone.

However, for clauses with other kinds of predicates, the correspondence between the grammatical relation and the thematic role is much less consistent. Consider, for instance, the following sentences:

$$\text{Noel} \left\{ \begin{array}{l} \text{liked} \\ \text{was fond of} \\ \text{enjoyed} \end{array} \right\} \text{those colors.}$$

There is no agent in these sentences. Noel doesn't do anything and *those colors* does not undergo an action. This is because verbs *like* and *enjoy* and the adjective *fond* express psychological states rather than actions. So the grammatical relation of subject does not correspond to the role of agent. With such psychological predicates as *like,* the subject is assigned a role called the *experiencer role,* while the role the object is assigned is called the *theme role,*[3] despite the fact that it undergoes no action. As we will see, it has been found useful to define the theme role more broadly as a typically inert entity that is in a certain state or position or is changing its state or position. An argument consisting of an embedded clause is also considered an inert entity—it doesn't do anything or feel anything. So it too is a theme.

An *experiencer* is an entity engaged in a mental process or state involving *cognition* (thinking, believing, knowing, understanding), *perception* (seeing, hearing, smelling), or *emotion* (liking, hating, fearing, being angry, trusting). In the example, then, *Noel*, the subject, is the experiencer and *those colors*, the object, is the theme.

So, for these psychological predicates, we could modify the strategy by replacing the agent role with the experiencer role. The first argument would be the experiencer, the second the theme:

Noel (experiencer) *liked those colors* (theme).

But now look at some examples with different psychological predicates:

The colors $\left\{ \begin{array}{l} \text{delighted} \\ \text{pleased} \\ \text{seemed delightful to} \end{array} \right\}$ Noel.

The predicates *delight, please, enchant, (seem) delightful*, and many others (*horrify, interest, frighten, gladden, (get) angry, disillusion, fascinate/be fascinating (to), deceive*, etc.) also express psychological processes or states. They differ from the earlier set in presenting the theme first and the experiencer second. The experience seems more like a reaction or an effect caused by the theme. The theme is now the subject and the experiencer the object:

The colors in the Marloff paintings (theme) *pleased Noel* (experiencer).

For many psychological predicates, then, the grammatical relation subject does not correspond to the thematic role experiencer nor the object relation to the theme. English predicates that express mental experience vary as to which thematic roles are assigned to which arguments. In fact, a similar variability is found in many other languages.

Although action predicates overwhelmingly assign roles in a consistent way, with the subject being assigned the agent role and the object the theme role, passive voice predicates of action do not conform to this generalization. Passive voice clauses do not have agents in subject position. They either omit them or relegate them to a *by* phrase after the passive verb unit, which is the combination of a form of *be* (or *get*) followed by a verb in its past participle form (e.g., *be eaten, get robbed, be attacked*). Note this example:

The Duke of Wellington was attacked (by Napoleon Bonaparte).

The predicate is not one of attacking but one of being attacked. This predicate requires only one argument slot to be filled, that of the entity being attacked, the theme. Since the sentence has to have a subject, the required theme argument can only be placed in the subject position. Other noun phrases or clauses can occur, but they would all be optional. In the example, the agent role is specified in the optional prepositional phrase *by Napoleon Bonaparte*.[4] So the passive verb *be attacked* has its theme as subject and may specify its agent as the object of an optional prepositional phrase.

Now we come to an interesting issue concerning the position of a certain type of theme. As we have seen, some predicates allow clauses to be arguments. The predicate *(is) important* can have a whole clause like *that you leave early* as its argument, assigning to it the role theme. Thus *(is) important* is a predicate that allows a clause expressing a proposition as its only argument, as in this next sentence:

That you leave early is important.

There is, however, the possibility of having the embedded sentence follow the predicate. If we simply placed the embedded clause after the predicate, as in the sentence following, it would not be grammatical:

*is important that you leave early

The sentence must have a subject, a requirement for English known as the *subject constraint*.[5] But English has a way to make the sentence grammatical without our having to have the theme in the subject position. To fill the empty subject slot, a form without a thematic role is used:

It is important that you leave early.

The noun phrase subject is the pronoun *it*, which has no intrinsic meaning of its own and isn't assigned a thematic role by the predicate *important*. We'll refer to this special *it* as **filler it,** since it fills the empty subject position. This *it* is not an argument of the predicate *important*. It just lets you know that the real thing that is important, the proposition expressed as *that you leave early,* will be specified later in the sentence.

At this point we should define more clearly what an argument is. We define *argument* as follows: *An argument of a predicate is a noun phrase or clause that is required by that predicate (in the absence of contextual information)* **and to which the predicate assigns a thematic role.**

The filler *it* in the example, *It is important that you leave early,* is a noun phrase that functions as subject, but it has no thematic role assigned to it by the predicate *important*. It is thus not an argument of that predicate.

The fact that a subject may lack a thematic role, as with filler *it,* and the variability of the roles assigned to subjects and objects make it clear that grammatical relations do not correspond on a one-to-one basis to thematic roles. Knowing the grammatical relation an argument noun phrase or clause bears doesn't automatically mean knowing its thematic role. We've seen already that predicates vary considerably as to:

1. the number of arguments they require;
2. the thematic roles assigned to the arguments;
3. the grammatical relations of the arguments to which roles are assigned.

Thematic Role Assignment

Someone who understands English sentences therefore knows the set of thematic roles assigned by the predicates. This is implicit rather than explicit knowledge. No speaker can specify with any certainty a list of the thematic roles that speakers actually use. Moreover, grammarians are unable to specify such a list. Different grammarians have come up with different lists. However, in most current analytical studies, what is important is not identifying the specific thematic roles but rather identifying the predicate from which a particular noun phrase obtained its thematic role. Unless it is a filler like *it* (or *there*), every noun phrase is assigned a thematic role. Otherwise the sentence in which it occurs would not be well formed. Sometimes the predicate assigning the role is not obvious. In the following sentence, for instance, the subject noun phrase *the party leaders* does not get its role (that of agent) from the verb *seem* but from the infinitive verb *deny:*

The party leaders seem to deny any responsibility.

Check this by trying to substitute other noun phrases as the subject of *seem*. Only noun phrases denoting mind-possessing entities can occur. Sentences like this one:

> *The cupboard seems to deny any responsibility.*

are asterisked because the verb *deny* has assigned the agent role to the cupboard. A cupboard cannot deny anything. *Deny* requires its subject to be a mind-possessor. Replace this verb with a predicate that does not assign an agent role to the cupboard and the sentence is fine:

> *The cupboard seems to be empty.*

The predicate *(be) empty* assigns a theme role rather than an agent role, and themes need not be mind-possessors. So it was not the verb *seem* that assigned the agent role to its subject but the second verb, *deny*.

In the sections immediately following this, the thematic roles common in current linguistic descriptions are listed and briefly explained.[6]

Thematic Role *Agent*

The agent is a mind-possessor who acts, usually intentionally. So *Emily Bronte* is the agent in these sentences:

> **Emily Brontë** *opened the drawer with that iron key.*
> *The drawer was opened by* **Emily Brontë.**

In an active voice sentence, the agent is typically the subject. A useful test for the agent role is to see whether the noun phrase can follow the verb *order* with its original verb following it in its active infinitive form, as in this sentence:

> *Branwell ordered* **Emily Brontë** *to open the drawer with that iron key.*

Thematic Role *Instrument*

The instrument is the thing with which the action is done. The argument *that iron key* is the instrument in these examples:

> *Emily Brontë opened the drawer with* **that iron key.**
> **That iron key** *opens the drawer.*
> *Emily Brontë used* **that iron key** *to open the drawer.*

Note, however, the differences in grammatical relations. In the first example, the instrument *that iron key* is the object of the preposition *with*, in the second it is the subject of the sentence, and in the third it is the object of the verb *used*.

In an active voice clause, the instrument is typically either the object of *with* or the clause subject.

Thematic Role *Theme*

The role of theme is the hardest to pin down. The broad definition of the role theme covers three somewhat different classes of theme. The first corresponds to a narrow definition. It is the role of the often inert entity, which is in a certain state or position or is changing its state or position:

The girders were rusting.
The ball rolled down the slope.
Cavour rolled *the ball* down the slope.
The news would have shocked that community.

The second is the role assigned to clauses. As previously stated, clauses can be arguments, and since clauses express propositions, which don't do anything and don't undergo anything, like other themes, clauses are inert entities. Look at the theme arguments shown in boldface in these sentences:

For Charlotte to outdo Branwell would shock that community.
Patrick believed *that Emily had the greatest talent.*

Chomsky's *Knowledge of Language* (1986) distinguished the class of clauses which are arguments as arguments with their own special thematic role. He calls this role *proposition.*

The third class is that of affected mind-possessing entities. Because this class is not a class of inert entities and seems different in nature, the term *patient* is sometimes used instead of the broader term *theme.* Patients undergo the action or process specified by their predicate and are affected by it. The argument *the Bengal tiger* would be described as having the patient role in the following examples:

A wealthy hunter killed *the Bengal tiger.*
The Bengal tiger died.

Note that even under a narrower definition of theme as only a role for inert entities, the theme role can be assigned to a living thing if it is treated in the same way as an inert object, as *Uncle Toby* is in this sentence:

They moved *Uncle Toby* into the corridor.

Unlike the Bengal tiger, Uncle Toby is *in this context* considered as being as inert as, say, an armchair or a potted plant.

In this grammar we have found it convenient pedagogically to use the term *theme* to cover all three classes. The three classes of themes have much in common when compared to the other roles. Moreover, it becomes too easy to confuse the patient role with the next role to be described, that of *experiencer.* In an active voice sentence, the theme is typically the subject of the verb *be* or the direct object of a verb.

Thematic Role *Experiencer*

The experiencer is the one who experiences a mental state or process such as thinking, knowing, believing, understanding, seeing, hearing, fearing, hoping, being surprised, etc.

The trooper hoped for a promotion.
Montaigne's words inspired *the young poet.*
They will see a huge bronze gate between two pillars.

Note that the experiencer in the first and third sentences occupies the subject slot; in the second, it occupies the object slot. In an active voice sentence, the experiencer is typically the subject.

Thematic Roles *Source* and *Goal*

The term *source* refers to the location from which someone or something originates and the term *goal* to the location that serves or should serve as the destination. We will assume that whenever a transfer of possession is involved (in verbs like *give, own, lend*), the original possessor is the source, unless it is a mind-possessing entity carrying out an action, and the receiver or potential receiver is the goal. Other kinds of shifts use these roles; for example, a change in personality or identity. The roles are illustrated in these sentences:

> *The delegates left* **Mexico City** *(source)* for **Buenos Aires** *(goal).*
> **The government** *(agent)* took over **a billion dollars** *(theme)* from **the poor** *(source).*
> **Marley** *(theme)* changed from **a heartless miser** *(source)* into **a philanthropist** (goal).

In an active voice sentence, the goal is typically the indirect object or the object of *to,* and the source is typically the object of *from.*

Thematic Role *Benefactive*

The *benefactive* is the role of the individual for whose benefit some action is undertaken:

> *The chef baked* **Jessica** *a cherry pie.*

The benefactive noun phrase is often introduced with the preposition *for:*

> *The chef baked a cherry pie* **for Jessica.**

In an active voice sentence, the benefactive is typically the indirect object or the object of *for.*

Thematic Roles for Nonargument Noun Phrases

Noun phrases which are not arguments of predicates also have thematic roles. What can be said about the roles of the boldface noun phrases in the following sentences?

> **The doctor's** *car was a Mercedes.*
> *Moses waited for them on* **the mountain.**
> *A truce will be declared for* **two weeks.**
> **Last year** *the government divided the huge estates among the peasants.*

They have the thematic roles of *location* and *time.* This should seem straightforward enough for *the mountain, two weeks,* and *last year,* but it is not easy to think of the possessive noun phrase *the doctor's* as a kind of location for the car. Although this analysis may not seem too obvious for English, it works well for a number of other languages. Recall that goal was defined as the role assigned to someone receiving something; that is, the transfer of something to someone else is treated as a *shift* in the *location* of that thing. If you give something to someone, that receiver is the destination (or goal) to which the gift is directed. Once the gift is located at that goal, the goal person is no longer a goal, but rather the person possesses the gift and functions as a kind of location for the gift.

Note that although all the noun phrases are semantically significant, none are arguments required by the main predicate of the clause. Except for *last year,* all are attached to their clause by prepositions.

They are, in fact, arguments of prepositions. This may seem strange, since all arguments discussed so far have been arguments of predicates. Prepositions are similar semantically to predicates. Like many predicates they take object arguments, but unlike those predicates, they take no subject arguments. The relation of the verb *approach* to *the hut* in the first example phrase following is very like the relation of the preposition *to* to *the hut* in the second:

> approach **the hut**
> to **the hut**

In both cases, *the hut* is the goal argument.

The time noun phrase *last year* in the sentence, *Last year the government divided the huge estates among the peasants,* does not follow a preposition. Noun phrases with time thematic roles can, and sometimes must, appear without prepositions. Examples are *last year, there, then, here, Tuesday, a month ago,* and *next week.* This characteristic is a relic of an earlier form of English in which time and location noun phrases were often marked by special case suffixes rather than prepositions. Puzzled grammarians have sometimes assumed that these phrases have an *understood* preposition preceding them, pointing to such alternations as the following:

> I'll come **Tuesday.** I'll come **on Tuesday.**
> He came **the next day.** He came **on the next day.**

There are a few predicates, such as *put* in the following example, *place,* and *be situated,* which actually *require* a location argument even if the argument must be introduced by a preposition:

> Cato put his sword on **the table.**

The prepositional phrase *on the table* cannot be dropped from the sentence. In these cases, the noun phrase following the preposition is a true argument of the predicate, despite the preposition. The predicate assigns the thematic role via the preposition.

SOME CONCLUSIONS ABOUT CORRELATIONS BETWEEN SEMANTICS AND GRAMMAR

The semantic units we've been discussing are propositions, predicates, and arguments. The arguments bear thematic roles assigned to them by their predicates. How closely do these semantic units correspond to grammatical forms? We have seen that there is not a one-to-one correspondence since the grammar and the semantics are two quite different systems with their own units and relations. Nevertheless, there are indeed some interesting correspondences, including the following:

1. Propositions in the semantic system are often expressed as clauses in the grammatical system.

2. Predicates are expressed as verbs, predicate adjective phrases, predicate noun phrases, or prepositional phrases.

3. Arguments are expressed as either noun phrases or clauses.

4. Thematic roles show a partial correlation with grammatical relations.

A REVISED NOTATION FOR PROPOSITIONAL CONTENT

It is now time to revise our logical notation to represent accurately more of the core grammatical information that native speakers of English have about the predicates of the language. For example: The verb *paint* has a valency of two, that is, it requires two arguments, one of which must be the agent, the person(s) doing the painting, and the other the theme, the entity undergoing the painting. In English, most predicates with a valency of two assign the theme role to the noun phrase or clause immediately following the verb. (This will be a very useful guideline for semantic analysis, as we'll see when we consider *deep structure* [or D-structure] in the next section of this chapter.) If an agent role is assigned, it is assigned to the noun phrase immediately before the verb, that is, to the subject.

Now let's make our notation more useful. The old notation *x* PAINT *y* does not tell us the thematic roles that are very much a part of the meaning of *paint*. The notation is not a good semantic representation. A better representation would be this one:

agent PAINT theme

But what about the passive voice form *be painted*? This predicate requires a theme argument but it does not require an agent argument. When an agent is specified in a passive voice clause, it appears as the object of *by:*

Her house has just been painted **by Thomas.**

If we just specified the agent but not the theme, the sentence would be ungrammatical:

*Has just been painted by Thomas.

On the other hand, specifying the theme but not the agent does no grammatical harm:

Her house has just been painted.

Clearly, English speakers must see *paint* and *be painted* as very much the same predicate semantically, more closely connected, for example, than *paint* and *be arrested*. One way to show this connection is to treat *be painted* as a more specialized form of *paint*, one which does not require an overt agent argument. For convenience, we'll show the predicate as BE PAINTED, although a more formal account would simply show the predicate as PAINT, as with the active voice verb. And similar to the active voice verb, the theme role would be assigned to the argument following the verb. We'll place a score line in the unfilled subject position:

___ BE PAINTED theme

This would make the assignment of the theme role the same as for PAINT. It would also show such passive verbs as conforming to the following generalization:

> *In English, active voice verbs with a valency of two and the corresponding passive voice verbs tend to assign the theme role to the noun phrase or clause immediately following the verb.*

But now we have a slight problem. This analysis wrongly suggests that the following sentence should be grammatical:

*Has just been painted her house.

However, other grammatical principles come into play here. English, as we noted earlier, has a subject constraint, which requires clauses with verbs in the past or present tense to have subjects. To satisfy this constraint, something must be inserted into the subject position. For certain kinds of sentences, we have seen that the filler *it* is inserted. But this is not possible here:

*It has just been painted her house.

So what needs to be done? The sentence contains just one argument, the theme noun phrase *her house*. If we move this theme noun phrase into subject position, we get this perfectly grammatical sentence:

Her house has just been painted.

So the theme argument becomes the subject of the passive clause. This kind of movement into an empty subject slot is quite common in English.

Consider a different verb, *prove*, and its passive form, *be proven*. The active and passive voice forms would be represented as follows:

ACTIVE VOICE: agent PROVE theme
PASSIVE VOICE: — BE PROVEN theme

The active voice formula corresponds to this sentence:

Thomas Young (agent) *proved almost three centuries ago* **that light is made up of waves** (theme).[7]

while the passive voice formula corresponds to this form:

*was proven almost three centuries ago **that light is made up of waves** (theme).

The theme argument in these examples is not a noun phrase but the clause *that light is made up of waves*. Both sentences conform to our generalization as to the position of the theme after the predicate. The passive voice sentence, however, is ungrammatical because it violates the subject constraint. This defect can easily be remedied in the same way that we used for the house-painting example. The sentence has a theme argument that can be moved into the subject slot:

That light was made up of waves (theme) *was proven almost three centuries ago.*

Note, however, another option for this example, one that was not available for the house-painting example. The subject constraint can be satisfied by inserting the filler *it* into subject position. As we pointed out earlier, this *it* is not an argument of the predicate and has no thematic role.

It *was proven almost three centuries ago* **that light was made up of waves** (theme).

This insertion of *it* is only allowed when the argument after the predicate is a *clause* rather than a noun phrase. That's why the following sentence is ungrammatical:

*It has just been painted **her house** (theme).

Our only option, if the theme argument is a noun phrase, is to move the theme *her house* into subject position. We cannot use the filler *it*. So that's how we get this sentence:

Her house (theme) *has just been painted.*

In Chapter 11 we will see just *why* there is this difference between noun phrase arguments and clause arguments.

DEEP AND SURFACE STRUCTURES

Now for a brief but more intensive consideration of linguistic theory. We have claimed that the theme role is assigned to the noun phrase or clause *following* the predicate. If, at that point, the clause has no subject, the theme noun phrase is moved into subject position. But if the theme argument is a *clause*, it need not be shifted since the filler *it* can be inserted into subject position.

Note that we are thus considering sentences at *two* stages or levels, one at which a predicate assigns the thematic role *theme* to the argument following it, and a second level of analysis at which either the theme argument has been moved into subject position or the filler *it* has been inserted. It is at this second level that we can identify which arguments end up as subjects and which as objects.

So, thematic roles are assigned on the first level, and the final grammatical relations are established on the second level. Not all theoretical approaches distinguish levels like this, but this approach, pioneered by Noam Chomsky, has been a very productive and influential one for the analysis of human languages.

The level at which thematic roles are assigned is called the *deep structure*, usually abbreviated as *D-structure*. At this level the verbs, predicate adjective phrases, predicate noun phrases, and prepositions assign thematic roles to the noun phrases or clauses that occur right next to them.

The level at which grammatical relations are established for each clause is known as the *surface structure*, or more commonly, *S-structure*. At this level, noun phrases like the filler *it* can occur without having to have any thematic role.

The two levels, D-structure and S-structure, are connected to each other by the kind of moving operation described earlier in this chapter, one moving the theme argument from the position after the predicate into the empty subject position. Such operations are called *transformations*, and they gave their name to an earlier version of Chomskyan syntax known as Generative-Transformational Grammar (a model current in the sixties and seventies).

SUMMARY

We need to posit separate systems for grammatical relations and thematic roles because they do not correspond on a one-to-one basis. This is especially the case for psychological predicates like *enjoy* and *please*. Except for fillers like *it*, all noun phrases are arguments and must be assigned thematic roles either by predicates or by prepositions like *to*, *with*, and *by*. Clauses may also function as arguments. In general, the theme role is assigned to the noun phrase or embedded clause following the predicate. Subsequently, if the subject position is empty, an argument following the predicate can be moved, via a process called transformation, into the subject slot, thereby satisfying the *subject constraint*. If the argument following the predicate is a noun phrase, the movement is obligatory. If it is an embedded clause, the movement is optional because the subject constraint can instead be satisfied by insertion of filler *it* into subject position. This is how passive voice clauses, which start off without subjects, can acquire themes as their subjects. It is at this stage that we see the final grammatical relations that the arguments have. This final stage, the S-structure, follows an earlier stage, D-structure, at which predicates assign thematic roles such as agent and theme to noun phrases and clauses that are arguments. A more adequate semantic representation is achieved if thematic relations are indicated in the logical notation that we have been using.

EXERCISE SET 3

1. Write one passive voice counterpart for each of the following sentences:
   a. *Her behavior frightened the child.*
   b. *The Council agreed that the matter was serious.*

2. The sentence you wrote for (1b) has two passive voice counterparts. One counterpart has as its subject the clause that *the matter was serious,* while the other has the filler *it.* Write the version that you did not use for (1a). Check to be sure that the propositional content remains the same.

3. What is the relevance of the following pair of sentences to the possibility of treating subjects and objects as thematic roles as well as grammatical relations?

  a. *Teresita feared the new governor.*
  b. *The new governor frightened Teresita.*

4. Use the new notation explained to represent the concepts expressed by the following predicates:

  TALL, IRRITATE, BELIEVE, ASTONISH,
  ANXIOUS, PERSUADE, BE PRAISED

Show only the arguments that are typically required.

5. List five predicates in (4) which can take something other than a noun phrase as an argument. Write an example sentence for each.

6. What thematic roles would you assign to the boldface forms in the following sentences?

  a. *Each year **the economy** gets worse.*
  b. *Sarah Higgins annoyed **me**.*
  c. ***Neubauer** killed the diseased cells.*
  d. *Gandhi was sad to find out **that the hatred still survived**.*
  e. ***To build a second nuclear reactor now** would be foolish.*

7. Suppose you were teaching a first-year class in German for English speakers. The German verb *liebt* is translated as "loves," while *gefällt* is often translated as "likes." Compare the following sentences with their English counterparts:

  a. *Hans liebt Maria.*   c. *Hans gefällt Maria.*
    "Hans loves Maria."   "Maria likes Hans."
  b. *Maria liebt Hans.*   d. *Maria gefällt Hans.*
    "Maria loves Hans."   "Hans likes Maria."

What difficulty might arise for the students and how might the teacher deal with it? Keep in mind that there is more than one way to deal with such problems.

8. In view of the data in (7), what information about such verbs would be needed by a German-English computer translation program?

NOTES

1. See G. Brown and G. Yule, *Teaching the Spoken Language: An Approach Based on the Analysis of Conversational English* (New York: Cambridge University Press, 1983), especially the discussion on p. 57.

2. See, for example, M. P. Maratsos and M. Chalkley, "The internal language of children's syntax: The ontogenesis and representation of syntactic categories," in K. Nelson, ed., *Children's Language*, vol. 2 (New York: Gardner Press, 1981).

3. Some writers distinguish between theme and patient. While the patient role is for mind-possessing beings capable of being consciously affected by actions, the theme role is reserved for entities, typically inanimate, that cannot be aware of any action or that the speaker considers to be functioning as if they were inanimate. The semantic distinction between theme and patient depends on the kind of notion expressed by the predicate (action, perception, cognition, state, process, etc.) and the kind of entity the argument refers to (living creature, inanimate object, proposition, etc.).

4. Here as elsewhere in the book, parentheses () are used to set off optional constituents.

5. English is one of the minority of languages that have a subject constraint. French and German have counterparts to the *it;* Italian, Spanish, Japanese, and Mandarin, for example, do not. In fact, in informal spoken English, subjects are often omitted, as in *Gotta go home early tonight* and *Seems like he's not going to pay for it.* We will assume here a slightly more formal register of spoken English which requires the subject slot to be filled. Written English, except in very informal notes, observes the subject condition strictly.

6. The discussion of thematic roles here is based primarily on the pioneer work of Jeffrey Gruber, "Studies in lexical relations" (1965), an M.I.T. dissertation fortunately reprinted in Jeffrey Gruber, *Lexical Structures in Syntax and Semantics* (Amsterdam: North-Holland, 1976), and also on Charles Fillmore's, "The case for case," in Emmon Bach and R. Harms, eds., *Universals in Linguistic Theory* (New York: Holt, Rinehart and Winston, 1968). This work is well worth reading. A useful account appears in R. S. Jackendoff, *Semantic Interpretation in Generative Grammar* (Cambridge, MA: M.I.T. Press, 1973), 29-46 and 214-226.

7. Note that the time noun phrase *almost three centuries ago* does not block the assignment of the theme role to the clause after it (*that light was made of waves*). Time and location phrases seem invisible when the predicate assigns the theme role. Such phrases are optional constituents of clauses and can easily be shifted around in the clause, e.g., **Almost three centuries ago** *Thomas Young proved that light was made up of waves.*

4

Some Properties of Sentence Structure

We all know how difficult it is, unless we are very young, to learn to speak a foreign language with a nativelike accent. It's too easy to transfer to a second language the pronunciation habits and rules of our first language, that is, the implicit knowledge of English phonology that we acquired when we were children.

Although the differences are sometimes more subtle, our grasp of the syntax of another language can be similarly flawed. In this chapter we will look at some general characteristics of sentence structure and see what kinds of likenesses and differences among languages we can observe. But first consider one kind of difference in word order that shows how different languages use different means to achieve the same goal — efficient communication.

LANGUAGE OPTIONS AND PARAMETERS

If the variations in form from language to language are regarded as *options* (or alternatives), then different languages have different combinations of options. For example, languages have different ways of distinguishing subjects and objects. English uses word order or position in the clause. Most subject noun phrases are easily identified by their position before the verb, and objects by their position after the verb. But some languages mark subjects and objects with special suffixes or other special markings. Such languages don't need to place subjects and objects in fixed slots. The word order can thus be fairly free. Whatever their position in a clause, subjects and objects are easily identifiable.

Latin is just such a language. Let's take a quick look at it before we get on to the more general properties of sentence structure. We'll look at forms corresponding to a single English sentence:

Cassius sees Brutus.

The major elements in the sentence are a subject noun phrase, a verb, and an object noun phrase. The Latin forms for this sentence can be arranged in six different ways, corresponding to these six orders:

Cassius Brutus sees.	*Sees Brutus Cassius*
Brutus sees Cassius.	*Brutus Cassius sees.*
Sees Cassius Brutus.	*Cassius sees Brutus.*

The sentences all mean "Cassius sees Brutus," though they vary in emphasis. We couldn't tell from these English equivalents whether Cassius sees Brutus or Brutus sees Cassius. The Romans, however, would have had no trouble figuring out the single meaning of the six Latin sentences.

How did they do this? The answer is that, instead of using word order to distinguish subjects from objects, they used suffixes. Look at the Latin forms; the suffixes on the nouns are shown with hyphens.

Cassiu-s Brutu-m videt.	*Videt Brutu-m Cassiu-s.*
Brutu-m videt Cassiu-s.	*Brutu-m Cassiu-s videt.*
Videt Cassiu-s Brutu-m.	*Cassiu-s videt Brutu-m.*

The *-s* suffix marks the subjects in these sentences, and the *-m* suffix the objects. If we switched the suffixes around, as in the following examples:

Cassiu-m Brutu-s videt.
Videt Cassiu-m Brutu-s.

the sentences would mean "Brutus sees Cassius" instead of "Cassius sees Brutus."

It is helpful for language professionals to be aware of the ranges of options from which languages "select" options for sentence structure. These different ranges are known as parameters. There are parameters for other dimensions of language—for phonology, for example.

There are also plenty of nonlanguage examples of parameters, that is, of interacting ranges of options. Looking at a nonlanguage example can provide insights into how language parameters work. Let's take the purchase of a house. One obvious parameter is the price parameter. How much can the buyer afford to pay? A second parameter might be the distance from work. Buyers might be willing to pay more if the house was close to their workplace. A third might be size, and a fourth the quality of schools in the area. Few of us can afford the largest house close to our work and in the best location for our children's education. The setting we choose on any of these parameters affects the range of options on the other parameters.

What kind of parameter setting occurs in language? English and Japanese, for example, differ significantly with regard to verb and object order. In English the verb precedes the object; in Japanese, the object precedes the verb. This verb-object parameter is a prominent one in sentence structure, one that is connected with settings on other parameters.

THREE BASIC PROPERTIES OF SENTENCE STRUCTURE

Parameters such as the verb-object parameter arise out of a very basic property of language—its linear structure, which derives from the fact that the parts of an utterance are necessarily produced in a time sequence. This and other basic properties of sentence structure should be considered before we look at the details of how the parameters are set in English and other languages.

We are interested in how the words of grammatical sentences are organized and how their organization corresponds to likenesses or differences in meanings. The grammarian determines the distribution of particular word types or combinations by look-ing for restrictions on their occurrence. The distribution of a noun phrase, for instance, is the set of positions in which noun phrases can occur.

To understand the internal organization of sentences and the distribution of the units forming them, we must consider three major properties of sentence structure:

1. *Linearity:* Sentences are produced and received in a linear sequence.
2. *Hierarchy:* Sentences are hierarchically structured, that is, they are not simply sequences of individual words but are made up of word groupings, which themselves may consist of lesser groupings.
3. *Categoriality:* Sentences are made up of parts which belong to a set of distinct categories, each with its special characteristics.

Linearity

No one can utter simultaneously all the words of a sentence. Nor could such an utter-ance be understood. Words are spoken (or written) and heard (or read) in a time sequence from early to later, a sequence represented in the English writing system by a procession of written forms from left to right. There is a standard order for subjects and objects. In the English sentence example used earlier:

Cassius sees Brutus.

the subject of the sentence, *Cassius,* precedes the verb, while the object, *Brutus,* follows the verb. Numbers of other languages follow the same order, *Subject-Verb-Object* (abbre-viated as SVO). We could try to switch around the subject and the object, converting the SVO order into OVS, as in this example:

Brutus	sees	Cassius.
O	V	S

But if we did, English speakers would identify Brutus as the subject. The order would still be SVO, but the meaning would be different.

Other languages may use different orderings. The range of possible orderings of these words or phrases is known as the *word order parameter*. The verb-object parame-ter discussed earlier is, in fact, part of this more general parameter. In many languages, word order is less crucial than it is in English because, as in Latin, there is greater reliance on suffixes and other ways of marking sentence constituents. Word order therefore appears to be a setting on a yet more general parameter of function marking. But in no language is word order totally insignificant.

The examples that follow show languages which are like English in that word order is quite significant, but differ from it in their settings for this parameter.

Welsh typically uses a *VSO* ordering:

Gwelodd	y	dynion	y ci
saw	the	men	the dog
V		S	O

"The men saw the dog."

Turkish typically uses *SOV* order, as in this next sentence:

Ahmet	bu kitabɨ	istiyor
Ahmet	his book	wants
S	O	V

"Ahmet wants his book."

In the Philippine national language, Tagalog, more variation is allowed in word order, but a very common order is *VOS*:

Pumili	ng estudyante	ang titser
chose	a student	the teacher
V	O	S

"The teacher chose a student."

Many languages fall into two major groupings regarding the verb-object parameter, those in which the verb precedes its object and those in which it follows its object. What is especially interesting is that this difference is associated with other differences in linear ordering. Thus the relative position of verbs and their objects is very significant. (Surprisingly, perhaps, subject position seems less important.) Let us focus now on the clusterings of properties of linear ordering that correspond to the relative order of verbs and their objects.

Although few languages are fully consistent, the following tendencies have been observed in languages such as Japanese and Turkish, whose verbs *follow* their objects:

1. Auxiliary verb forms typically *follow* main verbs, usually as suffixes. Thus the Japanese for *was kidnapped* would be literally translated as "kidnapped-was."
2. There are *postpositions* instead of *prepositions*. Postpositions *follow* their object instead of preceding it. The English prepositional phrase *in their house* is translated into Luiseño, a Uto-Aztecan language of California, as "their-house-in."
3. Adjectives (*red, quiet, circular*), relative clauses (*who was obstinate, that I wanted most*), and other modifiers of nouns *precede* rather than follow their head noun.

What about languages in which verbs precede their objects instead of following them? These reveal the following tendencies:

1. Auxiliary verbs *precede* main verbs (*will talk*, not **talk will*).
2. There are *prepositions* rather than *postpositions* (*in Jakarta*, not **Jakarta in*).
3. Adjectives, relative clauses, and other modifiers of nouns *follow* their head nouns.

We must emphasize that, especially when large numbers of languages are examined, we find quite a few exceptions. For example, since English is a language whose verbs *precede* their objects, we would expect adjectives, along with other noun modifiers, to *follow* their head nouns. In fact, however, adjectives *precede* their head nouns (e.g., *lively music* rather than **music lively*). But adjectives are special; other modifiers of nouns follow their head nouns, as we would expect.

Despite the irregularities, the correlations are consistent enough to be of interest for language acquisition research. The task of learning a second language with clusterings of properties similar to those in one's own language is presumably quite different from that of learning a second language with different clusterings of properties. Thus, non-native speakers of languages with linear orderings close to those of English should find this aspect of English easier than will speakers whose first language orders its constituents very differently.

This is not necessarily the case, however. Japanese students of English, for example, rarely seem to have problems with the different positions of modifiers in relation to their heads, while speakers of German, which is much closer to English, sometimes do. Perhaps similarities mislead some learners into assuming greater likenesses than actually exist.

What about first language acquisition? When children learn their mother tongue, one task confronting them is to find out, on the basis of a limited language input, the principles of constituent order to which their language conforms. During the so-called critical learning period,[1] the child figures out subconsciously the appropriate setting for each parameter in the language being acquired. For instance, the child must figure out the position of modifiers with respect to their heads. There are two major options: the head is to the left of the modifier(s) or the head is to the right of the modifier(s). There is no interference from knowledge of the parameter settings for another language.

Hierarchy

Words are not necessarily the only constituents of sentences; there are also higher-level constituents that form sentences. This kind of hierarchical organization, like linearity, represents a more general strategy the mind uses to organize experience. In sentences, lesser elements are parts of larger wholes, which are in turn parts of yet larger wholes. Things are easier to deal with if they can be placed within a larger frame, a part-to-whole strategy, or if they can be seen as consisting of distinguishable parts, a whole-to-part strategy. The latter strategy, for example, makes it easier for us to memorize this sequence of numbers:

36, 724, 215, 105, 142, 52, 0, 77

than this one:

3672421510514252077

Now think about the following sentence and look at the tree-style diagram below:

The government expelled the officers from Thailand.

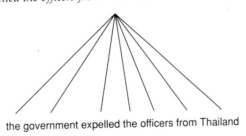

the government expelled the officers from Thailand

DIAGRAM 4.1

No two words in the diagram group together to form a higher-level constituent. Is this a correct reflection of sentence organization in English? Clearly not, since the lack of grouping fails to capture relationships that any native speaker of English can perceive.

English speakers know that the second *the* in the sentence is tied more closely to the noun *officers* than to the verb *expelled* that precedes it. The closeness of this tie is indicated by the fact that these two words, forming the phrase the *officers*, can be replaced with a single pronoun, *them*. In contrast, the words *expelled the* do not form a constituent phrase replaceable by any single word. The pair *the government* forms the same kind of phrase as *the officers*. Finally, the preposition *from* is more closely tied to the word following, *Thailand*, than to *officers*, which precedes it. A more accurate representation of the structure of our sentence would show these higher-level constituents too.

Look now at the following hierarchical structure:

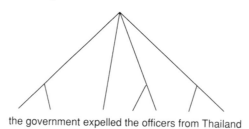

the government expelled the officers from Thailand

DIAGRAM 4.2

Note in Diagram 4.2 that the phrase *from Thailand* does not form a higher constituent grouping with the phrase *the officers*. The predicate *expel* here has one phrase indicating who was expelled and another indicating the place from which they were expelled. The object of *expelled* is *the officers*. There is evidence to support this constituent structure. First, the object can be replaced by a pronoun object, *them:*

> The government expelled **them** from Thailand.

Since *them* replaces the original object, that object must have been just *the officers*. Second, the sentence has the following passive voice counterpart:

> **The officers** were expelled from Thailand by the government.

In the passive voice sentence the object noun phrase, *the officers*, has been shifted to the subject slot. The prepositional phrase has not been shifted.

But note that the active voice sentence, *The government expelled the officers from Thailand*, has an alternative interpretation, one in which *from Thailand* does not indicate the place from which the officers were expelled but simply functions as further descriptive detail specifying *which* officers were expelled. Under this interpretation, *the officers from Thailand* is a constituent. It can therefore be replaced by the pronoun *them:*

> The government expelled **them**.

This interpretation corresponds to its own passive counterpart:

> The officers from Thailand were expelled by the government.

This time, the object noun phrase *the officers from Thailand* has been shifted to the subject slot. In this interpretation, the determiner *the* makes definite not just *officers* but the whole grouping *officers from Thailand*. So the sequence is a constituent whose structure can be shown like this:

the officers from Thailand

DIAGRAM 4.3

The constituents of *the officers from Thailand* together form a single higher-level constituent, that is, a phrase. On this interpretation, the constituent structure tree for the whole sentence must therefore show this constituent. The two interpretations of the sentence correspond to two distinct constituent structure trees.

There is yet another higher-level constituent, one headed by a verb. Note that the verb *expelled* is a *transitive* verb, that is, it takes an object. In our example, what the object is depends on which interpretation is chosen. For the interpretation in which the prepositional phrase *from Thailand* is separate from *the officers*, only *the officers* is the object. The higher-level constituent to which these phrases belong, the verb phrase, is made up of three separate parts: *expelled, the officers,* and *from Thailand,* as this next diagram shows:

expelled the officers from Thailand

DIAGRAM 4.4

Even though *from Thailand* is an optional constituent, it is just as closely tied to *expelled* as is the obligatory constituent *the officers*.

For the second interpretation, in which the object is *the officers from Thailand,* the verb phrase is made up of two separate parts, *expelled* and *the officers from Thailand,* as the following tree diagram shows:

expelled the officers from Thailand

DIAGRAM 4.5

For both interpretations there is an obvious dependence between *expelled* and the object constituent that follows. The verb *expel* requires an object and also allows a prepositional phrase to indicate the place from which someone is expelled. This special grouping relation is quite different from a relation between verbs and their subjects. Verbs are not categorized according to whether or not they take subjects; any verb can have a subject. So the verb and the constituents following it form a higher-level constituent in a clause.

Note, however, that not all constituents following a verb are necessarily part of the verb phrase. Forms like *yesterday*, which can be shifted to other positions in the sentence, *Yesterday the government...*, or, *The government yesterday...*, are outside the verb group.

Constituent structure trees can be revised to show the higher-level constituent as identified. Following are the revised constituent structure trees for the two interpretations. Which tree corresponds to which interpretation?

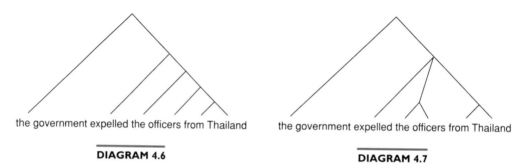

the government expelled the officers from Thailand   the government expelled the officers from Thailand

DIAGRAM 4.6   **DIAGRAM 4.7**

This analysis has demonstrated that the *linearity* property alone does not account for the relation between form and meaning in a sentence. The differences noted in *hierarchical* structure correspond to the differences between the two interpretations of the example sentence. A grammar of English that did not posit hierarchically organized constituents for sentence structures would find it hard to account for the ambiguity of sentences such as *The government expelled the officers from Thailand*. The differences in the groupings of the forms match up with the differences in meaning.

So, a hierarchical structure in syntax is a multilevel structure in which each individual constituent at the lowest level belongs—either on its own or together with adjacent constituents—to a constituent at the next higher level, and further to the highest level, which, in sentence grammar, is the category *sentence*.

To make the tree diagram system more useful for representing hierarchy, we need a few terms. The points on a tree where the branches come together are called *nodes*. Three feminine labels from the kinship system are used for the relations in the diagram between constituents. Two or more constituents attached to the next higher node on the tree are referred to as *sisters*. So, in the following tree for *expelled the officers:*

expelled the officers

DIAGRAM 4.8

the constituents *the* and *officers* are sisters because they are connected to the same next higher node. The larger constituent, *the officers*, is the sister of the verb *expelled*, since it is attached to the same higher node as *expelled*. Not surprisingly, the higher node to which sisters are attached is known as the *mother* node, and the sisters are *daughters* of the mother node. Thus, in our diagram, the word *officers* is a daughter of the higher node to which *the* and *officers* are attached.

Categoriality

The constituent structure trees studied so far represent (1) the linear ordering of the sentence and (2) native-speaker intuitions as to the hierarchical organization of the parts. But the trees fail to express crucial generalizations about sameness and differ-ence. Certain constituents are of the *same* kind, and they are *different* from others. Without conscious effort, native speakers exploit the samenesses and differences by using constituents of the same kind in the same positions within a sentence; that is, the constituents share the same distribution.

A descriptive grammar must differentiate between items that are the same and those that are different. Words, and the larger constituents they make up, belong to a set of distinct categories, each with its special characteristics. This is the third general property of sentence structures, *categoriality*.

The words *car* and *tree* are similar kinds of words, and their distribution—the range of positions in which they can occur—is very similar. They can, for instance, occur right after the words *a* and *the*. The two words also have counterparts with the *-s* suf-fix indicating plurality: *cars, trees*. This last similarity is not a matter of distribution but of the range of forms allowed for particular categories of words. The study of word forms, *morphology*, provides useful criteria for determining the category to which a word belongs. These supplement the distributional criteria for a particular category.

What about other words, for example, words like *this* and *unless?* Obviously these words don't belong in the same category with *car* and *tree*. They neither occur after *a* and *the* nor take the *-s* suffix. Moreover, the differences in their distribution indicate that they themselves fall into two separate *lexical categories*, the categories of words in the lexicon. While the lexical item or word *this* can follow prepositions like *after, on, before,* and *from*, the word *unless* cannot. We can say *after this* but not **after unless.*

To show categorial distinctions on constituent structure trees, the words must be labeled appropriately. The bottom part of the trees could look like this (DET stands for determiner, words like *the, this, a,* while N stands for noun, V for verb, and P for preposition):

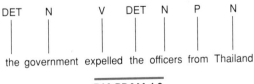

DIAGRAM 4.9

As we've already seen, the higher-level constituents—the phrases—also fall into categories, referred to as *phrasal categories*. For example, the two-word phrases *the government* and *the officer* clearly share enough properties to be included in a category. Both phrases have a noun as head, both can function as subject or object, and both can take a plural suffix. Since their head word is a noun (N), they are referred to as noun phrases (abbreviated NP). Now note that the noun *Thailand*, although a single word that doesn't normally take a plural suffix, shares not only key properties of the noun category but also distributional properties of noun phrases. *Thailand* has a noun as its head since it is the only word in the phrase. Moreover, it can function as subject or object and, like other noun phrases, can be replaced by a pronoun. It can be the object of a preposition like *from*, as other noun phrases can, and therefore can be considered to be a one-word noun phrase.

The phrasal category noun phrase also includes pronouns like *they, it,* and *them.* These pronouns have the same distribution as the phrases *the government* and *Thailand,* so pronouns, a special subcategory of nouns, can be, and almost always are, single-word noun phrases.

To go one step further in our example, the noun phrase *Thailand* is itself the object of a preposition, *from,* which is the head of the prepositional phrase *from Thailand.* The category prepositional phrase (PP) includes such phrases as *to Cortina, out of the village,* and *with her father.* The larger (mother) constituent to which both *expelled* and *the officers from Thailand* belong is *expelled the officers from Thailand.* For this larger phrase we can substitute the single intransitive verb *resigned:*

The government **expelled the officers from Thailand.**
The government **resigned.**

Like all the other phrase categories, except prepositional phrases, verb phrases (VP) can consist of just one word, for example, *resigned.* The sequence *expelled the officers from Thailand* is also a verb phrase, one organized around the transitive verb *expelled,* which is its head.

The sequence *fond of marshmallows* is organized around an *adjective,* the word *fond,* which requires a prepositional phrase like *of marshmallows* to follow it (and to be a sister of *fond* on a tree diagram). We can, however, substitute just an adjective for the phrase *fond of marshmallows.* Compare these next two examples:

The scoutmaster was **fond of marshmallows.**
The scoutmaster was **obstinate.**

The adjective *obstinate* is not only an adjective but an adjectival phrase (AP), just as *fond of marshmallows* is an adjectival phrase. It is also the head and only constituent of the adjectival phrase.

What exactly is a *head?* First and most important, the head of a phrase is the word around which the phrase is organized. This is why the head of a phrase cannot be omitted. Secondly, the category of the head is the category to which the phrase belongs. Thirdly, the head word is typically the semantic nucleus of the phrase. Single-word phrases, in which the word is also the whole phrase, consist of nothing but such a nucleus. Multiple-word phrases have other categories as constituents, and these constituents bear grammatical relations within the phrase. In fact, the notion *head* of a phrase is itself a grammatical relation, not a word or phrase category.

Let's return now to the sentence *The government expelled the officers from Thailand.* Constituent structures for the two interpretations of the sentence can now reflect categoriality as well as linearity and hierarchy. Just one of the alternative structures is shown here:

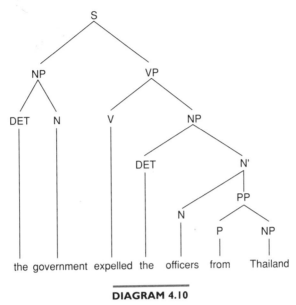

DIAGRAM 4.10

The constituent structure above shows the determiner *the* has as its sister constituent a unit consisting of the noun *officers* and the prepositional phrase *from Thailand.* In the diagram we have shown this unit as N'. (We will be discussing this category in Chapter 5.) All of these units together form a single, higher-level noun phrase. This higher-level noun phrase functions as the object.

SUMMARY

Sentences can be viewed as linear sequences of words. There are groupings within these sequences that result in hierarchical structures on which sister and daughter relations can be defined. A particular sequence may be structurally ambiguous, giving rise to more than one interpretation, each corresponding to a different constituent structure tree. In addition to these properties of linearity and hierarchy, sentences have the property of categoriality. The words of sentences fall into lexical categories, with each category (and subcategory) having its special properties and distribution. Moreover, there are higher-level phrasal categories that function as sentence constituents and which include one or more lexical forms. Phrasal categories are organized around a lexical head. The lexical category to which the head belongs determines the phrasal category. Languages tend to vary in systematic ways, some exploiting word order more intensively, others making greater use of affixes and case-marking. Word order itself varies fairly systematically, with interesting correlations, for example, between verb-object order and head-modifier order. These alternatives or options are viewed as settings on language parameters. They are of special interest to those involved in second language teaching and learning and in acquisition research, because they have to do with the ways we mentally process language data.

EXERCISE SET 4

1. Rewrite the following sentences using Japanese word order. Omit all articles. The first has been done for you.

    a. *Hiro took Masako to the school by the park.*
       Hiro Masako park-by school-to took.
    b. *Ota saw Tanaka in Kyoto.*
    c. *The man in the brown suit ate the sushi.*

2. List the verb phrases in the following sentences:

    a. *Two firemen entered the hall.*
    b. *A doctor with a huge stethoscope climbed up the cliff.*
    c. *Almost eighty percent of the individuals questioned had started smoking before age twelve.*
    d. *The news failed to impress his family.*
    e. *In the afternoon, the women will take over the assignments.*

3. Which of the following underlined strings of words form constituents?

    a. *<u>Carrie was</u> the leader of the group.*
    b. *Carrie <u>was the leader of the group.</u>*
    c. *Carrie was <u>the leader of the group.</u>*
    d. *Carrie was the leader of <u>the group.</u>*
    e. *Carrie was the leader <u>of the group.</u>*
    f. *Carrie was the leader <u>of the</u> group.*

4. Draw constituent tree structures for the following sentences:

    a. *An ostrich seized the ribbon.*
    b. *Those crocodiles came from Egypt.*
    c. *The woman in the boat jumped into the water.*

5. Look at the tree you drew for 4b. List the constituents (with their category names) that are sisters of each other and the category of the higher constituent whose daughters they are.

Example: The noun phrase *those crocodiles* and the verb phrase *came from Egypt* are sisters; they are daughters of the S.

6. To what lexical categories do the following words belong?

    a. *house*   b. *rope*   c. *dry*   d. *fast*   e. *slow*   f. *run*

7. The following two sentences are ambiguous:

    The lawyer looked at the judge with suspicious eyes.
    Phil hit the man with a red flashlight.

    State the two meanings for each sentence and explain how the ambiguity of each sentence is due to differences in hierarchical structure.

8. What can you tell about the grammar of this sample of the Southern Slonal language? Assume that this sample is representative of the language as a whole.

    a.

Ata-stasy	Karlosa	predai	nyui	kvarta-si
visit	Carlos	girl	that	morning-in

    "Carlos will visit that girl in the morning."

b.	*lla-stasy*	*preda*	*nyu*	*Karlosai*	*Tala-si*
	visit	girl	that	Carlos	Tala-in

"That girl has visited Carlos in Tala."

NOTES

1. Readable discussions of this acquisition and of the "critical period" hypothesis are to be found in Jean Aitchison, *The Articulate Mammal: An Introduction to Psycholinguistics*, 2nd ed. (London: Hutchinson, 1983), and also in Jill and Peter de Villiers, *Language Acquisition* (Cambridge, MA: Harvard University Press, 1978). At a more advanced level is Anne Peters, *The Units of Language Acquisition* (Cambridge, UK: Cambridge University Press, 1983). For an important consideration of related issues in second language acquisition, see M. Long, "Maturational constraints on language development," *Studies in Second Language Acquisition* 12 (1990): 251-85.

PART

II

CLAUSES IN ENGLISH

5

Clause Structures

One teaching exercise popular with many English language instructors provides students with a sentence structure or pattern that they must imitate. Here is a typical structure for transitive clauses (i.e., clauses with objects):

SUBJECT	FREQUENCY	VERB	DIRECT OBJECT	PLACE	TIME
Doctors	rarely	visit	patients	in their homes	at night
Britons	normally	prefer	fish and chips	overseas	during the summer

Then the students are given lists of forms that can fill the slots. For example, one list might include the following: *children, Americans, chefs, customs officials, wrestlers, cats.* Any one of these could be inserted into either the subject or direct object slots. Other exercises might have learners suggesting their own items for each slot. The same kind of exercise can be used for other types of clauses such as intransitive clauses. Grammarians looking at such exercises would notice that they exploit the kinds of properties discussed in the last chapter—*linearity, hierarchy,* and *categoriality.* Teachers would need to be aware of the ranges of options available for clause sequences.

In this chapter we start to look in more detail at the options for clause structure, not just the linear sequences but the hierarchical structures exploited in English, and the grammatical categories used. We are interested not only in the *units* employed but also in the grammatical *relations* between the units. We will be applying tests to check grammatical analyses and to distinguish between clauses that look structurally identical at first glance, yet are not treated as such by native speakers. Those learning English have to acquire these distinctions, and our grammatical analyses must reflect them.

WHAT ARE CLAUSES?

Clauses are constructions with one phrase constituent, typically a noun phrase, that bears the subject relation and another constituent, the verb phrase, bearing the predicate relation. This construction:

a woman in a 1993 Jaguar sedan

cannot be a clause because it lacks a verb phrase. Here is one example of a clause:

Clara delayed her graduation

The subject of the clause is *Clara* and the verb phrase is *delayed her graduation*. This clause can stand on its own as a sentence, but could also be embedded inside another clause. We could replace the object noun phrase *the rumor* in this sentence:

*I heard **the rumor.***

with the *Clara* clause:

*I heard **(that) Clara delayed her graduation.***

Now the *Clara* clause is the object of the verb phrase whose head is *heard*.

Notice that the embedded clause can be introduced with *that*. This introducing word, *that*, is known as the *complementizer*. The complementizer was optional in the last example, when the embedded clause was the object, but it can never be omitted when the embedded clause is *subject* of another clause:

***That Clara delayed her graduation** is unfortunate.*

Complementizers never occur when the clause is an independent clause, that is, one capable of being a full sentence on its own.

We need to mention here one important parameter for clauses that will be dealt with in more detail in a later chapter, the *finiteness* parameter. Clauses can be either *finite* or *nonfinite*. In the *Clara* clause, with or without the complementizer *that*, the verb phrase begins with *delayed*, a verb marked for past tense. Alternatively, the verb could have been preceded by *may, can, would, will, should, might, must, could*, or *ought to*, special verb forms known as *modals*. Clauses that have either modals or verbs indicating past or present tense are known as *finite* clauses.

What are *nonfinite* clauses then? They are clauses in which the predicate phrase begins not with a present or past tense verb or a modal but with a *to* before the verb. The verb with *to* is often called an infinitive verb. Nonfinite clauses are like finite clauses in that they have a verb phrase and a subject, though the subject is sometimes understood rather than overt. Also like finite clauses, they can be introduced by a complementizer. But their complementizer is not *that* but *for*. Here is an example:

***(for)** Clara to delay her graduation*

The subject is again *Clara* and the predicate phrase is *to delay her graduation*. The complementizer *for* enables us to embed this clause into a larger clause, as in these two examples:

***For Clara to delay her graduation** is unnecessary.*
*Mrs. Trowbridge was unwilling **for Clara to delay her graduation.***

Grammatical Relations Within Clauses

The terms *subject* and *object* are not names of categories. In contrast to terms like *noun phrase* and *verb phrase*, they are names of grammatical relations. A particular phrase may in one clause bear a different grammatical relation from one the same phrase bears in a different clause, just as the same person can be a father, a son, or a brother, depending on the family grouping being considered. A noun phrase like *that chemist* can bear the subject relation in a clause, as in this example:

***That chemist** is studying synthetic hormones.*

The noun phrase *that chemist* is in the subject position, in front of the verb. In the object position after the verb is another noun phrase, *synthetic hormones*. Note the effect of the first noun phrase on the verb. Since the noun phrase is singular, the present tense verb has the form *is* rather than *are*. The verb *agrees in number* with its subject, that is, its form shows it has a singular rather than plural subject. Of course, *that chemist* can bear some other relation within a clause, for example, that of the object of a preposition like *by:*

Synthetic hormones are being studied by that chemist.

SENTENCE AND PHRASE CONSTITUENTS

Structurally, English sentences are organized as two major constituents, as the following constituent structure tree indicates:

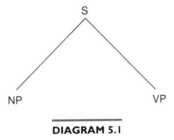

DIAGRAM 5.1

Heads of Phrases

As we saw in Chapter 4, each phrase must have a head. A noun phrase has a noun as head, a verb phrase has a verb as head, a prepositional phrase a preposition as head, and an adjective phrase an adjective as head. Here is a constituent structure tree in which the phrases contain only a head category:

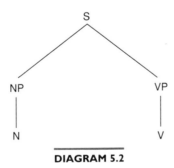

DIAGRAM 5.2

In this next sentence:

A wolf howled mournfully.

the subject noun phrase consists of a determiner, in this case the indefinite article *a*, followed by its head noun *wolf*. The verb phrase has as its head the verb *howled*, but there is also another constituent, the manner adverb *mournfully*, specifying the manner in which the wolf howled. So the constituent structure of the sentence would look like this:

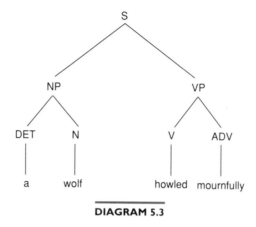

DIAGRAM 5.3

Additional Noun Phrase Constituents

Let's look now at some more complicated noun phrases that occur as subjects or objects. The following sentence:

The lonely ploughman talked to the cows.

has as its subject a noun phrase with three constituents: the definite article *the;* the head noun *ploughman;* and the adjective *lonely.* The adjective *lonely* is the head and only constituent of an adjective phrase. Here is a constituent structure for the noun phrase *the lonely ploughman:*

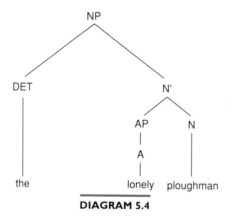

DIAGRAM 5.4

One feature of the tree structure shown for *the lonely ploughman* is the use of an intermediate label N′ between NP and N. This is because we believe that an adjective phrase and its head noun form a special unit, also a constituent. One way to check whether a group of words with a noun as its likely head actually forms a constituent is to see if it can be replaced by a pronoun. Instead of saying this:

Claudia was in love with this lonely ploughman while Isabel was infatuated with that lonely ploughman.

we can say this, with the pronoun *one* replacing *lonely ploughman:*

> *Claudia was in love with this lonely ploughman while Isabel was infatuated with that **one**.*

Since *one* substitutes for *lonely ploughman,* we have shown that *lonely ploughman* is indeed a constituent, one that is a sister of the determiner on the tree diagram. Clearly, *lonely ploughman* is not a full noun phrase, since it needs a determiner; but neither is it a single noun—an intermediate category is needed, one higher than noun and lower than noun phrase. We will show it here as N', and call it "N-bar."

The subject of this next sentence:

> **The man in the iron mask** *ate a watermelon.*

includes the determiner *the* and an N-bar constituent consisting of the head noun *man* and a prepositional phrase with its own head, the preposition *in:*

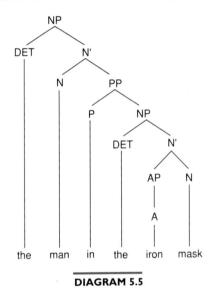

DIAGRAM 5.5

The determiner *the* thus has as its sister constituent an N' with two daughter constituents, the head noun *man,* and the prepositional phrase *in the iron mask.*

Finally, think about the object noun phrase *the news that Joan had escaped from Orleans* in the following sentence:

> *The messengers spread* **the news that Joan had escaped from Orleans.**

The object noun phrase consists of the determiner *the* plus an N-bar consisting of the head noun *news* and a whole clause introduced by the complementizer *that: that Joan had escaped from Orleans.* Following is a constituent structure tree for the entire sentence. The triangle shown for the embedded clause *that Joan had escaped from Orleans* saves us from having to specify details of the internal structure of the clause. Where the internal structure of a clause or noun phrase or verb phrase is not immediately relevant to the discussion, we will use a triangle.

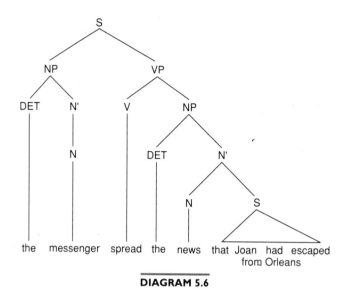

DIAGRAM 5.6

The embedded clause is the sister constituent of the head noun *news,* and they are both daughters of the N'.

TYPES OF CLAUSES

Noun phrases are not the only constituents made up of various combinations of phrases and even clauses. The verb phrase also allows a range of combinations. Thus, clauses are categorized as *intransitive, transitive, copular,* and *ditransitive,* depending on how many argument noun phrases or clauses, if any, follow the verb.

Intransitive and Transitive Clauses

Consider again the verb phrases in the examples:

> *Dogs **bark.***
> *A wolf **howled mournfully.***
> *The lonely ploughman **talked to the cows.***

None of these three contain a verb directly followed by an object. Here is a constituent tree for the sentence about the cows:

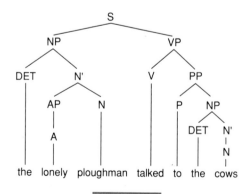

DIAGRAM 5.7

Clauses like these, in which the verbs do not take objects, are called *intransitive clauses*. The verbs are said to be used intransitively. *Transitive clauses* are clauses in which the verb is directly followed by a noun phrase or an embedded clause. Thus, the following are all examples of transitive clauses:

*The panther climbed **the tree**.*
*The mayor rejected **the petitions**.*
*Dr. Faustus knew **that Helen was unreliable**.*

But not all clauses with a sequence of a verb followed by a noun phrase are transitive clauses. Consider this clause in which the verb is followed by a noun phrase:

*Esmeralda arrived **the next day**.*

The noun phrase *the next day* is a time noun phrase that could be shifted to the beginning of the clause. It is not part of a verb phrase whose head is *arrived,* and it is not an argument of the predicate ARRIVE. It is thus not a daughter of the verb phrase. The clause is an intransitive clause and there is no sister slot for an object. Transitive clauses, however, have an object position after the main verb. The noun phrases after the verbs *climbed* and *rejected* in the previous two examples are objects of their verb phrases.

One useful way to test whether a clause is transitive is to see whether it has a passive counterpart. Look at these pairs of examples:

The panther climbed the tree.
The tree was climbed by the panther.
The mayor rejected the petitions.
The petitions were rejected by the mayor.

The first clause in each pair is a transitive clause. Only transitive clauses have passive voice counterparts. See what happens when we try to form a passive voice clause corresponding to the intransitive clause with the time noun phrase:

Esmeralda arrived the next day.
*The next day was arrived by Esmeralda.

Unlike the noun phrase objects in the other examples, *the next day* cannot be the subject of the passive voice clause. In the active voice clause it isn't the object of the verb phrase. Phrases like *the next day* are optional constituents known as *adjuncts*. Adjuncts are more freely moved than are required constituents. Thus *the next day* can be shifted to the front of the clause:

***The next day** Esmeralda arrived.*

The passive voice test is probably the most reliable way to check whether an active voice clause is transitive or intransitive. In the next section we'll examine another kind of clause that looks like a transitive clause but isn't. Again we'll apply the passive test.

Copular Verb Clauses

The verbs *be, seem,* and *become* are all copular verbs. In *copular verb clauses,* a copular verb is followed by a noun phrase but the noun phrase is not an object. Since transitive clauses are by definition clauses with objects, these clauses therefore cannot be transitive. We can predict that they have no passive voice counterparts.

Let's examine some copular verb clauses to see if this is the case. Look at the following active voice clauses, each with a noun phrase after a copular verb:

This animal is a pachyderm.
The burglar became an art connoisseur.

These clauses have no corresponding passive voice clauses. If there were such passives, they would look like these:

*A pachyderm is been (by this animal).
*An art connoisseur was become (by the burglar).

The passive test thus indicates that the noun phrases after the verbs in these sentences are not objects. Note, however, that they are required noun phrases, not adjuncts. That's why the sentences would sound strange if these noun phrases were moved in front of the subjects:

*A pachyderm this animal is.
*An art connoisseur the burglar became.

Copular verbs can only be in the active voice form, and noun phrases following them are never objects.

What, then, are these noun phrases? It's clear, first of all, that they have a different semantic function. They are not assigned thematic roles by the verb. They are never agents or goals or instruments. The role *theme* is so vaguely defined that it could seem to apply to these noun phrases. But a closer look reveals that it does not. In the example sentences, the semantic relationship between the copular verb and the noun phrase following is very different from those between other verbs we've looked at and subsequent argument noun phrases. The copular verb *is* in this sentence:

This animal is a pachyderm.

cannot be interpreted as the semantic predicate. The verb *is* carries very little meaning; nor do other copular verbs such as *seem, appear,* and *become.* What *is* does semantically is indicate time reference. The major semantic core of the predicate is expressed by the noun phrase following the verb, *a pachyderm.*

These noun phrases following copular verbs are called *predicate noun phrases.* There are other respects in which they differ from other noun phrases. For example, forms like *president* and *teacher* can be predicate noun phrases, but they cannot be subjects unless they are preceded by a determiner. That's why these two sentences are grammatical:

*Now Kelly is **president** again.*
*Travis is **teacher** today.*

while the next two are very strange:

Now **president is Kelly again.*
*Teacher is Travis today.

In fact, other kinds of constituents can fill this special predicate position. A copular verb need not be followed by a noun phrase. Thus, in addition to sentences like:

*The dormouse was **a sluggard.***

there are similar sentences with *a predicate adjective phrase* after the copular verb:

*The dormouse was **sluggish.***
*The dormouse was **angry about the cold tea.***

Prepositional phrases can also occur in this position:

*The dormice were **in the house.***
*The dormice were **in the mood for good runny cheese.***

Ditransitive Clauses

Ditransitive clauses have two argument constituents in the verb phrase. The first noun phrase immediately following the verb normally refers to a living creature, the second to something nonliving. We'll describe here the two major classes of ditransitive clause.

Goal ditransitive clauses have immediately following the verb an object noun phrase with the goal role. This object is called the *indirect object:*

*They gave **Angelica** a Golden Globe award.*
*The parlormaid will lend **Arabella** an umbrella.*
*The generals have sold **the rebels** twenty-three tanks.*

The second object argument is assigned the theme role. For most sentences like these, there are counterparts in which the first object has switched places with the second object and must be introduced by the preposition *to*. The noun phrase that was the indirect object is now the object of a prepositional phrase headed by the preposition *to*. Look at these examples:

*They gave a Golden Globe award **to Angelica.***
*The parlormaid will lend an umbrella **to Arabella.***
*The generals have sold twenty-three tanks **to the rebels.***

These noun phrases are no longer indirect objects of the verbs but instead are objects of the preposition *to*. However, they are still arguments in their clause and cannot be omitted unless the context makes their mention unnecessary. We referred earlier to such noun phrases as oblique arguments, abbreviating the term as *OBL-to*.

Some goal ditransitive clauses are idioms. These typically have *give* as their predicate, but allow other predicates such as *show* and *sell*. Examples are *give the house a coat of paint, give the child a scolding, give the school a bad reputation, show the visitors a good time* (meaning "arrange for visitors to enjoy themselves"), and *sell them a bill of goods* (meaning "deceive them"). These have no counterparts with the goal proposition following *to*.

The same is true when the direct object is a clause rather than a noun phrase, as in these next examples:

*They told Angelica **that she must arrive early for the award.***
*They told Angelica **to arrive early for the award.***

There are no grammatical counterparts with *to:*

They told **that she must arrive early for the award to Angelica.*
They told **to arrive early for the award to Angelica.*

The second class of ditransitive clause, *benefactive ditransitive clauses*, contains predicates which assign the thematic role benefactive to the second object. In such clauses the second object, which is called the *benefactive object*, refers to who the action was done *for* rather than who it was done *to*. Not surprisingly, the preposition counterpart uses *for* rather than *to* before the oblique object:

*Craig baked **the club** a guava-chiffon cake.*
*Craig baked a guava-chiffon cake **for the club.***
*She carved **Franz** a jade figurine.*

*She carved a jade figurine **for Franz**.*
*The weary soldier made/built **them** a crude shelter.*
*The weary soldier made/built a crude shelter **for them**.*

There are, in addition to the two major classes of ditransitive clauses, clauses that cannot be so neatly classified because of special properties of their verbs. For instance, the verb *cost* can be followed by two arguments, but unlike other verbs in transitive and ditransitive clauses, it has no counterpart with a preposition:

*That party may cost **you a lot of money**.*
That party may cost **a lot of money to you.*

The verb *cost* is also unusual in that it has no passive counterpart:

*You may be cost a lot of money (by that party).

Other ditransitives do have passive counterparts:

Angelica was told (by them) to arrive early for the award.
The club was baked a guava-chiffon cake (by Craig).

Since the verb may have two objects, we might expect there to be two passive counterparts. After all, the object of a transitive clause is the unit that functions as subject for the counterpart passive clause. Two objects in the active voice should correspond to two subjects in the passive voice.

But this is not the case. Only the noun phrase that functions as the first object (i.e., as the indirect object) can be subject of a passive counterpart. Following is an active voice example along with two candidates for its passive counterpart:

*The group awarded **the college two special scholarships**.*
***The college** was awarded **two special scholarships** (by the group).*
*****Two special scholarships** were awarded **the college** (by the group).[1]*

Actually, the noun phrase *two special scholarships* can be the subject of a passive, but only in the counterparts of the examples with *to*:

***Two special scholarships** will be awarded **to the college** (by the group).*

Subject and Object Complements

There are certain clauses that look as if they are ditransitive clauses but in fact are not. In these bogus ditransitives, there is a special semantic relationship between the two noun phrases following the verb. The second noun phrase after the verb is semantically a predicate that is *about* the noun phrase before it. This semantic relationship is often close to, but not identical with, that between the subject of a clause with *be*, the copular verb, and the predicate noun phrase following the copular verb. Here are some examples:

*The commission called **the proposal a sham**. (cf. The proposal was a sham.)*
*The group elected **Randall president**. (cf. Randall was president.)*
*Shaw considered **Chesterton a fool**. (cf. Chesterton was a fool.)*

What can we say about the last noun phrase in each of the examples? *A sham* is a predicate about the proposal, *president* is predicated about Randall, and *a fool* is predicated about Chesterton. Note also that it is often possible to insert *to be* in front of the last noun phrase:

*Shaw considered Chesterton **to be** a fool.*

This indicates that the relationship between the predicate noun phrase and the object noun phrase preceding it is the same as that between the subject of a copular verb clause and its predicate noun phrase. The verb *consider* really takes only two arguments, a "considerer" and a proposition that is considered, in this case the proposition that Chesterton was a fool. Noun phrases like *a fool* are predicates, not arguments; therefore, they have neither a referent nor a thematic role.

Grammarians refer to noun phrases used this way as *object complements* because they bear a semantic relation (predicate) to the *object*. (The term "complement" is often used for constituents whose relation to an argument or sometimes a predicate is not one of modifying but one of completing the meaning.) Consider these examples:

*The Council appointed **Wang** chairman of the new commission.*
*They elected **her** chairman of the committee.*

The constituent following the first object can be introduced with *as* or *to be:*

*The Council appointed Wang **as** chairman of the new commission.*
*They elected her **to be** chairman of the committee.*

Similar verbs are *nominate* and *choose.* Such sentences have no counterpart with *to:*

The Council appointed chairman of the new commission **to Wang.*

Once more, the semantic relation between Wang and the object complement *chairman of the committee* is essentially the same as that between the subject of a copular verb clause and its predicate noun phrase:

Wang is chairman of the new commission.

But a complement can also be a predicate about the subject instead of the object. Compare these two sentences:

*Mavis left the house **a dirty, smelly slum.***
*Mavis left the house **a smiling, confident woman.***

The predicate noun phrase in the first example, *a dirty, smelly slum,* refers to the object, *the house.* It is thus an object complement. In the second example, however, the predicate noun phrase, *a smiling, confident woman,* refers to the subject, *Mavis,* not to the object, *the house.* So it is a subject complement, not an object complement.

These subject and object complements have exactly the properties that would be expected of noun phrases acting as predicates after *be* and the other copular verbs noted earlier. Since these noun phrases are really predicates, they cannot function as subjects in the passive counterparts:

*The commission called the proposal **a sham.***
*The proposal was called **a sham** (by the commission).*
****A sham** was called the proposal (by the commission).*

As in clauses with copular verbs, other categories besides verbs and noun phrases can be predicates. The following sentences use a predicate adjective phrase and a predicate prepositional phrase respectively:

*Shaw considered Chesterton **foolish.***
*The group elected Randall **to the presidency.***

The adjective phrase *foolish* and the prepositional phrase *to the presidency* both function semantically as predicates for the object noun phrase; that is, they are object complements. In the sentences following, an adjective phrase and a prepositional phrase function as subject complements:

>   *She left the room* **very happy.**
>   *She left the room* **in a good mood.**

Clearly the adjective and prepositional phrases in these examples are predicated about the subject rather than the object. We wouldn't interpret the sentences as meaning that the room was happy or that the room was in a good mood.

SOME TEACHING ISSUES

In this book we are demonstrating how English sentences are structured to present propositional content. At this juncture we should point out that the kind of discussion and analysis used for briefing teachers and other English language professionals is not necessarily the kind of presentation suitable for those learning English.

In this chapter we have dealt, for example, with major clause types and the number of arguments occurring in the various types. Obviously the different clause types must correspond in some fashion to broad meaning differences.

How might such content be presented in the English language classroom? In an exercise question in Chapter 2, a teacher in Malaysia was reported to have asked his class to check in their classroom dictionaries the meanings of the following adjectives and verbs:

>   *soft, hard, short, dark, quick*
>   *soften, harden, shorten, darken, quicken*

In a subsequent class, we noted, he tried with only partial success to get the students to formulate some grammatical and semantic generalizations about the data they had obtained. Why was the material so difficult for many learners?

One likely reason is that the material the teacher was presenting was too complex for efficient absorption by many of the learners. The first five forms are adjectives, the others verbs. He had hoped that students might notice that the adjectives all referred to states while the verbs all referred to the causing or bringing about of the same states. But generalizations other than the presence or absence of a causative sense can be drawn from the data. The verbs used transitively can also be used intransitively, and when used intransitively they have no causative sense.

The different phenomena needed to be carefully separated and taught in a sequence of short presentations and discussions. The teacher should have looked more closely at his list of forms, consulted a good dictionary to see the range of meanings his students would be examining, and checked the forms in a good reference grammar.

This teacher's objectives were valid ones—to have his class learn to generalize inductively over a body of language data connecting predicates in intransitive clauses with the same predicate forms in transitive clauses. For those students unfamiliar with such constructions, the exploration would provide a useful introduction to these phenomena. For those students already able to understand passages in which these forms occurred, the procedure, if successful, would make them conscious of the grammatical structures they were reading and perhaps more capable of producing new structures modeled on them. The learner is viewed as an active language investigator exploring the new language.

An alternative procedure would have been to present the data already analyzed. Then the class could have concentrated on applying and practicing the patterns. Such an approach assumes that language learning is a matter of acquiring a new set of habits. This is a deductive procedure focusing on the teacher as the source of grammatical knowledge and as drill sergeant.

A third alternative would have been to present the forms in the context of a piece of English prose and to determine by questioning and discussion whether the class understood the semantic roles of the arguments occurring with each predicate. This could well involve no explicit grammatical presentation, yet the learners might still show that they understand, consciously or unconsciously, the grammatical factors involved. Foreign language learning is thus viewed as being more like first language learning. Such an approach seeks to make students learn about structures (and vocabulary) in context; if the approach works, no rule study is needed.

Each of these possible approaches thus reflects different assumptions about language learning and the role of the teacher. Yet, for any of these approaches to succeed, the teacher needs to be conscious of the grammatical rules and principles being applied.

SUMMARY

English clause structure is more complex than it initially appears. Clauses that look structurally identical at first glance may in fact be significantly different. Clauses are constructions with a subject and a verb phrase. When they are main clauses and can function as independent sentences, they need no introducing element. Embedded clauses are usually but not always introduced by complementizers. Finite embedded clauses, in which there is either a modal or a past or present tense verb, typically have *that* as their complementizer, while nonfinite embedded clauses, in which there is no modal or past or present tense verb, can and sometimes must take *for*. Noun phrases, whether subjects or objects, must have a noun as head of the phrase. But they also contain an intermediate constituent consisting of the head noun and its modifiers. This constituent, called N-bar (N'), in the appropriate context, can be replaced by the pronoun *one*. This substitution of pronouns for word sequences is a valuable way to establish that a sequence is a constituent.

We have discussed four major clause types: *intransitive, transitive, copular,* and *ditransitive*. These were classified according to the number of arguments a particular predicate requires. Two classes of ditransitives were discussed: goal ditransitives, which typically corresponded to clauses with *to*, and benefactive ditransitives, which typically corresponded to clauses with *for*. There are bogus ditransitive clauses, in which the second noun phrase actually functions as a predicate rather than an argument. This is why it cannot be the subject of the passive form of the clause.

In most cases, a predicate adjective or prepositional phrase can be substituted for the predicate noun phrase without making the clause ungrammatical. The predicate, whether it is a predicate adjective, noun, or prepositional phrase, is either about the object and called an *object complement,* or about the subject and called a *subject complement*. The semantic relationship between this predicate and the noun phrase to which it refers is very similar to the relationship between the subject of a copular clause and the predicate adjective, noun, or prepositional phrases that follow the copular verb *be*.

Although learners of English need to acquire an implicit knowledge of the phenomena described, the analytical approach taken in this grammar is not necessarily appropriate for the second or foreign language classroom. Teachers need the explicit knowledge, but such analysis will in many cases confuse learners.

EXERCISE SET 5

1. Draw constituent structure trees for the following three sentences. You may use a triangle where you don't wish to go into detail about an embedded clause.
  a. *That brown soup tasted delicious.*
  b. *The nurses hurried into the clinic.*
  c. *The people believed the rumor that the general was dishonest.*

2. State what kind of phrase each of the following is and specify the head of the phrase:
  a. *extremely tall*
  b. *sings all those songs*
  c. *a child with a bouquet*
  d. *beyond the distant hills*

3. Identify the following boldfaced phrases as subject or object complements:
  a. *We consider him **an idiot**.*
  b. *The reports were believed **false**.*
  c. *They made them **angry**.*
  d. *Cedric entered the room **in a foul mood**.*

4. Below are two clauses. How does the semantic function of *a masterpiece* in (a) differ from that in (b)?
  a. *Marcel lent his mother a masterpiece.*
  b. *Marcel called that book a masterpiece.*

5.
  a. Rewrite sentence 4a (about Marcel) using the preposition *to*.
  b. Try to rewrite sentence 4b using *to*.
  c. Take the first object of *lent* and try to write it as the subject of a sentence whose predicate is *is a masterpiece*.
  d. Take the first object of *called* and write it as the subject of a sentence whose predicate is *is a masterpiece*.
  e. Now comment on the differences you have noted between *lend* and *call* and on the differences between sentences 4a and 4b.

6. How are the following sentences ambiguous and what have the two meanings to do with grammatical distinctions discussed in this chapter?
  a. *I called him a taxi.*
  b. *Marcie found Edward a fascinating person.*

7. Consider the following data from the speech of English-speaking children under four:
  a. *I'll brush him his hair.*
  b. *Pick me up all these things.*
  c. *I said her no.*
  d. *Button me the rest.*
  e. *Mummy, open Hadwen the door.*

and the following utterance by an eight-year-old:

    f.   *Mattia demonstrated me that yesterday.*[2]

Assume that the children have not heard anyone else uttering these sentences. What do you think is happening?

NOTES

1. Some speakers of what we will henceforth refer to as Commonwealth English allow such constructions. Commonwealth English is the set of English dialects spoken in Great Britain, Australia, New Zealand, South Africa, and the Indian subcontinent, all of them past or present members of the British Commonwealth of Nations. It has been noted that some speakers of North American English accept these constructions, but their judgments are often not consistent. Our example might be accepted by speakers who would reject *A medal was awarded the fireman.*

2. The data here, originally collected and discussed by Irene Mazurkewich and Lydia White and by Melissa Bowerman, are cited in a useful discussion in J. Gropen, S. Pinker, M. Hollander, R. Goldberg, and R. Wilson, "The learnability and acquisition of the dative alternation in English," *Language* 65 (1989): 203-57. See also Betty Le Compagnon, "Interference and overgeneralization in second language learning: the acquisition of English dative verbs by native speakers of French," *Language Learning* 34 (1984): 39-67, and Irene Mazurkewich, "The acquisition of the dative alternation by second language learners and linguistic theory," *Language Learning* 34 (1984): 91-109.

6

Dependent Clauses

Clause units are the basic grammatical packages for communication. For making statements, asking questions, or issuing instructions and requests, a clause is usually the minimal syntactic unit needed. Lesser constructions such as *More coffee, please* fill some of these functions, especially where social conventions and the particular context provide any additional information needed. But where fuller information has to be provided, clauses have the appropriate positions or *slots* for it. We noted in Chapter 5 that clauses can be inserted into subject and object slots in other clauses. In addition, there is a wide range of devices for linking clauses with other clauses.

MAIN CLAUSES VERSUS DEPENDENT CLAUSES

A clause that can stand alone as a sentence is called a *main clause* or sometimes an *independent clause*. The latter designation is often used when the clause is the only one in its sentence. To simplify matters, we will use only the term *main clause*. Here are two examples:

> *A soft breeze rippled the lake waters.*
> *The aspen leaves quivered delicately.*

Dependent clauses, on the other hand, do not stand on their own as sentences. Here are some examples:

> *for Sharon's car to break down*
> *that Sharon's car had broken down*
> *because Sharon's car had broken down*

Each of these dependent clauses has an introducing word before the clause subject. All three introducing words mark their clause as being a dependent clause.

However, the first two, *for* and *that*, have little or no special meaning of their own, and they were referred to as *complementizers* in the previous chapter. The third, *because*, has a very specific meaning, one something like "the reason is." Introducers such as *because, although*, and *since*, all of which have quite specific meanings, are *subordinators.*

Complementizers and subordinators are associated with two distinct kinds of dependent clauses: *embedded clauses* and *subordinate clauses*. Both kinds of clauses have a special slot before the subject, one in which the complementizer or subordinator occurs. This slot, known as the *COMP slot* (after "complementizer"), turns out to be a very important one. Let's examine how the two kinds of dependent clauses differ.

Embedded Clauses

Consider first the clauses with the complementizers *for* and *that*:

> *for Sharon's car to break down*
> *that Sharon's car broke down*

These clauses can occur as subjects or objects of other clauses; that is, like noun phrases, they can be arguments of a predicate. In the next sentence, the clause *for Sharon's car to break down* is the subject of the clause containing it:

> **For Sharon's car to break down** *would be unfortunate.*

We can, of course, substitute a noun phrase for this kind of dependent clause:

> **A breakdown** *would be unfortunate.*

The noun phrase *a breakdown* bears the same grammatical relation and has the same thematic role as the dependent clause *for Sharon's car to break down*. Both are subjects and both have the theme role assigned to them.

In the next example, the clause *that Sharon's car had broken down* is the object of the larger clause containing it:

> *The police reported* **that Sharon's car had broken down.**

The object clause can be replaced by an ordinary noun phrase object such as *the breakdown:*

> *The police reported* **the breakdown.**

Again, the noun phrase and the dependent clause bear the same grammatical relations and have the same thematic role.

This kind of dependent clause is an argument clause, which has been embedded inside a larger clause. That's why it's called an *embedded clause*. Those clauses that contain embedded clauses are called *container clauses* or *matrix clauses*. We will be using the term *container* in this book.

Subordinate Clauses

Subordinate clauses, clauses with subordinators in the COMP slot, differ from embedded clauses in that *they are not arguments of a predicate*. They are thus not used as subjects or objects:

> *****Because Sharon's car had broken down** *surprised Eric.*
> **The police denied* **because Sharon's car had broken down.**

Instead such clauses are usually linked to the beginning or end of some other clause. Subordinators such as *because* subordinate the clauses, that is, they assign the clauses a lesser grammatical status. The clauses are therefore called *subordinate clauses*, after the Latin *sub*, "under," and *ordo*, "rank." The clause to which the subordinate clause is attached is sometimes called the *superordinate clause* from the Latin *super*, "above" and, of course, *ordo*, "rank." In general, just as a subordinate clause has a lower grammatical rank than the clause to which it is linked, so the *content* expressed by the subordinate clause is backgrounded or made "subordinate" to the content of the clause to which it is linked.

In many grammars, subordinate clauses are called *adverbial clauses*. The rationale is that just as adverbs modify verbs, so these subordinate clauses supply additional information modifying the more general content of the verb in the other clause. In fact, most subordinate clauses, like adverbs, could just as reasonably be said to modify the whole clause. The information subordinate clauses supply is relevant to the gist of the superordinate clause.

The subordinator indicates the kind of relevance its clause has to the superordinate clause. A *because* clause is relevant as a reason for the state of affairs described in its superordinate clause. A clause introduced by *in order that* is relevant as a purpose underlying the action expressed in its superordinate clause. Other kinds of relevance are indicated by other subordinators. Some of these are *after, where,* and *if.* Here are examples:

> The family returned to the villa **after Sharon's car had broken down.**
> Pavlova found the children **where Sharon's car had broken down.**
> Lord Aston only used his Rolls Royce **if Sharon's car broke down.**

The subordinator *after* indicates that it is the time aspect of the subordinate clause that is relevant; *where* indicates that the location where the children were found is the relevant relation of the subordinate clause to its superordinate clause; while *if* shows its clause to be relevant as the condition under which the Rolls Royce is used. This relevance relation will be called the *perspective* of the subordinate clause.

Nonfinite subordinate clauses often lack an overt subordinator. Compare the following sentences:

> She locked the doors **so as** to prevent any more intrusions.
> She locked the doors to prevent any more intrusions.

The perspective of the subordinate clause is clearly one of *purpose,* with or without the subordinator *so as.* Note that *in order that, in order for,* and *so that* actually include the complementizers *that* and *for.* Although this suggests an analysis in which subordinators precede complementizers, it is simpler here just to treat these overt so-called complementizers as part of the subordinator.

Typically, subordinate clauses are classified according to semantic criteria—whether their perspective on the content of the superordinate clause, as indicated by their subordinator, is one of time, location, manner, reason, etc. Here is a listing of subordinate clauses identified as to their perspectives:

TABLE 6.1

Subordinator	Clause	Perspective
after	Lee met them	TIME
before	Trollope died	TIME
since	I last met them	TIME
until	we meet again	TIME

(continued)

TABLE 6.1 (continued)

Subordinator	Clause	Perspective
when	you are in love	TIME
while	they were eating	TIME
where	Melville wrote it	LOCATION
because	Achilles was angry	REASON
since	you didn't pay me	REASON
as if	Carl was sick	MANNER
as though	Jill hadn't seen him	MANNER
so that	we'd miss them	PURPOSE
in order that	Joe would confess	PURPOSE
so as	to avoid the police	PURPOSE
in order	to avoid the police	PURPOSE
as (many) as	Jane had	COMPARISON
more than	Jane had	COMPARISON
(tall)-er than	Jane was	COMPARISON
(al)though	they refused	CONTRAST
even though	she was rich	CONTRAST
despite	(my) hating eggs	CONTRAST
so (that)	it was a success	RESULT
if	Sam had read it	CONDITION

SUBORDINATE CLAUSES VERSUS EMBEDDED CLAUSES

The following difference between embedded and subordinate clauses is an important one. If embedded clauses are omitted from a sentence containing them, the sentence is usually ungrammatical. This is because embedded clauses are arguments of a higher predicate, very often the subjects or objects of their container clause. Any finite clause sentence that loses its subject or object argument becomes ungrammatical. So the embedded clauses are indispensable for grammaticality.

Subordinate clauses, however, are adjuncts. Adjuncts, unlike required arguments, can be omitted without making their sentence ungrammatical. Just as adverbs and prepositional phrases can be omitted, so can subordinate clauses; they are not arguments of the predicate. Thus the three examples we discussed earlier are well formed even without their subordinate clauses:

The family returned to the villa.
Pavlova found the children.
Lord Aston used his Rolls Royce.

As we have seen, a subordinate clause is always attached to its superordinate clause. This superordinate clause is frequently the main clause of the sentence. Typically, the subordinate clause either immediately precedes or immediately follows its higher clause:

When we met them, the brothers were arguing about a football game.
The brothers were arguing about a football game when we met them.[1]

But there is also the option of inserting the adjunct inside the higher clause:

The brothers, **when we met them,** *were arguing about a football game.*

Although the subordinate clause is inside the higher clause, it has no grammatical function within the clause. It is not an argument of the predicate *were arguing,* nor is it part of an argument.

This is important because, as we've seen, embedded clauses are often arguments in their container clauses. Note that commas set off the subordinate clause from what is around it and show that it is not a structural part of the clause in which it occurs. In spoken English, a slight intonation break fills the same role as the commas. The clause is a separate intonation unit.

The different clause types we've discussed here are shown in the following chart:

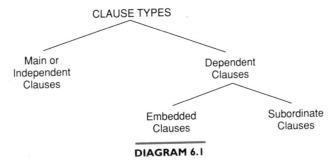

DIAGRAM 6.1

DEPENDENT CLAUSES IN CONSTITUENT STRUCTURE

What kind of constituent structure do sentences with dependent clauses have? We'll start with embedded clauses. Here are two sentences with embedded clauses:

That Sharon's car had broken down *astonished the mechanic.*
The police denied **that Sharon's car had broken down.**

These sentences have the following constituent structures:

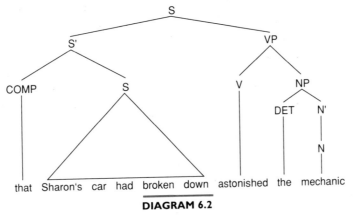

DIAGRAM 6.2

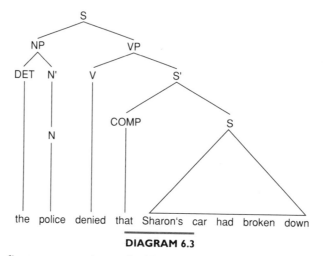

DIAGRAM 6.3

Note that in the first sentence the embedded clause is the subject argument of its container clause. In the second sentence, the embedded clause is in the object position, after the transitive verb *denied*.

We have made one innovation in the two trees just shown, the introduction of the label S´. Despite the fact that *that Sharon's car had broken down* is a clause and therefore an S, the sequence inside it, *Sharon's car broke down*, also looks like an S. To distinguish them, the full clause form with its complementizer is shown as S´ (call it S-bar). The complementizer is in the slot marked COMP.

The constituent structures of subordinate clauses are very similar to those of embedded clauses. Look at the following example:

We visited the Olympics, although we avoided the crowds.

The sequence *although we avoided the crowds* is a clause and therefore an S; the sequence inside it, *we avoided the crowds*, also looks like an S. So once again we will show the full clause form (with its subordinator in the COMP slot) as S´ (S-bar). Note that we also show an S-bar for the main clause. The comp slot for this S-bar is the slot into which auxiliary verbs move for questions. Question sentences are covered in a later chapter. For now we will focus on the lower S-bar.

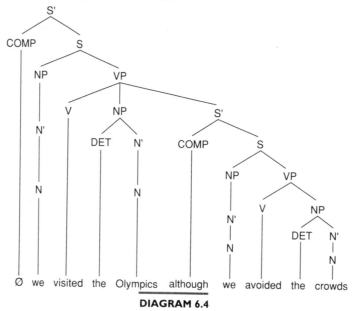

DIAGRAM 6.4

The whole S-bar in the subordinate clause is attached to the verb phrase in our constituent structure tree. However, when the subordinate S-bar is shifted so that it precedes the main clause, we will attach it to the main clause S-bar:[2]

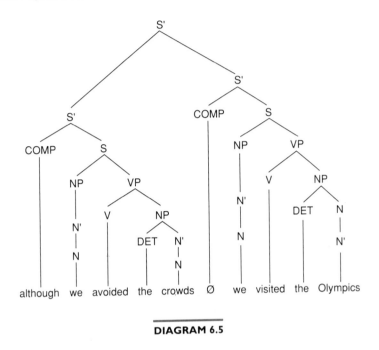

DIAGRAM 6.5

LEARNER CONFUSIONS

It's not uncommon for native speakers of English to write dependent clauses as if they were full sentences. Often, this represents just a misunderstanding of punctuation conventions, one that teachers sometimes try to remedy by having the writer read the "sentence" aloud. The student should realize from the intonation that something is wrong.

Non-native speakers, however, may not have acquired a mastery of the appropriate intonation and, in addition, may have more serious problems. Some forms used as subordinators have other functions. For instance, *(al)though* is a subordinator in the following sentence:

(Al)though Sharon's car had broken down, she was in good spirits.

But it also occurs in verbless constructions like *(al)though a young man, (al)though angry, and (al)though in a gloomy mood.*

There are other words with about the same semantic content that are not subordinators. *However* is close in meaning to *(al)though*, but it is never used as a subordinator. It functions instead as an introducer for an independent clause, one which contrasts semantically with the sentence preceding it, as in this next example:

They had expected Sharon to drive them to Ottawa. **However,** *Sharon's car had broken down.*

Non-native speakers can mistake *however* for a subordinator like *(al)though:*

*However Carl was old man, he could lift heavy weights.
*Mozart was working hard however he was very ill.

But the confusion can also work the other way, with both native and non-native speakers of English treating a subordinate clause as an independent sentence:

> *Although Sharon's car had broken down.

Although relevant, the information in subordinate clauses is, as we have seen, generally the less crucial information. A skillful writer can achieve interesting effects by reversing this general strategy of putting less crucial information into subordinate clauses. Consider the following example:

> It had been a quiet summer **until, one Sunday at 4:17 in the morning, a tornado struck the little Oklahoma township.**

The important information, that a tornado occurred, is in the subordinate clause beginning with *until*. Note that because the clause is an adjunct it can be omitted without rendering the sentence ungrammatical. Of course, the most important information would then be missing.[3]

Covert Subjects

Many subordinate clauses lack an overt subject, for example, *so as to avoid the police*, as in:

> Dominique left early **so as [e] to avoid the police.**

A subject is always understood in such clauses. We have used the symbol [e] (for empty) to mark where a subject might have occurred if the grammar had allowed it. In this last example, English speakers understand *Dominique* to be the subject of the subordinate clause *so as to avoid the police*. Such understood though not physically present subjects are referred to as *covert subjects*. Covert subjects are cognitively real, that is, real in the English speaker's consciousness, despite the lack of words standing for them.

Covert subjects also occur in subordinate clauses whose predicate is a present or past participle:

> **[e] pushing him aside,** Carol jumped onto the platform.
> **[e] battered by the heavy storm,** the ship limped into Southampton harbor.

These participial constructions express such perspectives as time and reason. Although they seem like modifiers of the noun phrase following them, both their position and their function show that they are not. They are nonfinite subordinate clauses marking a perspective. Sometimes, a more explicit marking of perspective appears:

> **After** [e] being battered by the heavy storm, the ship limped into Southampton harbor.

Clause Coordination and Conjunction Reduction

The sentences discussed so far have had just one main clause each, but it's not hard to find sentences with more than one main clause:

> Theodora is a saint, but she has no patience.
> The water jug's empty and Miss Chaffey hasn't got the legs to fetch more.

The first sentence consists of two clauses, each of which could have stood alone. They are conjoined (linked together) by the contrast conjunction *but*. The second sentence is more complicated. It consists of three clauses. One of them, *The water jug's empty*, is conjoined with a second, *Miss Chaffey hasn't got the legs to fetch more*, the linking being done by the conjunction *and*. Both clauses could have stood on their own. But the second clause has embedded inside it a third clause, *to fetch more*, with a covert subject.

Because neither of the conjoined clauses in these sentences is subordinate to the other (the two clauses are equal in rank), they are called *coordinate clauses*. The linking together of sentences in this way is known as *coordination*. However, intuitively, the conjunction seems more closely linked with the clause following it than with the preceding clause. Its position is similar to that of a complementizer, as the following constituent structure indicates.

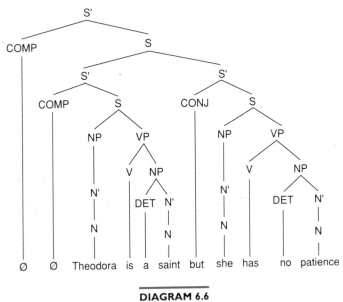

DIAGRAM 6.6

Coordination does not have to be at the main clause level, and the number of clauses conjoined is not limited to two. In the first example below, three *subordinate* clauses are conjoined; in the second, two *embedded* clauses are conjoined:

> *I will return to the house* **when Ludmilla has cleaned the oven, when Alyosha stops smoking that filthy pipe, and when Varvara has polished the samovar.**

> *They wanted* **Carl to report to the Halton air force base and Helena to wait in Norwich for instructions.**

Note that when more than two clauses are conjoined, the conjunction usually precedes only the last conjoined clause.

English allows conjoined clauses to be "reduced" where certain constituents are repeated. This phenomenon is known as *conjunction reduction*. Following are some examples. We'll use [e] (for "empty") to mark the gaps resulting from reduction. Which are the constituents represented by the gaps?

> *Today, Jeremy goes to an art exhibition, Melissa [e] to the Observatory, and the Steinbergs [e] to a Chopin recital.*

> *Wu visited Dorchester in March, [e] [e] Ringwood in April, and [e] [e] Piddletrenthide early in June.*

> *Interco won an award for increased productivity, and Sun Industries [e] [e] for sound employee relations.*

The first example has one empty slot. The verb *goes* is omitted from the slot after *Melissa* and its plural form *go* from the corresponding slot after *the Steinbergs*. But the second example has two empty slots; it omits both a subject and its verb (i.e., *Wu visited*) from the slots before *Ringwood* and *Piddletrenthide*. The third example also has two empty slots; it omits a verb and its object, *won an award*, from after *Sun Industries*.

Note that the constituents omitted need not be exactly the same forms as their counterparts earlier in the sentence. Thus in the first example, the first verb form was *goes*, but the third verb, had it been included, would have been *go*. The form of the verb can be figured out from its context. The other constituents need to have the same meaning, otherwise we wouldn't be able to figure out what the omitted verbs meant.

Clauses Embedded in Adjective Phrases

Look at the following sentences containing embedded clauses:

> *It was unfortunate* **that Sharon's car broke down.**
> *It is quite ridiculous* **for Harrison to go to Birmingham.**

In the previous examples, the embedded clause was an argument of a verb. But in this present one, the semantic predicates are adjectives: *unfortunate* and *ridiculous*. So adjectives also take clauses as arguments. These predicate adjectives assign the thematic role *theme* to the clause embedded after them. Take note of the following constituent structure for one of our examples:

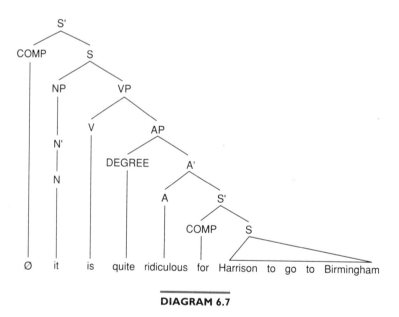

DIAGRAM 6.7

The S-bar appears inside the adjective phrase. It is a sister of the adjective.

We have now shown the full adjective phrase *quite ridiculous for Harrison to go to Birmingham* as made up of two parts, the degree word *quite* and the rest of the phrase, which, following the precedent set by N-bar and S-bar, it is useful to show as A-bar.

Now, if an adjective can have an embedded clause as its theme argument, shouldn't it be possible that adjectives also take noun phrases as theme arguments? If they could, wouldn't these arguments be rather like objects? It seems a little farfetched to think of adjectives as taking objects; however, it is certainly true that some adjectives, like *unfor-*

tunate and *ridiculous,* assign a theme role to a constituent following them, while others such as *dead* and *compassionate* cannot:

> *His dog is dead **that Sharon's car broke down.***
> *Florence was compassionate **for Harrison to go to Birmingham.***

There is certainly a parallel here with transitivity and intransitivity in verbs.

Think about the adjective *fond.* Its meaning is very close to that of the verb *like.* Now, *like* requires two arguments. Both would be noun phrases, such as *we* and *those muffins* in this next example:

> *We like those muffins.*

Replace *like* with the predicate adjective *fond* (introduced by *are*):

> *We are fond those muffins.*

The meaning of this sentence is clear enough, but grammatically the sentence is defective. For reasons we'll discuss in a later chapter, a preposition has to precede *those muffins:*

> *We are fond **of** those muffins.*

The preposition *of* differs from other prepositions in lacking any real meaning. It is simply inserted to allow the adjective to have a noun phrase as its complement. In fact, some grammarians have claimed that it is not a true preposition at all.[4] *Fond* resembles *like* in that it, too, takes two arguments. The noun phrases *we* and *those muffins* bear the same semantic relation to the predicate adjective *fond* as they did to the transitive verb *like.* Both *fond* and *like* assign the thematic role experiencer to their subject and that of theme to the argument after the predicate. It's not surprising, then, that for many English adjectives the nearest counterparts in some other languages are verbs. Semantically, adjectives are very close to being verbs in English.

In Chapter 3, we mentioned the use of the filler pronoun *it* without a thematic role. This phenomenon occurs when there is a predicate, often an adjective (introduced, of course, by a copular verb), followed by an embedded clause. Compare the following sentences:

> *It was unfortunate **that Sharon's car broke down.***
> ***That Sharon's car broke down** was unfortunate.*

The first example contains a noun phrase without a thematic role, the filler *it.* Not all languages have such fillers. If English did not, there might exist sentences like this:

> *Was unfortunate **that Sharon's car broke down.***

Sentences very like this are common in Spanish and Italian, which have no counterpart to filler *it.* Note that the English sequence is semantically complete as a proposition even though there is no subject. The sequence has a predicate and has the only argument that the predicate requires semantically. But it lacks a subject, and that is a grammatical defect. As we noted in Chapter 3, English has a strict subject constraint for finite clauses. There has to be an overt, a physically present, subject, even if the subject has no thematic role. Since the only thematic role, theme, has already been assigned to the argument after the verb, any noun phrase or clause filling the subject position would lack a thematic role. The *it* has no meaning.[5] Thus, in this sentence, *It was unfortunate that Sharon's car broke down,* the filler *it* appears to signal to us not exactly a meaning but something like a notification: "Don't worry about the thematic role here—it's been assigned to a later argument, one at the end of this clause."

The D-structure for our last example would have the subject position unfilled. The subject constraint allows two options when the theme argument of a predicate adjective is an embedded clause. Either the theme clause is shifted into the subject slot, or filler *it* is inserted into the subject slot while the embedded clause remains after its predicate adjective.

However, one of the options is not available if the theme argument of the predicate adjective is a noun phrase instead of an embedded clause. We'll show the D-structure like this:

...*was unfortunate* **that breakdown**

The subject constraint requires that something fill the subject slot. But filler *it* is not permitted:

It was unfortunate **that breakdown.**

The noun phrase *that breakdown* is in the position occupied by the embedded clause in the other sentence. But the sentence is ungrammatical because the last argument is a noun phrase instead of a clause. So the theme noun phrase has to be moved into the subject slot to satisfy the subject constraint:

That breakdown *was unfortunate.*

What has been described here is a difference between noun phrases and embedded clauses with respect to the occurrence of this *it*. Why should we be able to use filler *it* when the theme argument is a clause but not when it is a noun phrase? We'll be considering an explanation for this in Chapter 12, which concerns case in English.

PREDICATE ANALYSIS ON D-STRUCTURE TREES

We can draw a constituent structure tree to show how a sentence looks at D-structure and another to show how it looks at S-structure after, for example, a constituent has been moved to a different position on the tree. Most of the trees we use will be D-structure trees because they always have their predicates adjacent to the arguments they require. We have not so far shown on our trees that the predicates require a specific number of arguments, whether these arguments are clauses or noun phrases. Arguments are assigned thematic roles by the predicates that require them. On every D-structure tree we will in future mark under the predicates the thematic roles they assign to arguments and the positions the arguments occupy. It is unnecessary to mark the roles on S-structure trees. We'll refer to this D-structure marking as *predicate analysis.*[6] If you do this predicate analysis whenever you draw a D-structure tree, you should find it much easier to avoid mistakes. Abbreviate the roles, using EXP for experiencer, AG for agent, TH for theme, LOC for location, GO for goal, and BEN for benefactive. Mark the predicate position itself with a dash (—). Here are some examples:

see	laugh	seem	fond	award
EXP — TH	EXP —	. . . — TH	EXP — TH	AG — GO, TH

Here are two example D-structures:

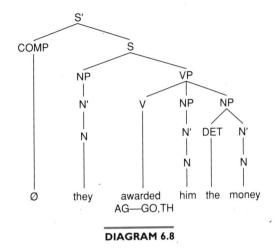

DIAGRAM 6.8

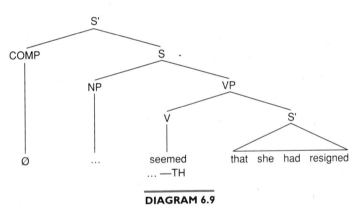

DIAGRAM 6.9

When you have finished the tree with its predicate analysis, check to make sure that the tree does indeed have noun phrases or embedded clauses corresponding to each of the thematic roles you have indicated. Remember that the passive voice verbs and predicates like *seem, apparent, obvious,* and *true* require no subject argument in D-structure. Mark the unfilled position with an ellipsis (. . .), as in diagram 6.9.

NOUN PHRASES AS CONTAINERS

We have seen that clauses can be embedded inside other clauses in verb phrases and adjective phrases. One final type of complex structure is left for discussion—clauses embedded inside noun phrases. We'll look at some examples. What are the subjects of the verb *astonished* in these sentences?

> ***The rumor that Sharon's car broke down*** astonished the mechanic.
> ***The request for Sharon's car to be repaired*** astonished the mechanic.

The subject of *astonished* is the whole complex noun phrase beginning with *the rumor/request*. It consists of a determiner (*the*), a head noun (*rumor, request*), and the embedded clause introduced by the complementizer *that* or *for*.

One special kind of finite clause embedded inside a noun phrase is known as a *relative clause*. These differ from embedded clauses in that relative clauses needn't begin with the *that* or any other complementizer but can instead have a *"Wh-*word," that is, a relative pronoun such as *who* or *which*. Here are two noun phrases with embedded relative clauses:

> the car **which/that broke down**
> the mechanic **who(m)/that Sharon employed**

These relative clauses provide more detail about the car or mechanic, detail that should assist in identifying correctly *which* car or mechanic is being referred to.

SUMMARY

Embedded clauses, one of the two major classes of dependent clauses, are embedded as arguments of a predicate. Some embedded clauses satisfy the subject constraint by moving from the theme position after the predicate into the empty subject slot of a finite clause. Otherwise the filler pronoun *it* must fill the subject slot. These clauses are typically introduced by a complementizer. The embedded clause and the complementizer, which is in its own COMP slot, together form a structure represented as S′ (S-bar). Clauses can be embedded as arguments of adjectives as well as verbs, and occur also in noun phrases. One special subclass of clause embedded in a noun phrase is known as a relative clause, a type of clause used to narrow down the reference of the noun phrase to which it belongs.

Subordinate clauses constitute the second class of dependent clause. They are introduced by subordinators such as *because* and *when* which, like complementizers, occur in the COMP slot. Whereas complementizers themselves have little semantic content, a subordinator presents the perspective of its clause, expressing such perspectives as time, location, reason, purpose, manner, and contrast. Subordinate clauses are not arguments but adjuncts, optional constituents similar semantically to adverbs and other optional constituents.

EXERCISE SET 6

1. Using columns like those in the clause perspective table on pages 67–68, analyze only the *subordinate* clauses in the sentences below. Remember, the clauses may lack overt subjects.

    a. *As Foulkes lay there, he groped for his knife where he had dropped it.*
    b. *He tried to strike a match to look for it, but the match was too damp.*
    c. *Although the hounds had gone, his fear remained, since the men knew he was somewhere in the forest.*
    d. *If he stayed where he was, they would find him, because the traces of his panic-stricken flight were obvious.*
    e. *Although Dorfman deplored the violence, he asserted that his party supported the reforms. If this government ignored the people, the people would despise the government.*

2. Draw D-structure trees for the two sentences below. Use a triangle to abbreviate embedded clauses. Be sure to do the predicate analysis for the container clause predicates.

    a. *Jacques thought that Menandez met Julia in Rangoon.*
    b. *For the government to abandon those refugees was heartless.* (Hint: *heartless* has no overt subject in D-structure.)

3. Look at the tree you drew for 2a. List the constituents (with their category names) that are sisters of each other and the category of the higher constituent whose daughters they are. You need not do this for the internal structure of the embedded clause.

4. We claimed in the text that the number of clauses that can be conjoined is not limited to two. The claim seems valid if the conjunction is *and*. Is it correct for other conjunctions?

5. In the sentence, *Hotchkiss is a lawyer and Coraggio is a talented pianist*, the coordinated clauses can be switched around to form *Coraggio is a talented pianist and Hotchkiss is a lawyer*. It's been claimed that the change does not affect the meaning of the sentence. How far is such a claim valid for this sentence: *The boy sat down and they ate supper*? How are the clauses in this sentence different from those in the other?

6. E. O. Winter has pointed out that the same logical relationships between clauses can be signaled in three grammatically distinct ways. One, which he refers to as Vocabulary 1, is the use of subordinators like *because* and *so that;* a second, Vocabulary 2, uses sentence linkers like *therefore* and *thus;* Vocabulary 3 uses phrases which explicitly specify the relation, such as the predicate phrases *was the reason, the result was,* and the rather less obvious *has led to*.[7] Here are examples of each:

   a. ***Because*** *Swanson had always enjoyed writing, she sought writing assignments from several magazines.*
   b. *Swanson had always enjoyed writing.* ***Therefore,*** *she sought writing assignments from several magazines.*
   c. *Swanson had always enjoyed writing. This* ***was the reason*** *she sought writing assignments from several magazines.*

   (1) Select a page of prose from a college textbook and state with examples how many of each of these three devices are used in your selection. Are they all used for the cause-effect relation? If not, what other semantic relations are expressed?

   (2) Write a paragraph speculating as to how teachers might be able to use their knowledge of these devices to help their students in reading comprehension.

NOTES

1. Note that the comma is almost always omitted here. The requirement for a comma (and the corresponding intonational break in speech) when the subordinate clause precedes its superordinate suggests that the more basic order is the one in which the subordinate clause *follows* its superordinate.

2. There are other options for capturing the constituent structures of sentences containing subordinate clauses. For instance, good arguments can be made for attaching some types of subordinate S-bars following the verb to the VP preceding them, or to the higher S or S-bar.

3. There are also superficially subordinate clauses that are not really subordinate at all; for example, *Rutherford had hardly opened the book when, to his surprise, Winston Churchill and Leonardo da Vinci came in*. Notice that inversion is possible—*when in came Winston Churchill and Leonardo da Vinci*—an option normally available only for independent clauses.

4. See, for example, Robert Freidin, *Foundations of Generative Syntax* (Cambridge, MA: M.I.T. Press, 1992), 48-55.

5. At a considerably more subtle level, there *is* meaning associated with *it*. For a sensitive discussion of these issues, see Dwight Bolinger, *Meaning and Form* (London: Longman, 1977), 66-89.

6. This is sometimes referred to in the technical literature as a *theta grid*.

7. E. O. Winter, "A clause relational approach to English texts: a study of some predictive lexical items in written discourse," *Instructional Science* 6 (1977): 1-92. For a more semantically oriented approach using college bioscience writing, see S. E. Jacobs, *Composing and Coherence: The Writing of Eleven Premedical Students* (Washington, D.C.: Center for Applied Linguistics, 1982).

7

Finite and Nonfinite Clauses

For non-native speakers, English clause types can be extremely puzzling and, at times, frustrating, especially when the clauses are embedded. English appears at first sight to offer a wide range of choices among various types of embedded clauses and other constructions. Sometimes it appears to make no difference what choice is made. There is, for example, little semantic difference between these next two sentences, the first with an embedded clause whose verb is an infinitive, the second with a gerundive after the container clause verb:

> *Judy preferred* **to swim in an unheated pool.**
> *Judy preferred* **swimming in an unheated pool.**

But more often than not, a particular choice has a significant effect upon the meaning communicated, as in these examples:

> *Judy stopped* **to buy lunch.**
> *Judy stopped* **buying lunch.**

The first sentence tells us why Judy stopped; the second sentence tells us what Judy stopped doing.

In this chapter we will focus on three important constructions. First, there are *finite clauses*, which are clauses with either a modal or a verb in present or past tense. Second, there are *nonfinite clauses*, which have infinitive verbs, that is, verbs immediately preceded by *to*.[1] Finally, there are *gerundives*, which have verbs ending with the *-ing* suffix. Gerundives, like nonfinite clauses, often lack overt subjects; if they do have a subject, it is often in its possessive form; for example, *Jackson's* in *Jackson's refusing to surrender*, as in this example:

> **Jackson's refusing to surrender** *infuriated Lee.*

The choice of which of these constructions to embed after a predicate depends in part on the particular predicate and in part on the meaning to be communicated. Some container clause verbs allow any of the three forms to be used after them. The verb *like* is an example:

> FINITE :   *Tom Wolfe didn't like it* **that his son repeated gossip.**
> INFINITIVE :   *Tom Wolfe didn't like* **his son to repeat gossip.**

GERUNDIVE: *Tom Wolfe didn't like **his son's having repeated gossip.***
    or: *Tom Wolfe didn't like **his son repeating gossip.***

But, with other container clause predicates, the use of one of these forms instead of another can make the sentence ungrammatical:

Tom Wolfe wanted **that his son told the truth.*
Tom Wolfe appreciated **his son to tell the truth.*
Tom Wolfe forced **his son telling the truth.*

Now we come to the major point of the chapter. Unlike many languages, English makes a very sharp distinction between finite and nonfinite clauses.[2] This distinction is important for an understanding of many aspects of English syntax. But before we go into this, we need to determine the status of the construction we labeled as gerundives.

WHY GERUNDIVES ARE NOUN PHRASES, NOT CLAUSES

As we've seen, English provides many alternative ways to present propositional content. Look at the following sentences:

That Galahad had arrived late offended the king.
For Galahad to have arrived late offended the king.
Galahad's having arrived late offended the king.

All three sentences have the same propositional content: Galahad arrived late and this late arrival offended the king. In all three, the form expressing the late arrival proposition serves as subject of the container clause. These embedded forms are thus arguments of the verb *offended*. Each of these subjects also has inside it its own subject, *Galahad*, and its own predicate, a form of *arrive* (*late*).

Yet despite these similarities, linguists have claimed that gerundives like *Galahad's having arrived late* are very different from the other two types of embedded construction. Such a claim, if supported, could have interesting implications for language teaching. Suppose, for example, that second language learners had more trouble acquiring the gerundive construction than either of the other two. If basic differences between gerundives and the other constructions are found, the findings could suggest a slightly different organization of teaching materials, to help students overcome the problem. Similarly, a computer program handling natural language might need to treat these constructions rather differently.

There are three major differences between gerundives and the finite and nonfinite clauses we have been discussing. The first major difference is a straightforward one:

1. *Clauses with finite or infinitive verbs are introduced by the complementizers **that** and **for**, respectively, but the gerundive has no complementizer and no COMP slot for a complementizer.*

The second difference is less obvious. We saw in Chapter 6 that if a finite clause with an unfilled subject slot has another clause embedded after its predicate, the subject constraint can be satisfied if the embedded clause is shifted into the unfilled slot. Otherwise, the filler pronoun *it* must fill the subject slot. So, a clause starting out like this:

*... was unfortunate **that Sharon's car broke down.***

ends up as either of these two sentences:

*It was unfortunate **that Sharon's car broke down.***
***That Sharon's car broke down** was unfortunate.*

We'll try this on our three example sentences. The embedded finite clause in D-structure would be like this:

> ... *offended the king* **that Galahad had arrived late.**

Either the embedded clause is shifted into the unfilled subject slot or the embedded clause remains at the end and the filler pronoun *it* is inserted into the subject slot. Here are the two sentences produced:

> **That Galahad had arrived late** *offended the king.*
> *It offended the king* **that Galahad had arrived late.**

As for the nonfinite clause (the one with the infinitive verb), it starts out at D-structure like this:

> ... *offended the king* **for Galahad to have arrived late.**

and ends up as either of these two sentences in S-structure:

> **For Galahad to have arrived late** *offended the king.*
> *It offended the king* **for Galahad to have arrived late.**

It's clear that the finite clause and the nonfinite clause share the same characteristics in these constructions. Now we will see whether the gerundive also shares these characteristics:

> ... *offended the king* **Galahad's having arrived late.**
> **Galahad's having arrived late** *offended the king.*
> **It offended the king* **Galahad's having arrived late.**

The gerundive cannot be left in its original position after the predicate. It has to be shifted into the subject slot. So the filler pronoun *it* does not occur in the subject slot with a gerundive following the predicate. Obviously there is something different about the construction *Galahad's having arrived late*, a difference that requires the gerundive to be moved into the subject slot. Let's state this as the second major difference between gerundive constructions and finite and nonfinite clauses:

2. *For finite and nonfinite embedded clauses, movement into the empty subject slot of a container clause is optional. If they are not moved, filler **it** must fill the subject slot. For gerundive constructions, this movement is obligatory.*[3] *Thus they do not occur with filler **it.***

The third major difference between gerundives and embedded finite and nonfinite clauses has to do with their occurrence after prepositions. The gerundive can be the object of a preposition:

> *The king was offended AT* **Galahad's having arrived late.**

But neither finite nor nonfinite clauses can be objects of a preposition:[4]

> **The king was offended AT* **that Galahad had arrived late.**
> **The king was offended AT* **for Galahad to have arrived late.**

So the third difference is as follows:

3. *Unlike finite and nonfinite clauses, the gerundive can be the object of a preposition.*

We have thus found three major differences between finite and nonfinite clauses on the one hand and gerundives on the other. But if gerundives are not clauses, then what are they? The differences we have found suggest that gerundives are a type of noun phrase.

The first difference we found between gerundives and embedded clauses was that gerundives don't have a complementizer or a COMP slot. Ordinary noun phrases like *the false report* also lack a COMP slot. In this respect, then, gerundives conform to the noun phrase structure. The second difference was that for gerundives movement into the empty subject slot of a container clause is obligatory; they do not occur with filler *it*. Compare now the gerundive example with an example having an ordinary noun phrase. Here are the two D-structures:

> ... *offended the king* **Galahad's having arrived late**
> ... *offended the king* **the false report**

In both cases, the theme has to be shifted into the subject slot, since the alternative with filler *it* is not acceptable:

> **Galahad's having arrived late** *offended the king.*
> **It offended the king* **Galahad's having arrived late.**
> **The false report** *offended the king.*
> **It offended the king* **the false report.**

In this respect too, gerundives are like noun phrases rather than embedded clauses. The third difference was that, unlike finite and nonfinite clauses, a gerundive can be the object of a preposition. Ordinary noun phrases can, of course, also be objects of prepositions. Here are the relevant examples:

> *The king was offended AT* **Galahad's having arrived late.**
> *The king was offended AT* **the false report.**

Although gerundives express propositional content very close semantically to their embedded clause counterparts, we see that syntactically they behave like ordinary noun phrases.[5] Our constituent tree structures should show them under the NP node.[6]

DIFFERENCES BETWEEN FINITE AND NONFINITE CLAUSES

Let's return to the two major types of embedded clause and consider some likenesses and differences in form and function.

Both types of clause have a subject followed by a verb. Both thus express a proposition. Although both types may be introduced by a complementizer, under certain conditions the complementizer can be omitted. We'll use parentheses around the omissible complementizer:

> *Guinevere believed (that) Galahad had arrived late.*
> *Guinevere hated (for) Galahad to arrive late.*

But here the similarities end.

First, finite embedded clauses typically begin with the complementizer *that*. The first verb in each finite clause either is a present or past tense form or is preceded by a modal (*will, must, can, may, should,* etc.). Neither past or present tense verbs nor modals occur in nonfinite clauses. (We mark finiteness on constituent structure trees as [+FINITE].) Nonfinite embedded clauses take the complementizer *for* before their subject (if they have one). The verb is preceded by *to*. (We mark nonfiniteness on constituent structure trees as [-FINITE].)

Second, if the complementizer is omitted, finite clauses can function on their own as grammatical sentences or as the main clause of a larger clause. A nonfinite clause cannot:

Nora left her husband.
*Nora to leave her husband.

Third, there is a difference in communicative function. Finite clauses are likely to be either statements or questions, that is, they are either *declarative* or *interrogative*. Nonfinite clauses are neither. They are often used as the embedded counterparts of orders and requests:

*Wooster ordered him **to leave immediately**.*

Finally, and perhaps most significantly for the present discussion, the two clause types differ as to whether one other constituent, the subject, has to be overt. Finite clauses need to have overt subjects; nonfinite clauses do not. Sentences with nonfinite clauses are grammatical even if the subject position in the nonfinite clause is not filled by an overt subject:

*Guinevere hated **[e] to arrive late**.*

The subject constraint thus does not apply to nonfinite clauses. The empty position, the position shown with an [e], is interpreted as referring to the subject of the container clause, *Guinevere*. Guinevere is not only the one who hates, but also the one who might arrive late.[7] Call the [e] a *covert subject*. Both *Guinevere* and the covert subject [e] have the same referent. *Referents* are entities to which noun phrases refer. *Guinevere* and [e] refer to the actual individual named *Guinevere*. But to interpret the [e], we have to go back to its antecedent noun phrase, *Guinevere*.

The subject constraint does not allow a covert subject in finite clauses:

*Guinevere believed that [e] had arrived late.

Finiteness and Meaning

There is often a significant semantic distinction corresponding to the grammatical contrast between finiteness and nonfiniteness. While the situation expressed in a finite clause may or may not be a real situation, one expressed in a nonfinite clause is typically assumed not to have happened, at least, not yet. Compare the following sentences, the first with a finite clause embedded in it, the second with a nonfinite clause:

*Gunther forgot **that he had locked the door**.*
*Gunther forgot **[e] to lock the door**.*

The finite clause, *he had locked the door*, typically refers to a *real* event at some *real* point in time. In contrast, the nonfinite clause [e] *to lock the door* has no obvious time reference in the past, present or future, and the event referred to probably did not happen. The event is a hypothetical one, and its *reality status* depends on the verb in the container clause. The distinction thus has to do with the reality status of the situation expressed by the clause.

Container predicates can force an interpretation on an embedded nonfinite clause. For instance, use of the container clause predicate *forced* communicates that the incident actually took place, while use of the predicate *refused* communicates that it didn't:

*The janitor forced the psychiatrist **[e] to lock the door**.*
*The janitor refused **[e] to lock the door**.*

The difference in the semantic interpretation of the embedded clause is signaled by the container clause predicate, not by the nonfinite clause, whose form remains the same. Nonfinite clauses themselves involve no claim by the utterer that they report a real situation. If the container verb is *wanted*, the door locking is *not* being presented as a *real* event:

> *The psychologist wanted [e] to lock the door.*

A speaker uttering this sentence is not indicating that the psychologist actually locked the door; indeed, in many contexts the speaker may be implying that he did not. But the sentence does not actually assert this. The reality status is left open. The sentence can also be used in contexts in which it becomes clear that the psychologist did lock the door.

Other languages make similar distinctions. Many languages belonging to the Uto-Aztecan branch of the Amerindian languages show the same contrast. In his account of the Hopi language (spoken in Arizona), Benjamin Whorf, who worked on this language in the first half of this century, pointed to the same basic distinction, calling the contrasting moods the "assertive" and the "expective."[8] English itself used to make frequent use of special forms of the verb called *subjunctives*. They were said to be in the *subjunctive mood* and, like nonfinite clauses, made no reality claims. Like nonfinite clauses, they were in contrast with ordinary finite clauses, which are still referred to as *indicative mood clauses*. In such Indo-European languages as Russian and Persian, the contrast between the subjunctive mood and the indicative mood remains important.[9] For situations presented as real, whether past, ongoing, or future, the verb is marked for the indicative mood and the clause is an indicative mood clause. If the verb is in its subjunctive mood form, the reality status is left open, unsettled.

The old subjunctive mood forms have disappeared from English, but there are still traces of this mood in clauses that look like finite clauses but lack a present or past tense verb or a modal. They occur after just a few verbs such as *fear, prefer, suggest, demand, order*, and *command*. We say, *I suggested that she leave* (instead of *leaves* or *left*). Such subjunctive usages occur mainly in formal English.

After most container clause verbs that used to allow subjunctive embedded clauses, the subjunctive mood clauses have been replaced by nonfinite clauses with *to*. The reality status distinction in English is chiefly made through the finite versus nonfinite contrast.

Most teachers of English as a second or foreign language have encountered sentences like this from non-native speakers:

> **I suggested her to leave.*

—forms which have also been known to occur in the writing of some native speakers. This is because the more general pattern for container clause verbs like *tell, order, ask*, and *force* is with an infinitive and the learner assumes that *suggest* also belongs to this class of verbs.

IMPERATIVES AND [e] AS SUBJECT

The nonfinite clauses considered so far have had infinitive verbs introduced by *to* and have all been embedded clauses. In contrast, the finite clauses discussed have included both embedded and main clauses. The next question is whether nonfinite main clauses exist.

In fact, they do. Like their embedded counterparts these main clauses never have modals or present or past tense verbs. Like the embedded nonfinite clauses, they do not have reality status assigned to them, so they certainly should qualify as nonfinite. The state of affairs described in these clauses is always assumed not to have happened yet because of the way they are used. These clauses are called *imperative* clauses. Here are some examples:

> *Tighten the wheel nuts.*
> *Lend me some more money, please!*
> *Don't drive so fast!*

Obviously, the wheel nut tightening and the giving of money haven't yet occurred. The function of the imperative clause is to get the addressee to do what is asked. If it has already been done or is underway at the time of utterance, there is little point in asking. The third imperative given above is addressed to someone driving faster than the speaker likes. The situation of the addressee driving less fast has not yet become reality.

But not all imperatives are orders, even though the word *imperative* comes from the Latin verb meaning "to order." Imperative clauses can also be used to beg or plead—the second example above, *Lend me some more money, please,* can be used as a plea. Imperatives can be used to give instructions, as in a recipe or in a leaflet telling you how to assemble a microcomputer. If negative, imperatives can be used as prohibitions or warnings.

There is no *to* before the verb, since the clauses are not embedded, nor, very often, is there an overt subject. Although the clauses usually lack overt subjects, they are always understood as if they had overt subjects. In this respect too, imperative clauses are no different from embedded nonfinite clauses.

There is some mental reality to such subjects, so they are referred to as covert subjects, where the covert subject is understood to refer to someone or something in the speaker's mind. In the following examples, the covert subject position is marked with an [e] for empty:

> *[e] wash the windows!*
> *[e] don't give her a peach!*

The typical speech context for such utterances is an interchange in which one person is directing or pleading with one or more others to do or not to do something. So the speech situation requires that the [e] be interpreted as referring to the addressee(s).

When these imperative clauses are converted to indirect speech, they are ordinary nonfinite clauses:

> *Maria ordered the superintendent **[e] to wash the windows.***
> *A bystander begged the manager **[e] not to give her a peach.***

Traditional grammar used the label *"you* understood" to refer to the missing subjects of imperative clauses but did not connect them with the covert subjects in embedded nonfinite clauses. The newer analysis covers a wider range of data, and the link it makes between the main and embedded nonfinite clauses could be exploited pedagogically. For example, a teacher might hand a student a slip of paper with one of the following sentences on it:

> *Order Abdul to open the windows.*
> *Warn Abdul not to open the windows.*
> *Beg Abdul to open the windows.*
> *Ask Abdul politely to open the windows.*

The student should be able to practice not only the appropriate imperative form corresponding to the embedded clause but also the intonation appropriate for warning, ordering, begging, and polite requesting. Moreover, other students should be able to report what happened in sentences using the embedded clause:

Chao ordered Abdul to open the windows.
Chao warned Abdul not to open the windows.

and so forth. Not all grammatical generalizations are as easily translated into classroom practice, but we should certainly take advantage of whatever we can. Perhaps more important is the need for the teacher to be familiar with reasonably current grammatical findings.

Interpreting [e]

We apply complex strategies in interpreting utterances. These strategies involve the context of the utterance as well as its semantic and grammatical properties.

Let's consider a grammatical dimension. How do we interpret the [e] subjects? Think about these two examples:

Carlos tried [e] to visit the Queen.
Conchita ordered Carlos [e] to visit the Queen.

For these examples, the strategy is probably to go back to the last noun phrase in the container clause to determine the identity of the person represented by the [e].

Is this the correct generalization? As the next example will demonstrate, the strategy won't always work:

Conchita promised Carlos [e] to visit the Queen.

In this case the referent of the [e] is Conchita rather than Carlos, even though *Carlos* occurs immediately before the embedded clause. The only difference between this example and the previous one with *ordered* is in the container clause verb. It appears, then, that the referent of the covert subject in an embedded clause is determined differently, depending on the particular verb (or other predicate) used.

However, there is one situation in which the reference of the covert subject is not grammatically determined. The container clause in the next example has no plausible noun phrase to indicate the referent of the [e]:

It's strange [e] to be talking to you here.

What happens in sentences like this is that the general context usually indicates the appropriate reference. This kind of interpretation is called *pragmatic inference*. Even with an isolated sentence like this, hearers know enough about situations in which it would be uttered to identify the [e] as the speaker, as *me*. The embedded clause can, of course, have an overt subject:

*It's strange for **me** to be talking to you here.*

The subject of the clause is grammatically specified, not pragmatically inferred. There is a difference between the two embedded clauses but it is a subtle one, one primarily of emphasis. Think about situations where the last example might be more appropriate than its counterpart with a covert subject. One obvious case is where the emphasis is on how strange it is for the *speaker* to be talking.

CLAUSE INFLECTION—THE *I* CONSTITUENT

The constituent structure trees discussed so far have all shown clauses to consist of a subject constituent, usually a noun phrase, and a verb phrase, as in this representation:

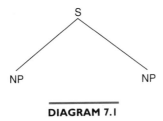

DIAGRAM 7.1

The trees, however, have not shown whether the clauses are finite or nonfinite, a contrast we referred to earlier in this chapter as a *mood* contrast. As we have seen, clauses are inflected (i.e., marked) for mood, the mood distinction corresponding to finiteness or nonfiniteness of the clause. We need to represent the mood on the tree. Let's assume that each clause has a mood marker, which we will refer to as the *Inflection*, abbreviated as *I*. The *I* is a constituent of a larger unit consisting of *I* and the verb phrase. We'll call the larger unit the *predicate phrase* (abbreviated PRED.P). Now the mood can be shown like this on constituent structure trees:

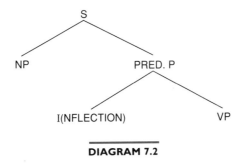

DIAGRAM 7.2

The Inflection constituent shows the finiteness or nonfiniteness of the clause:

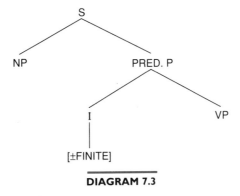

DIAGRAM 7.3

The specification of present or past tense or a modal appears under the *I* constituent of a finite clause, while a nonfinite *I* may specify *to* under it. Look at the embedded clauses in the two sentences following:

*Eiko says **the baby walks.***
*Eiko wants **the baby to walk.***

The constituent structures for the clauses would look like this:

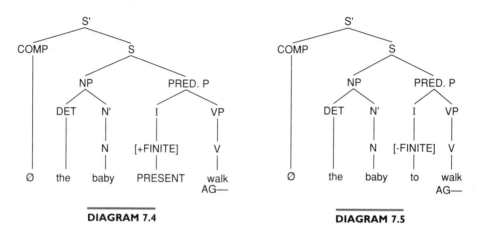

DIAGRAM 7.4   **DIAGRAM 7.5**

Note that in the verb phrase, the verb is shown only in its uninflected form, the same form as that appearing in infinitives after *to*. Here is one final example, the constituent structure for *that the group from Oregon liked that new play,* an embedded clause with an overt complementizer:

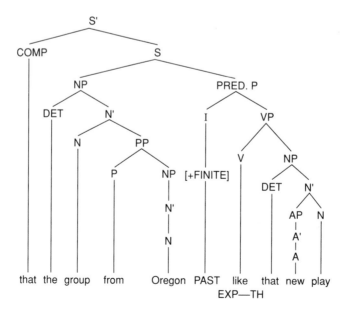

DIAGRAM 7.6

SUMMARY

The contrast between finite and nonfinite clauses is an extremely significant one for English. It is exploited by the grammar as a way to mark the reality status of the propositional content of a clause. The constituent structure tree for clauses now has a branch called Inflection, on which the reality status and the tense or modal is indicated. Together with the verb phrase it forms the predicate phrase of the S. Finite clauses (labeled [+FINITE] on the Inflection branch) are clauses with either a present or past tense verb or a modal. When they are embedded, they typically begin with the complementizer *that*. They cannot have a covert subject. Nonfinite embedded clauses (labeled [-FINITE] on the Inflection branch) can have a covert subject. If instead they have an overt subject, they usually take the complementizer *for* before their subject; their verb is always in the infinitive, normally preceded by *to*. Both clause types differ significantly from gerundives, which express a proposition but, as a type of noun phrase, lack a slot for a complementizer. Gerundives, if they have an overt subject, often mark it as a possessive, while the verb gets the *-ing* suffix.

Nonfinite clauses differ semantically from their finite counterparts in that the situation expressed in the nonfinite clause is typically assumed not yet to have happened. The contrast is thus one of reality status. In English, nonfinite clauses have taken over most of the functions formerly filled by subjunctive mood clauses, which were widely used to represent unrealized situations. We can say that finite clauses are in the indicative (or reality) mood, while nonfinite clauses are in the hypothetical mood. If, however, nonfinite clauses are embedded after container verbs like *force*, the container verb overrules the hypothetical status of the clause, and the event it represents is assumed to have occurred.

Imperative sentences, which also have covert subjects, are essentially the main clause counterparts of nonfinite embedded clauses, so they too are in the hypothetical mood. The referent of the covert subject of an imperative is understood to be the addressee in the speech situation. The referent of the covert subject of an embedded nonfinite clause is determined either on the basis of the container clause predicate or, if the container clause has nothing that could be a referent, by pragmatic inference.

EXERCISE SET 7

1. Draw D-structures for the following clauses. Be sure to show the Inflection constituent and to do the predicate analysis.

    a. *The plumber should come in the evening.*
    b. *for the lawyers to charge high fees*

2. Look at the tree you drew for 1b. List the constituents (with their category names) that are sisters of each other and the category of the higher constituent whose daughters they are.

3. Analyze the following sentence into clauses. Write out each clause separately and specify whether it is finite or nonfinite, what its subject is (even if it's just [e]), and what tensed verb or modal it has, if any. Where the clause has another clause embedded in it, include the embedded clause in parentheses.

    a. *Although Sebastian thought that his sister must have drowned, he sailed to Salonica [e] to search for her.*
    b. *Elliot ordered his deputy [e] to arrest the smugglers.*
    c. *Tell the doctors that they must help the poorest patients.*

4. Examine these sentences carefully:

    a. *Alexander begged the girl [e] to leave.*
    b. *Alexander begged [e] to leave.*

What do you notice about the reference of the covert subject in the nonfinite clause in each sentence? How is *beg* different from *promise?*

5. Look at all the following sentences containing clauses with covert subjects. What difficulties might they present for students of English as a second language? Not all of the sentences present the same level of difficulty. What makes some of the sentences easier to interpret?

    a. *They persuaded Teresita [e] to drive to Yokohama.*
    b. *Who did they promise Singh [e] to promote?*
    c. *It is always discouraging [e] to lose.*

6. Compare the following sentences with respect to who is claimed to be working and enjoying the work. For each sentence, tell how reference is determined. Could all of these have been produced by native speakers of English?

    a. *Working and enjoying the work is an important dimension of living.*
    b. *Working in an orphanage and enjoying the work, Derek Croft was now finding life more exciting.*
    c. *Working in an orphanage and enjoying the work, the children now became a part of Derek's family.*

NOTES

1. The infinitive verbs discussed so far have all been preceded by a *to.* However, a few container predicates, primarily the sensory verbs *see* and *hear,* the verb *make,* and sometimes the verb *help* omit the *to:*

$$\text{The police} \left\{ \begin{array}{c} \text{saw} \\ \text{made} \end{array} \right\} \text{Stella climb that wall.}$$

Note, though, that the *to* is required in the passive counterparts of these sentences:

$$\text{Stella was} \left\{ \begin{array}{c} \text{seen} \\ \text{made} \end{array} \right\} \text{to climb that wall.}$$

2. The notions underlying this account of finiteness in English are discussed in Roderick A. Jacobs, "On being hypothetical," in R. Hendrick, C. Masek, and M. Miller, eds., *Papers from the 17th Regional Meeting of the Chicago Linguistic Society* (Chicago: Chicago Linguistic Society, 1978), 99–117.

3. A few exceptions exist, such as *It's been nice knowing you.*

4. Hubbard, however, has presented strong arguments for considering *before, after,* and *until* as prepositions even when they introduce embedded clauses. See Katherine Hubbard, "The Syntax of English Temporal Constructions Introduced by AFTER, BEFORE, SINCE, UNTIL, WHEN, and WHILE" (Ph.D. diss., University of Hawai'i, 1986). So our generalization would not be valid for these three prepositions.

5. The gerundives considered here are actually part of a wider range of constructions. Our examples have all had possessive markers on the noun preceding the verbal form (e.g., *Galahad's having arrived late*). The possessive marker does not always occur and there are forms which are so like ordinary noun phrases that they are introduced by the definite article: *the shooting of the hunters.* Note that *shooting* has become a true noun here and so must be linked to its following noun phrase with an *of.*

6. However, we will, to avoid complex questions concerning their internal structure, show gerundives as triangles when we come to deal with constituent structure trees later in this chapter.

7. Interestingly, the [e] has a different thematic role from that of *Guinevere*. While *Guinevere* is an experiencer, the verb *arrive* must assign the agent role to its subject, [e].

8. Benjamin Whorf, "The Hopi Language, Toreva Dialect" (1946), in H. Hoijer et al, eds., *Linguistic Structures of Native America* (New York: Viking Fund Publications in Anthropology, 1946), 158–183.

9. See the discussion in Michael Noonan's chapter on complementation in Timothy Shopen, *Language Typology and Syntactic Description,* vol. 2 (Cambridge, UK: Cambridge University Press, 1985), 95–97.

THE NOUN PHRASE

8

The Structure of Noun Phrases

Noun phrases are used to refer to things people want to talk about, things as varied as boiled eggs, petroleum, hopes for a lasting peace, and the prime minister of Sweden. As we noted in the last chapter, the entities that noun phrases refer to are known as their *referents*. Sometimes a noun phrase has no referent. The noun phrase *the president of the United States in 1941* has the man Franklin Delano Roosevelt as its referent. However, the noun phrase *the president of the United States in 1066* has no referent, although someone writing a fantasy might imagine one.

Referring is important. Speakers need to refer to people, objects, concepts, processes, and all kinds of entities, and noun phrases serve this function.

DETERMINERS AND DETERMINER COMBINATIONS

Many noun phrases in English are simple forms consisting perhaps just of a noun like *cabbages* or a pronoun like *they*. Actually pronouns are a special class of noun, so both *cabbages* and *they* are nouns. When there is nothing else in the noun phrase, nouns are also complete noun phrases, as in these examples:

> The truck was loaded with **cabbages.**
> **They** flew down to Aiken, South Carolina.

Almost as simple in structure are noun phrases consisting of a noun introduced by an article (the definite article *the* or the indefinite article *a(n)*) or a demonstrative (e.g., *this* or *that*):

> **This dish** is prepared at **the table** by **a waiter**.

Words called quantifiers, such as *one, two, first, last, many, every, several,* and *all,* appear in this position too, sometimes with other introducers. Quantifiers are constituents specifying how much or how many. Here is a sentence whose noun phrases include quantifiers:

> **Every** student was charged **three** dollars for the **second** glass.

Notice that in the last noun phrase of our example, the quantifier (*second*) appears with another introducing form, the article (*the*).

All of these introducing forms are grouped together under the general label *determiner*. As the preceding example shows, certain determiner combinations are possible. Determiners that are *not* quantifiers include:

a(n)	*the*
this	*these*
that	*those*
a certain	*some* (with a singular NP)
which	*what* (e.g., *What woman would refuse the job?*)

The definite article *the* can occur before either singular or plural nouns, but the indefinite article *a(n)* occurs only before singular nouns. Thus, whereas the singular definite noun phrase *the river* has the plural definite form *the rivers*, the indefinite plural corresponding to the singular indefinite noun phrase *a river* is simply *rivers* (e.g., *Rivers carry the chemicals down to the ocean*). Rather than say there is no indefinite plural article, grammarians find it convenient to say that the plural indefinite article is a zero (0) article.

Below are some determiners that are quantifiers. Note that many have to use *of* plus an article or demonstrative to be linked to definite nouns (i.e., to nouns introduced by definite determiners such as *the, this, that, these, those*). For others, the *of* phrase is optional.

one	*two*	*fifth*	*several*
few	*many*	*half*	*much*
little	*all*	*each*	*every*
no(ne)	*plenty*	*any*	*several*
less	*more*	*most*	*fewer*

Here are four noun phrases containing quantifiers:

> DEFINITE NOUN PHRASES: *several of the dogs*   *all (of) the money*
> INDEFINITE NOUN PHRASES: *several dogs*   *all money*

The noun phrases listed as definite refer to dogs or money mentioned previously or assumed to be known to the addressee. Those listed as indefinite refer to dogs or money that may not have been previously mentioned or that the addressee is not assumed to be aware of. We pointed out that these indefinite noun phrases are often analyzed as having a covert indefinite article (e.g., *several 0 dogs* and *all 0 money*).

The Order of Determiner Words in Noun Phrases

As we've already shown, determiner words can cluster together. Some of the combinations are quite complicated. For example, in *all of the nineteen chairs*, the noun, the head of the phrase, is introduced by a complex determiner consisting of three determiner words and the preposition *of*. The number and range of combinations allowed depends primarily on the type of head noun in the noun phrase. But the following two schemas provide useful guidelines for the order in which the determiner words typically occur (optional constituents are shown inside parentheses).

FOR DEFINITE NOUN PHRASES:

(Quantifier-of)	*Definite article* *Possessive NP* *Demonstrative*	(Quantifier) Noun

(e.g., *several of those trees, none of the four psychologists, all of Terry's money, some of his relatives*).

Note that a possessive noun phrase like *Terry's* or *his* can occur instead of the definite article or demonstrative.

FOR INDEFINITE NOUN PHRASES:

| *(Quantifier)* | Noun *(of Possessive NP)* |
| *Indefinite article* | |

(e.g., *a knapsack, no money, ravens,* and *several books of his*).

Phrases like *all knapsacks* and *several dogs,* which have the quantifier *several* before the covert indefinite article according to some grammarians, probably have an omitted *of* before the article. (Compare *several of the dogs.*) When the article is the covert indefinite, the preposition must be omitted.

To go further into the structure of noun phrases, we need to discuss two more general notions, which apply not only to noun phrases but also to adjective phrases, prepositional phrases, and verb phrases. The two notions are grammatical functions, the *complement* function and the *modifier* function. We have already dealt with complements in earlier chapters, but now it is time to examine the complement notion in more detail, since we need to distinguish it from the modifier notion.

COMPLEMENTS AND MODIFIERS

A complement is the phrase following the predicate and linked very closely to it; it is the constituent that "completes" the predicate. For example, the adjective *fond* requires a complement. In the adjective phrase *fond of marshmallows,* the adjective *fond* is the head and the prepositional phrase *of marshmallows* is its complement, that is, its "completer."

A grammarian would say that the actual adjective (the A, not the A-bar or AP), noun, preposition, or verb *selects* its complement, if it requires one; that is why complements are shown as sisters of the actual word rather than of the higher level A', N', P', or V'. This is an important difference between the complement function and the modifier function.

Let's look more closely at the prepositional phrase *of marshmallows,* which is the complement of *fond* in *fond of marshmallows.* Some adjectives require complements, as does *fond.* Others, like *extinct,* do not. This is why we say the adjective itself, not the larger phrase, selects its complement and is therefore its sister. In this prepositional phrase, the noun phrase *marshmallows* is itself the complement or completer of the preposition *of.* Note that we also say that the function of *marshmallows* in the phrase is that of *object* of the preposition. Objects are really a kind of complement; thus the objects of transitive verbs are also complements. Recall that verb complements are not always object *noun phrases,* but are sometimes whole clauses, as a comparison of these two sentences makes clear:

> *Martin Becker now believed* **the news stories.**
> *Martin Becker now believed* **that the company was not making a profit.**

Now we are ready to look at noun complements. The container verb used in the last example, *believe,* has a noun counterpart, *belief.* Like the verb, this noun can take the clause *that the company was not making a profit* as its complement:

> *this belief* **that the company was not making a profit**

Many other nouns, often without verb counterparts, take complement clauses or complement prepositional phrases:

the story **that Eleanor had met with the senator**
the news **of her marriage**

Head nouns taking clauses as complements are abstract nouns like *fact, belief, rumor, story,* and *news.* A noun complement is also known as a *contentive,* so called because the complement clause (or phrase) normally specifies the *content* of its head noun. Thus, in our last examples, the clause *that Eleanor had met with the senator* is the content referred to as *the story,* and *of her marriage* is the content referred to as *the news.* Here is a tree diagram showing the first example:

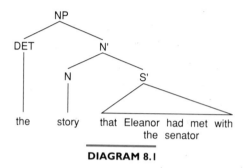

DIAGRAM 8.1

Compare the following two noun phrases:

the story **that Eleanor had met with the senator**
the story **that Eleanor had given to the senator**

The second noun phrase is different in that the clause *that Eleanor had given to the senator* does not supply the content of the story. Instead, it functions as a modifier identifying the story.

Modifiers supply a description which is added to the meaning of the head word and its complements and that pinpoints more narrowly the content of the head by adding identifying detail. For noun phrases, modifiers *identify* who or what the whole noun phrase refers to. Here are some examples:

the man **in the iron mask**
a box **which was delivered here yesterday**
a scoutmaster **fond of marshmallows**

The modifier *in the iron mask* is a prepositional phrase, the modifier *which was delivered here yesterday* is an embedded clause, and the modifier *fond of marshmallows* is an adjective phrase.

Here are constituent structure trees for the noun phrases *the story that Eleanor gave to the senator* and *a scoutmaster fond of marshmallows:*

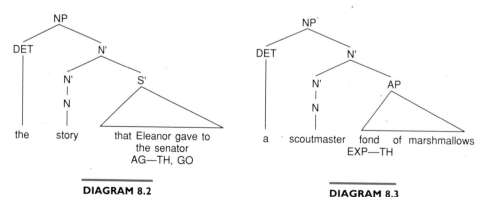

DIAGRAM 8.2   **DIAGRAM 8.3**

Compare especially Diagram 8.2 with 8.1. Notice that 8.2 and 8.3 have an additional N': the modifier phrases are attached to the higher N'; the noun itself is attached to lower N'. If the noun had also had a complement, it would have been attached to this lower N' as a sister of the N. On constituent structure trees, noun modifiers are shown as sisters of N', while noun complements appear as sisters of the head noun, the N. This requirement means that when both modifiers and complements follow a head noun, the complement comes first at D-structure (though a re-ordering is sometimes possible at S-structure if the complement is longer than the modifier). This is why the first of the following sentences, with the complement before the modifier, sounds better than the second:

> *the story* **that Eleanor had met with the senator** *which was reported on the evening news*
>
> **the story** **which was reported on the evening news** *that Eleanor had met with the senator*

The first example, which follows the normal order, would have the complement clause attached as a sister of the head noun *story*, while the modifier would be attached as a sister of the higher N-bar.

Not all modifiers in English follow their head word. Adjective phrases, for example, often occur before the head they modify. The head noun *plums* of the noun phrase *those juicy plums* is modified by an adjective phrase consisting just of the single adjective *juicy*.

There are two kinds of adjective phrase: those that precede their head noun and those that follow their head noun. Those that precede are shorter. They consist of adjectives, perhaps preceded by *intensifiers* such as *very, rather,* and other degree words:

> *a* **very tall** *building*   *three* **silver** *spoons*

If the adjective phrase contains an adjective followed by a prepositional phrase or embedded clause, it must follow the head noun:

> *a scoutmaster fond of marshmallows*

Let's now look at a tree for a more complicated noun phrase:

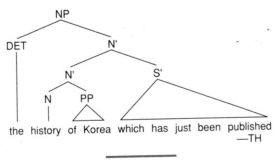

DIAGRAM 8.4

The noun phrase *the history of Korea which has just been published* contains the determiner *the* and the N-bar (N') to which is attached the modifier *which has just been published*. The lower N-bar consists of the head noun *history* plus its complement, in this case the prepositional phrase *of Korea*.

PROPOSITIONAL NOUN PHRASES AND COMPREHENSION

Some head nouns with a prepositional phrase as complement express predicate notions. In such cases, the whole noun phrase expresses a proposition. Consider, for example, the noun phrase *Cooper's denunciation of corruption*, which expresses the proposition *Cooper DENOUNCE corruption*. In the noun phrase, the head noun *denunciation* expresses the predicate notion of the verb *denounce*, and the possessive noun phrase *Cooper's* is understood as the subject of *denounce*. Inside the prepositional phrase *of corruption* is another noun phrase, *corruption*, which is understood as the object of *denunciation*. Thus the noun phrase *Cooper's denunciation of corruption* corresponds to the proposition *Cooper DENOUNCE corruption*.

With such noun phrases, it's not hard to identify the propositions expressed. For example, *Teruya's report of a break-in* corresponds to the proposition:

Teruya REPORT a break-in

AGENT   THEME

and *the Romans' destruction of the city* corresponds to the proposition:

the Romans DESTROY the city

AGENT   THEME

The noun phrases we've considered so far have all included predicates that, as verbs, take two arguments, that is, have a valency of two. In our examples, we've seen that the nouns in the noun phrases occupy the same positions relative to the predicate as they do in the clauses expressing the propositions. For instance, in *the Romans' destruction of the city*, the noun phrase *the Romans'* precedes the "predicate" *destruction*, which in turn is followed by the noun phrase *the city*; this order of elements is the same as that in the clause corresponding to the proposition, that is, *the Romans destroyed the city*.

But now consider a noun phrase whose head noun, *death*, corresponds to an intransitive verb, *die*:

the archbishop's death

This noun phrase corresponds to the following proposition:

the archbishop DIE
EXPERIENCER

In *The archbishop died*, the noun phrase *the archbishop* would have to be the subject of *die*. In the noun phrase *the death of the archbishop*, the noun phrase *the archbishop* is understood as the subject of *death*, the one who dies.

Some noun phrases expressing propositions do not specify their "subject." Compare the noun phrase *Livingstone's shooting of the hunters*, in which the subject is the possessive noun phrase *Livingstone's*, with the noun phrase *the shooting of the hunters*. The hunters could be either the shooters or the ones shot, that is, they could be understood either as the subject or the object of the verb *shoot* in the corresponding clauses:

Someone (unspecified) *shot the hunters.*
The hunters shot someone (unspecified).

The same ambiguity can occur in noun phrases in which a possessive noun phrase precedes the head noun. For example, Beecham in *Beecham's operation* could, assuming a medical context, be understood to be either the doctor who performed the operation (the subject of the verb *operate*) or the patient undergoing the operation (the object of *operate*). In the latter case the proposition expressed has an unspecified agent.

Noun phrases expressing propositions can present interesting challenges to non-native learners of English. Faced with such constructions, learners must identify the proposition and the thematic roles of the arguments, including those left unexpressed. The comprehension process involves not only identifying the possible interpretations allowed by the grammar, but also using contextual clues to eliminate some interpretations.

On the grammatical side, this means that learners must somehow have acquired knowledge of what we have referred to as *predicate analysis,* the ability to determine the properties of the predicate corresponding to the head noun, including the arguments associated with it and their thematic roles. This should enable learners to narrow down the range of possibilities. They will not, of course, do this the way we have in this book, since much of the comprehension process is unconscious. They may indeed refer back to forms in their native language that they believe could be counterparts to the English expression. Moreover, the learners must combine and integrate their grammar-based conclusions with their pragmatic knowledge of what is to be expected in situations such as those expressed by the noun phrase and also the knowledge provided by the context in which the noun phrase occurs. At present, second language acquisition researchers know little about these processes.

Nevertheless, teachers can help their students with these constructions whenever comprehension problems occur. Take the following horrendous noun phrase from an immunology textbook:

> *successful restoration of immune responsiveness by administration of the mixture of bone marrow and thymus cells* [1]

The construction is about a success in restoring a failed human immune system. The noun *responsiveness* corresponds to the predicate RESPOND, which takes two arguments:

x RESPOND to y

The x must refer to the immune system, while the y refers to an attack by some organism (which was specified elsewhere in the text as an antigen used to arouse response by the immune system). The noun *administration* corresponds to the predicate ADMINISTER, which here means something like "give" (as a treatment). It also takes two arguments:

x ADMINISTER y

This time the x (the agent) is unspecified, but the convention in such writing is that the agent is understood to be the researcher or physician. The y is the bone marrow and thymus cell mixture. The noun *mixture* itself refers to the product of a mixing process involving someone mixing two ingredients. Finally *successful restoration* involves the predicate RESTORE:

x RESTORE y (BY MEANS OF z)

in which x (the agent) is again understood to be the researcher or physician, y is the immune responsiveness, and z is the administration of the mixture.

Non-native students in an immunology course are probably going to understand much of the propositional content from their own background knowledge and reading, probably more than would an ESL teacher. But they may also misinterpret some part of the complex construction, perhaps by associating it with the wrong chunk of their own knowledge. A teacher with syntactic training should be able to help such students work out the probable meaning. The key word here is "help," since the students must provide much of the relevant scientific knowledge.

Noun phrases are rather more complex structures than you might have thought at first. The complex forms that correspond to propositions with predicates and arguments contribute to the reading difficulties presented in much academic prose. However, it is not too hard to break down these complex forms. Presumably, automatic translation devices and computer processing of natural language will need to do this. As for the teaching of reading comprehension, training and practice in the recognition of propositions expressed as noun phrases should be a valuable pedagogical technique.

SUMMARY

Noun phrases can be simple constituents consisting of just one overt element, perhaps a word like *cabbages*, although grammarians posit that the indefinite plural noun phrase *cabbages* has a covert article (shown as 0) in its determiner slot. The determiner itself may include not only an article *(the, a(n))* but also a quantifier (e.g., *three, several*). Noun phrases can also be very complex. They sometimes have a possessive noun phrase instead of a determiner, like *Yeltsin's* in *several of Yeltsin's supporters*, and they may also contain prepositional phrases, adjective phrases, and embedded clauses.

Two kinds of relationship to a head noun should be distinguished. *Complements*, shown as sisters of the actual word rather than of a higher level, are *selected* by their head noun, that is, the type of head noun determines whether it can take a complement and what complements it can take. *Modifiers*, on the other hand, are sisters of a higher N-bar level and are allowed by almost any head noun. They are optional. Prepositional phrases, adjective phrases, and embedded clauses can occur as either complements or modifiers in noun phrases. Semantically, noun phrases can also be quite complex. The noun phrase *Cooper's denunciation of corruption* expresses a proposition, Cooper DENOUNCE corruption, and the semantic predicate of the proposition is expressed by the head noun *denunciation*. Not all noun phrases expressing propositions specify the full set of arguments associated with the predicate. In such cases, ambiguity can result, as in *the shooting of the hunters*. While the context usually disambiguates such noun phrases, there is always a possibility for confusion for non-native learners, especially in complex technical prose. Teachers can sometimes help by discussing informally the propositions expressed by these propositional noun phrases.

EXERCISE SET 8

1. Using columns with the headings DETERMINER COMBINATION, HEAD NOUN, COMPLEMENT, and MODIFIER, write the constituents of the following noun phrases in the appropriate columns:

  a. *that heavy suitcase*
  b. *several of those batteries*
  c. *none of the books about space that she had read*
  d. *the surprising news of her marriage*
  e. *the fierce hatred of hypocrisy which you expressed*

2. Write five definite noun phrases which conform to the definite noun phrase formula given in the chapter. Each must correspond to a different option in the formula.

3. Find six predicates, two each of verbs, nouns, and adjectives, that take a clause as their complement and create a head-complement combination for each. Use the definite article before the two nouns.

4. Identify the propositions expressed in the following noun phrases. (The first one is done for you.)

> a. *the killing of the whales*

someone KILL the whales

AGENT   EXPERIENCER

> b. *the Dutch ban on nuclear weapons*
> c. *their resentment at the insult*
> d. *Abdul's gift from Ismail of a stereo*
> e. *the narration of the story by Laurence Olivier*

5. Convert the following sentences into noun phrases.

> a. *The partners purchased a minicomputer.*
> b. *He suspended the rules.*
> c. *I was impatient with his laziness.*
> d. *The young executive was obstinate.*

6. Now compose five more sentences for students to convert into noun phrases. Give the corresponding noun phrase for each one.

7. What could students learn from converting sentences into noun phrases and vice versa?

NOTES

1. Eli Benjamini and Sidney Leskowitz, *Immunology: A Short Course* (New York: Alan R. Liss, 1988), 156.

9

Types of Nouns

We will now shift from noun phrase structure to properties of individual types of nouns in English. Non-native speakers have problems with noun forms and the articles and quantifiers that go with them. The resulting errors can sound incongruous:

I have much headache tonight and a fever so I will drink many waters.

These problems with the determiner system, in contrast, for example, with problems with the verb system, do not hinder communication and are not associated with problems in learners' comprehension. Nevertheless, frequent determiner errors do pose questions of English language mastery that may disturb employers, admissions personnel, and teachers of other courses. The goal of this chapter is to cast some useful light on the determiner system and the types of nouns that allow or prohibit particular determiner constructions.

THE COUNT-NONCOUNT DISTINCTION

Why can't we say *much headache* instead of *a bad headache?* What's wrong with *many waters?* Both forms relate to an important distinction in many languages, that between *count nouns* and *noncount nouns*. Unfortunately, languages having the count versus non-count distinction vary as to which entities are viewed as units that can be counted. Learners acquiring vocabulary in a new language, therefore, have to sort the new nouns differently into count and noncount categories.

In English, there can be *one umbrella, two mice, three questions, four analyses,* and so on, but there's something strange about specifying *one butter, two waters, three furnitures, four rices, five desperations,* and *six equipments.* In fact, though, nouns in English are not inherently count or noncount, but rather are used countably or uncountably. (As we'll see shortly, when a noun that is normally used uncountably is instead used countably, its meaning is somewhat different.) For convenience, however, we'll start by treating the count-noncount distinction as a clear one.

Count nouns, not surprisingly, refer to entities viewed in English as individual units. They are sometimes described as having the feature [+COUNT]. The entities they refer to can be abstract (an idea, suggestion, belief, prejudice) as well as concrete (a house, child, potato, finger). If there is just one entity being referred to and the noun phrase is indefinite, we use the article *a(n)*, a determiner descended from the same older form as the numeral *one*. The question form beginning *How many...?* is used to ask about quantity for count nouns only:

> How many guests are coming tonight?
> *How many butter do you want?

Noncount nouns typically refer to entities that are viewed not as individual units but as something having no specific shape or boundary. They are described as having the negative value for the count feature [-COUNT]. Indefinite noncount nouns cannot take the indefinite article *a(n)*. Noncount nouns are used to designate abstract or very generalized referents such as *starvation, naturalization, gravity, desperation, pollution, happiness, humanity, time, information, vegetarianism, ugliness, social studies, integrity*. They are also used for concrete things viewed as mass or bulk rather than as countable units, for example, *butter, water, flour, rice, furniture, carbon monoxide, equipment*. The question form *How much ...?* is used to ask about quantity for noncount nouns:

> How much butter do you want today?
> *How much man will work today?

Proper nouns, names for particular people, places, times, and other entities (e.g., *Kennedy, Chicago, January*), are a somewhat special case of noncount nouns. They normally refer to a unique entity and therefore do not occur as plural forms. Because of their uniqueness of reference, they occur alone in their noun phrase without modifiers or any determiners. In writing, of course, they differ from other nouns in beginning with a capital letter. As with most categories in English grammar, there are significant exceptions. Some proper nouns are also count nouns and can therefore occur in the plural with determiners before them: *two Arabs, those Spaniards, several Buddhists*. Most proper nouns, however, are noncount nouns.

DETERMINERS WITH COUNT AND NONCOUNT NOUNS

The count-noncount distinction helps us understand the uses of the indefinite article *a(n)*. Unlike count nouns, noncount nouns do not take the indefinite article *a(n)*. Nonnative speakers unaware of this distinction or of how a particular noun can be classified may mistakenly use *a* or *an* with a noncount noun like *money*, as in this sentence:

> *She have a money in her handbag.

Noncount nouns that are also proper nouns, such as *Mr. Schwartz* or *Fifth Avenue*, are even more restrictive—they generally take no determiner at all. A few major exceptions are the names of certain organizations and some well-known buildings, such as *the United Nations, the Pentagon*, and *the Eiffel Tower*, along with river names (e.g., *the Mississippi* and *the Rhine*).

Count nouns, since they refer to units viewed as countable, can be singular or plural, a property referred to as the *number property*.[1] The singular form of a count noun must be introduced by an overt determiner. This is a major difference between singular count nouns and noncount nouns, which do not require a determiner, although some determiners—the definite article, the singular form of demonstratives like *this* and *that*, and certain quantifiers—often do introduce them.

Singular count nouns require either the indefinite article *a(n)* or a definite determiner like *the, this*, or *that*. For plural nouns, the only indefinite article allowed is the zero form, for example, *houses* rather than **a houses*. Some quantifiers, like *each* and *every*, can occur with singular count nouns, while other quantifiers, such as *several, both,* and *few,* occur with plural count nouns:

each house	*each houses
every house	*every houses
*few house	few houses
*both house	both houses
*several house	several houses

Teachers of non-native speakers have probably heard asterisked phrases like these from their students. Note, however, that certain ungrammatical plural phrases would be grammatical if *of* plus a definite determiner were inserted after the quantifier, for example, *each of those houses.*

THE INDEFINITE ARTICLE

Singular indefinite noun phrases have several basic uses:

1. The *specific indefinite use* indicates a specific entity that is not yet familiar to the addressee and not uniquely identified by the noun phrase:

    She saw **a tall tree with purple blossoms.**
    A young accountant interviewed her.

2. The *generic indefinite use* refers not to anyone or anything specific but to a *class* of entities.

    They advertised for **a three-bedroom apartment.**
    A car can be very expensive.

3. The *generic predicate noun phrase* use provides a classification; this is really a special case of the generic indefinite use:

    Toby was **a deerhound.**
    Denver is **an interesting city.**

Since indefinite noun phrases can be understood as either specific or generic, there is certainly a possibility of misunderstanding. But the interpretation of a noun phrase as specific or generic depends heavily on the predicate it occurs with, the time reference of the clause, and, of course, the broader context. Thus, in these examples:

    The young couple have **a baby girl.**
    The wealthy orthodontist drives **a 1934 Jaguar convertible.**

it should be clear that the reference is to a specific baby girl and a specific 1934 Jaguar convertible. However, in these next examples, in which the verbs are *hope* and *want* rather than *have* and *drive,* the reference is less clear, though, in the absence of other information, we might interpret the object noun phrase as generic:

    The young couple are hoping for **a baby girl.**
    The wealthy orthodontist wants **a 1934 Jaguar convertible.**

The ambiguity disappears when the noun phrase is replaced by a pronoun. The pronoun *it* would be used for the *Jaguar* noun phrase if the reference is to a specific car, while *one* would be the choice if the reference was generic:

The wealthy orthodontist wants a 1934 Jaguar convertible, and my English teacher wants
it *as well.*

The wealthy orthodontist wants a 1934 Jaguar convertible, and my English teacher wants
one *as well.*

Essentially, the same uses can be listed for plural indefinite noun phrases. Once again, the different uses seem to blur at the boundaries:

1. The *specific indefinite* use indicates specific entities that are not yet in the mind of the addressee. In this use, plural nouns have either the zero indefinite article or the determiner *some* (often pronounced with very weak stress *(sm)* as if it had no vowel):

   She saw **0 tall trees with 0 purple blossoms.**
   She saw **some (sm) tall trees with some (sm) purple blossoms.**

This *some* is *not* being used as a quantifier. When *some* is used as a quantifier, it is in contrast to *all*—it focuses on the notion of being part of a larger specific group. This is clearly not the case for *some tall trees* in the sentence above. As a quantifier, *some* is never pronounced with weak stress.

2. The *generic indefinite* use refers to a class of entities:

   0 Cars *can be very expensive.*

Note that *some* in a generic noun phrase is used solely as a quantifier; it refers to part of the class:

   Some cars (i.e., not all) *can be very expensive.*[2]

3. The *generic predicate noun phrase* use indicates a classifying predicate. This again is a special case of the generic indefinite use:

   Toby and Finster were **0 deerhounds.**
   Denver and Chicago are **0 interesting cities.**

Once again, there is a possibility of misunderstanding. The noun phrase *supporters* in the first clause of the next example could be specific or generic; the second clause clears up the ambiguity:

   The candidate searched for supporters but he didn't find **them.**
   The candidate searched for supporters but he didn't find **any.**

THE DEFINITE ARTICLE

The definite article *the* can occur with almost any kind of noun—count or noncount, singular or plural—except for noncount proper nouns. There is no well-defined set of principles governing all the situations in which it is used. In general, however, the definite article is used when its noun phrase refers to an entity that should be identifiable. The entity may be considered identifiable for any of several reasons:

1. It has previously been identified to the addressee.
2. There is only one such entity or event, at least in our everyday experience. Examples of such noun phrases include *the sun, the earth, the Republican party, the United Nations, the Olympic Games, the USA, the Pacific Ocean.* We may be aware of other suns or other republican parties, but normally when someone refers to the

sun, we know the one thing the noun phrase refers to; and when someone discussing U.S. politics talks about *the Republican party,* native speakers of American English have no trouble identifying which party is meant.

3. Within a particular context, the entity is something we assume exists. For example:
    *   In the context of a family, we can talk about *the father, the mother, the grand-parents,* and *the daughter(s);*
    *   in the context of a human body, we can talk about *the head, the nose,* and *the feet;*
    *   in the context of a law court, we can talk about *the judge, the defendant, the prosecution,* and *the courtroom;*
    *   in the context of a process, event, book, poem, or anything else viewed as a linear sequence, we can talk about *the beginning, the middle,* and *the end;*
    *   in the context of things viewed as occupying space, we can talk about *the front, the top, the left-hand side,* and *the exterior.*

4. The entity has been referred to previously. Thus, *A tall woman entered the room* may be followed by the statement *Oscar noticed that* the *woman looked angry.*

5. The entity is represented as unique in some context by modifiers like the superlatives *strongest, most beautiful, thickest, least valuable,* or by other words designating uniqueness, such as *only* and *sole* in *the only reporter* and *the sole representative.*

6. The entity is present at the time of the utterance or within a reasonable time before the utterance. This allows us to speak of *the brown jacket,* or *the boy over there.*

7. The entity is expressed as a noun with a specific rather than generic reference, followed by an identifying modifier, as in *the anger that he felt.*

QUANTIFIERS, THE COUNT-NONCOUNT DISTINCTION, AND REALITY STATUS

Some quantifiers are restricted to count nouns, others to noncount nouns. Yet other quantifiers such as *all, some,* and *no(ne)* allow either count or noncount nouns to follow. Of course the number quantifiers (*one, two, three, first, second, third,* etc.) go only with count nouns. But also restricted to count nouns are *many, several, few, each,* and *every.* That's why, for example, only the first of these next two sentences is grammatical:

> *The hospital took every* **penny** *he had.*
> **The hospital took every* **money** *he had.*

On the other hand, *much* and *little* (referring to quantity, not size) occur only with non-count nouns:

> *Bradshaw had little money left.*
> **Bradshaw had little pennies left.*

The last example is not grammatical where *little* is meant to express quantity, that is, to mean the same as *few.* As for *much,* note that, except in subject position, as in this sentence:

> *Much trouble could have been avoided if they had planned more carefully.*

and after *so* or *too:*

> *They've put too much money into that house.*

the quantifier *much* is restricted to questions and negative clauses:[3]

> *James Warren had much money.
> James Warren didn't have much money.
> Did James Warren have much money?*

Quantifiers like *a lot of* or *a great deal of* are preferred:

> *James Warren had **a lot of**/*much* money.*

Like *much, any* is associated with negatives, interrogatives, conditional clauses, and other constructions, most of which deny, question, or leave unresolved the reality status of the entity to which the noun phrase refers. It does not occur in ordinary affirmative statements; the quantifier *some* is used instead:

> *William Tell had **some**/*any apples.
> William Tell didn't have **some/any** apples.*

But it would be inaccurate to posit a rule converting *some* to *any* in negatives, interrogatives, and conditional clauses. This is because *some* can also occur in these. Furthermore, there is often a subtle difference in the way they are used:

> *Does William Tell have **some** useful skills?
> Does William Tell have **any** useful skills?*

The first question seems more positive than the second. The speaker may expect an affirmative answer. The same contrast can be noted for these conditional clause examples:

> *If William has **some** apples, I'd like them.
> If William has **any** apples, I'd like them.*

In the first of these two examples, the speaker may believe that William has apples; in the second, there is no hint as to the speaker's belief about the existence of the apples.

SWITCHING THE COUNT FEATURE

We noted earlier that, strictly speaking, nouns were not inherently count or noncount nouns but instead could be used countably or noncountably. Not all nouns can be used both ways, but there are a great many nouns usually used as noncount nouns that are also used as count nouns and vice versa. Such nouns are said to switch the count feature, that is, [-COUNT] becomes [+COUNT], and vice versa.

Abstract nouns such as *demand, acceleration, priority, success, damage, gravity,* and *increase* can be used either way, although for many of them there is some difference in meaning. *Gravity,* for example, is normally used as a noncount noun referring to a natural force. But when it is used as a count noun it refers to a unit of measurement for this force:

> *The rocket casing fell at a rate of **4.5 gravities.***

With *success,* in contrast, the difference in meaning is very slight, with the count use referring to individual successful achievements and the noncount use to an overall evaluation of an effort.

Many nouns referring to concrete entities can also switch. The normally noncount noun *butter* can be used as a count noun to refer to types of butter:

*Two **butters** that we especially favor are a slightly sweet one from New Zealand and a richly creamed one from Wisconsin.*

or to portions or units of butter:

*"Marilyn, take **two more butters** to those customers over there."*

Other such nouns are *cheese, coffee, wine, chocolate, candy, fish, poison,* and *food*. With concrete nouns, the switch from [-COUNT] to [+COUNT] tends to be a switch in reference from the actual substance to types or units of the substance.

Counting Noncount Nouns

Even when nouns are used as noncount nouns, they can be counted. The device used is similar in some respects to one used in Chinese, Vietnamese, and other Asian languages and also in many Amerindian languages. These languages have words or suffixes known as *classifiers*. A classifier is often attached to a quantifier. It is an element that specifies the noun as belonging to a particular class. One classifier might mean something like "long object" and can be used for nouns referring to long round objects such as needles, cigarettes, pencils, and sticks. In Japanese this classifier is *hon*. The word for "five" in Japanese is *go*. So, to specify five needles, the word for needle is followed by the form *go-hon*. The classifier *hiki* is used for fish, birds, and four-legged animals. So, to specify five dogs the form *go-hiki* follows the word for "dog."

In English, the counting phrase precedes rather than follows the noun and is linked to it by *of*:

four bags/cubes/pounds of sugar
a drop/glass/gallon of water
two pieces of furniture

In these noun phrases, the classifying noun (*pound, drop, piece*) is itself a count noun, typically designating an appropriate unit of measure or a container; such nouns can be called *counters*. The noun phrase *three bags of wool* contains two nouns, the counter *bags* and *wool*. Which noun is the head noun? We can find out by checking to see what the verb agrees with if this noun phrase is the subject of a clause:

*Three bags of wool **are** in the barn.*

The *are* cannot be replaced by *is*, so the head noun can only be the counter. The prepositional phrase beginning with *of* functions as the complement of the head noun.

The choice of the right counter isn't always simple or predictable, as many non-native speakers have discovered. For example, the counters *chunk* and *piece* are both used for solid material often cut up or broken into segments (e.g., *a chunk/piece of cheese*). However, *piece* but not *chunk* is also used for solid objects such as furniture and equipment, which are seen as unsegmentable. So, while *two pieces of equipment* is acceptable, *two chunks of equipment* sounds wrong. The counter *bar* can go with *candy* but not with *cheese*. We talk about a *candy bar* but not about a *cheese bar*. For the most part, non-native speakers must learn the appropriate counters item by item.

SOME PROBLEMS FOR NOUN CLASSIFICATION

Here is a diagram showing the noun classes discussed:

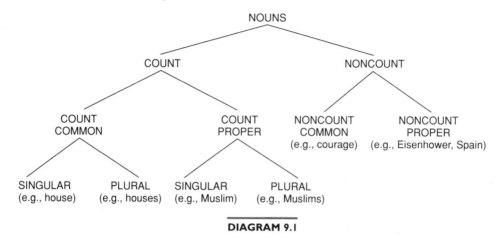

DIAGRAM 9.1

Not all nouns fit neatly into the classes shown in the diagram. Some noncount nouns are always plural, except for a few specialized usages. The nouns *scissors, shears, trousers, pants, pyjamas, jeans, knickers, binoculars, bellows, scales, compasses* (geometrical), and *glasses/spectacles* require *a pair of, two pairs of,* etc., to precede them if they are to be counted. People in the business of manufacturing and selling these objects do, however, use the singular form, usually to mean a particular kind of scissor, etc. Other nouns are always plural. Perhaps the most common is *clothes,* but *thanks, arms* (when used to signify weapons), *manners* (as in *good manners*), and *lodgings* are also common examples.

On the other hand, nouns like *police, people, cattle,* and *vermin* are used as plural nouns, though they do not take plural endings. Because they are plural, third-person present tense verb forms that have them as their subjects cannot be in the singular form:

> *The police are coming immediately.*
> **The police is coming immediately.*

Since these nouns are count nouns, they permit the use of quantifiers restricted to count nouns (*many, several,* and *a few*):

> **Two police** arrived on the scene, and at once **several people** came forward to report what they had seen.

However, they cannot be used to refer to a single entity:

> **A police arrived.*

The noun *people* causes non-native speakers more difficulty than a noun should. The problem is that it can also be used to refer to a tribal or national group, and then it is a normal count noun allowing the plural suffix:

> *There should be a bond of friendship between the Azerbaijani and Kurdish peoples.*

One last significant problem for classification concerns *collective nouns,* which refer to groups of individuals. In American and Canadian English, when singular nouns like *administration, government, public, committee, crowd, audience, board* (of directors), and *junta* are used as subjects, present tense verbs are almost inevitably in their singular form, while in British English plural forms also occur frequently, especially when the members of the group are being viewed as individuals rather than as an undifferentiated grouping:

> *The government has announced a new initiative.* (American)
> *The government has/have announced a new initiative.* (British)

However, speakers of both kinds of English vary considerably in this respect. The noun *faculty*, for example, occurs with either singular or plural present tense verbs in both American and British usage, and speakers of both may be choosing one or the other on the basis of how they view the grouping. Interestingly, plural pronouns are commonly used for many of these nouns in both varieties of English:

> *The committee was arguing that their proposal was more practical and that they should be allowed to implement it immediately.*

SUMMARY

The count-noncount distinction is important for nouns, especially with respect to use of the indefinite article *a(n)* and of quantifiers such as *several* and *many*. Only count nouns can have the indefinite article *a(n)*. For noncount nouns, the indefinite article is the covert *0*.

Most nouns in English are not inherently count or noncount but, rather, are used countably or uncountably. Some count nouns are used as plural nouns, though they do not take plural endings; examples are *police* and *people*. Noncount nouns, of course, are never plural. Many nouns can be used both as count and noncount nouns, but there are interesting and not easily predictable variations of meaning between the count form and the noncount form. For concrete nouns, the switch from [-COUNT] to [+COUNT] tends to be a switch in reference from the actual substance to types or units of the substance. Noncount nouns can actually be counted if counters like *bag, cup,* and *piece* are used. These counters designate units appropriate for the entity referred to.

There are three major uses for indefinite noun phrases: (1) as specific indefinites indicating a specific entity not yet known to the addressee and not uniquely identified by the noun phrase; (2) as generic indefinites referring to a class of entities; and (3) as generic predicate noun phrases providing a classification.

Definite determiners like *the, this,* and *those* are used when the entity to which the NP refers is or should be identifiable either from the speech context or from what the addressee should know about the world.

Nouns seem to resist neat classification. As with another major category, verbs, nouns have many properties that are idiosyncratic and acquired item by item. However, the generalizations discussed here at least provide a useful schema that should enable non-native speakers to use the appropriate forms for most situations.

EXERCISE SET 9

1. Which of these nouns are *typically* used as count nouns and which as noncount nouns:

hill	*recession*	*optimism*
envy	*culture*	*turf*
turbulence	*liquor*	*victory*

2. Write pairs of sentences for each noun below. In the first sentence of each pair, use the noun as a count noun; in the second, use it as a noncount noun:

    a. *coffee*

    b. *glass*

   c. *chicken*
   d. *fruit*

3. What semantic difference can you see between the following two sentences?
   a. *Don't you have some warm clothes?*
   b. *Don't you have any warm clothes?*

4. Select the first five noncount nouns from any book or article and write a sentence for each using it as a count noun. Some of your sentences will be unacceptable. For those that are reasonably acceptable, explain the differences in sense between the noncount forms and the count forms.

5. The following passage has numbers where an article might or might not be appropriate. For each number, specify which article, if any, you would use and explain your answer.

> It is clear that despite (1) civil rights legislation enacted in (2) last twenty-five years, (3) Native Americans continue to suffer from (3) severe discrimination. I recently met (4) elementary school teacher from (5) Mojave reservation. He said (6) school he taught in was (7) firetrap. He had asked in vain for (8) textbooks for (9) children. (10) Bureau of Indian Affairs had ignored pleas by (11) principal of (12) school.

6. Write two 6–9 line dialogues, one of which requires students to practice using count forms while the other requires noncount forms. Include examples of such forms as *How many* versus *how much*, *as many* versus *as much*, *a few* versus *a little*.

7. The following paragraph was written by Soraya, an Iranian student. First, read it through to get an overall sense of the piece. Examine each noun phrase or series of noun phrases of the same type, decide whether it is specific or generic, singular or plural, count or noncount, and then evaluate the choice of determiner, or the lack of a determiner. Finally, write a paragraph discussing the writer's grammatical successes and failures with noun phrases. State any generalizations you can make about Soraya's usages.

> Most of the peoples in my country Iran, especially the peoples who are very religious, believe that the ghost appears after the dead. It is very important to mention that the ghost has a meaning of religious among these peoples. According to the peoples of religious if the man or woman die, a soul of his or her raises to sky and then the soul of man appears like the ghost with two of different shapes and characters. One refers to the good persons and another to persons of the bad character.

NOTES

1. At some stage, an ancestor of English may have had a DUAL number, as well as singular number and plural number. But even in Anglo-Saxon, the dual distinction was a minor one, perhaps a relic of a more pervasive system. The quantifier *both* and forms such as *twice* reflect an earlier stage when there were also dual pronouns.

2. Plural noun phrases with the zero indefinite article can also be used this way. Generic plurals with *some* are far less common. They sound informal and are often used when the addressee might already know what class of entities is being referred to:

> *These are 0 snowplows.*
> *These are some (=sm) snowplows.*

The first sentence could be said to someone who doesn't know what snowplows look like. The second would be more appropriate if the addressee were being taken around a warehouse and the speaker opened a door to show one of the storage compartments.

3. There is also a formal and somewhat old-fashioned usage, as in *Charleston has much to be thankful for.*

10

Pronominals and Reference

We use noun phrases to refer to any entity we want to talk about. But right after we've made the reference, we might need to refer again to that entity. Having to repeat the exact noun phrases needed for initial identification would be clumsy and tedious. Languages are more efficient than this. Thus in English, instead of repeating a noun phrase, we might use a pronoun. But there are dangers to this avoidance of repetition. Pronouns don't contain as much information as most full noun phrases. So there is the possibility of ambiguity of reference, as in this example:

> *Teresa* told **Mrs. Harper** that **she** had to release the information.

The *she* here could refer to Teresa, Mrs. Harper, or even to some other female. Does this mean that the full meaning can't be communicated? Of course not. The sentence would probably occur within a context that allowed the reference of *she* to be clear. Notice that if we switched around *she* and *Teresa*, the *she* could not refer either to Teresa or Mrs. Harper:

> **She** told **Mrs. Harper** that *Teresa* had to release the information.

Clearly, the positioning of pronouns and the noun phrases to which they refer is extremely important. We call the noun phrase to which a pronoun refers its *antecedent*. The antecedent itself is not normally a pronoun.

English has principles covering the positioning of pronouns and their antecedents. To see just what these principles are, we will examine the ways in which pronoun reference works across clauses and within clauses and noun phrases. But first we'll look at the actual pronoun forms.

WHAT IS A PRONOUN?

Pronouns are a specialized kind of noun. We show them as N on a tree diagram. But since pronouns are almost always the only constituent of their noun phrase, they would look like this on a tree:

DIAGRAM 10.1

Traditionally, English pronouns have been called "personal pronouns" because they indicate the notion *person*, or the role of the referent in the speech situation. The pronouns *I, me, we,* and *us* are called *first person* pronouns. They refer to the speaker, either alone or with others.[1] The *second person* in a conversational exchange is the addressee (or addressees), the "you." Everyone and everything else is *third person*. Ordinary nonpronominal noun phrases are also third person.

Noun phrases like *Celia's,* as in *Celia's apartment,* are *possessive noun phrases*. They occur either inside another noun phrase, in which case we refer to them as *NP-internal,* as in this example:

That is **Celia's** apartment.

or outside, as in this example:

That apartment is **Celia's**.

We'll refer to possessives not inside another noun phrase as *independent*. As the corresponding sentences with pronouns reveal, *her* is an internal form, while *hers* is an independent possessive:

That is **her** apartment.
That apartment is **hers**.

NP-internal pronouns like *her, their,* and *my* are possessive noun phrases that occur instead of the definite article in the noun phrase containing them. Like the article *the,* they mark the noun phrase as being definite. The noun phrase *their friend* owes its definiteness to the possessive noun phrase *their* preceding the head noun *friend*. If the reference to the friend is intended to be indefinite, then the indefinite article (*a* for singular, *0* for plural) is used, and the independent possessive follows the head noun in an *of* phrase, as in *a friend of mine*.

It will be helpful to have a more general label for all of these forms—the personal pronouns, the NP-internal possessive pronouns, and the independent possessive pronouns. We will use for them all the term *pronominal*.

PRONOMINALS AND CASE

In Chapter 4 we noted that instead of using word order to distinguish subjects from objects, Latin used suffixes, as in these examples, all of which mean "Cassius sees Brutus":

Cassiu-s Brutu-m videt.   Videt Brutu-m Cassiu-s.
Brutu-m videt Cassiu-s.   Brutu-m Cassiu-s videt.
Videt Cassiu-s Brutu-m.   Cassiu-s videt Brutu-m.

The -s suffix marks the subjects in these sentences, and the -m suffix the objects. If we switched the suffixes around, as in the following examples:

Cassiu-m Brutu-s videt.   *Videt Cassiu-m Brutu-s.*

the sentences would mean "Brutus sees Cassius" instead of "Cassius sees Brutus." These suffixes are known as *case suffixes*. The subject-marking -s suffix in the examples above marks the noun phrase with the *nominative case*. Direct objects in Latin have *accusative* (or *objective*) *case* endings, like the -m in the examples above. There was a *genitive case* suffix for possessive noun phrases. We won't specify all the Latin cases, since only those named here have counterparts in English.

The notion of grammatical case has been used in grammatical analysis for centuries. Current theoretical research has led to a special use of this notion, one that accounts for otherwise unexplained word orders in English and a great many other languages, including even Chinese, which has no overt markings for case. This more specialized notion of case will be explored in Chapter 12.

Now we are ready to see how case comes into play with English pronominals. First, look at this pronominal paradigm, that is, a table of pronominal forms:[2]

TABLE 10.1

Person and Number	Nominative Pronouns	Objective Pronouns	Independent Possessive Pronouns	NP-Internal Possessive Pronouns
1st sg	I	me	mine	my
pl	we	us	ours	our
2nd sg	you	you	yours	your
pl	you	you	yours	your
3rd sg	he, she it, one	him, her, it, one	his, hers	his, her its, one's
pl	they	them	theirs	their

The nominative pronouns occur as subjects, the objective pronouns as objects of either verbs or prepositions, and the possessives (sometimes referred to as genitive pronouns) indicate various kinds of possessive relationships. Our pronominal paradigm omits some forms that are traditionally referred to as pronouns, reflexive forms like *herself*. We'll see in the next chapter that reflexives differ from the pronominals just shown in ways that justify their being placed in a different class.

THE TRADITIONAL VIEW OF PRONOUNS

Traditional school grammars used to describe pronouns as taking the place of nouns. Instead of repeating a noun, speakers would replace the repetition with a pronoun. But this traditional account is oversimplified and misleading. Consider the following sentence:

Gladstone wanted him to leave.

The pronoun *him* is not a way to avoid repeating *Gladstone*. It can refer to any male creature in the universe *except* Gladstone. The school grammar rule doesn't provide any explanation for this important fact. Indeed, if Gladstone is to be both the person wanting to leave and the person who would leave, the position after *wanted* must be "occupied" by an covert noun phrase, the [e] discussed in the previous chapter:

Gladstone wanted [e] to leave.

However, the school grammar rule sometimes does work. Notice that the *him* is fine for a second reference to Gladstone in the following example:

Gladstone thought that Montgomery wanted him to leave.

In this example the *him* can indeed refer to Gladstone. Notice that the pronominal *him* is much closer to the noun phrase *Montgomery*, yet it *cannot* refer to Montgomery. What is happening? Obviously, English does not just have a rule that says, "If you want to refer to someone or something just referred to, use a pronoun." The system used in English is orderly but more complex than this, as the rest of this chapter will demonstrate.

In written language as well as in speech, we use pronominals to cross-reference, to point back (or occasionally forward) in a discourse to another noun phrase. Note in the following example how the woman described is referred to in the first sentence by a lengthy descriptive noun phrase and then is assigned a name. In the second sentence a further noun phrase description is added. From then on, her identity having been established, she is referred to by pronominals:

The old woman conducting the Bournemouth Symphony Orchestra is Dora Hotchkiss. Dora Hotchkiss is one of the greatest conductors of our time. Renowned for her Beethoven interpretations, she has been brought here to extend and deepen the orchestra's experience with Beethoven's late symphonies.

Once the old woman has been identified as Dora Hotchkiss, it is no longer necessary to repeat the long noun phrase beginning *the old woman conducting*. By the third sentence, it is possible to refer to her with pronominals such as *her* and *she*. Pronouns should provide enough information to allow them to be connected with the more fully specified noun phrase having the same referent.

PRONOMINALS AND THEIR ANTECEDENTS

One way, then, to identify the reference of a pronominal is to look for an eligible noun phrase, normally a more fully specified noun phrase not too far off in the stretch of language in which the pronominal occurs. To be eligible, the full noun phrase has to match the pronoun in number (singular or plural) and gender (masculine, feminine, or neither). Consider the following example:

The director told Peter that she could visit that prison.

Assuming that Peter is male, the most eligible antecedent for *she* is *the director*.

In some contexts, however, *the director* is not the only possible antecedent for *she*. The antecedent might be some other person mentioned in an earlier remark. As we saw from the Dora Hotchkiss example, the antecedent need not be in the same sentence as the pronominal. Here we provide a context:

Yesterday Peter interviewed Henry Schmidt, the director of prisons. Peter mentioned that his daughter Celia wanted to write an article about Newgate Prison. After some discussion, the director promised Peter that she could visit that prison.

The most likely antecedent for *she* is clearly the noun phrase *his daughter Celia*, which is in the preceding sentence.

The issue now is where pronominals and their antecedents can be placed in relation to one another. One crucial factor determining when a pronominal can or cannot legitimately refer to a particular antecedent is whether or not they occur within the same linguistic unit. Two kinds of linguistic units are relevant for this reference relationship: the *clause* and the *noun phrase*. We'll make two tentative generalizations. The first generalization concerns clauses:

1. *A pronominal and its antecedent cannot be in the same clause.*

This generalization explains why *her* cannot have *Olivia* as its antecedent in this next example:

Olivia was looking at her in the long mirror.

The pronominal *her* and *Olivia* are in the same clause. Therefore *her* cannot have *Olivia* as its antecedent. A pronoun has to be free of any antecedent in its clause. Notice in the example that follows, *her* is in a different clause and *Olivia* can thus be its antecedent:

Olivia knew that the woman had looked at her in the long mirror.

Our second tentative generalization concerns noun phrases:

2. *A pronominal and its antecedent cannot be in the same noun phrase.*

Strictly speaking, our first generalization already rules out this possibility since, if they are in the same noun phrase, they are in the same clause. But we will see that there are some complications that make it useful to consider clauses and noun phrases separately. Our second generalization accounts for the fact that *him* cannot have *Orsino* as its antecedent in the example below:

Orsino's eloquence about him pleased Viola.

The pronominal *him* is inside the same noun phrase as *Orsino* (*Orsino's eloquence about him*) and therefore cannot have *Orsino* as its antecedent.

But an examination of more complex cases shows that we'll need to revise these tentative generalizations. For example, what happens when the pronominal is inside a noun phrase that is itself inside a noun phrase? Look at this next example:

We know nothing about a play that Marlowe wrote about Shakespeare's treatment of him.

In this example, just as we would expect, *him* cannot have *Shakespeare* as its antecedent because they are in the same noun phrase, *Shakespeare's treatment of him*. But notice that *him* can have *Marlowe* as its antecedent. Indeed, that is a likely interpretation. And yet, *him* and *Marlowe* are also together in a noun phrase, that is, in the larger noun phrase *a play that Marlowe wrote about Shakespeare's treatment of him*, and in the same clause. So our tentative generalizations as phrased cannot be correct.

Look at the following constituent structure tree for the sentence:

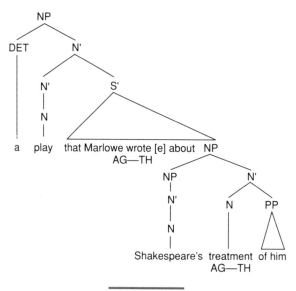

DIAGRAM 10.2

The pronominal *him* is inside a noun phrase, which is inside a clause (shown as an S'), which is, in turn, inside another noun phrase. The antecedent of *him* must not be inside the smaller of the noun phrases containing it, but it can be within a larger constituent. Thus *Marlowe* and *him* are in the same clause and the same larger noun phrase, and *Marlowe* can still be the antecedent. The fact is that our generalization applies to the *smallest* noun phrase or clause containing the pronominal.

Let's revise our generalizations in two ways. First, we need to phrase them as a single generalization applying to both clauses and noun phrases. Let's use a single label, *domain*, to cover both the clauses and the noun phrases involved. Second, we need to phrase our generalization in terms of the smallest domain containing the pronominal. We'll call this smallest domain the *local domain*.[3] Now we can restate our generalization as a single statement: *A pronominal and its antecedent cannot be in the same local domain.*

To see how our generalization works, let's look at several examples. First consider the following two sentences:

> *Voinevich believed that he could do well in that business.*
> *Voinevich's belief in his capabilities surprised me.*

In the first example, *he* can have *Voinevich* as its antecedent. Since *Voinevich* is in the container clause while *he* is in the embedded clause, this is as we would expect. The local domain of *he*, the clause *that he could do well in that business*, doesn't contain *Voinevich*. The same situation holds for *his* and *Voinevich* in the second example, except that the local domain is a noun phrase, not a clause. The noun phrase *Voinevich's belief in his capabilities* contains the smaller noun phrase *his capabilities*, which in turn contains the pronominal *his*. So *his capabilities* is the local domain. As *Voinevich* is not in the local domain for *his*, it is eligible to be its antecedent.

Now we need to look at one more example:

> *Orsino's eloquence pleased him.*

Here *Orsino's* can be the antecedent for *him*. The local domain for *him* is the clause containing it, which also contains *Orsino's*:

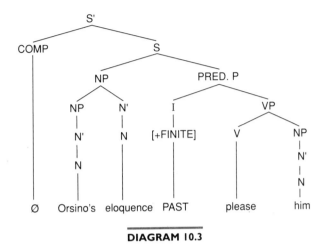

DIAGRAM 10.3

However, the local domain for the possessive noun phrase *Orsino's* is the noun phrase *Orsino's eloquence*, which does not also contain the pronominal *him*. So the pronominal and its antecedent are not in the same local domain, and *Orsino's* can indeed be the antecedent for *him*.

This relation between a pronominal and its antecedent is described as one in which the antecedent *binds* the pronominal. Where a pronominal lacks an antecedent, it is said to be *free*. If the generalization just specified is correct, then within a local domain a pronominal must be free rather than bound. As we've just seen, any antecedent must be outside the local domain.

There is no grammatical rule requiring that any pronominal must have a particular noun phrase as its antecedent. Our generalization just indicates when a noun phrase is *allowed* to be the antecedent of a specific pronominal. Where a pronoun seems to have a particular antecedent, often this interpretation may be required or at least favored by the nonlinguistic facts of the situation.

Effect of Order and Rank

In both of the following examples, the pronominal *her* can have as its antecedent the noun phrase *Janet Dunbracken*:

> **Janet Dunbracken** *admitted that the reporters had interviewed* **her.**
> *The agents reported that* **Janet Dunbracken** *had arrived in Beirut. The reporters were looking for* **her.**

In the first example, the antecedent is in the same sentence but not the same clause. In the second example, the antecedent is in an earlier sentence. Thus, in neither example are the pronominal and its antecedent in the same local domain—in neither arguments of the same predicate.

Now let's look at some examples in which the pronominal *she* cannot have *Janet Dunbracken* as its antecedent even though, as before, the two noun phrases are *not* in the same local domain. Consider, for example, this sentence in which the pronominal *she* occurs *before* the full noun phrase:

> **She** *admitted that the reporters had interviewed* **Janet Dunbracken.**

The *she* cannot refer to Janet Dunbracken. We could speculate that a pronominal must follow its antecedent.

But this isn't correct, as these next three examples show:

*While the reporters were looking for **her** in Cincinnati, the agents believed **Janet Dunbracken** to be hiding in Beirut.*

*Because the agents felt **she** was concealing certain facts, **Janet Dunbracken** was ordered to appear at security headquarters.*

*That **she** had been cheated was now obvious even to **Janet Dunbracken**.*

What's happening? What is the difference between this last set of examples and the previous example? This last set differs in one relevant respect: The pronominals which precede eligible antecedents are in either embedded or subordinate clauses, that is, clauses which would be lower in a constituent structure tree than the clause in which the eligible antecedent appears. When this is the case, a pronominal can precede its antecedent. Such clauses are sometimes referred to as having a lower *rank*. We can now formulate the following generalization regarding pronominal reference across clause boundaries:

A pronominal can follow its antecedent, but it can only precede its antecedent if the pronominal is in a lower ranked clause.

We'll repeat our other pronominal generalization here:

A pronominal and its antecedent cannot be in the same local domain.

Our two generalizations cover pronominal reference within both noun phrases and clauses, as well as across clauses in the same sentence.

English pronominals can cause serious communication problems for ESL/EFL learners, especially in reading comprehension. Learners may know the meaning of every word in a passage but still not understand the passage. Because pronominals are often ambiguous, especially in sentences considered separately from their context, non-native speakers need to draw for their interpretation on both grammatical principles and pragmatic knowledge.[4] To help them do this, we need to provide training and practice in general reading strategies as well as the grammatical principles described in this chapter and the next. This is not to argue that the formulations presented in this chapter be taught in an ESL/EFL classroom. They should not; they are intended as briefing for teachers and other language professionals, not as ESL/EFL learning materials. Careful exposure to the appropriate language data along with focused questioning is likely to be far more effective for most learners.

SUMMARY

Pronouns are specialized nouns. They are almost always the only constituent in their noun phrase. There are nominative and objective pronouns such as *we* and *me*, NP-internal possessive pronouns like *your* and *my*, which occur inside other noun phrases, and independent possessive pronouns like *yours* and *mine*, which can stand alone as noun phrases. NP-internal possessives make the noun phrase in which they occur a definite one, while attaching the independent possessive in an *of* phrase after the head noun allows for the use of an indefinite article before the head. The general term for all these forms is *pronominals*.

Pronominals enable us to cross-reference the entities we refer to in a discourse. In the speech situation, once an identity has been established, either by reference to prior knowledge or by explicit identification in the discourse, a pronominal can be used to refer to that entity. The full noun phrase to which a pronominal refers is known as its *antecedent.* But there are a number of conditions upon the use of a pronominal, the major grammatical ones being constraints on the positions a pronominal may occupy relative to its antecedent. These conditions must be met if a pronominal is to be understood as referring to the intended antecedent.

What are the right positions for a pronominal and its antecedent? First of all, they cannot be in the same local domain, that is, in the same smallest clause or noun phrase. Second, a pronominal can follow its antecedent but can only precede it if the pronominal is in a lower ranked clause.

EXERCISE SET 10

1. For each italicized pronominal below, tell whether it is in the first, second, or third person singular or plural and whether it is a nominative, objective, NP-internal possessive, or independent possessive.

a. Abraham took *their* offering and burned *it*, and the priestess left *him* by the altar, and the people obeyed *her* commands and shouted that the offerings were *theirs* alone.

b. *We* insisted that *he* return whatever was *yours*, but *his* father asked *us* to be patient.

2. What is an antecedent? Give the antecedent of *them* in the following sentence:

Bogart and Bacall told the reporters that no one would speak to them.

3. Explain any meaning difference you detect between the following sentences:

a. *Marion is a friend of his.*
b. *Marion is his friend.*

4. Why is the following generalization inadequate?

A pronominal and its antecedent cannot be in the same clause.

What kinds of phenomena won't it cover? Give one or more examples and provide a more accurate generalization.

5. For each italicized pronominal, tell whether the other italicized noun phrase in the sentence can or cannot be its antecedent and explain why. The italicized noun phrases in each sentence are all third person singular and of the same gender.

a. Because *she* had trained as an engineer, the company sent *Jasmine* to supervise the project.
b. Yesterday *Ruggles* was pleased with *him*.
c. Yesterday *Ruggles* was pleased that the club had chosen *him*.
d. Sturtevant resented *Ruggles's* attack on *him*.
e. *Li* noticed *his* book on Korean pottery.
f. Chauncey believed *Heisenberg's* claim that *he* had argued against the bombing.

6. We expect pronouns to have antecedents in a text. Comment on the effectiveness of the following as the *first paragraph* of a novel:

She was a typical Glasgow girl. She had met a pilot, then married him right away, that fast. The pilot was a man—a boy really—from Dover, New Hampshire. He was shot down maybe two or three weeks after the marriage. Still, he had left behind the start of a baby. I grew up with just one image of him, standing next to his girl bride and smiling awkwardly at the photographer. They never found the body. I used to think he would bang on our back door some day and tell us how he'd crawled out of the wreckage but had lost his memory until now. But he never came.

7. Write an eight-line narrative paragraph to test learners' ability to use the appropriate pronominal forms. Your instructions can achieve this by asking the students first to change *Jack* to *Janet* and every masculine pronominal to a feminine pronominal, and then to change *Janet* to *Janet and Jack* and every singular into a plural. Here is an example sentence:

> *Jack found **his** coat in the garden, but **he** did not at first recognize **it** as **his**.*

The changed versions would read:

> *Janet found **her** coat in the garden, but **she** did not at first recognize **it** as **hers**.*

> *Janet and Jack found **their** coats in the garden, but **they** did not at first recognize **them** as **theirs**.*

Can you think of a grammatical unit other than pronominals that you could ask students to change? What is the value of such exercises?

NOTES

1. Some languages have two first-person plural pronouns. An *exclusive* pronoun is used by speakers to refer to themselves and others but not to the addressee. An *inclusive* form includes the addressee. English, in this case, relies more heavily on context than do these other languages.

2. Note the gaps in the possessive pronoun column for *it* and *one*. Some speakers use *its* as an independent possessive pronoun, as in *Their paws are swollen but, as for the tiger's, its are fine.* Most speakers queried rejected this usage.

3. Another common term for this in the Principles-and-Parameters (or GB) framework is *governing category*.

4. The ideas in this section draw heavily on a report of an interesting study of the relationship between overall comprehension and the comprehension of pronominals; see M. Demel, "The relationship between overall reading comprehension and comprehension of co-referential ties for second language readers of English," *TESOL Quarterly* 24 (1990): 267-92.

11

Empty Noun Phrases and Anaphors

In the last two chapters we considered two types of noun phrases. First, there are full noun phrases such as *an engineer, the woman who was elected president,* and *Mozart.* These noun phrases, sometimes called *referring expressions,* are used when the speaker or writer believes we should be able to identify from the noun phrase who or what is referred to. Second, there are pronominals, like *her* and *their,* which are specialized nouns functioning as noun phrases. A pronominal is interpreted either by reference to an antecedent somewhere else in the sentence or from the context outside the bounds of that sentence, perhaps from a full noun phrase elsewhere in the discourse or from the broader situation. We saw in Chapter 10 that English is quite strict regarding the reference possibilities allowed for pronominals.

There is a third major type of noun phrase, which appears similar to pronominals but in fact has quite different conditions on where antecedents can be positioned. This is the category of *anaphors,* which includes reflexives like *herself* and *themselves* and reciprocals like *each other* and *one another.* In addition to the three major types, there are the so-called covert noun phrases shown as [e] in earlier chapters. We'll start our discussion with an examination of covert noun phrases.

COVERT NOUN PHRASES [e] AND THEIR ANTECEDENTS

Consider the function of the empty position, shown as [e][1] in the following sentence:

The director of prisons promised Peter [e] to visit that prison.

The director's promise refers to a specific person who is to visit the prison, but the embedded clause has no overt noun phrase subject. However, this very absence of an overt subject in an embedded clause is a signal that some other noun phrase, a noun phrase in the container clause, determines the reference of the empty noun phrase. The relevant noun phrase here is *the director of prisons,* the subject of the container clause. The director is the person who is supposed to visit the prison. So the [e] refers back to the subject of the next higher clause.

However, it isn't always the container clause subject that is the relevant noun phrase. The predicate in the container clause is the verb *promised.* Suppose we replaced it with the verb *persuaded:*

The director persuaded Peter **[e] to visit the prison**.

Now which of the two noun phrases in the container clause determines the reference of the [e]? In this case, the person who is to visit the prison is not the director but Peter. The noun phrase *Peter* is an object in the container clause. So while the predicate *promise* requires the antecedent of the covert noun phrase to be the container clause subject, *persuade* requires the antecedent to be a container clause object. The predicate in the container clause thus *controls* which of the container arguments is to be the antecedent of the covert noun phrase.

Notice one difference between the pronominals and this empty noun phrase, [e]. Third person pronominals are free in a way that the [e] is not: These pronominals are not required to refer to some particular noun phrase elsewhere in the sentence. So the *she* in *Holly said she was leaving early* doesn't have to have *Holly* as its antecedent. The *she* could refer to some other female individual mentioned elsewhere in the discourse or to someone not even mentioned in the discourse, for example, to someone standing near the speaker. The "antecedent" in this last case is not a linguistic unit but a person. First person pronominals are restricted to referring to the speaker and others he or she includes, while second person pronominals refer to the addressee(s).

Covert noun phrases, in contrast, typically must have an antecedent in their container clause. However, there are exceptions. In the filler *it* construction or a similar construction with an embedded clause instead of *it*, an [e] can refer to some unspecified entity paraphrasable with an indefinite form like *anyone, anything, someone,* or *something*:

> *It's unusual [e] to see snow at this time of year.*
> *[e] to see snow at this time of year is unusual.*

We could replace the [e] in the example with *anyone* without changing the sentence's propositional content. However, we will need to introduce it with the complementizer *for*.

> *It's unusual for **anyone** to see snow at this time of year.*
> *For **anyone** to see snow at this time of year is unusual.*

Furthermore, empty noun phrases can also refer to the speaker or others in the speech situation, much as the pronominals *I, you, we, me,* and the other first and second person pronominals do:

> *It's sad [e] to see them leave so early.*

The conditions for this kind of interpretation are pragmatic, not grammatical.

In Chapter 10, we referred to the smallest clause or noun phrase containing the pronominal as its *local domain*. The covert noun phrases we have been discussing have one important property in common with pronominals: If a covert noun phrase has an antecedent in the sentence, it must be outside its local domain, whether this domain is a clause or noun phrase.

ANAPHORS[2]

Like pronominals, anaphors are forms whose main function is to indicate reference; but their distribution is much more limited. An anaphor is a kind of pronoun that has its antecedent in the same minimal clause or noun phrase. In this respect, it is totally different from the pronominal category. Here is an anaphor paradigm:

TABLE II.I

Person Number	Reflexive Anaphors	Reciprocal Anaphors	NP-Internal Reflexives	NP-Internal Reciprocals
1st sg	myself		my own	
pl	ourselves	one another, each other	our own	one another's, each other's
2nd sg	yourself		your own	
pl	yourselves	one another, each other	your own	one another's, each other's
3rd sg	himself, herself, itself, oneself	one another, each other	his, her, its	one another's,
pl	themselves	one another, each other	one's own their own	each other's

To see how the distribution of anaphors differs from that of pronominals, let's start by looking at these sentences with anaphors:

*The cats washed **themselves** delicately.*
The cats thought that Josephine washed **themselves delicately.*

*Julian and his friend visited **each other** regularly.*
Julian and his friend wanted Josephine to visit **each other regularly.*

Trudeau washes his own hair.
*I wash his own hair.

Notice that in the acceptable sentences, the reflexive and reciprocal anaphors occur in the same clauses as their antecedents, whereas in the sentences asterisked as ungrammatical, the anaphors and antecedents are in different clauses.

Anaphors must have antecedents within the same smallest clause. They contrast with pronominals in this regard. Anaphors must be bound by antecedents within their smallest clause, whereas pronouns must be free of any antecedent in their smallest clause. The two groups thus complement each other.

In Chapter 10, we saw that the same kind of generalization about pronominals in clauses could be made about pronominals inside noun phrases. We noted that in the noun phrase *a play that Marlowe wrote about Shakespeare's treatment of him*, the pronominal *him* could not have as its antecedent the noun phrase *Shakespeare's*, because both are in the same smallest noun phrase, *Shakespeare's treatment of him*. In contrast, *Marlowe*, which is not in the same small noun phrase, could be the antecedent.

Let's change our example so that it contains an anaphor instead of a pronominal:

a play that Marlowe wrote about Shakespeare's treatment of himself

Here the only possible antecedent to bind *himself* is *Shakespeare's*, which is within the same local domain noun phrase; *himself* cannot refer to Marlowe. The notion *local domain* is thus valid for anaphors too.

So let us formulate the following generalization: *An anaphor must be bound within its local domain; a pronominal must be free within its local domain.*

SOME POSSIBLE COUNTEREXAMPLES

There are some apparent counterexamples to the generalizations made so far. Consider the following sentence:

*Faust persuaded Mephistopheles [e] to untie **him**.*

Why can't the pronominal *him* have *Mephistopheles* as its antecedent? After all, they are not in the same clause. Here are the two clauses:

Clause 1:   *Faust persuaded Mephistopheles* (embedded clause)
Clause 2:   *[e] to untie him*

The answer has to do with the reference of the covert noun phrase, [e]. The verb *persuaded* requires that the empty subject of its embedded clause have the same referent as the object of *persuaded* in the container clause, that is, *Mephistopheles*. Now, if the subject of the embedded clause, [e], refers to Mephistopheles, then the object *him* in that same clause cannot also refer to Mephistopheles. This is because its antecedent would be in the same local domain. Personal pronouns like *him* cannot have their antecedent in the same clause. So the sentence isn't really a counterexample.

The discussion above also explains the following apparent counterexample, in which a reflexive pronoun seems to have as its antecedent a noun phrase in a different clause, a binding relationship forbidden for anaphors:

*Helen didn't try [e] to free **herself**.*

The verb *try*, like *promise*, requires that the covert subject of its embedded clause have the container clause subject as its antecedent, so the covert noun phrase [e] must refer to Helen. Since the [e] refers to Helen, it is therefore the antecedent of the reflexive anaphor *herself*, and the sentence does not constitute a counterexample.

There are, however, examples in which the subject of an embedded clause is a reflexive anaphor and yet has as its antecedent the subject of the container clause:

*The biochemist believed **herself** to be honest.*

Surely the subject of the embedded clause in this last example, *herself*, is bound by an antecedent in a different clause, a binding relation claimed to be forbidden? No straightforward explanation exists. We have here an exception rather than a counterexample because the binding generalization works for the great majority of verbs. There is simply a small group of verbs—*believe, think, expect*, and *consider* are examples—that allow the general principle to be violated.[3] Within the Principles-and-Parameters framework, a more complex definition of our notion "local domain" is used, one that results in the local domain being defined for this small group of verbs as the container sentence.

One other possible exception or counterexample remains to be discussed. Look at the following sentence:

Marlowe resented the book about himself.

The anaphor *himself* is inside the noun phrase *the book about himself*. However, *Marlowe*, the antecedent, is outside this noun phrase. Our generalization that anaphors must be bound within their smallest noun phrase does not work for this example. How does this example differ from *Marlowe resented Shakespeare's talk about himself*, where, in keeping with our generalization, *himself* can refer only to Shakespeare and not to Marlowe? Like clauses, noun phrases expressing propositions may have subjects, though the subjects are possessive. The relevant difference between the two sentences is that in one case the noun phrase in which *himself* occurs has as its subject the possessive noun phrase *Shakespeare's,* while in the other there is no subject but only the article *the.*

Our generalization is valid, except for these subjectless noun phrases. There is something different about such noun phrases that puts them outside this generalization. We can capture this difference by specifying that to be a local domain a noun phrase, like a finite clause, must have an overt subject.[4]

Counterparts in Other Languages

In this chapter and the previous one we've looked into an intricate linguistic cross-referencing system that operates to make referring to someone or something very straightforward. We've seen that pronominals, anaphors, and empty noun phrases are the crucial categories in the system for English. Each category has its own special distribution and reference possibilities, and the categories mesh together remarkably neatly to provide users of English with an elegant and economical system for referring.

All languages share certain features, and some logically possible referring systems never occur in human languages, presumably because they violate restrictions imposed by human mental structure. Such features and such restrictions form part of what is called Universal Grammar, the set of grammatical principles underlying all human languages.

Languages of all types are being examined to provide data for a universally valid account of pronominals and anaphors. But care is needed. A word listed as meaning "himself or herself" in a dictionary of another language may have some properties very different from the apparent counterparts in English. Mandarin Chinese, for example, has a word *ziji,* which is usually listed as the appropriate form for any of the English *self* words. But Chinese is less strict than English about where reflexive forms can occur, since the Chinese counterparts of these ungrammatical English sentences are also perfectly grammatical:

> *Alice wanted the king to look at herself in the glass.
> *Alice was angry that the king just ignored herself.

In the Mandarin versions of these sentences, the antecedent of *herself* can be *Alice.*
The anaphor *himself* in the following English sentence can only refer to Wangwu:

> *Zhangsan believed that Lisi knew that Wangwu had no confidence in himself.*

But in the corresponding Mandarin sentence:

> *Zhangsan xiangxin [Lisi zhidao [Wangwu dui **ziji** mei xinxin]].*

Zhangsan believed [that Lisi knew [that Wangwu had no confidence in self]].

the anaphor *ziji,* "self," can refer to Wangwu, Lisi, or Zhangsan.

Speakers of languages with less stringent restrictions on reflexives must adapt to stricter conditions when acquiring English. Some learners may initially apply to their English the looser rules of their first language. Others may, for example, apply the strict rules to finite clauses but treat nonfinite clauses differently. Obviously, a great deal more research is needed on how non-native speakers acquire these forms.

As we noted in the previous chapter, pronominals and anaphors can be confusing, especially to readers of complex prose. Non-native speakers may mistake the antecedent of a pronominal or anaphor and perhaps misunderstand an important part of the propositional content of a text or utterance. For most learners, patient testing and the careful correcting of misinterpretations are needed. For those students accustomed to learning from explicit grammatical rules (often a minority), a very simplified version of our generalization regarding pronominals and anaphors in clauses might be helpful. For instance, an instructor could refer to pronominals and anaphors as just two types of pronoun, using many examples of each. Fortunately, the contexts in which these forms occur should make it clear who or what the pronominals and anaphors are referring to. For learners, the ability to exploit contextual clues is at least as valuable as knowledge of the grammatical rules for these elements.

SUMMARY

There are three types of noun phrases. First, there are full noun phrases, also called referring expressions, such as *an energetic teacher* and *Margaret Thatcher*. These need no antecedents since the addressee is assumed to be able to identify from the noun phrase who or what is referred to. Second, there are the pronominals, such as *theirs* and *she*. These must be free within their local domain, that is, they cannot have an antecedent within the smallest noun phrase or clause which contains them. Third, there are anaphors, which include reflexives like *ourselves* and reciprocals like *one another*. Anaphors must be bound (i.e., have an antecedent) in their local domain. Covert noun phrases in the subject position of an embedded clause typically have to have as their antecedent either the subject or the object of their container clause, depending on the container clause predicate. But like pronominals, covert noun phrases can sometimes refer to someone or something not mentioned elsewhere in the sentence, such as the speaker, the addressee, or an indefinite entity that could have been expressed as *anyone* or *someone*. The reference is pragmatically rather than grammatically determined.

Cross-referencing categories with similar properties have been identified in many other languages. The restrictions on their distribution vary from language to language. If indeed all human languages follow the same basic principles, varying only in the degree of restrictiveness on reference and in certain other details, then these principles and the *types* of restrictions form part of Universal Grammar.

So, speakers of other languages should find the general reference system of English not too difficult to acquire but would have to get used to different degrees of restrictiveness and differences in the use of pragmatic information.

EXERCISE SET 11

1. Who is the referent of the covert noun phrase in each of these sentences?
   a. *It was foolish [e] to report that to the agency.*
   b. *It was foolish of you [e] to report that to the agency.*

2. According to this chapter, reflexives must have their antecedent in the same local domain. How then can the imperative sentence *Wash yourself now!* be accounted for? Why is **Wash himself now!* not grammatical?

3. Describe and explain the possible interpretations of *she, her,* and *herself* in the following sentences:
   a. *Susan greeted her father.*
   b. *Susan admired her.*
   c. *Her father greeted Susan warmly.*
   d. *She greeted Susan's father warmly.*
   e. *Susan wanted Agnes to improve herself.*

    f. *Susan told George to treat herself to a luxury cruise.*

    g. *Susan believes that she is healthy.*

4. From the point of view of native speaker competence and of second language acquisition, what justification is there for positing a covert unit [e]?

5. Draw a D-structure tree for sentence 1a above.

6. Devise a set of five sentences that might help teachers determine whether their students are having problems interpreting pronominals and anaphors.

7. Examine the treatment of pronominals and anaphors in an ESL/EFL grammar textbook or a grammar handbook for native speakers and specify the phenomena not covered. How important for the intended readership are these phenomena?

NOTES

1. These [e] noun phrases, which are typically subjects of nonfinite clauses, are called PRO in the technical linguistic literature. PRO is always written in capital letters and is sometimes referred to as "Big PRO." The conditions regarding the positioning and interpretation of this PRO form part of the Control Theory module of the Principles-and-Parameters Theory. For a useful but technical account of this module, see Liliane Haegeman, *Introduction to Government and Binding Theory* (Oxford: Basil Blackwell, 1991), chapter 5. There is another type of covert noun phrase with different properties in other languages. The Italian *ho mangiato*, literally "have-1st person eaten" is assumed to have a "small pro" subject referring to the speaker. The English counterpart to this sentence, like those in French and German, has to have an overt form before the verb: *I* in English, *je* in French, and *ich* in German.

2. Unfortunately, *anaphor*, along with the adjectival *anaphoric*, is more often used as a cover term for both pronominals and the forms referred to here as anaphors. The related form *anaphora* is used as a general label for the whole phenomenon of cross-referencing within discourse. In this sense, *anaphoric* is in opposition to *deictic*, which covers reference in a text beyond the sentence or reference to a nonlinguistic entity. The more restricted usage of *anaphor* here conforms to that in Chomsky's Principles-and-Parameters framework.

3. The embedded clause subject—*herself* in our example—could be regarded as also being the container clause object. It could therefore be a reflexive anaphor having the container subject as its antecedent. Such an analysis does not fit into the Principles-and-Parameters framework, but earlier models of transformational grammar posited a rule called Subject-to-Object Raising, which promoted or raised the embedded clause subject into the higher clause, converting it into an object in S-structure. Certain modern approaches, most notably Relational Grammar, adopt a similar formulation. The Principles-and-Parameters approach of Chomsky allows no rules that create new noun phrase slots after D-structure. An alternative, having verbs like *believe* specify in their lexical structure a nonthematic slot to be filled later, is similarly rejected. Both formulations are seen as violating the Projection Principle. For a relevant discussion, see Noam Chomsky, *Knowledge of Language* (New York: Praeger, 1986), 84 and 189–190. The goal is to have the most restrictive grammar able to generate the sentences of a language. It should be noted, however, that empty *subject* positions occur in D-structure without thematic roles and are later filled by *it* or *there*. The issues are complex. The verbs involved are a very small class and their counterparts in other Indo-European languages lack this exceptional characteristic.

4. Note that, for most speakers, the sentence *Marlowe resented the talk about him* is also acceptable. This presents a serious problem for the framework, since the object noun phrase has no subject, so the local domain for the pronominal *him* would have to be the whole sentence. In that case, *him* should not have its antecedent in that sentence. But it does. Similarly the sentence in the text—*Marlowe resented the book about himself*—may not be acceptable to many speakers. Some readers may also have noticed that reflexive and reciprocal anaphors in the determiner slot, as for instance, *her own house* and *each other's achievements*, cannot be bound inside their noun phrases—they actually start their noun phrase. Noun phrases in which the anaphor is itself the subject cannot be minimal noun phrases. A helpful discussion of these issues is to be found in V. J. Cook, *Chomsky's Universal Grammar* (Oxford: Basil Blackwell, 1988), 43–49.

    We are not dealing with the use of the emphatic reflexive in sentences like *I myself watched the satellite launch.* The occurrence of emphatic reflexives is pragmatically rather than grammatically determined. Fortunately, emphatic reflexives are unlikely to present difficulties for learners. The occurrence of ordinary reflexive anaphors can also be pragmatically determined, as in sentences like *A number of nurses, including myself, have objected to this procedure.*

12

Noun Phrases and Case

English does not allow noun phrases to occur just anywhere in a sentence. The object of a verb or preposition always starts out in the position following the verb or preposition. Certain sentence processes, for example, movement of the object to the front of the sentence for a question—as in *Which car did she ride in?*—may shift noun phrases to other positions. But as we will see, there are strict constraints as to the positions to which a noun phrase can be moved. It's not hard to see why this is so for English, because English relies so heavily on word order to signal semantic relationships. The set of positions in which a constituent can occur is known as its *distribution*. Noun phrase distribution is more complex than it might at first sight seem. Three distributional characteristics of noun phrases come to mind as requiring explanation; all three are related to constructions we've already discussed.

First, there are certain positions in sentences in which overt noun phrases do not occur. If noun phrases were placed in those positions, English speakers might be able to figure out the meaning intended but would judge the sentences ungrammatical. Here are some examples with noun phrases in "illegal" positions:

> ***Betty** to resign was unfortunate.*
> *Rosamond was fond **Anatole**.*
> *I was surprised **Jacqueline** to be innocent.*
> *The captain persuaded the soldiers **the passenger** to board the ship.*

It's not hard to correct these sentences and make the noun phrases acceptable. The first two just require the addition of a preposition—*of* or *for*:

> *For Betty to resign was unfortunate.*
> *Rosamond was fond of Anatole.*

But *why* are such additions needed? The third and fourth sentences require finite *that* clauses, instead of nonfinite clauses:

> *I was surprised that Jacqueline was innocent.*
> *The captain persuaded the soldiers that the passenger should board the ship.*

Why can't *Jacqueline* and *the passenger* be the subjects of nonfinite clauses? After all, *Jacqueline* can be the subject of the same nonfinite clause in the sentence *I believed*

Jacqueline to be innocent. So, the first phenomenon requiring explanation is this inability of noun phrases to occur in certain positions.

A second phenomenon requiring explanation is the distribution of various pronoun forms in clauses. Why are the following sentences ungrammatical?

> *The citizens believed **she** to be a murderer.
> *Tony persuaded **he** that his wife should sing.
> *The citizens considered that **her** had killed Caligula.

Again these sentences are easy to correct.

The third phenomenon involves *covert noun phrases*, which, like overt noun phrases, have positions in which they can or cannot occur. Their occurrence is related according to clause type. As we've seen, nonfinite clauses allow covert noun phrases in subject position (*[e] to err is human*) but not overt noun phrases (**People** *to err is human*). Finite clauses, on the other hand, do not allow empty noun phrases in subject position[1]—*That [e] make mistakes is natural enough*—although they always allow overt noun phrase subjects.

There is good reason to believe that these distributional differences all have to do with the grammatical notion of *case*. We will see that all overt noun phrases have to be in positions where they can be assigned a case, whereas covert noun phrases don't get case and therefore occur in positions in which the noun phrase cannot be assigned case.

CASE ASSIGNMENT AND PRONOMINALS

In Chapter 10, we saw that noun phrases in many languages show a special marking—frequently a suffix—which is called *case marking*. A subject noun phrase gets a nominative case suffix, an object noun phrase gets an accusative (or objective) case suffix, and a possessor noun phrase gets a genitive (or possessive) suffix. The case-marked noun phrases can be referred to as nominative noun phrases, accusative noun phrases, and so forth. The precise number of cases and their labels vary according to the language.

In English, pronouns and possessive determiners have special nominative, objective, and possessive forms. Look at the italicized third person singular forms in the following example:

He	took	**him**	to	**his** office and talked to **him.**
NOMINATIVE		OBJECTIVE		POSSESSIVE OBJECTIVE

In this sentence the subject pronoun is in the nominative case form *he*. The pronoun right after the verb is the object of the verb and so is in its objective case form *him*. The next pronominal is inside the noun phrase *his office* and, signifying the "possessor" of the office, is in the possessive case form. The last pronominal is also an object, the object of the preposition *to*, so it too is in the objective case form *him.*[2] How do these pronominals get their case? As we shall see, there are various ways.

Pronouns in the objective case—object pronouns—are assigned their case only by active voice transitive verbs and by prepositions. The verbs and prepositions are therefore called *case assigners*, while the object pronouns that get the case are called *case receivers*.

What about pronouns in the possessive case? Possessive noun phrases, remember, occur in the determiner slot of a larger noun phrase:

the teacher's notebook
his notebook

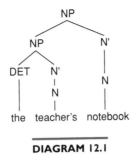

DIAGRAM 12.1

Pronouns get possessive case if they are in the determiner slot. They are, however, noun phrases, not determiners. In the example *his notebook*, the pronoun *his* is in the determiner slot for the head noun *notebook*. The pronoun is in the possessive case. Possessive case is not assigned by a verb or preposition but is automatic for pronouns (or any kind of noun phrase, since full noun phrases in this slot get a possessive marker like *'s*) in the determiner position. As we will see later in this chapter, this special kind of case is actually assigned at D-structure and is connected with the thematic role of the noun phrase. The general phenomenon is known as *inherent case*.[3]

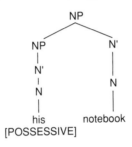

DIAGRAM 12.2

No explanation has been provided so far for nominative case. We know that either verbs or prepositions assign objective case to pronouns, and we have seen that possessive case is assigned to pronouns in a determiner slot. Which constituent is the nominative case assigner?

The most useful way to answer this last question is to look at language data. Consider the pronoun subjects of the embedded clauses in the following examples:

*For **them** to arrive so late was unfortunate.*
*That **they** arrived so late was unfortunate.*

The first embedded clause is nonfinite. The pronoun subject *them* immediately follows the preposition *for*, which assigns objective case. As this example makes clear, not all subjects are assigned nominative case. The second embedded clause is finite, and its pronoun subject is in the nominative case. The subject is immediately preceded by the complementizer *that*, but it does not get its case from the complementizer. Note that even if nothing preceded the pronoun subject, it would be in its nominative form:

***They** arrived late.*

So what is the crucial difference between the clause embedded after *for* and the clause embedded after *that*? The difference is that the first embedded clause is inflected as a nonfinite clause, whereas the second clause, with a nominative subject, is inflected as a finite clause. Recall from Chapter 7 that the Inflection constituent is either [+FINITE] or [-FINITE]. If the Inflection constituent is [+FINITE], it contains past or present tense or a modal verb; if it is [-FINITE], it contains *to*.

Thus it is the [+FINITE] Inflection constituent that assigns nominative case. In other words, finite Inflection is the case assigner that requires subjects to have nominative case.

As we noted earlier, the Inflection constituent is in the predicate phrase. There is thus a difference in the direction of case assignment. For objective case the case assigner—a transitive verb or preposition—must precede the case receiver. For nominative case, the case assigner—Inflection—always follows the case receiver.

To summarize, the case of a pronominal depends on the kind of structure in which it occurs. The constituent assigning case is always adjacent to the pronominal, either immediately following it or immediately preceding it. Possessive case, however, is an inherent case: these pronominals have case not because of a case assigner, but because of their occurrence in the determiner slot.

CASE ASSIGNMENT AND NONPRONOMINAL NOUN PHRASES

So far, we have focused on only pronominals. What about other kinds of noun phrases? Do they receive case?

Some noun phrases obviously have case. Specifically, we know that possessor noun phrases have possessive case because they have a possessive case suffix. In *the teacher's notebook*, the possessor noun phrase is in the determiner slot before the head noun *notebook* and has the *'s* suffix.

There is reason to believe that *all* noun phrases get case. When native speakers replace a noun phrase like *the teacher* with a pronominal, they know which case form to use. They know because the information relevant to the choice is provided by the structure in which the pronominal would appear.

The fact that the structures provide this information suggests that case is also assigned to full noun phrases, even though, with the exception of possessives, their form seems unaffected. If this is true, the noun phrases must be in the right position to get case. So we conclude that, in English, a noun phrase, whether pronominal or nonpronominal, either is inherently possessive by virtue of its position in the determiner slot or is assigned (a) objective case by an immediately preceding active voice transitive verb, (b) objective case by an immediately preceding preposition, or (c) nominative case by a [+FINITE] Inflection immediately following.

EMBEDDED CLAUSE SUBJECTS AND CASE

Look at the following pair of sentences and think about how the subjects of the embedded clauses get assigned their case:

> The police believed that **they** had left.
> The police believed **them** to be leaving.

The first example is straightforward. The embedded clause is finite and there is therefore a [+FINITE] Inflection after the subject to assign nominative case to it. In the second example, since the clause in which it occurs is nonfinite, there is no [+FINITE] Inflection to assign nominative case to the subject. However, the pronoun happens to be immediately preceded by the transitive verb *believed*. Since having an immediately preceding transitive verb is one of the two contexts for objective case assignment, the noun phrase is assigned objective case by that verb. The verb *believe* is one of an exceptional class of verbs that assigns objective case to the subject of the next clause down, if that clause is nonfinite. Other verbs in this class are *report, expect, consider, think, prove, show, proclaim,* and *imagine.*

Now consider this example:

Emily was anxious for them to leave.

Here the pronoun subject is also in a nonfinite clause. But this time it follows the preposition *for*. Since prepositions are also case assigners, the pronoun subject of the embedded clause must be assigned objective case.

In the next example, the preposition *for* is optional for many speakers:

Ivan would like (for) them to leave.

If *for* is chosen, it must assign case to the embedded clause's subject. If it is omitted, then the active voice transitive verb *like* in the container clause does the job.[4] In this last respect, the class of verbs including *like, dislike, want,* and *hate* resembles *believe,* although *believe* doesn't allow the *for* complementizer:

*The police believed for them to be going.

ADJECTIVES AND CASE

Adjectives are not case assigners. Only transitive verbs, prepositions, and Inflection assign case in English. Look again at these two examples:

*Emily was anxious **for** them to leave.*
*Ivan would like **(for)** them to leave.*

Why is the preposition *for*, which functions as the complementizer introducing the embedded clause, optional in one sentence yet obligatory in the other?

Suppose the preposition were omitted from both examples. In the sentence with the verb *like* as predicate, the subject of the embedded clause would get its case from the transitive verb immediately preceding it. But the other sentence has as its main predicate the adjective *anxious*. If the preposition were omitted, the subject of the embedded clause would be preceded by an adjective, so the subject could not get case. But the embedded clause is nonfinite. Since the embedded clause is nonfinite, there is no [+FINITE] Inflection constituent to assign case. As a result, there would be no way for case to be assigned to the subject. That's why sentences like the following are ungrammatical:

*Emily was anxious them to leave.

So, when a predicate adjective precedes a noun phrase, a preposition must intervene. Noun phrases *must* be assigned case by an adjacent assigner or the sentence in which they occur will be ungrammatical.

The same point can be made with the Ivan sentence in which *for* is optional. Put the adverbial phrase *very much* between the verb *like* and the noun phrase following it and the sentence is ungrammatical:

*Ivan would like very much them to leave.

The pronoun cannot get its case from the adverbial phrase and the verb *like* is not immediately adjacent to it. To remedy the situation, the preposition *for* can be inserted before the embedded clause subject, to which it assigns objective case. So all the noun phrases in the sentence have been assigned case and the sentence is grammatical:

Ivan would like very much for them to leave.

THE CASE FILTER

The principles regarding case that we have been discussing form the central part of what is known as *Case Theory*, which specifies a prohibition against overt noun phrases that have not been assigned case. This prohibition is referred to as the *case filter*. Sentences that have noun phrases without case are assumed to be "filtered out" as ungrammatical. The case filter has a wide range of applications.

Possessive case, remember, is assigned to a possessor noun phrase by virtue of its position in the determiner slot of a larger noun phrase. This is what happens in noun phrases like *the composer's daughter*. But suppose the possessor noun phrase follows the noun phrase for the thing possessed:

*the daughter the composer

Now the possessor noun phrase cannot be assigned possessive case because it isn't in the determiner slot. However, English does provide a way for case to be assigned. The noun phrase *the composer* can be converted into the object of a preposition by inserting *of*:

the daughter of the composer

As object of the preposition, the noun phrase *the composer* can be assigned objective case. This possessor construction with *of* is a useful alternative to the form with a possessive noun phrase, though it isn't always available (notice how awkward *the pen of my aunt* sounds). Speakers generally prefer *'s*, that is, possessive case, when the possessor is a living thing or a time notion (e.g., *today's winner*).[5]

CASE AND COVERT NOUN PHRASES

One type of noun phrase is not, and must not be, assigned case. These noun phrases, therefore, appear only in positions in which case can't be assigned. We're talking about covert noun phrases ([e]),[6] noun phrases that have no overt form, although they correspond to components of the meaning of a clause.

The following example with *anxious* is ungrammatical because the embedded clause subject is not [e] but an overt noun phrase, *the men*:

She was anxious **the men to leave.*

This noun phrase cannot get case from the predicate preceding it because the predicate is an adjective, *anxious*. It cannot get case from the Inflection following it because the Inflection isn't a finite one. If, however, the subject of the embedded clause, *the men*, were replaced by the empty subject [e], the sentence would be perfectly grammatical:

She was anxious [e] to leave.

As we've seen, the embedded clause subject, the [e] noun phrase, cannot be assigned case by the preceding predicate or by the following Inflection. But this is fine with the empty noun phrase because it doesn't *need* case and, in fact, cannot appear in any position where it could get case.[7] That's why this next sentence is ungrammatical in English:[8]

*She was anxious for [e] to leave.

The [e] follows directly after the complementizer, which happens to be the case-assigning preposition *for*. The sentence is therefore ruled out.

Clauses with covert subjects can be embedded after predicate adjectives and intransitive verbs, forms that don't assign case. The empty subject follows immediately after these adjectives or verbs. So an empty noun phrase can occur in this position without any chance of being assigned case. This is why empty noun phrases can appear in sentences like the following, which have as container clause predicates either an adjective or an intransitive verb:

It is unusual [e] to find such artists in a place like this.
The laborers tried [e] to earn their suppers.

Where an embedded nonfinite clause is the subject of a container clause, [e] can be subject of that embedded clause:

[e] to struggle against this tyranny is a duty.

This is because there is no case assigner to give case to the [e] subject.

Ditransitive Verbs and Inherent Case

As discussed in Chapter 5, ditransitive verbs are verbs like *give, lend, cook,* and *make,* which can have two objects:

The landlord gave the fireman a fried chicken. (= *to the fireman*)
Mrs. McTavish cooked Ian a young chicken. (= *for Ian*)

In these sentences the direct object (*a fried chicken, a young chicken*) has the theme role and the other object has either the goal (*to*) role (*the fireman*) or the benefactive (*for*) role (*Ian*).

What is special about these verbs is that their direct objects, the theme noun phrases, cannot get their objective case from their verbs since they don't immediately follow them. This is a problem for the grammatical theory because these noun phrases have to have case or the sentences in which they occur will be ruled out by the case filter. Since the sentences are perfectly grammatical, they should not be ruled out.

Interestingly, languages allowing clauses with two objective case noun phrases are exceptions. Such languages (e.g., English, Chinese, Malay) are, in technical phraseology, more highly marked in this respect. Consequently, grammatical theorists have felt justified in positing an exceptional analysis for them. They claim that the second object, like possessive noun phrases in determiner slots, already has case assigned at D-structure because of its position. The verb *give* and similar verbs occurring in ditransitive clauses (e.g., *tell, lend, ask, cook,* and *promise*) can all have a second object, a *theme* noun phrase, which has inherent case. The regular kind of case assignment by verbs and prepositions occurs at surface structure and has nothing to do with any thematic role. In fact, the filler pronoun *it,* which has no thematic role and doesn't appear at D-structure, must also get case. Regular case assignment depends on the *structure* in which the noun phrase occurs, not the noun phrase's role. Thus it is known as *structural case assignment.* This distinction between inherent and structural case preserves a generalization that works well for many languages: Verbs can assign case to only one noun phrase.

But does this answer *explain* anything about ditransitive clauses in English, or is it just a devious way to avoid having these clauses incorrectly ruled out by the case filter? We'll see, in the next section, that this inherent case hypothesis does indeed have some explanatory value.

D-STRUCTURE, DITRANSITIVES, AND CASE THEORY

Our summary at the end of Chapter 3 noted that the theme role is assigned to the noun phrase following the predicate. Subsequently, because of the *subject constraint*, if the subject position is unfilled, a noun phrase or a clause must be moved (via a process called transformation) into subject position (or, alternatively, filler *it* is inserted). This is how passive voice clauses, which start off without subjects, acquire themes as their *subjects*. It is at this stage, S-structure, that we see the final grammatical relations the arguments have. This final stage follows the earlier stage, D-structure, at which predicates assign thematic roles such as agent and theme to noun phrases and to clauses which are arguments.

What happens to passive clauses with ditransitive verbs? Can both objects get case? Look at the following D-structures of two such passives:

> ... was given the fireman a fried chicken
> ... was cooked Ian a young chicken

As we pointed out earlier, active voice transitive verbs can assign case. Passive voice verbs, like adjectives (to which they bear some resemblance), cannot assign case. This doesn't matter for the theme objects (*a fried chicken* and *a young chicken*) since they are claimed to have inherent objective case. But the only way *the fireman* and *Ian* can get case is if they are *moved* into subject position for surface structure:

> **The fireman** was given a fried chicken.
> **Ian** was cooked a young chicken.

Of course, the moved noun phrases can now get nominative case since the subject slot of the finite clauses is assigned nominative case by the finite Inflection constituent. The case filter is satisfied by the result of this movement. Moreover, the movement satisfies the *subject constraint*.

What if the *theme* object instead is moved to subject position? The results will sound ungrammatical to most native speakers:

> *__A fried chicken__ was given the fireman.
> *__A young chicken__ was cooked Ian.

For most speakers, the first sentence could be open to the nonsensical interpretation that someone gave the fireman to a fried chicken; a parallel interpretation is remotely possible for the second sentence. But pragmatic factors such as real world knowledge would normally exclude these interpretations and, for some speakers, would overpower the grammar to introduce a more likely interpretation. The grammatical explanation that Case Theory provides for the strangeness of these examples is that the theme noun phrases, which received inherent objective case at D-structure, cannot move into a position where they would be assigned an additional case, nominative. A noun phrase, remember, can only have one case. Moreover, the other object noun phrases, which aren't assigned case by the passive voice verb, have to be moved into the subject position or they will violate the case filter. The inherent case hypothesis thus predicts which clause forms will be grammatical and which ungrammatical.

Now notice that when the goal noun phrase is preceded by *to*, only the *theme* can be the subject of the passive clause:

*A fried chicken was given **to** the fireman.*
**A fried chicken was given to the fireman.*

The D-structure is as follows:

... was given a fried chicken to the fireman

This is the word order for the active voice verb too. Since inherent case is not assigned to the noun phrase adjacent to the verb, *a fried chicken* has to move into the subject slot to get case. On the other hand, *the fireman* cannot move into the subject slot because it already has case from the preposition *to*. It seems, then, that the grammar allows either the theme or the goal to serve as subject of a passive clause but only allows the goal to move when it is not in a prepositional phrase, and only allows the theme to move when it is adjacent to the passive verb. The inherent case hypothesis neatly accounts for the differences.

One kind of construction that looks deceptively similar to the ditransitives we have just discussed actually contains predicate noun phrases rather than theme noun phrases with inherent objective case. As we noted in Chapter 5, predicate noun phrases are predicates, not arguments. They therefore receive no thematic roles and can get no case. They are similar in function to other kinds of predicates, most notably verb phrases. The similarity can be seen in the following sentences:

*That dormouse is **a sound sleeper**.*
*That dormouse **sleeps soundly**.*

As mentioned in Chapter 5, there is another respect in which some predicate noun phrases differ from ordinary noun phrases. Forms like *president* and *teacher* can be predicate noun phrases but they cannot be subjects unless they are preceded by a determiner. That's why these two sentences are grammatical:

*Now Kelly is **president** again.*
*Travis is **teacher** today.*

while the next two are not:

Now **president is Kelly again.*
***Teacher** is Travis today.*

We now come to the resemblance to ditransitive constructions. Predicate noun phrases also occur in clauses that look very much like ditransitive clauses:

*They elected George **president**.*
*Cyril called the man **a fool**.*

Since *president* and *a fool* are predicates, they receive neither a thematic role nor objective case. Note that they cannot be replaced by pronouns, either nominative or objective. Moreover, since they cannot occur in slots to which case is assigned, they cannot be surface structure subjects of passive voice verbs. Thus, while the following sentences are grammatical:

*George was elected **president**.*
*The man was called **a fool**.*

the following clauses are not:

President *was elected George.*
A fool *was called the man.*

In the last two examples, the predicate noun phrase was shifted into the subject slot, a slot assigned nominative case by the finite Inflection. Since, according to Case Theory, predicates are not allowed case, the sentences are unacceptable.

A NOTE CONCERNING CLAUSES

In Chapter 3, we pointed out that if a finite clause lacks a subject, the sentence is only grammatical if the subject slot is filled by a noun phrase, typically a theme noun phrase, or if the theme argument is a *clause*, by movement of the clause or by the insertion of the filler *it* into subject position. Why is there this difference between noun phrases and clauses? Consider the following examples:

*Associated Press reported this morning **that the government had been overthrown**.*
*Associated Press reported **the story** this morning.*

Note that *this morning* can precede the clause *that the government had been overthrown* but cannot precede the noun phrase *the story*. It cannot precede *the story* because that noun phrase could not then get case from *reported*, since it would not be adjacent to it. On the other hand, the embedded clause *that the government had been overthrown* need not follow directly after the active voice transitive verb because it does not need to be in a case-marked slot. This is why the embedded clause in the following construction:

*... was reported this morning **that the government had been overthrown**.*

can stay where it is, provided filler *it* is inserted into the subject slot:

*It was reported this morning **that the government had been overthrown**.*

or can be shifted into the case-marked subject slot:

That the government had been overthrown *was reported this morning.*

A noun phrase theme does not, of course, have such a choice. It must move into the subject slot; it cannot stay after the passive voice verb, leaving the subject slot to be filled by *it*:

It was reported this morning **that story.*

Here again Case Theory supplies an elegant explanation.

SUMMARY

This chapter has specified a range of positions in which an overt noun phrase can appear. Case Theory specifies that every such position must be one to which case could be assigned. Prepositions and active voice transitive verbs assign objective case to their object noun phrases. The finite Inflection constituent assigns nominative case to noun phrases in the subject slot. Inherent possessive case is assigned to noun phrases in the determiner slot, while inherent objective case is assigned to theme noun phrases in the second object slot for a ditransitive verb. In Case Theory, the case filter ensures that all overt noun phrases (except those serving as predicates) have case.

In contrast, covert noun phrases and noun phrases serving as predicates cannot get case, and therefore cannot occur in slots which get case, whether from a verb or preposition or from a finite Inflection constituent.

The positions in which overt noun phrases, covert noun phrases, and predicate noun phrases can occur are complementary. Each can occur only in positions in which the others can't. Finally, clauses functioning as arguments can appear in case-marked slots but do not need to. This is why clauses sometimes appear where noun phrases can appear but can also occur where noun phrases are forbidden.

Case thus plays a central role in determining the distribution of noun phrases. The generalizations described here amount to a theory as to *why* the different kinds of noun phrase occur in the particular positions in which they occur. What seems like an arbitrary distribution actually has a principled explanation.

EXERCISE SET 12

1. How does Case Theory rule out the following as well-formed sentences of English? For each sentence, indicate the specific problem involved.

   a. *The citizens considered that her had killed Caligula.
   b. *The citizens considered she to be a murderer.
   c. *Tony persuaded he that his wife should sing.
   d. *Tony persuaded him his wife to sing.
   e. *It was certain Olga to win.
   f. *A cake was baked Tony.

2. Draw a D-structure tree for *That she lost her job was very unfortunate*. Treat the modifier *very* as a sister of the A-bar in the AP *very unfortunate* and label its node DEGREE.

3. Drawing on what you now know about Case Theory, explain why the sentence:

   a. *That she lost her job was very unfortunate.*

has a counterpart with *it*:

   b. *It was very unfortunate that she lost her job.*

whereas the following sentence:

   c. *Her situation was very unfortunate.*

has no grammatical counterpart with *it*:

   d. *It was very unfortunate her situation.*

4. Explain what the following are:

   a. Inflection
   b. inherent case
   c. the case filter

5. Imagine that a computer has generated the following strings of words:

   *was believed Sarah to have been a great actress.
   *I knew was certain Kennedy to run for the presidency.
   *will be captured that dog.
   *seems the situation to be serious.
   *was unlikely the public to support that legislation.

Now carry out the following two tasks:

    a. By moving certain words, write down a form for each string that would be a grammatical sentence of English. Do not add or remove words.

    b. Immediately after each corrected string, explain why Case Theory rules out the asterisked string but permits the version that you wrote. (Note that the ungrammatical sentences also violate another rule for English—the rule that finite clauses must have overt subjects.)

6. Examine the following sentences uttered by native speakers of French:

    a. *I lost yesterday evening my raincoat.*

    b. *My friend closed quickly the door.*

    c. *Claudine went very happily with Edward.*

French also has a case filter. But the French counterparts to the sentences above are all grammatical. What can you infer about case-marking in French and English?

7. Construct two exercises that will help learners understand and use the equivalence between sentences with filler *it* and their counterparts with embedded clauses as subjects.

NOTES

1. There are actually a few contexts in which a finite clause can appear without a subject, most notably comparative constructions like the following:

    Fewer people turned up for the meeting than [e] had signed up for it.

2. The form *him* was originally the old dative case form meaning "to him," the accusative case form being the now extinct pronoun *hine*. In Anglo-Saxon, not only pronouns but all noun phrases were marked for their case.

3. For discussion of contextually assigned case for possessor noun phrases, see E. Reuland, "Governing *-ing*," *Linguistic Inquiry* 14.1 (1983) and, for a more general account, N. Fabb, *Syntactic Affixation* (Ph.D. diss., M.I.T., 1984).

4. Alternatively, we might argue that *for* assigns case and is deleted later. This is a common analysis in the theoretical literature.

5. Note, however, that our explanation does not cover constructions like *a friend of my aunt's* and *a cousin of mine* in which the possessive noun phrase isn't in the determiner slot yet shows possessive case. These typically occur in indefinite noun phrases.

6. We will not be discussing here empty slots from which noun phrases have been moved. These slots are treated as another kind of empty noun phrase and have very different properties. They are usually referred to as *traces* (abbreviated on trees as [t]). We will be considering them briefly in later chapters.

7. The verb *want* poses problems for the claim that [e] cannot occur where it could be assigned case. In this sentence, *She wanted [e] to leave*, the [e] appears to be in a case-marked position and should get accusative case from the container verb. I know of no convincing explanation for this.

8. The grammar was somewhat different earlier in the history of English, when the *for to* combination was not uncommon. Chaucer wrote, *Thanne longen ... palmeres for to seken straunge strondes* ("Then pilgrims long to seek strange shores").

PART IV

ORGANIZING THE INFORMATION

13

Information Structure

Language learners must acquire some formidable skills, including the ability to produce and comprehend the propositional content of sentences of the language, a sensitivity to the often very different cultural and pragmatic assumptions of speakers of the language, and the ability to recognize the ways in which the propositional content of the target language is packaged grammatically to indicate the informational functions of the various constituents.

The first of these skills, the production and comprehension of propositional content, is a major focus of our whole examination of English syntax; the second, which is concerned with the social use of language, goes far beyond the scope of this book and is the subject of much ongoing research; the third is the main subject matter of this chapter and the next two.

Speakers or writers need to take into account whatever relevant knowledge their audience already possesses. Some of what they say must be new information for the audience, or else why bother to say it? But other information included is "old" news that may be needed as background for the new content. Addressees must be able to determine what the main thrust of each sentence is and what is background, as well as what connection it has to what was said before and what is said after.

Information thus has different functions, which are indicated through specialized language forms. The grammatical forms may indicate three major informational functions:

- Information Status: old information[1] versus new information
- Reference/Assertion: content that is just referred to versus
                                    content that is asserted
- Topic/Comment: what the speaker or writer intends a
                           sentence (or larger discourse unit) to
                           be about to be about versus what new
                           information is asserted about the topic

The three informational functions frequently seem to overlap as dimensions of utterances. The notions *topic* and *old information* are not the same. While the information in the topic is always old information, there can be old information outside the topic, and the grammatical forms used may be slightly different. *New information* is asserted in the *comment* and expresses either the speaker's main message for that sentence or information considered relevant to the main message.

THE GRAMMATICAL PACKAGING OF INFORMATION

English uses grammatical forms to package information in such a way as to make clear its information status as old or new information. Learners of English, therefore, need to be aware of the signals given by the grammatical forms.

Let's consider an example. One grammatical form often used to encode old information is the definite noun phrase. The writer of a newspaper editorial began with the following definite noun phrase:

> *The recent troubles in the Middle East...*

She could instead have begun with this finite clause:

> *There have been troubles recently in the Middle East.*

If the writer had used the finite clause, instead of the definite noun phrase, she would have been presenting the content as new information, *asserting* that there have been troubles in that region. Such an assertion would have suggested that her readers were not already familiar with the troubles.

On the other hand, by using the noun phrase *the recent troubles in the Middle East,* the writer is assuming, rightly or wrongly, that her readers are already aware of the recent Middle East troubles; in other words, the information is *old* information. The function of the noun phrase is simply to *refer* to the particular familiar situation. Then the writer can go on to *assert* new information about the familiar situation, as in this example:

> *The recent troubles in the Middle East* **are having serious effects on several East African nations.**

The *new* information here concerns the *effects* of the troubles on the East African nations. The writer believes—or writes as if she believes—that her readers are unaware of any impact on East Africa, that this part of the information will be new to them.

The old information is referred to and is clearly the topic about which the speaker intends to communicate something. The new information is being asserted as the main thrust of the sentence, the comment about the topic. The three kinds of function correspond neatly to each other. But it is also likely that the addressee knows about the existence of several East African nations, that is, the noun phrase *several East African nations* is old information, although it is not the topic of the sentence.

Just about every utterance is organized to communicate both old and new information. The utterance must refer and it must assert. The old information is needed if the new information is to be adequately understood. The typical informational function of a noun phrase is the referential function, while verbs serve to mark the assertive function. Thus it is not surprising that noun phrases, especially definite noun phrases, typically encode old information, while finite predicate phrases communicate the new information.

Think about the noun phrases and the verbs in the following sentence:

> *Your father saw a burglar leave the house.*

Two of the noun phrases represent old information, *your father* and *the house.* The speaker assumes that the addressees know their own father and the house being referred to.

These are definite noun phrases. A third noun phrase, *a burglar*, represents new information. The indefinite article *a* marks this clearly here. If *the* had been used instead, this noun phrase too would have represented old information, indicating that the addressee already knew about the burglar:

> Your father saw **the** burglar leave the house.

Although *a burglar* is new information, the speaker is not asserting the existence of a burglar as new but rather that the father witnessed the burglar's departure. The central markers of the new information status are the two verbs *saw* and *leave*.

The function identifying content as *old* and *new* is thus very closely connected to that specifying *reference* and *assertion*. The third function, that distinguishing *topic* from *comment*, is less obvious from the examples cited because English, unlike, for example, Japanese, often does not mark topics and comments grammatically. To know for sure what topic the example sentences are related to, we need to know more about the context in which this sentence was uttered. However, we need first to clarify what is meant by Topic-Comment structure.

TOPIC-COMMENT STRUCTURE

Some languages, most notably Japanese, Korean, and Chinese, organize almost all their sentences so that one part, the *topic*, represents what the speakers want the sentence to be about, while the other part, the *comment*, contains the major information asserted about the topic. At the beginning of the sentence is a special topic slot marked by the topic particle *wa*, as in this example (note that the subject noun phrase is marked with the particle *ga*):

Kono hon	wa	John	ga	yonda[2]
this book	TOPIC	John	SUBJ	read

"Speaking of this book, John has read it."

Such sentences are called *Topic-Comment structures*. The topic is *kono hon*, "this book," while the comment is the rest of the sentence, which contains both a piece of old information, *John*, and new information, *yonda*, "read." Thus the comment part of the sentence may include both old and new information.

The noun phrases have the appropriate thematic roles: *John* is the agent, and *kono hon* ("this book") is the theme. Moreover, *John* is the subject and, since *yonda* is a transitive verb, *kono hon* is the object. The subject noun phrase could have been in the topic slot instead:

John wa	kono hon o	yonda
John TOPIC	this book OBJ	read

"As for John, he read this book."

in which the topic corresponds to the subject.

But sometimes the topic does not correspond to any of the arguments of the predicate:

Sakana wa	tai ga	oisii	desu
fish TOPIC	red-snapper SUBJ	delicious	is

"Speaking of fish, red snapper is the most delicious."

For sentences like this, the topic slot must be filled in D-structure. Note that there is a semantic relationship between the topic and one of the noun phrases in the comment, a relationship of inclusion. The class of fish includes red snapper.

English also uses Topic-Comment structures, especially in speech, but to a far lesser extent than Japanese. When these structures occur, they are easy enough to pick out. In the examples below, both the topic and any noun phrase referring to it in the comment are in bold type:

> As for **the tapes,** we should destroy **them.**

> With respect to **the wall you have built,** I must inform you that **it** violates current F14 zoning restrictions.

> **Drunk drivers,** we ought to rid the state of **them**.

Note that the next example has no overt pronoun referring to the topic. Instead, there is a gap (shown as 0) after *take up*:

> **This matter** we will take up **0** at the next meeting.

The next sentence has neither a pronoun referring to the topic nor a gap, but a noun phrase, *our deficit*, which refers to something included in the topic's more general notion of foreign trade:

> As far as **foreign trade** is concerned, **our deficit** is still growing.

Each of the sentences above starts with a topic phrase; the new information in each of them is presented in the comment. There is an intonational break, often marked with a comma, between the topic and the comment. The comment does also contain old information: *we, I, you, the next meeting,* and *our deficit* are entities the addressee is assumed to know about already.

In the examples above, *the tapes, the wall you have built,* and *this matter* are all definite noun phrases. *Drunk drivers* and *foreign trade,* in contrast, are indefinite noun phrases, but notice that, like the definite noun phrases, they are assumed to be completely identifiable for the addressee. This is because they are *generic* noun phrases referring to the total class of drunk drivers and *to all* our foreign trade. Topics are always either definite or generic.

In each of the first three examples, there is in the comment a pronoun (*them, it,* and *they*), which has the topic as its antecedent. We'll refer to these pronouns as *counterparts* of the topic noun phrase. In the fourth example, the topic noun phrase has no counterpart pronominal but simply a gap where we might expect an object noun phrase to occur. For such sentences we assume that the noun phrase has been moved out of the clause and placed in front as a special topic phrase. The last example, with neither a gap nor a counterpart pronominal, is somewhat similar to the Japanese sentence about fish and red snapper: There is a semantic relationship of inclusion between the topic, *foreign trade,* and *our deficit* in the comment.

In both the third and fourth sentences, the topic noun phrase has no topic-introducing words such as *as for* and *speaking of.* The contexts in which they are likely to occur are somewhat different. The third sentence, in which the topic has a pronominal counterpart in the comment, would be likely to occur in an informal speech setting. The fourth, whose topic has no counterpart in the comment, represents a usage more typical of formal prose or formal speech situations.

We can now formulate the following conclusions about Topic-Comment structure in English:

1. The topic noun phrase does not need an overt counterpart in the comment.

2. If the topic does have an overt counterpart, the counterpart can be a subject or an object (or the object of a preposition).

3. When the comment lacks an argument noun phrase, the missing noun phrase is the one that would be the counterpart. In such cases, the sentence looks as if one noun phrase has been shifted into topic position, leaving an empty position behind.

4. Various introducing words or phrases indicate topics (e.g., *as for, regarding, with reference to, as far as ... is concerned*). One option is for the topic to have no introducing phrase at all.

SENTENCE-INITIAL POSITION

In English, as in many other languages, old information tends to precede new information. The topic phrase is always old information, and when topic phrases occur, they occupy the initial position in their sentence. It's not surprising that topics occupy this position. The sentence-initial position is a particularly prominent one, a good site for "what the sentence is about," that is, the topic.

Sentence-initial position also has other uses:

1. Sentence-initial position is often occupied by adverbial phrases or clauses indicating a time or place, like *before 1980, in Ottawa,* and *when Hubel first started his work on perception.*

2. Simple linkages between separate sentences are also common in sentence-initial position. They typically indicate logical relations of contrast, exemplification, elaboration, and so forth:

however	*for instance*
furthermore	*incidentally*
on the other hand	*to be more precise*
in conclusion	*in short*
similarly	*with this in mind*

Some, like *(un)fortunately* and *happily,* are judgmental linkages, as in *Happily, Mavis had already deposited the pearls in her safe-deposit box.*

3. Sentence-initial position is also a place for direction-setting linkages—phrases or clauses indicating the direction the text will now take, such as *to understand these higher levels of neural activity, in approaching a new discipline,* and *in the forefront of recent research.*

The occurrence of these other sentence-initial forms does not rule out a topic phrase. In fact, these forms are often followed by a topic phrase:

*Furthermore, **as far as foreign trade is concerned**, our deficit is still growing.*

SUBJECT NPs AS TOPICS

When there is no topic noun phrase and the subject is old information, then the subject, as the first major constituent in the sentence, easily takes on the topic function. So the subject and topic functions often coincide in English in sentence-initial position.

Consider, for example, the informational role of the subject noun phrases printed in bold type in the following passage:

The specialized regions of the brain investigated in the greatest detail are those involved in language. **Broca's area,** on the side of the frontal lobes, is susceptible to damage leading to aphasia because it is adjacent to the face area of the motor cortex. **A stroke destroying Broca's area** almost always severely damages the neural mechanisms required for speech articulation. **A patient of mine who recently suffered such a stroke** is still able to read, write, and comprehend, but cannot speak.

The first two subject noun phrases are definite noun phrases—*the specialized regions of the brain investigated in the greatest detail* and *Broca's area.* They are old information, and they function informationally as the topics of their sentences. Structurally, of course, they are different in that they do not have topic-comment structuring. The third subject, *a stroke destroying Broca's area,* although an indefinite noun phrase, also functions informationally as the topic of its sentence. It is a generic noun phrase. Generics, like definite noun phrases, are old information. The writer assumes that readers are familiar with such strokes. The modifier *destroying Broca's area* designates an identifiable subset of strokes, a subset whose relevance is clear from the sentence preceding. Thus, the third subject also functions informationally as the topic of its sentence.

The final subject—*a patient of mine who recently suffered such a stroke*—is quite different. This complex noun phrase is not the topic of its sentence. Like the previous subject, it is indefinite, but it is a nongeneric noun phrase referring to a specific person, one the writer assumes is not known to the addressees. The *whole sentence* is new information and hence the noun phrase cannot be a topic. The indefinite noun phrase tells something new and is close in meaning to an assertion like the following: *I have a patient who recently suffered such a stroke.* To summarize, the examples show that subjects *can* represent old information and *can* function as topics, but they can also be new information and thus ineligible for topic status.

SUBJECTS, TOPICS, AND NON-NATIVE TOPIC-CREATING STRATEGIES

The special role of sentence-initial position has interesting consequences for English. Take the following construction:

> *... is always difficult [e] to please Mr. Williams.*

The requirement that finite clauses have an overt subject in S-structure can be fulfilled by using the filler pronoun *it*:

> *It is always difficult to please Mr. Williams.*

But the initial absence of a subject opens up two other possibilities. Which one is chosen depends on what is seen as the topic of the sentence.

If the topic of the sentence is pleasing Mr. Williams, then the whole embedded clause can be moved into subject position:

> **To please Mr. Williams** *is always difficult.*

An embedded clause in the subject slot is *always* old information and *always* the topic.[3] Interestingly, embedded *finite* clauses in subject position seem to correspond to definite noun phrases in that they refer to real and definite situations, whereas embedded *nonfinite* clauses are closer to generic noun phrases. Compare the following sentences:

> **That Glenda Grymes stole the diamonds** *is undeniable.*
> **For Glenda Grymes to steal the diamonds** *would be disgraceful.*

The finite embedded clause refers to a definite occurrence, whereas the nonfinite embedded clause refers to a hypothetical situation, to a *kind* of behavior rather than to a definite occurrence of that behavior. Both, of course, function as topics for their sentences.

Returning to our sentence about Mr. Williams, we could also have as our topic a noun phrase in the embedded clause, that is, *Mr. Williams.* In that case, *Mr. Williams* can be moved into subject position:

> **Mr. Williams** *is always difficult to please.*[4]

Such a sentence might appear in an exchange like the following:

> Ellen : *What can you tell me about Mr. Williams and Dr. Tremaine?*
> Brian: *Mr. Williams is always difficult to please, but Dr. Tremaine is wonderful.*

Note that subjects which have been shifted by this process are always topics of their sentence, which is why they can only be definite or generic. Thus the subject of the following sentence, *a good mechanic*, can only be interpreted as generic:

> **A good mechanic** *is hard to find.*

The subject of the sentence cannot be understood to refer to a specific good mechanic.

Non-native speakers of English, especially Chinese, Japanese, and Koreans, sometimes write strange sentences like these:

> **Those people have been arranged for me to talk to (them).*
> **The doctor was obvious that they did not trust (her).*

instead of:

> *It has been arranged for me to talk to those people.*
> *It was obvious that they did not trust the doctor.*

If native speakers of English want these topics in sentence-initial position, they would probably use Topic-Comment structures like the following:

> *Regarding those people, it has been arranged for me to talk to them.*
> *As for the doctor, it was obvious that they didn't trust her.*

Evidently, these non-native speakers intend *those people* and *the doctor* to be topics in sentence-initial position. But *be arranged* and *be obvious* do not belong to the very small group of predicates like *be difficult* and *be tough* that allow a noun phrase from a lower clause to move into their subject position. Non-native speakers may be over-generalizing from sentences with predicates that do allow such movement.

Moreover, the first language of these speakers seems always to be one in which topic-comment structuring is predominant. Such languages are often characterized as *topic-prominent languages*, in contrast to English, which is a *subject-prominent language*. Subject-prominent languages are languages in which subject-predicate phrase structuring is predominant and topic-comment structuring is much less pervasive. So it is also very likely that the speakers are transferring their native language topic-creating strategies to their English.

INITIAL POSITION AND PASSIVE CLAUSES

Sentence-initial position has been shown to be an important position for structuring information. Writers and speakers need to remind their addressees of key old information so that the new information will be understood appropriately and efficiently. There is one other very common structure that enables a topic to be shifted into sentence-initial position.

As we saw earlier, a definite noun phrase in subject position can be the topic. In the following transitive clause, *the twelve-year-old girl* is a subject filling this topic function:

> **The twelve-year-old girl** *stole the crown.*

The noun phrase *the twelve-year-old girl* has the agent role, and agents are almost always in subject position. But suppose the speaker or writer wants the noun phrase *the crown* to be the topic. How can this noun phrase appear in sentence-initial position as a topic? One way is to use the passive counterpart of the sentence:

> **The crown** *was stolen (by the twelve-year-old girl).*

Like Topic-Comment structures, passives enable speakers to place crucial constituents in sentence-initial position in response to discourse needs. Passive constructions play an important role in English syntax, as they do in the grammars of many languages. We shall explore these forms in more detail in the following chapter.

SUMMARY

This chapter has dealt with the ways English grammar packages propositional content so as to indicate three informational functions of the various constituents of a sentence. The first is the information status of the part of the content packaged. The content may be assumed by the speaker to be *new* to the addressee or *old*, that is, already known to the addressee but included to provide necessary background. The second is the reference/assertion function. Utterances are typically intended to *assert* something, but to communicate the assertion the speaker needs to *refer* to contextualizing information. The key category for communicating assertions is the verb phrase, while that for making references is the noun phrase. The third function is indicated by the topic/comment split. The *topic* is what the speaker or writer intends a sentence to be about, while the *comment* is what is asserted about that topic. The topic is always old information, and a topic noun phrase must be either definite or generic.

Topic-prominent languages are languages in which the Topic-Comment structure is predominant. English is a subject-prominent language, that is, subject-predicate structure is predominant. English does have Topic-Comment structures such as *These objections we will deal with in a later chapter*, where the topic noun phrase has been shifted from the comment, *Teenagers, I hate them*, where there is a counterpart pronominal and the topic noun phrase is assumed to have been in the topic slot at D-structure, and *As for operas, Tosca is my favorite* in which an inclusion relation holds between the topic *operas* and its counterpart *Tosca*. But in sentences lacking Topic-Comment structure, subjects can, if they are either definite or generic, function as topics.

Embedded clauses serving as subjects are also always topics of their sentence. In addition, for certain predicate adjectives such as *tough*, the object of a clause embedded beneath it can be shifted into the subject slot. So, instead of *It will be tough to win that race*, we can say, *That race will be tough to win*. In such cases, the subject is always the topic.

Sentence-initial position is an especially prominent position. This makes it especially useful for topics. But topics are sometimes preceded by time or location phrases, logic-indicating adverbial forms (*moreover, therefore*), or direction-setting linkages (*to prove this*). The passive voice and processes which convert nonsubject constituents into subjects permit arguments that belong semantically elsewhere in the sentence to be shifted into the more prominent sentence-initial position.

EXERCISE SET 13

1. Draw two columns, one headed TOPIC, the other COMMENT. Then copy the topics of the sentences below into the first column, and the comments into the second:

 a. *Speaking of our annual meeting, it seems that some stockholders wish to oppose our proposals.*
 b. *As for Gildenstern, he didn't have a chance.*
 c. *Regarding those expenses, Carmody won't pay them.*
 d. *With reference to your last letter, the president has authorized me to inform you that he will pay no attention to it.*
 e. *About that dinner, I can't stand roast turkey.*
 f. *That rock they cannot lift.*

2. In three of the sentences of Question 1, the clause following the topic contains a counterpart noun phrase. Find these sentences. Then, for each of the three, tell (a) which noun phrase is the counterpart and (b) what grammatical relation it bears in the comment clause.

3. Sentence (f) in Question 1 is different from the others. How is it different? What evidence does the *verb* provide regarding this difference?

4. Which of the underlined constituents in the following sentences can be interpreted as *old* information and which as *new* information? Copy each constituent and label it OLD or NEW.

 a. *Doctors, they just can't be trusted!*
 b. *It was Clarence who was drowned in a barrel.*
 c. *In that garden there was a stone fountain.*
 d. *Happy that villain may be, but not for long.*
 e. *What surprised the investigators was the incredibly fast growth of the microbes.*

5. Change the following sentences so that the underscored noun phrases are topics in sentence-initial position. You may change the word forms, but you should not change the propositional content of the sentences.

 a. *It is hard to argue with Jeffrey.*
 b. *We will not discuss politics here.*
 c. *It seems that victory is impossible.*
 d. *Mildred saw a wolf on the roof.*

Why does this task seem more difficult for sentence (d)?

6. Gibson (1975) suggests a "strip story" activity that should serve a number of learning goals.[5] The teacher finds or writes a short narrative, types each sentence of the narrative on a separate line, and then cuts the paper into strips, each containing one sentence. The students are asked to talk with one another to figure out the order in which the strips should be arranged so as to form a reasonable story. The original order is not necessarily the only plausible order. How might this kind of activity help students master the forms used for the identification of old and new information?

7. Choose, write, or revise a suitable piece that could be used for this activity. If you select, say, a ten-sentence extract from a published source, you might want to adapt it using some of the forms described in this chapter. You may find nonfiction writing more useful for this specialized use of the strip-story technique.

NOTES

1. Old information is sometimes referred to as *given information*. The account of information provided here is close in some respects to that of H. H. Clark and E. V. Clark, *The Psychology of Language* (New York: Harcourt, Brace, Jovanovich, 1977). They specify that "given information should be identifiable and new information unknown.... Listeners should be confident that the given information conveys information they can identify uniquely. They understand that it is information the speaker believes they both agree on and that the speaker is asserting his beliefs about." (92) For an important discussion of these matters, see Gillian Brown and George Yule, *Discourse Analysis* (Cambridge: Cambridge University Press, 1983).

2. The Japanese examples are from Susumu Kuno, *The Structure of the Japanese Language* (Cambridge, MA: M.I.T. Press, 1973).

3. For a detailed discussion of this and related matters, see Jeanette K. Gundel, "The role of topic and comment in linguistic theory" (Ph.D. diss., University of Texas, Austin, 1974) and also Jeanette K. Gundel and Roderick A. Jacobs, "Why *seem* and *be* aren't what they seem to be," *Centerpoint* 4 (1980): 115-23.

4. But this movement of a noun phrase from object position in an embedded clause into subject position in the container clause, sometimes called *tough* movement, is limited to just a small class of predicates—*be tough, be easy, be impossible, be hard,* and *be good* are other examples.

5. Robert Gibson, "The strip story: A catalyst for communication," *TESOL Quarterly* 9 (1975): 149-54.

14

Passive Voice

We've seen that passive voice clauses allow speakers and writers to place at the beginning of a clause a noun phrase that would otherwise come after the verb. Look at the following transitive verb clause:

A hungry rhinoceros ate the bamboo shoots.

The corresponding passive clause is the following:

The bamboo shoots were eaten (by a hungry rhinoceros).

The verb *ate* in the first clause is said to be in the *active voice*, and its clause is an active voice clause. The verb combination *were eaten* is in the *passive voice* and its clause is a passive voice clause. Passive voice verbs begin with the copular verb *be*, which is followed by the main verb in its past participle form (e.g., *eaten, promoted, sung*). In passive voice clauses, it is not necessary to specify the agent. The *by* prepositional phrase containing the agent can be omitted, as the parentheses around it indicate.

The passive clause with the *by* phrase has the same propositional content as its active voice counterpart, but the information is arranged differently. The theme or entity affected by the event occupies the prominent first slot in the sentence, while the agent is placed at the end or even, as we have seen, omitted. Yet an agent is responsible for the action described by the clause. Why would such an important participant be omitted? This is a question we will try to answer.

Somehow, the active voice order agent-action-theme seems to most English speakers the more "natural" order. It's certainly the more common order. Many writing handbooks disapprove of passives. "Use active verbs," urges William Zinsser in his highly respected text on nonfiction writing, "unless there is no comfortable way to get around using a passive verb. The difference between an active-verb style and a passive-verb style—in pace, clarity and vigor—is the difference between life and death for a writer."[1]

Additionally, since the agent need not be specified in passive clauses, the passive voice has been stigmatized by George Orwell and other writers as a form used by unscrupulous politicians and others to deceive and confuse the public. Orwell's charges and Zinsser's recommendations have some validity. However, as we shall see, these critics overlook the fact that in some contexts a passive clause may be stylistically superior to its active counterpart.

COMPARING ACTIVE AND PASSIVE VOICE CLAUSES

Look again at our examples of active and passive clauses:

> A hungry rhinoceros ate the bamboo shoots.
> The bamboo shoots were eaten (by a hungry rhinoceros).

In both clauses the noun phrase assigned the agent role is *a hungry rhinoceros,* while the theme role is filled by *the bamboo shoots.* Both clauses use forms of the verb *eat* as their predicate, both have the same propositional content, and either could be used to refer to the same bamboo-eating incident.

There are three major differences of interest to us between the active and passive voice examples just given. The first is in the form of the verb. The verb in the active voice clause is its ordinary past tense form, *ate,* whereas in the passive voice clause the verb unit is a sequence of a form of the copular verb *be* plus the past participle form, *eaten.* Participles alone cannot serve as finite verbs. Like adjectives, they must be introduced by a copular verb, usually a form of *be.* But they are unlike adjectives in one very crucial respect. Compare these sentences:

> The bamboo shoots were brown.
> The bamboo shoots were eaten.

Like the predicate *were brown,* the predicate *were eaten* has only one argument, the theme *the bamboo shoots.* But this predicate clearly refers to an *event* in which an agent is also involved. The word that tells us this is the participle *eaten;* it tells us there was an eater.

In passive clauses, then, the verb includes within itself the information that there is an agent.[2] So, unless the speaker wants to make a special point of who the agent is, it is optional rather than obligatory to specify the agent in a prepositional phrase like *by a hungry rhinoceros.* Therefore, passive clauses can specify one fewer argument than the corresponding active clauses.

Prepositional phrases are useful containers for the agent because they are almost always optional constituents. If you don't want to mention the agent, choose the passive voice, where the agent occurs in an omissible constituent. As we noted in Chapter 6, such optional constituents are said to bear an *adjunct* relation to their clause. Adjuncts can be omitted from a sentence without making it ungrammatical. Typically, they add information about such perspectives as time, location, manner, reason, or purpose. Examples include such forms as *immediately, there, this evening, at the ranch,* and *in order to leave.* The *by* phrase in a passive is a prepositional phrase adjunct.

This possibility of omitting the agent argument when it occurs in a prepositional phrase is the second way in which passive clauses differ from active clauses.

The third major difference is the order of the constituents. In passive clauses, the theme noun phrase comes before the verb since it is the subject, whereas in active clauses the theme comes after its verb since it is the object. As we shall see in the next section, the difference in word order between the active and passive voices arises from their difference in verb form.

THEMES, EXPERIENCERS, AND CASE

In Chapter 3, we noted that in D-structure most transitive verbs (e.g., *paint* and *prove*) assigned the theme role to the right, to their object, and the agent role to the left, via the verb phrase, to the subject. Thus, regardless of whether the verb is in the active or passive voice, the argument that follows such verbs is the theme. A smaller class of transitive verbs (e.g., *annoy, please, exasperate, amuse*) assigns the experiencer role to the right, while the noun phrase that functions as subject in S-structure is the theme.

Consider now the following D-structures with passive voice verbs:

> *... were eaten the bamboo shoots (by the giant panda)*
> *... were annoyed the nurses (by the arrogant surgeon)*

The *by* phrases are adjuncts (i.e., optional constituents) at the D-structure stage. If they are selected, they will, of course, appear at surface structure too. But the D-structures cannot yet become surface structures for two reasons. First, they are finite clauses with an empty subject slot; thus they violate the subject constraint. Second, unlike their active voice counterparts, the passive voice participles *eaten* and *annoyed* are not transitive verbs, so they cannot assign objective case to their theme or experiencer noun phrase. As we saw in Chapter 12, the case filter rules out sentences having noun phrases without case. The way to remedy both problems is to move the object noun phrase into the empty subject slot. There it is assigned nominative case by the finite Inflection constituent. The following grammatical surface structures result:

> *The bamboo shoots were eaten (by the giant panda).*
> *The nurses were annoyed (by the arrogant surgeon).*

DITRANSITIVES AND PASSIVE VOICE

Ditransitives like *give* and *tell* take two objects, a goal and a theme, as in the example used in Chapter 12:

> *The landlord gave the fireman a fried chicken.*
>   GOAL   THEME

We saw in Chapter 12 that in the passive counterpart of this two-object clause the theme noun phrase, *a fried chicken,* was not moved into subject position. Instead, it was the goal noun phrase, *the fireman,* which was moved, so that this D-structure:

> *... was given **the fireman** a fried chicken.*
>   GOAL   THEME

became the following surface structure:

> **The fireman** *was given a fried chicken.*
> GOAL   THEME

In the next two examples, goal arguments have also been moved into the subject slot:

> **The three victims** *were offered compensation.*
> GOAL   THEME

> **The families** *were told the news at three o'clock.*
> GOAL   THEME

In the examples above, the themes *a fried chicken, compensation,* and *the news* remain in their original D-structure position. The passive verbs *be given, be offered,* and *be told* started off in D-structure with their two objects in the same order as required for the active verbs:

... VERB - Goal - Theme

The goal, rather than the theme, had to be shifted because the theme noun phrase already had inherent case—objective case—so it didn't need to be moved. Normally, case is assigned *after* D-structure. But inherent case (as we noted in Chapter 12) is an exceptional kind of case that noun phrases already have in D-structure, provided they occur in certain constructions. If the theme noun phrase, which already has objective case, were moved into the subject slot, it would then have two cases—its original inherent case, objective, and the nominative case it would get after it had been moved into the subject position. Just as a pronoun can't simultaneously have two different forms, for example, *hehim*, so a noun phrase cannot have two cases. This difference between the two noun phrases—the goal needs case while the theme already has it— accounts neatly for the forms that actually occur.

PREPOSITIONAL VERBS

Look at the predicates (in boldface) in the following pairs of sentences:

1 a. *The prosecutor will **investigate** these charges.*
b. *The prosecutor will **look into** these charges.*
2 a. *Dr. Holmes **reached** the following conclusions.*
b. *Dr. Holmes **arrived at** the following conclusions.*
3 a. *We will not **tolerate** this behavior.*
b. *We will not **put up with** this behavior.*
4 a. *Dombey **despised** such people.*
b. *Dombey **looked down on** such people.*
5 a. *The people really **respected** that old woman.*
b. *The people really **looked up to** that old woman.*

The (a) sentences of each pair have transitive verbs as their predicates. Each (b) sentence is a fairly close paraphrase of its (a) sentence. But instead of a single transitive verb, each has a verb followed by a preposition or by a directional adverb like *down* or *up* followed by a preposition. Since the (a) sentences are transitive clauses, they obviously can have passive counterparts like *These charges will be investigated by the prosecutor.* The interesting thing is that the (b) sentences also have passive counterparts, as for example, *These charges will be looked into by the prosecutor.*

It seems that some verbs or verb plus directional adverb combinations have combined with the preposition heading the prepositional phrase following. These combinations have become two- or three-word transitive verbs. These *prepositional* verb sequences function like ordinary transitive verbs and therefore have passive counterparts.

Now look at the following sentences in which an intransitive verb is followed by a prepositional phrase:

*Seven monarchs have **slept** in that four-poster bed.*
*A surveyor **walked** through the forest.*

The sentences make an assertion that includes a specification of the location in which the monarchs slept or through which the surveyor walked. Thus, syntactically and semantically, these sentences should not have passive voice counterparts. They have an intransitive verb plus a preposition, and they don't seem to have a suitable candidate for subject, since the subjects of passive voice clauses are prototypically the entities affected by the action expressed by the verb. Yet such counterparts exist:

> *That four-poster bed has been slept in by seven monarchs.*
> *The forest was walked through by a surveyor.*

We may not think of the bed as being affected by the sleeping, and certainly the forest seems unlikely to be affected by someone walking through it. But in fact we can envisage a slept-in bed with its rumpled sheets. We understand the bed to have been somehow affected by having had so many high-ranking people sleep in it. Its value as an antique must surely have been enhanced. Notice that *slept in* cannot be replaced by *died in*. We don't normally visualize a "died-in" bed. In the second passive sentence, *walked through* can be understood as meaning "measured," as a surveyor might measure off land by counting the number of paces. Something is being done to the forest.

So, semantically, these sentences *are* like other passives. What seems to be happening is that the active intransitive verbs followed by prepositions are sometimes reanalyzed as prepositional verbs (*sleep in, walk through*). The resulting sentences offer interesting insights into the basic semantic nature of the passive voice. Passive voice clauses typically focus on the *end result* of an action (or process) rather than on the action itself, although the action is still an important part of the propositional content.

MIDDLE VERBS

The last pair of verbs we considered was unusual in that, despite their apparent intransitivity, they also occurred in the passive voice. Now we have some verbs that appear to be transitive, in that they are followed by a noun phrase, and yet do not occur in the passive voice. These verbs include *have, lack, fit, cost, weigh, equal, measure, possess, suit,* and *resemble*:

> *Fielding resembled his mother.*

If they are followed by a pronominal, the pronominal is in the objective case; that is, these verbs assign objective case to the noun phrase argument following them:

> *That dress fits **her** perfectly.*

Yet they have no passive counterparts:

> **His mother was resembled by Fielding.*
> **She is fitted by that dress perfectly.*

Because these verbs seem intermediate between transitive and intransitive verbs, they are sometimes called "middle verbs." They all refer to states rather than actions or processes. Some middle verbs, however, can also be used as ordinary action transitives. In such uses they have passive counterparts:

> *The customs officials **weighed** twenty pounds of rice.*
> *Twenty pounds of rice **were weighed** by the customs officials.*

> *Her assistants **measured** the younger children.*
> *The younger children **were measured** by her assistants.*

These sentences all refer to actions or events rather than to states.

✓ Some of the verbs also occur in idiom like these below with the verb *have*, with both active and passive forms:

> *Everyone* **had** *a good time.*
> *A good time* **was had** *by everyone.*
>
> *That swindler really* **had** *you.*
> *You've really* **been had** *by that swindler.*

Note that these passives too refer to the results of actions or events rather than just to states. They refer to something that has happened.

STATIVE AND DYNAMIC PASSIVES

The state versus nonstate distinction is a very significant one for English predicates. Before looking at its particular significance for passives, let's look briefly at the general distinction.

Verbs like *know* and *believe* and predicate adjective or predicate noun phrase combinations like *be tall* or *be my cousin* are used to refer to states, not actions or processes. As a result, they aren't normally used to give orders. An order like *Know Chinese!* or *Be my cousin!*, if it is grammatical, can only be understood as requiring action.

Predicates used statively, that is, to represent states, also do not normally occur with the progressive aspect combination of *be* and the suffix *-ing*:

> **Soseki was knowing Chinese.*
> **Kim is being my cousin.*

✓ Predicates used dynamically, to refer to actions or processes, can be used as imperatives and do allow progressive aspect. Examples are *learn, persuade, be tactful,* and *be a good girl*:

> *Learn Chinese!*
> *Lee was being tactful.*
> *Be a good girl, Tanya!*
> *Tanya is being a good girl.*

We have already seen that some verbs can be used in both dynamic and stative senses. One example is *run*:

> *The women will* **run** *from Ann Arbor to Detroit.*
> *Route 94* **runs** *from Ann Arbor to Detroit.*

Run refers to an activity in the first sentence, but not in the second. Being in a particular location is not an activity.

Many passive voice forms, like their active voice counterparts, reveal the stative-dynamic distinction. Look at the following pairs of sentences:

> *The village* **was surrounded** *by coniferous trees.*
> *The village* **was** *(quickly)* **surrounded** *by the guerrillas.*
>
> *The area of settlement* **was separated** *from the rest of the region by a mountain range.*
> *The outer layer* **was separated** *from the nucleus by physicists using laser beams.*

The passive is sometimes described as typically emphasizing the state resulting from some prior action. But this description is inadequate for two of the passives just cited. The first sentence in each pair contains a stative passive, one that refers to a state not resulting from any prior action, while the second contains a dynamic passive, referring to both the state and the prior action.

Stative passives, like their active voice counterparts, cannot be used as imperatives and do not allow progressive aspect. When progressive aspect is used, the sentences with stative passives, like their active counterparts, are ungrammatical:

> *The village **was being surrounded** by coniferous trees.
> *The area of settlement **was being separated** from the rest of the region by a mountain range.

These examples can be grammatical if the verb can be understood as a cumulative process rather than as a state. So the trees are seen as gradually coming to be around the village, and, perhaps, volcanic action is causing the separation from the rest of the region.

In the sentences above, as in all previous examples, the passives differ in word order from their active voice counterparts. There are, however, a few verbs that, when used statively, allow their noun phrases to stay in the same slots whether they are active or passive:

> The kneebone **connects** to the thighbone.
> The kneebone **is connected** to the thighbone.

> The old Kiangsi tunnel **joined** the Suchow tunnel here.
> The old Kiangsi tunnel **was joined** to the Suchow tunnel here.

Other such verbs are *attach* and *separate*. They belong to a class of predicates known as *symmetric predicates*, which can have the order of their arguments reversed without a major change of meaning, just a shift in perspective:

> The thighbone **connects** to the kneebone.
> The kneebone **connects** to the thighbone.

> The kneebone **is connected** to the thighbone.
> The thighbone **is connected** to the kneebone.

In isolation the passive voice forms of such predicates are ambiguous between the stative and a dynamic interpretation. The insertion of *by* followed by an agent argument forces the dynamic interpretation:

> The kneebone was connected **by the surgeon** to the thighbone.

But the active voice forms, which do not permit a *by* agent:

> *The kneebone connects to the thighbone **by the surgeon**.

have only the stative interpretation.[3]

This stative–dynamic contrast also occurs between certain passive verbs and other forms that look like passive voice verbs, and yet are not. We'll call these forms pseudo-passives.

PSEUDO-PASSIVES

Pseudo-passive sentences are sentences that look at first glance somewhat like passives but actually have predicate adjectives instead of the past participles of verbs. In fact, some of these adjectives were participles in earlier stages of English. *Rotten* is one such adjective; the past participle function is now filled by *rotted*. We can say this:

*The rope had been **rotted** by the damp salty air.*

but not this:

The rope had been **rotten by the damp salty air.*

The sentence containing the participle *rotted* specifies both a result, the state of the rope, and a process, the process of rotting caused by the dampness. The adjective *rotten*, however, refers only to the state. This is why it cannot occur with the *by* phrase, a phrase used in the first example to specify the entity responsible for the process of rotting.

There is a similar relationship between the participle *opened* and the adjective *open*. Compare these two sentences:

*The door was **opened.***
*The door was **open.***

The first sentence is simply a passive clause without a *by* phrase. If a *by* phrase such as *by the butler* is added, the sentence remains grammatical. The clause refers to an action that had a specified result—the door was in the state of being open. The second sentence is not a passive clause. The phrase *by the butler* cannot be added to make it a clause about an action. A speaker using the second sentence is simply making an assertion about the state of the door.

In the examples above, it's easy enough to distinguish between the passives and the sentences with adjectives because the participles are at least slightly different from the adjective forms. But quite often the past participle and the adjective are identical. Look now at these pairs of examples:

*The door was **shut** by the butler.*
*The door was **shut.***

*The factory was **closed** by the inspectors.*
*The factory was **closed.***

The first sentence of each pair refers to the actual event of door-shutting or factory-closing. The second sentence of each pair, however, is ambiguous. If *shut* and *closed* are interpreted as adjectives, the door and the factory are just not open. But these words could be past participles, in which case the sentence would refer to the event, the action of closing.

The same ambiguity occurs for *smashed* and *broken*:

*The lock was **smashed** yesterday.*
*The window was **broken** yesterday.*

Without more information, we cannot tell whether *smashed* is being used as a participle in a passive construction—the actual smashing of the lock took place yesterday—or as a stative adjective—the lock was discovered yesterday already smashed. Similarly, the second sentence could be used to mean either that someone broke the window yesterday, with *broken* as a participle, or, if *broken* is used as a stative adjective, that it was discovered yesterday that the window was already broken (and might have been broken for weeks). *Was broken* is understood in the first case as referring to the actual breaking event as well as to the resulting state, but in the second case it refers only to a state, without any focus on the event that presumably caused it.

THE *GET* PASSIVE

Passives using a form of *get* before the past participle occur mainly in informal English:

> *She got arrested by the Feds last night.*
> *Yesterday Cyril's house got broken into by some drunks.*
> *Somehow his whole bill got charged to her credit card number.*

This kind of passive is like the *be* passive in that the theme noun phrases end up in the subject slot, having been moved from the position after the verb. As with *be* passives, the agent can be specified in an optional *by* phrase.

As we'll see in our discussion of Japanese passives in the next section, passives in some languages communicate an unfavorable attitude toward the event being described. The referent of the subject is considered to have been adversely affected by the event. *Get* passives in English often have a similar connotation, one of somewhat accidental misfortune. This is not always the case, however, as shown by the following sentences:

> *She got awarded a Nobel Peace Prize.*
> *They got praised by the president in his broadcast last night.*
> *The long-delayed housing legislation finally got voted on last night.*

Three of our six examples with *get* have *by* phrases. In fact, this proportion is misleading. The agent phrase is even less common in *get* passives than in passives with *be*. This lack of a *by* phrase makes it easy to confuse *get* passives with uses of *get* before a past participle or an adjective. In the following examples, *get* occurs before adjectives and means "become":

> *Leslie got angry at the naval officer.*
> *Leslie got irritated at the naval officer.*

In the first example, the adjective is easily identified as such, but in the second example, the adjective has the same form as a participle. Notice, however, that *very* can be inserted before *irritated*; this helps us identify the apparent participle as an adjective.

The problem for language analysis, and for learners, increases when we look at constructions like this next one:

> *Kermit got (very) confused by Ernie's explanation.*

Here the *by* phrase looks very much like an agent phrase in a passive. Again, though, the apparent participle, in this case the word *confused*, allows *very* before it, suggesting that it is an adjective.

To make matters worse, *get* can be used in a causative sense, meaning "cause to become" or "cause to happen." In this use it functions as a container clause verb, which takes as its complement a nonfinite passive clause with a passive participle as its predicate:

> *Terwilliger got **Josephine arrested by the security police**.*
> *Terwilliger got **himself arrested by the security police**.*

There are similar constructions with other verbs:

> *Terwilliger wanted **Josephine arrested by the security police**.*

The *get* phenomenon is one of the areas of English syntax that remains a challenge for language analysis.

A Note on Passives in Japanese

For comparison, let's take a brief look at the corresponding constructions in Japanese. When teaching the English forms, it is always useful to know something about similar constructions in the first language of our students. While this is not practicable for many teaching situations, it is certainly worth attempting if the class is composed of speakers of a single language, such as Japanese.

There is a passive construction in Japanese that is like the English construction in that it has an active counterpart with the same propositional content. The following sentences are examples:

Hattori sensei-ga	*Higa-o*	*home-ta.*
Hattori teacher-SUBJECT	Higa-OBJECT	praise-PAST
"Professor Hattori praised Higa."		

Higa-ga.	*Hattori sensei-ni*	*home-rare-ta.*
Higa-SUBJECT	Hattori teacher-to/by	praise-PASSIVE-PAST
"Higa was praised by Professor Hattori."		

It would seem that Japanese learners should have no serious problems with English passives. But look at this sentence written by a Japanese student:

For her unbelievable beauty, she was suffered from several misfortunes.

Is this strange sentence a result of special features of the native language of the student? Or does it simply reflect the difficulties of English passives?

Both factors are involved. Japanese has a second kind of passive, which is actually more common than the one we have just discussed. This passive is known as the *adversative passive*, because the situation described is almost always an unfortunate one for the referent of the subject. In most cases, these adversative passives have no obvious active voice counterpart.

The passive verb in the example below is recognizable because it has *-are-* just before the past tense suffix *-ta*:

Yuube	*Hanako-ga*	*kodomo-ni*	*nak-are-ta.*
last-night	Hanako-SUBJECT	child-to/by	cry-PASSIVE-PAST
"Last night, Hanako suffered from/was bothered by the baby crying."			

It is the passive marker *-are-* that carries the sense "suffered" or "was bothered." A more colloquial translation of the passive verb might be "got cried on (by)," but that would hardly be normal English.

Moreover, many Japanese students learn that their adversative passive corresponds to the notion "suffer" in English. They also learn that the English passive consists of a main verb in its past participle form preceded by a form of *be*. It shouldn't be surprising that, in the ungrammatical sentence given earlier, the Japanese student used a passive form for *suffer*. In Japanese, such a sentence has no active voice counterpart.

Semantic Differences between Active and Passive Voice

So far, we have assumed that active voice clauses and their passive counterparts have the same meaning, or at least the same propositional content.

But for certain active-passive clause pairs this assumption is not correct. Think about the following sentences:

*Five students in that room **spoke** three languages.*
*Three languages **were spoken** by five students in that room.*

Let's assume that the sentences are presented to us out of any context. Focus your thinking on the number of languages. The active clause easily allows an interpretation in which up to fifteen different languages were known by the five students. The passive clause, on the other hand, is more easily interpreted as being about just three specific languages. This semantic distinction between the two sentences is evidently the result of the relative order of the two quantifiers *five* and *three*, not the active-passive distinction itself.

There are also differences in the interpretation of active-passive pairs containing the negative forms of some modal verbs such as *will* and *can*. The modal *will* and its negative form *won't* can express prediction (i.e., an event will or won't happen) or volition (i.e., the agent is or isn't willing to act). The following active clause allows either interpretation:

> *Celia won't paint the bishop.*

This could mean either that the speaker predicts that there will be no such painting or that Celia refuses to paint the bishop. In contrast, the passive counterpart of the active clause has the prediction interpretation but cannot be understood as indicating that Celia is refusing:

> *The bishop **won't** be painted by Celia.*

Note that this passive voice clause, unlike the active, could also mean that the bishop refuses to be painted by Celia. It seems that the refusal sense can only be predicated of the subject argument.

What about *can* and *can't*? These modals include in their range of meanings the notions of both permission and ability. So the clause *Celia can't paint the bishop* can mean either that Celia does not have permission to paint the bishop or that Celia lacks the ability to paint the bishop. Now consider the passive counterpart:

> *The bishop **can't** be painted by Celia.*

This can mean that *permission* has been denied but, for most of us, it is less likely to mean that Celia lacks the *ability* to paint the bishop, since the ability interpretation normally applies to the subject. Notice that our example has a theme as its subject. The same peculiarities are seen when the subject is a goal:

> *Jeanette won't be given a commendation.*
> *Jeanette can't be given a commendation.*

The volition and ability interpretations are normally ruled out when a passive clause has a theme or goal as its subject.

In general, however, passive voice clauses and their active counterparts have the same propositional content. The choice between them normally depends on such factors as the topic organization of the discourse and the speaker's beliefs about what the addressee already knows.

SOME DISCOURSE FUNCTIONS OF PASSIVE VOICE

With all these complications, it hardly seems surprising that the passive voice presents difficulty for non-native speakers and, in some contexts, even for native speakers. You might indeed wonder why passive constructions are used, since there are alternatives. Perhaps William Zinsser is right in his condemnation of the passive. Let's look at why a writer or speaker might want to use a passive voice clause.

As we've seen, using the passive voice is one way to have the *theme* argument in subject position at the front of its clause. If the theme argument is also the sentence topic, then the subject slot is a good place for it. The following sentence is from a description of an experiment in which the previous sentence has specified equipment to be used.

> *The bulb is filled with hydrogen at an initial pressure of 86 cm of mercury, density 13.6 gm per cc.*

The sentence is about the bulb and gives instructions on what to do with it. The topic—the bulb—is specified in clause-initial position, a good place for a constituent representing old information to orient the reader.

If the agent were specified for this sentence, it would have to be in an adjunct phrase, a *by* phrase:

> *The bulb is filled with hydrogen by the experimenter at an initial pressure of 86 cm of mercury, density 13.6 gm per cc.*

In science writing like this, there is little point in specifying that an experimenter carry out the experiment. The information in the *by* phrase is redundant, given what we know about how experiments are carried out. The agent isn't specified in the original sentence because the agent role isn't relevant here and because readers naturally assume (unless told otherwise) that it is the experimenter who will fill the bulb. The active voice counterpart of the sentence not only specifies the experimenter unnecessarily, like the passive with the *by* phrase, but it goes one step further by giving the experimenter the unneeded prominence of subject position:

> *The experimenter fills the bulb with hydrogen at an initial pressure of 86 cm of mercury, density 13.6 gm per cc.*

Inclusion of the understood experimenter is in effect redundant. The tendency in scientific writing of this kind to avoid redundance therefore may explain why, for example, as pointed out in a linguistic study, the passive voice verb *be filled* is far more likely to occur in scientific text than its active counterpart *fill*; a study of 130,000 words of written scientific English found that *be filled* occurred more than three times as often as *fill*.[4]

In some situations the passive is used, not because the agent is unimportant, but, on the contrary, because the agent is *new* information that readers would need or want to know. In English, new information typically *follows* old information. The two most informationally prominent positions in a clause are the beginning and the end. While the clause-initial position makes *old* information prominent in English, the clause-final position provides the prominence a writer might want for *new* information. When the theme argument is new information, active voice has it as the clause-final argument. Where the agent argument is new information, passive voice provides a position for it in a clause-final *by* phrase. Compare these two examples:

> *The leadership of this department and the responsibility for implementing the complex reforms needed to make our new program work will be taken over* **by Jessica Hewitt**.
>
> **Jessica Hewitt** *will take over the leadership of this department and the responsibility for implementing the complex reforms needed to make our new program work.*

The clause-final position is the better place for emphasizing as new the agent's identity.

As for the observation, common in handbooks of style, that passive voice is clumsier and less clear than active voice, some kind of qualification is needed for sentences in which one argument is an embedded clause rather than a noun phrase. Compare now these examples:

ACTIVE: *That the president was willing to nominate such poorly qualified judges aston-ished the Judiciary Committee.*

PASSIVE: *The Judiciary Committee **was astonished** that the president was willing to nominate such poorly qualified judges.*

Note that the embedded clause is not introduced with the preposition *by*, as it would be if the clause had been in a noun phrase beginning *the fact that*. *By* cannot introduce clauses, so the prepositional phrase cannot be used. The passive voice version is far less awkward than its active voice counterpart. It appears that a whole clause not embedded in a noun phrase is a rather difficult construction to digest in subject position. The use of passive voice enables writers to place such clauses in clause-final position. In our example, it also enabled the writer to treat as the topic the Judiciary Committee rather than what they were astonished at. Of course, the passive voice is not the only way to keep the clause out of subject position. The clause could have been positioned at the end of the active voice sentence and the filler *it* placed in subject position:

It astonished the Judiciary Committee that the president was willing to nominate such poorly qualified judges.

The point is that it is misleading to label particular grammatical constructions as stylistically defective without considering the contexts in which they occur and the uses to which they are put. While passive voice can be used clumsily, in the hands of a good writer it can be a useful and even elegant option.

SUMMARY

Passive constructions give prominence to noun phrases that are not agents by placing them in the subject position at the beginning of the clause instead of in their D-structure position inside the verb phrase. The active voice counterpart of the main verb of such a clause may be an ordinary transitive verb, a two- or three-word prepositional verb, or a ditransitive. The passive verb unit is a sequence consisting of a form of *be* or *get* followed by the past participle form of the next verb. The agent may be included in a *by* phrase or omitted altogether, as it most often is. In D-structure, the subject position is unfilled, but, to satisfy the subject constraint and to acquire case, the argument following the verb is shifted into the subject slot. Typically, this argument has either the theme role or the experiencer role.

In ditransitive passive clauses, the argument that is shifted usually has the goal role. *Middle verbs* like *have* and *cost*, which refer to states rather than actions or processes, have no passive counterparts. The general distinction between *stative* predicates (representing states) and *dynamic* predicates (representing actions or processes) is significant also for passives. Some passive forms allow either a stative or dynamic interpretation. Like their active counterparts, stative passives do not occur with progressive aspect.

Pseudo-passives have a copular verb followed by a predicate adjective that looks similar or identical to the past participle. They refer to states without reference to past events bringing about the states.

Students whose first language has a different kind of passive voice (such as Japanese) may experience difficulties with English passives.

When clauses contain quantifiers or modals, active and passive clauses may differ in propositional content. The surface order of quantifiers, which differs between actives and passives, is semantically significant. The volitional and ability interpretations are normally ruled out when a passive clause has a theme or goal as its subject.

The passive can be used whenever it seems undesirable or unnecessary to specify the agent. This means that the occurrence of the passive is in part determined by the larger context in which it would be used.

EXERCISE SET 14

1. Discuss the semantic and grammatical facts (relevant to this chapter) about the sentence *The peas were frozen.*

2. For each of the following sentences, if there is a passive counterpart, write it. Be sure to include a *by* phrase in all your sentences. Some of the sentences will sound strange, even though they are grammatical.
  a. *The police stopped each car on the freeway.*
  b. *Two justices will consider this case.*
  c. *The baby weighed seven pounds.*
  d. *The prosecutor considered them criminals.*
  e. *The judge fined Sugita one hundred thousand yen.*
  f. *Several companies sent Calexco detailed proposals.*
  g. *They believe that tariff boundaries are harmful to international trade.*
  h. *People have denied that she was guilty of any crime.*

3. Sentences (g) and (h) actually have two passive counterparts each. Write the other passives. Comment on whether they sound better than the forms you wrote for (g) and (h) in the first question. What effect would omission of the agent phrase have for the four passive sentences?

4. Here is an activity from an ESL/EFL grammar textbook[5] for high-intermediate learners:

Imagine that you have the opportunity to interview some thinking robots. In small groups, write a short dialogue interviewing one or more robots. Practice the interview and then role play it for the entire class. Here are some suggested questions to ask. Be sure to add more of your own.

  • *What are you programmed to do?*
  • *Are you being taught new skills?*
  • *Have you been programmed to smell (see, taste, etc.)?*
  • *How was your nose designed?*

The activity is intended to help the class master passives. Form into groups of three or four, discuss how effective you think the activity might be, and jointly develop another activity for the passive. Report on your group's activity to the class.

5. The following excerpt from a paper written by a Chinese student at an American university reveals a number of problems. Write a paragraph discussing what you notice about her use of passive voice. Discuss your conclusions in groups.

Child abuse can hardly define because it depend on purpose for which definition being asking for. Child abuse not consider as problem at first but now it is become serious problem in our society and action now being take. As the population grow, more child abuse reporting. Those who have been abuse as child may be become dangerous in our society. Cause of child abuse is cause when child bad and discipline by parent. Then this may become too frequent and be turn into child abuse.

6. The writer of the paragraph in (5) obviously needs help with the passive. She has had some formal training in English grammar in China but has not incorporated all that knowledge into her spoken or written English. Devise a sequence of three exercises that should help the student master passive voice. For each exercise write a brief explanation of your specific objective(s) for that exercise.

NOTES

1. William Zinsser, *On Writing Well*, 2nd ed. (New York: Harper & Row, 1980), 101.

2. Researchers working within the Principles-and-Parameters framework have argued that the past participle marker, usually shown as *-en*, is itself an anaphor whose referent is the agent entity. For a complicated but useful discussion of this rather abstract analysis, see M. Baker, K. Johnson, and I. Roberts, "Passive Arguments Raised," *Linguistic Inquiry* 20 (1989): 219-51.

3. Actually, in special contexts, forms like *This pipe connects to that valve* can be used as instructions to someone on how to do something and, hence, have an active interpretation. We might want to distinguish between the general grammatical property of a form and specialized uses. Our example here would thus be a special use of the verb rather than a general grammatical property of the verb.

4. Reported in Rodney Huddleston, *The Sentence in Written English: A Syntactic Study Based on an Analysis of Scientific Texts* (Cambridge: Cambridge University Press, 1971), 115-120.

5. P. Werner, *Mosaic I*, 2nd ed. (New York: McGraw-Hill, 1990), 162-163.

15

Information Status and
Syntactic Structure

Syntactic structures have been shown to signal the information status of particular constituents of a sentence. We are concerned in this chapter with how specific syntactic structures can highlight those parts of the propositional content that represent *new information*.

We saw in Chapter 14 that passive voice clauses are convenient structures for making more prominent a theme or experiencer argument representing *old* information. Instead of following the verb, this argument is, in the passive voice, at the front of the clause, in subject position, which typically serves as the topic when there is no separate topic. Compare the following active sentence with the two passive voice counterparts:

> *Last night, the C.I.A. arrested the attorney general of the United States.*
> *The attorney general of the United States was arrested last night by the C.I.A.*
> *The attorney general of the United States was arrested by the C.I.A. last night.*

In the passive voice sentences, the theme noun phrase, *the attorney general of the United States*, is in the subject slot and is therefore more prominent than in the active voice form. These passive sentences also highlight new information. The most prominent new information slot, the clause-final position, is filled by *the C.I.A.* in one and by *last night* in the other. In the first case, the focus is on the agent argument; in the second, the focus is on the recentness of the event.

The same new information can be presented in a variety of ways. Instead of baldly stating this:

> *A unicorn is in the garden.*

speakers can introduce the animal more prominently by using *there* as an introducer:

> *There is a unicorn in the garden.*

This is the more common alternative.

The choice may be between an active or a passive or between a *there* clause and one beginning with an indefinite noun phrase. Whichever the choice made, the propositional content remains the same (assuming the alternatives include the same arguments). What is different is the way in which the information is presented to the addressee. This is true of all the structures considered in this chapter. The emphases may differ, but the propositional content is unchanged.

EMPHASIS AND ASSERTING NEW INFORMATION

Spoken English provides options that the written language cannot. Speakers can use their voice to stress the parts of an utterance they wish to emphasize. Think of the many different ways you could say the following sentence:

Wilson was president of the United States in 1913.

Generally, the main stress in a clause is on the last word. In declarative clauses and questions beginning with *wh* words like *who, what,* and *when,* the stress is accompanied by a falling tone. We'll use bold print to show this stress:

*Wilson was president of the United States in **1913**.*

The main stress falls on the first syllable of *1913*.

But stress can also be used contrastively to focus on new information that the speaker wants to assert, especially if that information is in subject position, where old information is the norm. We'll use bold capitals to mark this stress. For example, if someone had claimed that Harding was president of the United States in 1913, you could place a contrastive stress on *Wilson:*

***WILSON** was president of the United States in 1913.*

Contrastive stress is usually marked by a rising tone. Someone who utters this last sentence assumes that the addressee is already aware that the identity of the president is under discussion. The speaker's focus, then, is on asserting what the addressee is assumed *not* to know, or, at least, not to have in mind at that moment. The old information is referred to because it provides the necessary context. Think about specific speech situations in which other constituents of the sentence take contrastive stress.

Spoken English can use both stress and syntactic structure to focus on a constituent. Pronounce the following sentences aloud:

a. *The bulldozer destroyed the **cottage**.*
b. *The **BULLDOZER** destroyed the cottage.*
c. *What destroyed the cottage was the **bulldozer**.*
d. *It was the **BULLDOZER** that destroyed the cottage.*

In example (a) the main stress is where we would expect it to be—on the last constituent of the verb phrase. The verb phrase contains the major new information. In sentence (b), contrastive stress has been placed on the last constituent of the subject noun phrase. The subject is most typically old information; contrastive stress identifies this constituent as containing the major new information. The (c) sentence employs both stress and syntactic structure to mark the major new information in the sentence. That is, a special *what* clause is used to place *the bulldozer* in sentence-final position where it will receive main stress. Finally, in (d), *the bulldozer* has contrastive stress and is also in a special structure involving *it* and *that.*

Sentences (b), (c), and (d) all contrast with sentence (a) in marking *the bulldozer,* rather than the verb phrase ending with *the cottage,* as the locus of the major new information. Although the definite article in *the bulldozer* indicates that the addressee is expected to know that there was a bulldozer, the bulldozer's *role* in the destruction of the cottage is new information.[1]

Written English is essentially limited to *syntactic* devices for communicating different focuses, since stress is not marked in writing, except for the occasional use of italics. Let's look at these syntactic devices in more detail.

IT CLEFTS

Consider again the following sentence:

It was the bulldozer that destroyed the cottage.

As we've seen, this sentence is an alternative to *The bulldozer destroyed the cottage*. It would most likely be used if the addressee knows that the cottage has been destroyed but doesn't know what has done the destroying. Note that the *it* doesn't refer to the bulldozer, but is instead the filler *it*.

The sentence is an *it cleft*. In such constructions, the phrase that the speaker wants to assert is separated ("clefted") from the rest of its clause by *that/which* and put after *it's* or *it was/is*. The clefted phrase is followed by a relative clause. Basically, then, a cleft sentence consists of two information units, one containing the old information, referred to in order to provide context, and the other communicating the new information being asserted.

In our example, the unit with new information is the noun phrase *the bulldozer*, which in speech receives a contrastive (rising tone) stress on the first syllable, and the unit expressing old information is the relative clause *that destroyed the cottage*. This relative clause has no head noun—*the bulldozer* is actually a predicate noun phrase that does not combine with the relative clause following it to form a larger noun phrase. The separate information units correspond to separate sentence constituents, as shown in the following D-structure tree:

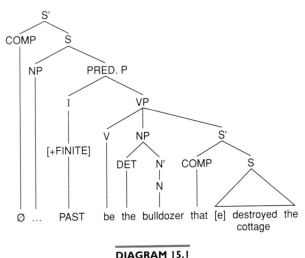

DIAGRAM 15.1

There is, of course, another sentence, *It was the bulldozer that destroyed the cottage*, in which the *it* is not filler *it* but refers to something previously mentioned or something obvious in the speech context. You might say the sentence in response to a question, as in this next example:

Which machine did they sell her? Was it the bulldozer with the faulty transmission?
No, it was the bulldozer that destroyed the cottage.

Note that the stress of this sentence is quite different from that of the *it* cleft sentence. Instead of a special stress on *bulldozer*, there is a main stress on *cottage*.

What kind of grammatical constituent can the new information unit be? In our example it was a noun phrase. It can also be a prepositional phrase, as can be seen by considering clefted versions of the following sentence:

The federation is sending Celia to Singapore on Thursday.

The cleft sentences below all express the same propositional content but have quite different focuses. In the first two examples, the new information units are noun phrases; in the other two, they are prepositional phrases. (The constituent focused on is boldfaced in the following examples, and capital letters indicate the stressed syllable.)

*It's **the federAtion** that is sending Celia to Singapore on Thursday.*
*It's **CElia** that the federation is sending to Singapore on Thursday.*
*It's **to SINGapore** that the federation is sending Celia on Thursday.*
*It's **on THURSday** that the federation is sending Celia to Singapore.*

The boldfaced constituents represent the new information. Note that the complementizer *that* cannot be replaced by *which* in the last two examples. In both cases, the *that* clauses are adjuncts, one of time and the other of place.

WH CLEFTS

In *wh* clefts (sometimes called "pseudo-clefts"), the old information is contained in a *wh* clause while the rest of the sentence is the new information. The two units are separated by a form of the copular verb *be*. The old information *wh* unit, which refers to needed context, can come either before or after the new information, although the former order is more common:

*What the colonists wanted was **freedom from external taxation**.*
***Freedom from external taxation** was what the colonists wanted.*

The two orderings differ in the degree of emphasis on the new information. When the new information unit comes first, it is more strongly emphasized. This is both because subject position is more prominent and because of the surprise factor—we don't normally expect the new information to precede the old. This construction can also be used when the addressee is being *reminded* of the content of the *wh* clause. Like the other focus constructions described here, *wh* cleft constructions are used for a number of distinct though related functions.

In the last example, the crucial new information was expressed as a noun phrase, but it can also be expressed as a clause, an adjective phrase, a verb phrase, or a prepositional phrase. Clauses with the new information can be either finite or nonfinite:

*What the colonists wanted was **to be free from external taxation**.*
*What the colonists believed was **that they should be free from external taxation**.*

Adjective phrases tend to occur in more informal speech:

*What he was was **obstinate**.*

When the new information unit is a verb phrase, the *wh* clause ends with a form of *do* instead of another verb:

*What Henry has **done** is **develop a better mousetrap**.*

Other *wh* forms besides *what* occur in *wh* clefts:

> **New Jersey** *was where we met.*
> *Where we met was* **New Jersey.**
> **January** *is when we visit Cortina.*
> *Why Todd sold his house was* **to get money for his wife's hospital costs.**
> *How they found out was* **by hiring a private detective.**

Although the last two examples may not be accepted by all speakers as "good" English, they are certainly native speaker English.

When a noun phrase referring to a human being is the focused item, the *wh* clause is normally embedded in a noun phrase beginning with *The one who, the person who,* or a similar phrase:

$$
The \left\{ \begin{array}{l} one \\ person \\ man \end{array} \right\} \textit{who advocated stronger action was Palmerston.}
$$

The major point about both *it* clefts and *wh* clefts is that they provide ways to make new information more prominent.

EXISTENTIAL *THERE* CONSTRUCTIONS

Some sentences present only new information. When a fairy tale starts, it typically assumes that the reader or hearer has no information on the story. So all information is new information:

> *Once upon a time there was a beautiful princess who lived in a castle on the top of a hill.*

We mentioned earlier this sentence:

> *A unicorn was in the garden.*

The subject slot contains *a unicorn*, which is clearly new information. Usually the new information occurs as a predicate and follows a subject referring to something familiar. But there is no such subject available here. What happens if the new information noun phrase *a unicorn* is placed after the verb? The result is a sentence that might, with appropriate modifications, have been grammatical in Anglo-Saxon but is not grammatical in modern English:

> **was a unicorn in the garden*

Since the clause is finite, some constituent must fill the subject position. What is used is the filler word *there*, which is always unstressed (unlike the stressed *there* indicating location):

> *There was a unicorn in the garden.*

The sentence has the same propositional content as our first example, but it marks more prominently as new information the noun phrase *a unicorn*. This filler *there*, sometimes called *existential there*, generally occurs when the noun phrase that would otherwise be subject is an indefinite noun phrase expressing new information. It provides a useful way to announce that what follows is going to be new.

Although *there* fills the subject slot, the verb agrees in number with the noun phrase that follows:

There **is** just **one unicorn** in the garden.
There **are** exactly **two unicorns** in the garden.

This indicates that, despite the occurrence of *there* in subject position, the noun phrase after the verb still retains the subject property of determining agreement for the verb. However, in informal usage, the verb may be singular even when the noun phrase following it is plural; in such cases the copular verb *be* is almost always contracted to *'s*:

Guess what! There's termites in that wall.

Filler *there* can occur not just with main verb *be* but also when some form of *be* is an auxiliary verb:

There **was a man arrested** yesterday with a suitcase full of heroin.
There **was a soldier coming** toward me with a nasty look in his eye.

Other verbs can precede *be* in these existential *there* constructions, verbs such as *appear, seem, happen,* and *come*:

There $\left\{\begin{array}{l} \text{appeared} \\ \text{seemed} \\ \text{happened} \\ \text{came} \end{array}\right\}$ to be a shortage of medical technicians.

Predicate adjectives such as *(un)likely, certain,* and *sure* occur in this position also:

There is $\left\{\begin{array}{l} \text{(un)likely} \\ \text{certain} \end{array}\right\}$ to be an inquiry into the incident.

These more complex constructions have D-structures similar to the following surface structures:

It is $\left\{\begin{array}{l} \text{(un)likely} \\ \text{certain} \end{array}\right\}$ that there will be an inquiry into the incident.

except that the embedded clauses are nonfinite:

... is $\left\{\begin{array}{l} \text{(un)likely} \\ \text{certain} \end{array}\right\}$ there to be an inquiry into the incident.[2]

Although *be* has occurred in all the examples so far and is the most common verb for this construction, *there* can occur with certain other verbs. These all have to do with notions of existence or position; they include *exist, arise, emerge, ensue, remain, live, stand, sit,* and *lie*. Here are some examples:

There emerged from that tunnel a beast with a long shiny neck.
There sat waiting for them in the parlor three anxious Persian cats.
There ensued a demonstration that was eventually to drive the government from power.
There remain a few minor issues that we should discuss.

The use of such verbs in existential *there* clauses is particularly common in literary prose. Like *be*, they are used in combination with *there* to introduce new information, typically expressed as indefinite noun phrases.

✓ However, not all occurrences of introductory *there* introduce indefinite noun phrases. Occasionally, *there* introduces definite noun phrases, typically as part of a list:

> Of course, there's the Tate Gallery on the Embankment, the National Gallery in Trafalgar Square, and the Whitechapel collection of old photographs of the East End.

The noun phrases introduced in this way can be used to represent information that the speaker thinks is familiar to the addressee, but not in the addressee's mind *at that time*. Sometimes only one definite noun phrase occurs, but it is normally understood to be the first of several that the speaker could specify. For example, in answer to the query, "What's the best museum to visit in Bournemouth?" someone might say:

> Well, there's the Russell Cotes Gallery near the Pleasure Gardens. It has some wonderful nineteenth-century stuff!

✓ This use of *there* with definite noun phrases is almost entirely confined to the spoken language.

Although in the examples so far *there* has been followed by a finite clause, it can also introduce a nonfinite clause as the new information:

> The divers believed **there to be a sunken Spanish galleon in the bay**.

Nonfinite clauses are usually embedded as object arguments after verbs like *believe, know, expect,* and *want.*

SUMMARY

This chapter has been concerned with special ways to mark and focus on new information. The structures used to highlight the status of content as new information differ from the basic subject-predicate structures we have studied so far. For example, in *existential there* constructions, the filler *there* plus either *be* or certain other verbs is used to introduce indefinite noun phrases having the status of new information. Although not in subject position, the indefinite noun phrase still determines the verb agreement. In embedded sentences, *there* can be in the subject slot of a nonfinite clause.

Whereas written English must rely on syntax, in speech stress can also be used to mark new information. The normal stress marking for a declarative sentence or a *wh* question is main stress, which is marked by a falling tone on a syllable of the last word. Contrastive stress, which is applied to constituents representing content the addressee is assumed *not* to be aware of, is marked by a rising tone.

In an *it cleft*, the focused new information follows a form of *be* and is itself followed by the old information, contained in a relative clause form. A *wh cleft* (or *pseudo-cleft*) typically starts with the old information, in a *wh* clause, which precedes the copular verb *be* that introduces the new, asserted content. Sometimes the order of the two clefted constituents is reversed so as to emphasize more strongly the content being asserted.

EXERCISE SET 15

1. Write three revisions of each of the following sentences so as to communicate different focuses. Do not use passive voice.
   a. *The Ottawa police were looking for a yellow Volvo.*
   b. *That woman held up the First National Bank.*
   c. *The social workers believed that unemployment would demoralize the youth of the nation.*

2. Explain what the ambiguities are in the following sentences:

    a. *It's the plumber who came to repair the sink.*
    b. *It's the conveyor belt that carries the screwtop lids.*
    c. *What I don't know is what worries me.*

3. Convert the following sentences into *it* clefts:

    a. *Leonardo drew that sketch.*
    b. *His plan failed.*
    c. *She appeared at the castle gate that morning.*

4. Convert the following sentences into *wh* clefts:

    a. *Crashaw wanted to sell off all the agricultural land.*
    b. *George was born in New Jersey.*
    c. *The plant manufactured automatic transmissions.*
    d. *Darlene used mud to patch up her walls.*

5. Develop an exercise in which students can practice using the filler *there*.

6. Different kinds of knowledge are needed for the interpretation of the following paragraph. In what respects does the writer's use of the underlined forms draw upon (a) syntactic/semantic knowledge, (b) knowledge about information structure, and/or (c) pragmatic knowledge? The paragraph is part of a discussion of presidential campaigns in the United States and follows immediately after a description of the 1988 presidential campaign.

> *The early part of the 1992 <u>campaign</u> was as ferocious as the later stages. Bush charged that Perot was deliberately distorting <u>his</u> domestic positions, was presenting a false picture of <u>himself</u>, and had hired detectives to investigate <u>his children</u>. "<u>Perot's unscrupulous behavior,</u>" he said, "was beyond the pale." As Clinton pointed out, <u>the wild accusations</u> on all sides had caused the popular discontent.*

7. The passage labeled A is from an essay by James Baldwin,[3] while the passage labeled B is a paraphrase provided just to help you isolate the effects of the relevant stylistic choices made by Baldwin. Look at the two versions. Then describe the effects Baldwin achieves by his choice of *wh* cleft constructions and his manipulation of active and passive voice.

    A.

> *And yet, it became clear as the debate wore on, that there was something which all black men held in common....What they held in common was their precarious, their unutterably painful relation to the white world. What they held in common was the necessity to remake the world in their own image, to impose this image on the world, and no longer be controlled by the vision of the world and of themselves, held by other people. What, in sum, black men held in common was their ache to come into the world as men.*

    B.

> *And yet, that there was something which all black men held in common became clear as the debate wore on. They held in common their precarious, their unutterably painful relation to the white world. They held in common the necessity to remake the world in their own image, to impose this image on the world. The vision of the world and of themselves, which other people held, would no longer control them. In sum, black men held in common their ache to come as men into the world.*

NOTES

1. Actually, (b), (c), and (d) differ somewhat in what the speaker assumes about the addressee's knowledge and beliefs about the situation, but these are subtle and highly variable differences that go far beyond the scope of this book.

2. For convenience, we show *there* as being in the D-structure, although our label *filler* might suggest otherwise.

3. James Baldwin, *Nobody Knows My Name* (New York: Dell, 1961), 35.

PART

V

INSIDE
THE PREDICATE PHRASE

16

Understanding Tense

"Every language has its peculiar problems of meaning," writes Geoffrey Leech, refer-ring to areas of difficulty for language learners. He identifies verb tense and aspect, dis-cussed respectively in this chapter and the next, as two of the most troublesome areas of English.[1] One serious problem in dealing with the English tense system is our ten-dency to treat the verb forms as directly corresponding to the semantic properties of time reference. Form and meaning should be treated as distinct dimensions, since in no language do tenses and time references match up on a one-to-one basis.

Tense and aspect have to do with *form*. Tense is the grammatical marking on verbs that usually indicates time reference relative to either the time of speaking or the time at which some other situation was in force. When we deal with *tense*, we're dealing with actual language *forms* used to represent time reference notions. Indeed, we're not even concerned with *all* the kinds of language forms used for time reference, but just the verb forms. After all, English has adverbs like *yesterday, later, meanwhile,* and phras-es like *the following day* and *last Tuesday*. None of these fall under the category of tense. Aspect, as we shall see, is the grammatical marking on verbs of the internal time struc-ture of a situation.

Time reference, unlike tense and aspect, has to do with *meaning* rather than *form*. Languages need ways to refer to time. Events and situations are located in time, perhaps *prior* to our speaking about them, perhaps *while* we are speaking about them, perhaps at some *later* time. Moreover, we may need to locate situations and events relative not just to the time of speaking but also to some other reference point.

In this chapter and the next, we'll be considering both form and meaning. We'll see that it is not possible to match up each verb form with a particular kind of time reference.

THE GRAMMATICAL TRADITION

Aristotle is said to have been the first to recognize the category *tense*. He observed that there were systematic variations in the forms of Greek verbs, variations that could be correlated with time notions such as *past* and *present*. Although English has many fewer such verb forms than Classical Greek, there are still systematic correlations.

Grammarians treated these notions as simple and obvious. We will discuss the grammatical tradition here because it continues to influence both the popular view of language and much English language teaching and research. This tradition was based on practices of Latin and Greek grammarians, though in important respects English is quite different.

Traditional Latin and Greek grammars listed in tables—now known as *paradigms*—the forms for each verb in a large number of tenses. The tables gave forms for the first, second, and third person, singular and plural. Here are the present tense forms of the Latin verb *portare*, "to carry":

PORTARE "TO CARRY"

Person	Singular	Plural
1st	porto ("I carry")	portamus ("we carry")
2nd	portas ("you carry")	portatis ("you carry")
3rd	portat ("he, she, it carries")	portant ("they carry")

In addition to the present tense, tenses distinguished for Latin included the future, the perfect tense (meaning "have V-ed" or just "V-ed"), the future perfect ("will have V-ed"), the pluperfect or past perfect ("had V-ed"), and the imperfect tense ("was/were V-ing"). These tenses were all in the *indicative mood* (corresponding fairly closely to finite verb forms in English). There was another set of four tenses in what is called the *subjunctive mood* (meaning something like "might V" and "might have V-ed"); English has only a relatively rare counterpart.[2] In addition, there were five more sets in the passive voice. With six forms in each set, this made a total of ninety verb forms, excluding participles and other nonfinite forms.

In the seventeenth and eighteenth centuries, grammarians writing English grammars for schools believed that the English language should be described in the same way as Latin and Greek. However, there are a number of problems with such an approach. First, in no language do the verb forms directly correspond to the semantic properties of time reference. An accurate and insightful grammar must be based on more than logical criteria. Second, English differs from Latin and Greek in having only *two* inflections on verbs to show tense. The past tense is usually but not always marked with an *-ed;* the present tense is marked with an *-s* agreement suffix for third person singular forms. Corresponding to other Latin and Greek verb inflections are auxiliary verbs such as *will* and *should*. To some early grammarians, English seemed an impoverished language, one lacking the range and precision of tense forms in the classical languages.

A typical attempt to remedy the defects of English was made by S. W. Clark, principal of the Cortland Academy in upstate New York in the mid-1800s. In his textbook, *A Practical Grammar*, which went into many printings, Mr. Clark filled pages and pages with verb paradigms, using combinations of auxiliaries, verbs, and other forms to fill in gaps in the tense system. His paradigms for the verb *recite* alone take up four pages of small print. The present subjunctive paradigm, for example, consists of six identical verb forms preceded by *if* (*If I were reciting*, etc.).

Later writers and teachers developed a more sensible version of this Latin-based classification, one which reflected more accurately the English verb data. Though still relying more on semantic or logical criteria than on the actual combinations and verb forms of English, the newer version turned out to be a useful framework for familiarizing learners with the range of verb forms available to express time relationships. This version listed twelve tenses. Here is a listing of the tenses for the verb *wash*, with the first person singular form representing each set of tense forms. Note that the tenses are categorized according to past, present, and future, in combination with what we shall be referring to as the perfect and progressive aspects:

1. Simple Present: *I wash*
2. Simple Past: *I washed*
3. Simple Future: *I will wash*
4. Present Progressive: *I am washing*
5. Past Progressive: *I was washing*
6. Future Progressive: *I will be washing*
7. Present Perfect: *I have washed*
8. Past Perfect: *I had washed*
9. Future Perfect: *I will have washed*
10. Present Perfect Progressive: *I have been washing*
11. Past Perfect Progressive: *I had been washing*
12. Future Perfect Progressive: *I will have been washing*

TOWARD AN ACCOUNT BASED ON LANGUAGE FORMS

The twelve-tense approach to describing the English tense system assumes that tense and time are really the same and that the perfect and progressive aspects are little more than devices to form additional tenses. But these assumptions are wrong, as we'll see both in our discussion of time and tense here and when we look in more detail at aspect and the modal verbs.

First, consider past tense and its relation to past time. Does past tense always refer to past time? It very often does, but not always. Take the past tense form *came* in this next example:

*If Roosevelt **came** into this office tomorrow, he'd find everything exactly the same.*

Clearly in this example the time reference is to the future. The word *tomorrow* makes this explicit, but, even without *tomorrow*, the word *if* would indicate that the speaker is referring to a hypothetical situation rather than to one that has already happened.

The following example also has a past tense form and refers to a hypothetical situation:

*If Justice Brandeis **examined** recent Supreme Court decisions, he would feel depressed.*

Again the time reference is not past, though here it is present rather than future. It is the hypothetical character of the situation (marked with the *if*) that allows the past tense to be used this way. Somewhat parallel is the use of past tense when someone, say a professor, addresses a question like the following to a person standing outside her office:

***Did** you want to see me now?*

The professor is not asking about a past desire; obviously, the time reference is present. The past tense *forms* are easy to recognize: Either the vowel is changed or there is a past tense suffix. But, as the preceding examples show, the time reference for past tense forms isn't as straightforwardly determined.

When we turn our attention to present tense, we see that even the forms are less obvious. The only overt marking is the *-s* that marks agreement with third person singular subjects, as in this sentence:

*Lady Godiva **rides** on a snow-white horse.*

Given this lack of overt marking, it could be argued that there is no present tense, that finite verbs simply are or aren't marked for past tense. This would amount to saying that finite verbs are either in the past tense or in a non-past tense. Since the arguments on either side are inconclusive, we'll adhere to the more traditional account and assume that there is a present tense, one marked by a zero (0) ending on all forms except for the third person singular.

But this is not to claim that present tense always corresponds to present time. Our "Lady Godiva" sentence would normally be used to describe not what is going on *now*, but what *usually* happens. The present tense of verbs signifying actions or processes does not in ordinary usage refer to present time. Such forms usually refer to habitual action. Only the present tense of verbs like *know*, representing states, normally refer to present time. Note that the same sentence can refer to future time, especially if an appropriate time adverb is added:

*Lady Godiva **rides** on a snow-white horse **tomorrow**.*

This combination use of present tense forms with future time adverbs is used for events that are scheduled in advance, and it suggests that nothing will be changed. We can call it the *prearranged present usage.*

As for a future tense, if we are using the term *tense* to refer to a set of verb forms, there really isn't a future tense. We use many kinds of verb forms and combinations when we refer to future time, and most of these can also be used to express notions not connected with future time reference. English has no special future tense forms. Traditional grammarians, searching for a future tense corresponding to those in Latin and Greek, noted that the modal *will* (and sometimes *shall*) could be used with a verb to refer to future time. So they decided that the *will* + verb combination (and sometimes the *shall* + verb combination) was the English future tense.

But *will* and *shall* are only two of the modal verbs that occur in combinations used to refer to future time. *May, could,* and *would* are other such modals. *Will* and *shall* behave just like the other modals; they differ from regular verbs in not allowing the -*s* or any of the other suffixes that go on verbs, and they have no present or past participle forms. The main differences among the modals are in the degree of certainty expressed and other dimensions which we shall discuss in Chapter 18.

In short, once grammatical tense is distinguished from semantic time reference, English can be seen to have a two-tense system consisting of past and present tenses. Past tense verbs need not refer to past time, and present tense verbs often do not refer to the time at which the sentence is uttered.

Our account of the allowed sequences of modals, tense-marked forms, and other items that can precede the main verb of a clause will start from the actual forms and combinations that can occur. When a finite clause contains a modal verb, the modal verb precedes the main verb:

*Dupont **will perform** a lab test on the used product.*

But when it contains instead tense, say past tense, as in:

*Dupont **PAST perform** a lab test on the used product.*

it has to be shifted onto the following verb, where it usually appears as a suffix:

*Dupont **perform** + **-ed** a lab test on the used product.*

The constituent *past tense* is realized not as a word but as a suffix. With verbs like *sing*, past tense changes the vowel so that the verb becomes *sang*.[3] In both cases, the tense combines with the verb. We can summarize this in the following schema:

TNS - V => V + TNS

where the plus sign (+) indicates that the verb and tense marking are combined.

But the tense or a modal does not always immediately precede the main verb of the clause. Look at the following examples:

The president **will have extended** *a helping hand to Japan's prime minister.*
The president **PRESENT have extended** *a helping hand to Japan's prime minister.*

In both examples, an additional verb *have* intervenes between the modal or tense and the main verb. Moreover, the *have* is that special form known as the perfect, which requires that the verb following it be in its past participle form. The *have* plus past participle combination indicates *perfect aspect,* which we discuss in some detail in the next chapter.

If the Inflection contains a modal such as *will,* the *have* following it does not change. But if the Inflection contains a tense, then that tense is marked on the next verb that follows it, whether or not that verb is the main verb. So, in our second example, the present tense is marked on the verb *have:*

The president **has extended** *a helping hand to Japan's prime minister.*

We'll show perfect aspect *have* on a tree this way:

have
.<-en>

We call the past participle form the *-en* form, since the *-en* suffix on verbs like *eaten* and *broken,* unlike the more common *-ed* suffix, is used only for the past participle form. So *-en* stands for whatever changes are needed to convert the verb following the *have* into its past participle form. The *-en* is included with the *have* because if this *have* is omitted, then *-en* is too. We can say that, for perfect aspect, the *-en* associated with *have* goes onto the verb following, as in this schematic representation:

have - V = have - V + -en
<-en>

Now we can use a more comprehensive schema. After the subject constituent of a finite clause there is the option of having either a tense or a modal. Nonfinite clauses require *to* in this position unless they are independent clauses. This gives us the following schema:

| TNS |
| MODAL | *have*   V ...
| to | <-en>

What about the *be* in the following sentence:

The African National Congress **is facing** *considerable pressure from its friends.*

Note that *be* is marked for present tense, so it comes from the sequence PRESENT–be. The tense combines with *be* to form *is* in this sentence. The *be* itself affects the form of the verb following, which takes on an *-ing* suffix. The combination of *be* and the *-ing* suffix on the following verb is known as *progressive aspect.* The *be,* known as *progressive be,* appears after the specification for tense, a modal, or *to.* So we'll show this progressive *be* on trees as follows:

be
<-ing>

Note that if perfect aspect *have* also occurs in a sentence, the progressive *be* must follow it:

Hawai'i **has been searching** *for new markets for its gourmet coffees.*
*Hawai'i **was having searched** *for new markets for its gourmet coffees.*

The second sentence shows what happens when progressive aspect *be* is allowed to precede perfect aspect *have*. So we can further expand our schema:

$$
\left\{
\begin{array}{l}
\text{TNS} \\
\text{MODAL} \\
\text{to}
\end{array}
\right\}
\quad
\begin{array}{c}
have \\
\text{<-en>}
\end{array}
\quad
\begin{array}{c}
(be) \\
\text{<-ing>}
\end{array}
\quad
\begin{array}{c}
\text{V} \ldots
\end{array}
$$

The parentheses indicate optional constituents. If a tense is chosen, it combines with whatever verb form immediately follows it. The <-en> and <-ing> must also combine with the immediately following verb.

One last constituent pair must be added to represent the possibility of passive voice. For passive voice, the verb *be* precedes the main verb, which must be in its *-en* form:

The Tigers **were beaten** *by an Arizona team.*
The rescuers had expected the streams to **be swollen** *by the melting snows.*

This constituent pair follows perfect aspect *have* and progressive aspect *be*, if they also occur. Now our formulation can cover the major combinations for the sequence of tense, aspect, passive voice, and main verb constituents. If the schema is followed, the constituents will always be in the correct order:

$$
\left\{
\begin{array}{l}
\text{TNS} \\
\text{MODAL} \\
\text{to}
\end{array}
\right\}
\quad
\begin{array}{c}
have \\
\text{<-en>}
\end{array}
\quad
\begin{array}{c}
(be) \\
\text{<-ing>}
\end{array}
\quad
\begin{array}{c}
(be) \\
\text{<-en>}
\end{array}
\quad
\begin{array}{c}
\text{V} \ldots
\end{array}
$$

However, it would be very hard to find examples with *all* the options selected and they would sound a little strange, as these do:

The cows **should have been being milked** *at that time.*
They reported the cows **to have been being milked** *at that time.*

USES OF TENSE

We've been dealing with the *forms* of the past and present tenses. Now look at some of their major *functions*. At the most basic level, past tense marks situations as distanced either in time or reality from the speaker or writer, while present tense (the absence of past tense) indicates the absence of such distancing. To make a past incident seem less distant and more real to her addressee, the person telling this story uses present tense for all verbs, except for the first verb, which sets the scene and indicates that the incident is not occurring now:

> *Yeah, I was standing right by the counter when this big dude comes up behind me and he says, "Excuse me, lady, I gotta go ahead of you." Well, I don't even look round, I just say, "The heck you do! You can wait your turn." Then I feel a paper bag against the back of my neck and there's something hard in it and it feels like a gun, and I tell you I want to be out of there, and he says, "Excuse me," and the teller is looking at us, her eyes wide as dinner plates.*

The speaker's use of present tense instead of past tense conveys immediacy rather than time distance. The event is being rerun for the addressee's benefit. This use of the present tense is sometimes referred to as the *narrative present.*

The tense switch can go in the opposite direction too, with the past tense being used for a present situation. The effect is to make the present event seem more distant and therefore less pressing. A speaker who says, *Do you want to see me now?*, may seem too direct. The speaker appears to expect an affirmative answer, so the addressee feels a negative answer is inappropriate. As we pointed out earlier, the past tense counterpart can be used; this distances the question from the here and now and makes a negative answer less inappropriate:

> *Did you want to see me now?*

The difference between the present and past tense forms of the questions is not one of time distance but of social distance. The past tense indicates greater social distance, making the question seem less confrontational.

Tense Shifting in Indirect Discourse

When speech or thought is being reported rather than quoted, a different kind of distancing can be observed. In finite embedded clauses reporting someone's thoughts or speech, the tense of verbs in embedded clauses is often shifted from present to past. We'll refer to reports of thoughts or speech as *indirect discourse*. Compare the following pairs of examples in which the thoughts or speech are presented first as if they are directly quoted and then more indirectly.

> *He **is** behaving like a conceited pig, she thought.*
> *She thought that he **was** behaving like a conceited pig.*

> *"I **don't** ever want to see you again," she told him.*
> *She told him that she **didn't** ever want to see him again.*

In the indirect discourse version, first person pronouns have become third person and the tense has been shifted from present to past. The shifting of tenses makes the tense in the embedded clause "harmonize" with the tense of the container clause.

This shifting of tenses doesn't always happen. For example, either of the following is well formed:

> *Aristotle announced that the earth **was** a globe.*
> *Aristotle announced that the earth **is** a globe.*

Yet in the next pair, there is something a little strange about the sentence whose tense has not been shifted:

> *Aristotle announced that the earth **was** a cubical object.*
> *?Aristotle announced that the earth **is** a cubical object.*

The reason is that use of the present tense removes the distancing, so that the speaker can be understood to be associating himself or herself with the belief expressed in the embedded clause. The result is fine when Aristotle specifies the earth as a globe, since this is still the current view, but not when he describes it as a cubical object.

Just as the present tense is used in indirect discourse when what is reported is for the speaker a universal truth, so it is used to describe a situation that is still ongoing:

> *Mrs. Brunner told me that he still **refuses**.*

Present tense has been described as occurring when the situation described is of "current relevance to the speaker." The past tense reflects a past point of view.[4]

Tense and Reference Points

If it now seems that tense is used for everything but simple time reference, this impression needs to be corrected. The major function of tense is still to locate situations in time relative to some fixed reference point. Typically, this reference point is "now," the time at which the sentences are uttered. We can call this kind of time reference *absolute time reference*. When the reference point is some other time, the term used is *relative time reference*.

To understand better the notions of absolute and relative time reference, let's look at an example situation. Assume Inspector Robichaud is investigating the murder of Sebastian Simms. The following sentences are taken from statements to the inspector:

Absolute Time Reference (relative to *now*):

*Jonathan Klein **left** the house at three o'clock.*
*Susan **was** cleaning her hunting rifle.*

The speaker is referring to a time past relative to now, the interrogation time.

Relative Time Reference (relative to *some time prior to now*):

*Maurice **had** already **left** when Sebastian telephoned.*

As the *already* indicates, Maurice's departure occurred in a past prior to the past time of Sebastian's telephone call, the reference point time.[5]

Relative Time Reference (relative to *some time after now*):

*The murderer **will have been arrested** when she arrives next week.*

The arrest of the murderer will have occurred prior to the time of her arrival, though not prior to now. The reference point is the time of her arrival next week.[6]

Tense, Aspect, and the Learner

English does not have three tenses corresponding directly to past, present, and future. It uses two tenses as part of a complex system for marking time reference. In fact, relatively few languages have a three-tense system. Far more common are two-way splits—past versus nonpast, or future versus nonfuture—similar to the system in English.[7]

For learners, difficulties arise because of the complexity of the relationships between the tenses and time reference, and because of mismatches between the native language system and the English system they are trying to acquire. For example, in English, there are two translations for each of these French sentences, which contain present tense verbs:

Que manges-tu, Alphonse?
Je mange des oeufs frites.

The two English versions are these:

What do you eat, Alphonse?
I eat fried eggs.
What are you eating, Alphonse?
I am eating fried eggs.

The first translation uses present tense to indicate habitual activity rather than an event happening at the moment of speech. The second translation combines present tense and progressive aspect to locate the events at the moment of speech. French uses a single set of forms to express both kinds of time relations.

These features of the English verb system can be very confusing for learners. Teachers have tried to reduce the confusion by labeling the present tense–progressive aspect combination (e.g., *I am eating*) as the present tense for English. Although this may be helpful in some situations, it can easily lead to confusion in others, because not all predicates allow progressive aspect forms. As discussed earlier, it is the stative-dynamic distinction that is responsible for this superficially confusing phenomenon.

Stative predicates use the simple present tense to refer to present time, whereas dynamic predicates use the present tense–progressive aspect combination for present time reference. When the simple present tense is used with dynamic predicates, it normally indicates habitual actions or processes rather than actions or processes underway at the time the sentence is uttered. Teachers thus need to help students distinguish between predicates signifying actions or processes and those signifying states.

SUMMARY

English uses its two tenses as part of a complex system for marking time reference, one which also includes modals like *will* or *can* preceding the verb and also other auxiliary verb forms, as shown in the summary schema:

$$
\left\{ \begin{array}{c} \text{TNS} \\ \text{MODAL} \\ \text{to} \end{array} \right\} \quad \begin{array}{c} have \\ \text{<-en>} \end{array} \quad \begin{array}{c} (be) \\ \text{<-ing>} \end{array} \quad \begin{array}{c} (be) \\ \text{<-en>} \end{array} \quad \text{V ...}
$$

All of these constituents preceding the main verb locate events in relation to some time reference point, frequently but not always, the time defined by the moment of speech (or, for written language, the time of writing). But as we have seen, tense can have other functions, for example, indicating the degree of immediacy the speaker is communicating or marking politeness by distancing an utterance.

For English, it is important, then, to distinguish between tense *forms* and *functions*. The tense forms are not simply time reference markers, but bear a more complex relation to the speech situation.

The traditional school grammar portrayal of English as having a twelve-tense system confuses tense with time reference and conceals the nature of the aspectual system that we'll be investigating in the next chapter.

EXERCISE SET 16

1. Indicate which sequences of the schema given in the chapter occur in the sentences below.

Example:
a. *Maureen was being praised for her inventiveness.*

PAST	be	be	praise
	<-ing>	<-en>	

b. *Mozart had been living with his father then.*
c. *Lady Macbeth could have been comforted.*

d. *for her to have been stealing all that money*
e. *The president may have been avoiding those questions.*
f. *Those envoys will be kidnapped.*
g. *Wittgenstein defines the problem differently.*

2. Rewrite the following sentences. For each sentence use the combinations specified under it.

Example:

a. *The milk boiled.*

MODAL	be
	<-ing>

Answer: *The milk might be boiling.*

b. *Dr. Foster examined Henry.*

PAST	be
	<-ing>

c. *Francisco lies.*

PRESENT	be
	<-ing>

d. *Yeltsin greeted the new ambassador.*

PRESENT	have	be
	<-en>	<-ing>

e. *They take the horse to Shanghai.*

PAST	have	be
	<-en>	<-ing>

3. Sandra McKay suggests an interesting exercise to help more advanced students practice tense and aspect usage. Students prepare a time line chart of important events in their life. They draw a three-column chart with the year in the first column, the personal event in the second column, and a world event that occurred in the same year in the third column.[8] Explain how such a chart could be used to practice tense and aspect usage. You might form small groups to discuss your conclusions.

4. Invent a writing assignment (perhaps also requiring a subsequent oral report to the class) that will test students' mastery of tense and aspect forms referring to the past, present, and future.

5. Give your own example of each of the following:
   a. paradigm
   b. perfect aspect
   c. narrative present
   d. indirect discourse
   e. absolute time reference
   f. relative time reference

6. Consider the predicates *write, be tactful, argue, know, run, be tall,* and *contain.* Which of these might present difficulties for non-native speakers who have learned that the present tense–progressive aspect combination is the main way to refer to present time in English? Explain why.

7. How would you describe the semantic differences between the members of the following pairs? Discuss each pair separately.

a. *He thinks now that the constitution should be revised.*
b. *He is thinking now that the constitution should be revised.*

a. *She hates those group sessions.*
b. *She is hating those group sessions.*

a. *They believe everything that Trevor says.*
b. *They are believing everything that Trevor says.*

a. *He lives in Aspen, Colorado.*
b. *He is living in Aspen, Colorado.*

NOTES

1. Geoffrey Leech, *Meaning and the English Verb*, 2nd ed. (London: Longman, 1987), 1.

2. There was a productive subjunctive mood in Anglo-Saxon, traces of which survive as a nonfinite verb in an exclamation (e.g., *Long **live** democracy in Costa Rica!*) and in nonfinite *that* clauses embedded as complements of a small group of verbs including *suggest, demand,* and *request.* For example, *They demanded that he **surrender** the remaining profits* and *Antonescu suggested that the region **be returned** to Romania.*

3. Chomsky formulates this as a process in which the verb is raised into the Inflection constituent, where it later combines morphologically with the tense element. See Noam Chomsky, *Barriers* [monograph] (Cambridge, MA: M.I.T. Press, 1986), 4–5 and 68–71.

4. Elizabeth Riddle, "The meaning and discourse function of the past tense in English," *TESOL Quarterly* 20 (June 1986): 267-86.

5. Without the *already*, both events reported—Maurice's departure and Sebastian's telephone call—could be understood to have occurred simultaneously. The past tense perfect aspect *had* is used only for the first verb, even if the second has exactly the same time reference. The *had* sets the relative time for what follows, much as the past tense form was used to open the present tense narrative about the bank robbery in an earlier example in this chapter.

6. One phenomenon that confuses many learners is that in subordinate time and condition clauses the tense used for future time reference is present tense:

*The murderer will have been arrested when she **will/may/could arrive** next week.*

7. A useful comparative discussion of tense, as well as aspect and mood, in a wide range of languages, appears in Sandra Chung and Alan Timberlake, "Tense, aspect, and mood," in Timothy Shopen, ed., *Language Typology and Syntactic Description*, vol. 3 (Cambridge, UK: Cambridge University Press, 1985), 203-258.

8. Sandra McKay, *Teaching Grammar: Form, Function and Technique* (New York: Pergamon Press, 1985), 11-13.

17

Understanding Aspect

"I have gone to have my hair cut yesterday," Olga said to me, *"where the hairdresser all wrong my hair was being cut. So I did not tipped her and she was being very distress."* Olga is having trouble with more than just her hairdresser. We can easily supply a more grammatical version:

> *I went to have my hair cut yesterday, and the hairdresser cut my hair all wrong. So I didn't tip her and she was very upset.*

But suppose Olga asks us to explain the rules covering the constructions above. That task is harder than simply providing a more grammatical version. In addition to other errors we will not dwell on, Olga has used incorrectly both perfect aspect *(I have gone)* and progressive aspect *(she was being)*.

In Chapter 16 we distinguished between the tense forms and their functions. We saw that in English tense has present and past forms. We then looked at the functions and found that the tense forms had other functions beside indicating time reference. In this chapter we'll adopt the same approach for aspect, dealing first with the forms and then with their functions.

Aspect is the general name given to verb forms used to signify certain ways in which an event is viewed or experienced. An event can be seen as a completed whole, as in progress, or as being repeated intermittently. English has two such aspects, *perfect* and *progressive*.

PERFECT AND PROGRESSIVE ASPECT FORMS

Perfect aspect is shown in the verb phrase by means of the verb *have*. When *have* is used to indicate aspect (rather than, say, possession), the verb immediately following it must be in its past participle form, the so-called *-en* form. In the formula presented in the last chapter, perfect aspect was shown like this:

have
<-en>

Now, let's look at some D-structures. We will show these structures as linear arrangements. We'll begin with a structure *without* perfect aspect:

Joyce Smaby **PAST eat** *the pumpkin.*

The past tense inflection gets marked on the verb immediately following it, converting *eat* into *ate*:

Joyce Smaby **ate** *the pumpkin.*

The next D-structure includes perfect aspect:

Joyce Smaby PAST have eat *the pumpkin.*
                        <-en>

Here, the past tense converts *have* into *had,* and the *<-en>* that goes with perfect *have* shifts onto the next verb, converting it into *eaten*:

Joyce Smaby **had eaten** *the pumpkin.*

Progressive aspect is shown in the verb phrase by means of the verb *be,* which, when used to indicate aspect, requires the verb immediately following it to be in its present participle form, the so-called *-ing* form. In the schema presented in the last chapter, progressive aspect was shown like this:

be
<-ing>

If in D-structure, the verb phrase has the verb *eat* after the progressive aspect form, as in the sentence shown here:

Joyce Smaby PAST   be   eat *the pumpkin*
                           <-ing>

then, in addition to the past tense converting *be* into *was,* the *<-ing>* converts *eat* into *eating*:

Joyce Smaby **was eating** *the pumpkin.*

PERFECT AND PROGRESSIVE ASPECT FORMS COMBINED

Let's see what happens when the two aspects occur together. The schema given in Chapter 16 for possible combinations of tense, aspect, and voice shows the perfect aspect always preceding progressive aspect, as well as passive *be <-en>*:

$$\left\{ \begin{array}{l} \text{TNS} \\ \text{MODAL} \\ \text{to} \end{array} \right\} \quad \begin{array}{l} \textit{have} \\ \textit{<-en>} \end{array} \quad \begin{array}{l} \textit{(be)} \\ \textit{<-ing>} \end{array} \quad \begin{array}{l} \textit{(be)} \\ \textit{<-en>} \end{array} \quad \text{V ...}$$

This allows such combinations as the following, with a modal and perfect and progressive aspects:

Joyce Smaby **may have   be** *be very careful about the publicity.*
                     <-en>   <-ing>

Since a modal requires the infinitive without *to* to follow it, the perfect aspect *have* remains *have,* while the *<-en>* converts progressive *be* into *been* and the *<-ing>* converts the main verb *be* into *being*:

Joyce Smaby **may have been being** *very careful about the publicity.*

In an alternative combination, infinitive *to* replaces the modal:

Colby believed Joyce Smaby   *to*   *have*   *be*   *be very careful about the publicity.*
                                        <-en>   <-ing>

which comes out as this somewhat bizarre sentence:

*Colby believed Joyce Smaby **to have been being** very careful about the publicity.*

The borderline acceptability of some sentences should not blind us to the general use-fulness of the schema, which works for the majority of the tense-aspect-voice combinations we encounter.

THE CORE SENSE OF PERFECT AND PROGRESSIVE ASPECT

Let's turn now to the kinds of situations in which perfect and progressive aspects are used. What dimensions of situations do the two aspects express?

Broadly speaking, predicates refer to actions, processes, and states. Does an action or process seem to occur once, like being born or exploding, or as a repeated activity, like striding or breathing? Is it momentary, like winking, or does it have the property of duration, like humming or vibrating? Is a state being referred to, such as knowing something or being Bolivian? Is the event viewed as a completed whole or is it viewed as ongoing at some time?

Notice that these are all questions about the "shape" or "time contour" of a situation, not about its time reference. These are all dimensions communicated by using some kind of aspect. Initially the term *aspect* was used to describe a specific kind of contrast in Russian grammar. An event could be presented in its clause as a completed activity or as an activity in progress.

A parallel contrast occurs in English. Compare the following examples:

*Jane Austen **was writing** her greatest novel.*
*Jane Austen **had written** her greatest novel.*

In both sentences the tense is past tense; the sentences refer to a time in the past. In the first sentence, the writing was going on at the time referred to. The progressive aspect verb *be* and its effect on the following verb indicate the ongoingness of the situation at that time. In the second sentence, the writing event was completed. This is indicated by the perfect aspect verb *have* and its effect on the following verb.

This same contrast occurs if present tense is used:

*Maureen Duffy **is now writing** a novel about two friends.*
*Maureen Duffy **has now written** a novel about two friends.*

Both sentences use present tense and refer to now, to the present. In the first sentence the writing of the novel is ongoing, whereas in the second it is completed. Thus progressive aspect presents an activity as ongoing, while perfect aspect presents it as completed.

FOUR FUNCTIONS OF THE PRESENT TENSE–PERFECT ASPECT COMBINATION

Aspect is a complicated phenomenon not because of the forms used to represent it, but because it is often impossible to separate the contribution of aspect to sentence interpretation from the contributions of the predicates that occur with the aspect. Consequently, the four major functions of perfect aspect described in this section are really only approximations, functions artificially ripped out of contexts that include not only a predicate but also a sentence and a discourse. A further complexity is that the functions of the past tense with perfect aspect (the *past perfect*) and present tense with perfect aspect (the *present perfect*) are not always parallel. Most of our discussion of perfect aspect will focus on the present perfect, since the use of the past perfect has been found to be rare in speech and relatively uncommon in written material.[1]

However, even approximations can be useful, both for our general understanding of perfect aspect and for pedagogy. The four functions of perfect aspect we'll look at are the past indefinite, state, change of state, and recurrent event usages. The examples chosen for discussion correspond well to our account of these usages, but you should be aware that other examples may be less clearcut.

In its *past indefinite* usage, the *present* perfect refers to events recent enough to be new and relevant to the present, thereby connecting the present to these past events. This function is sometimes called the "hot news" usage. The time the event happened is always left unspecified. Compare the following sentences:

> The Canadian prime minister **has taken** his family to visit New Brunswick.
> ?George Washington **has taken** Martha to visit the Marquis de Lafayette.

There is a Canadian prime minister, so it's quite possible that his family visit might be directly connected to some current situation. But the second sentence sounds strange. It implies that George and Martha Washington are still alive and that their visit is relevant to the present. The sentence has a question mark before it rather than an asterisk because it would be perfectly acceptable in a play about Washington's life. The past event could then be relevant to the time defined as present for the action of the play.

As our label *past indefinite* might indicate, the past time being referred to is not a definite point of time such as May 29, 1934, or last Tuesday evening. This explains the strangeness of the following example:

> The Canadian prime minister **has taken** his family to visit New Brunswick **on May 29, 1993** (or **last Tuesday**).

The perfect in this past indefinite usage contrasts in implication with the ordinary past tense. The contrast is shown by the next pair of sentences:

> Have you seen the Monet exhibition?
> Did you see the Monet exhibition?

The first sentence implies that the exhibition is still going on, while the second implies that it is over already.[2] (Notice again that *last Tuesday* can only be added to the second sentence, the one with the simple past. The simple past is thus a definite past.)

This contrast between a present tense perfect aspect indicating current relevance and an ordinary past tense is explicit in a comment by literary critic Christopher Ricks, writing just *after* the death of playwright Samuel Beckett:

> Beckett and I go back a long way. Not, though, in one another's company. Did I meet him? (Until just now, it was 'Have you ever met him?' Students have a way of asking.)[3]

Use of perfect aspect indicates that Beckett is still around, while the simple past makes no such commitment.[4]

The reason that no definite specification of a point of time is possible for perfect aspect is that otherwise a conflict in time reference would occur. Consider the following sentence:

On December 20, 1992, Maureen Duffy has written a novel about two friends.

The sentence sounds wrong. Two situations happening at different times are involved. The present situation in which the novel is already complete is seen in the light of a past event—the actual writing of the novel. But the major time perspective is that of the present. This is why we can't use point of time adverbials like the prepositional phrase *on December 20, 1992*. This date refers to the past, so it would contradict the present time reference indicated by the use of the present tense of *have*. We could, however, use the adverb *now*, since this adverb refers to the present time.

Olga's remark at the beginning of this chapter, *I **have gone** to have my hair cut yesterday*, contains the same kind of error. The adverb *yesterday* doesn't fit with the present time reference of *have gone*. There is a contradiction. From the context, we realize that Olga is really talking about a past event rather than a present situation seen in the light of a past event. So past tense should have been used without perfect aspect: *I **went** to have my hair cut yesterday*.

The second usage is the *state* usage. In its state usage, perfect aspect can be used to report the existence of a stable state of affairs over a continuous period of time up to the present. The following sentence is an example:

*Bangkok **has been** the capital of Thailand for many centuries.*

Note that the time phrase used here, *for many centuries*, is not a point of time phrase but one of duration. If the simple past tense had been used instead of the present tense with perfect aspect, the sentence would imply that Bangkok is no longer the capital of Thailand:

*Bangkok **was** the capital of Thailand for many centuries.*

Sometimes time duration *must* be specified for this state usage:

*George Washington has been dead **for almost two centuries.***

Without the duration prepositional phrase *for almost two centuries*, the sentence above would be unacceptable.

In the *change of state* usage, perfect aspect refers to a present state of affairs that has changed from an earlier state as the result of a past event. For this reason, it is sometimes called the *resultative perfect*.[5] Here are two examples:

*The two schools **have merged.***
*The owners **have agreed** to sell the property.*

The present tense form of *have* here indicates that the major focus of the clause is not the past event but the present result of that event. The present state of affairs described in the first example is that there is now only one school; the past event leading up to this result is the actual merging event. The present state of affairs described in the second example is that the property is for sale, as a result of a past agreement. Similarly, this sentence:

*Kirsten **has been chosen** as the new director.*

presents the present state of affairs (Kirsten is or will soon be the new director) as the result of the events involved in making the choice.

Finally, in its *recurrent event* usage, perfect aspect is used with predicates that refer to actions that are habitual or can be repeated more than once:

*Jonathan **has visited** his cousins daily.*
*The valley **has been flooded** every year since 1979.*

Frequency adverbials like *daily* and *every year* are almost always needed for this usage. The second of the two examples just given would have a state interpretation if the frequency adverbial *every year* had been omitted. The valley would be understood to have suffered continuously from a single flood.

PERFECT ASPECT IN MODAL CONSTRUCTIONS

What happens when perfect aspect combines not with past or present tense but with a modal? Once again, perfect aspect introduces an additional time reference. Compare the following sentences:

$$\text{When Louella March comes, she} \left\{ \begin{array}{l} \textit{may} \\ \textit{will} \\ \textit{might} \end{array} \right\} \text{confess.}$$

$$\text{When Louella March comes, she} \left\{ \begin{array}{l} \textit{may} \\ \textit{will} \\ \textit{might} \end{array} \right\} \text{have confessed.}$$

In the first sentence, the time of the confession follows the time of Louella's future arrival, but in the second sentence the use of perfect aspect shifts the confession back to a time previous to Louella's arrival.

Because of the rather tangled semantics of modals (to be discussed in the next two chapters), the interactions of modals and perfect aspect can be quite complex. Look, for example, at the following sentences with the modal *should*:

> The delegates should reject Yeltsin's proposals when they meet in Novosibirsk.
> The delegates should have rejected Yeltsin's proposals when they met in Novosibirsk.

In the first example *should* is generally interpreted as indicating that the speaker or writer believes rejection is advisable. When perfect aspect is added, as in the second example, the advisability interpretation is still valid, but additionally the sentence usually (but not always) indicates that the delegates did not reject the proposal. The same difference distinguishes *could*, *would*, and *ought to* from *could have*, *would have*, and *ought to have*.

Past Time Reference in Nonfinite Clauses

In embedded nonfinite clauses, perfect aspect, instead of past tense, is used to indicate past time reference. Look at the following pair of sentences:

> She believes that Clarissa **was born** at midnight on March 25.
> She believes Clarissa **to have been born** at midnight on March 25.

In the second sentence, which closely paraphrases the first, perfect aspect has replaced the past tense in the embedded clause. Note that this perfect aspect form allows a definite time phrase, *at midnight on March 25*. In finite clauses a time phrase like this cannot occur with the present tense–perfect aspect combination:

> *She believes that Clarissa **has been born** at midnight on March 25.

The reason the definite time phrase *at midnight on March 25* is possible with the *nonfinite* embedded clause is because perfect aspect in that clause stands for past tense rather than just aspect, so the two times referred to are both past. There is thus no present time–past time conflict.

Perfect Aspect in Narrative Finite Clauses

When past tense is used with perfect aspect, we do find time markers like *on December 20, 1992*:

> *Ackroyd was surprised when he checked the records in April 1993. A supercomputer had written the novel about Silicon Valley* **on December 20, 1992**.

Two times, both past, are involved—the time of the writing of the novel and the time when the records were checked. The use of perfect aspect in the second sentence marks the past writing event as being prior in time to the record checking event, even though the later event is reported first. The past perfect is a useful way to indicate the relative time reference of events not presented in chronological order.

This is clear when we compare the following two examples. In the first, past tense is used with perfect aspect, whereas in the second, past tense only is used:

> *General Rodriguez spurred his horse and rode to the wooden fort. The defenders had left, and the place was empty and desolate.*

> *General Rodriguez spurred his horse and rode to the wooden fort. The defenders left, and the place was empty and desolate.*

In the first version, when General Rodriguez arrives, the defenders are no longer in the fort, whereas in the second version, the defenders leave after General Rodriguez arrives. Thus, in the first version, the past perfect enables the writer to describe the state of affairs at a particular time by referring to a relevant previous event.

Notice that the explanation of the second version uses the word *after*. Like the tense and perfect aspect combinations discussed here, time introducers like *after* and *before* are used to mark the time relation of one event to another. These time introducers, then, can be alternatives to perfect aspect. Subordinate time clauses introduced by *before* and *after* may also use perfect aspect to relate past times to each other:

> *After the defenders had left, the general arrived.*
> *After the defenders left, the general arrived.*

This isn't surprising if we think about the meaning of *before* and *after*. These words themselves mark the relative order of events.

When past events are reported in the order in which they occurred, there is no need for perfect aspect. Consider, for example, this excerpt from a Hemingway novel:

> *When he was even with him and had the fish's head against the bow he could not believe his size. But he untied the harpoon rope from the bitt, passed it through the fish's gills and out his jaws, made a turn around his sword then passed the rope through the other gill, made another turn around the bill and knotted the double rope and made it fast to the bitt in the bow.*[6]

The excerpt reports a sequence of actions, all in the past tense.

However, when events are reported out of their time sequence, the past perfect can be very useful. Here is another excerpt from the same novel:

> *They sat on the Terrace and many of the fishermen made fun of the old man and he was not angry....The successful fishermen of that day were already in and had butchered their marlin out and [had] carried them laid full length across two planks, with two men staggering at the end of each plank....*

*"Santiago," the boy **said**.*
*"Yes," the old man **said**.*[7]

Hemingway uses ordinary past tense forms to report each event occurring in the *main* sequence from the time "they" sat on the Terrace. The events that had occurred prior to their arrival are reported in clauses with the past tense–perfect aspect combination. These events, which occur *out of the main sequence*, form a background to the main sequence. Apart from two participles, the only other verb form in this background sentence is *were already*, in which the adverb *already* renders unnecessary a perfect aspect construction. The past tense–perfect aspect combination, then, is used in narrative to mark past events that are out of sequence. Typically, events reported out of sequence serve as background for the main narrative, the foreground, in which ordinary past tense is used. Perfect aspect can play a useful role in providing a "setting" for a segment of narrative. Here is one example, a newspaper paragraph:

*"We **have lost** a lot of our authority as a leader in the world," says James O'Leary, an economic consultant to United States Trust Company. "Ten or fifteen years ago we **didn't** have to pay much attention to what happened elsewhere. Now we **are** just one of the boys."*

The present tense–perfect aspect combination in the first sentence refers to the *present* situation in which it is claimed this country no longer has the leadership authority it once had. Because of its dual time reference, it also refers to the *past* process of losing much of that authority. Two distinct times are thus referred to in the first sentence, which, in this way, provides the setting for the contrast between the past and the present expressed in the next two sentences. The second sentence, which uses just the past tense, refers to the earlier, more advantageous situation, while the third, using the present tense, refers to the present apparently unfortunate situation. An obvious causal relation is implied between the present state of affairs reported in the third sentence and the past events in the first sentence. There is a similar clear causal relation between the following two sentences, one with the past perfect, the other with the ordinary past tense:

Grendel was not hungry. He had devoured three warriors just an hour earlier.

The causal implication remains even if the order of the two sentences is reversed.

Progressive Aspect and the Stative–Dynamic Contrast

To understand progressive aspect, we need to recall the distinction between the *dynamic* and *stative* uses of predicates discussed in Chapter 14. Predicates that are used dynamically signify actions, processes, and events, that is, situations in which something happens. Examples of predicates that are normally (in some cases, always) used dynamically include *talk, jump, persuade, be tactful, become, be a coward, decide, die, deteriorate,* and *prosper*. Predicates that are used statively signify states (mental and physical), relations, and attributes. Nothing is viewed as happening, it just "is." Examples of predicates that are normally (in some cases, always) used statively include *know, believe, be equal, resemble, be tall, be angry, own, be in/on/at, signify, be a teacher,* and *be dead*.

Keep in mind that most predicates are not inherently dynamic or stative but, rather, are *used* dynamically or statively. Many predicates that are generally used statively can also be used dynamically, and vice versa. For convenience, however, we'll use the terms "dynamic predicate" for predicates that are used dynamically and "stative predicate" for predicates that are used statively.

Dynamic predicates differ from stative predicates in that, to refer to the time of utterance, they normally require both present tense *and* progressive aspect. Of the two examples that follow, only the first, which includes progressive aspect, is used to refer to the time of utterance:

> "Amy and Rudolph **are dancing** the polka," Gretchen told us.
> "Amy and Rudolph **dance** the polka," Gretchen told us.

In the first example Gretchen is telling us what is happening at the moment of utterance. But in the second, Gretchen is talking about habitual activity. Amy and Rudolph may not be dancing at the moment of utterance.

The same situation holds when the dynamic predicates are adjectives or noun phrases. The predicate adjective *tactless* refers in the first example below to behavior at the time of utterance and in the second to characteristic behavior:

> Emilio **is being** tactless.
> Emilio **is** tactless.

In the following two examples, we see the same contrast with the predicate noun phrase *a reckless idiot*:

> Emilio **is being** a reckless idiot.
> Emilio **is** a reckless idiot.

This use of a present tense–progressive aspect combination to refer to the time of utterance has led some textbook writers to redefine the combination as the "real" present tense. This redefinition mistakenly treats tense and time reference as essentially the same. Moreover, it does not take into account the fact that the combination rarely occurs with stative predicates.

Here we'll use a notion from phonology, that of *markedness*. A grammatical construction or usage that is *unmarked* is the one native speakers regard as the norm. One that is *marked* is a less ordinary form or usage. Markedness is not a simple two-way distinction, however. There are degrees of markedness. A very unusual form or usage may be characterized as *more marked* than a slightly unusual form or usage.

There are more marked usages of the present tense with dynamic verbs, usages that can refer to the time of utterance without using progressive aspect. They occur in limited contexts such as play-by-play commentaries by sportscasters:

> Holmes **races** toward the net and Perez **moves** left to intercept. But it's no use. Holmes is veering to his left and now he **leaps** forward and …yes …he **scores**. Holmes has done it again!

or stage directions:

> The ghost **enters** and **marches** ponderously toward Horatio.

As we noted in Chapter 16, present tense forms like these can also refer to past time, when the speaker removes the distancing effect of past tense inflection to create a closer, more vivid impression of a sequence of events.

To refer to the time of utterance, stative predicates take present tense form without progressive aspect:

> Holly Vasquez **is** tall now.
> *Holly Vasquez **is being** tall now.
> Bronwen **knows** Welsh.
> *Bronwen **was knowing** Welsh.
> 423 divided by 9 **equals** 47.
> *423 divided by 9 **is equaling** 47.

With these predicates, progressive aspect also cannot occur with past tense forms or modals:

> *Holly Vasquez **was being** tall.
> *Bronwen **should be knowing** Welsh.

What happens when predicates that are normally stative are used dynamically? As the following sentences show, such predicates can then be used with progressive aspect (with a few exceptions such as *know*):

> Kimio **is believing** that he was mistaken.
> Zacchary **is seeing** the dean right now.
> Zacchary **was seeing** the dean then.
> Zacchary **should be seeing** the dean now.

The sentence about Kimio has a variety of possible interpretations depending on the context in which it is uttered. It can mean something like "believes more and more" or "is coming to believe" or "believes at this moment (but this may change)." Belief is being treated as a process rather than a state. Similarly, in the sentence about Zacchary, *see* does not have its usual stative meaning, but instead refers to an action, that of having an interview or a consultation. *See* can also have another dynamic meaning—that of having dates with someone—in which case progressive aspect is again possible:

> **Is** Jane **seeing** anyone nowadays?

Some Other Functions of Progressive Aspect

We've seen that for dynamic predicates present tense must be used with progressive aspect if the time referred to is the time of utterance. If, however, future time adverbs accompany present tense progressive forms, the sentences are interpreted as referring to future time, usually in the sense of a present plan for future action:

> *Tomorrow* she **is leaving** for Kuala Lumpur.

A tighter kind of scheduling is indicated by present tense without progressive aspect:

> *Tomorrow* she **leaves** for Kuala Lumpur.

As you might expect, stative predicates can't be used for this, even without progressive aspect:

> ***Tomorrow* she **knows** Welsh.

Dynamic predicates with past tense–progressive aspect usually refer to activity in progress at some time prior to the moment of utterance. Compare these two sentences, one with just past tense, the other with past tense and progressive aspect:

> Jason **cooked** an omelette.
> Jason **was cooking** an omelette.

The first version tells us that Jason completed cooking the omelette. An end point is clearly indicated, one prior to the moment of utterance. The omelette-cooking thus had a beginning and an end. The progressive aspect version doesn't necessarily tell us that the omelette actually got cooked. No end point is indicated. What the progressive version does is focus on duration, stretching out the time so that we "see" a segment of that time rather than a completed event.

This property of duration makes progressive aspect very useful when relating two or more situations expressed as separate clauses. The two events reported in the following sentence without progressive aspect occur sequentially. First one happens and then the other:

*When Turpin entered the hall, the choir **sang** a medieval chant.*

But the events are not sequential when progressive aspect is used in the main clause:

*When Turpin entered the hall, the choir **was singing** a medieval chant.*

No starting point or end point is indicated for the singing in the second sentence. The two situations—the choir singing and Turpin's entry—overlap in time. The duration of the singing activity was from before Turpin's entry until some unspecified time after his entry.

The same properties can be seen in sentences with modals, like the following:

*When Turpin enters the hall, the choir **might sing** a medieval chant.*
*When Turpin enters the hall, the choir **might be singing** a medieval chant.*

In the first sentence the singing starts after Turpin enters, while in the second the singing event is already underway when he enters and provides a temporal frame for his entry.

Because of its focus on duration, progressive aspect suggests a certain temporariness to the situation referred to. Compare these two pairs of sentences:

*Jagdish **lives** in Calcutta. He **works** for a steel company.*
*Jagdish **is living** in Calcutta. He **is working** for a steel company.*

Speakers would use the second pair of sentences if they viewed Jagdish's location and employment as temporary. *not all the time, however*

THE FUNCTIONS OF COMBINED PERFECT AND PROGRESSIVE ASPECT

The functions of the combination of perfect and progressive aspects are more or less what might be predicted from the functions of the individual aspects. Suppose that we are reading a paragraph beginning:

Alison and Laura arrived at the apartment at seven o'clock.

and that this beginning is followed by one of these three sentences:

a. *Eric **had cooked** an omelette.*
b. *Eric **was cooking** an omelette.*
c. *Eric **had been cooking** an omelette.*

In the (a) sentence, which has only perfect aspect, the omelette was in a finished state at the time the sentence refers to. The cooking activity was already over. In the (b) sentence, which has only progressive aspect, the cooking was still underway. What about the (c) sentence, in which perfect and progressive aspects are combined? The question is whether the *completion* sense of the perfect overwhelms the *ongoing* sense of the progressive.

We understand the sentence to mean that, at the time the two women arrived, Eric had finished all the cooking he was going to do then for an omelette, but we can't tell from the sentence whether the cooking of the omelette had been completed. He might conceivably go back later to cook it. The completion sense of the perfect has applied to the duration sense of the progressive, not to the sense of the main verb following. The *duration* of the cooking was over. Here is the schema given in the last chapter, this time with the positions numbered from 1 to 5:

$$\left\{ \begin{array}{c} \text{TENSE} \\ \text{MODAL} \\ \text{I} \end{array} \right\} \quad \begin{array}{c} have \\ \text{<-en>} \\ 2 \end{array} \quad \begin{array}{c} (be) \\ \text{<-ing>} \\ 3 \end{array} \quad \begin{array}{c} (be) \\ \text{<-en>} \\ 4 \end{array} \quad \begin{array}{c} V \dots \\ \text{to} \\ 5 \end{array}$$

The perfect aspect *have* in position 2 for *had been cooking* affects the interpretation of the constituent in position 3, progressive *be -ing*. In its turn, the progressive aspect *be* affects the main verb *cook* in position 4. In other words, each aspect directly affects only the constituent following it.

EXPLAINING THE ORDER OF THE CONSTITUENTS IN THE SCHEMA

The schema shows the order of the constituents, but we also need to *explain* this ordering. Why can't modals follow perfect aspect instead of preceding it? Why can't progressive aspect precede perfect aspect instead of following it? Surely there must be reasons. What we have is essentially a sequence of verbs, since, with the exception of tense and the suffixes associated with aspect and voice, all the constituents are verbs of one sort or another. If we look at these verbs one at a time, we may understand the reasons for their ordering.

The first constituent in a finite clause sequence must be either a modal or a verb that carries the tense suffix. This means that all the other verbs must be in their nonfinite form. Since modals don't have a nonfinite form, a modal must precede any other verbs and cannot be followed by another modal:

> *She **might could** jump over that fence.[8]

This is the explanation for the position of the modal.

Next, why does perfect *have* occupy position 2? For a possible answer to this we must go to nonfinite clauses. Earlier in this chapter we compared the following sentences:

> She believes that Clarissa **was born** at midnight on March 25.
> She believes Clarissa **to have been born** at midnight on March 25.

We noted that in the embedded nonfinite clause of the second sentence, perfect aspect replaces the past tense. The tense, indicating the time reference, appears as *have*. Like any other tense marking it must precede any sequence of verbs.

In position 3 we find progressive *be*. As we've seen, progressive *be* can only be used with dynamic predicates, those signifying actions and processes. To affect the predicate, progressive *be* should therefore be after perfect *have* and next to the verb standing for the action or process. This is usually the case, except when the clause is passive. In that case, the passive voice *be* intervenes in position 4. The passive voice *be* is in this position because only the main verb is in the passive voice.[9]

CONSTITUENT STRUCTURES

The constituent structure for sequences of aspect and voice constituents shows them as verbs, each with an embedded verb phrase following it. Leaving aside the tense, since that belongs to the Inflection constituent, the sequence *have been watching* looks like this:

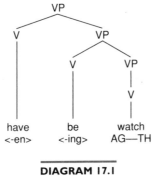

DIAGRAM 17.1

So the sentence *The students may have been watching the orchestra* should look like this:

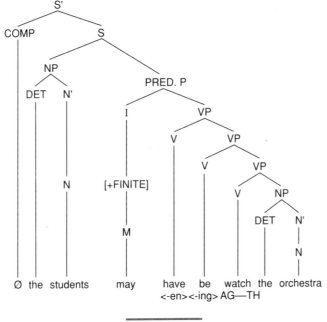

DIAGRAM 17.2

Finally, the passive voice sentence *The measure has been passed by a large majority* should look like this (in D-structure, remember, the theme argument, in this case, *the measure*, occurs right after the main verb, which assigns its thematic role):

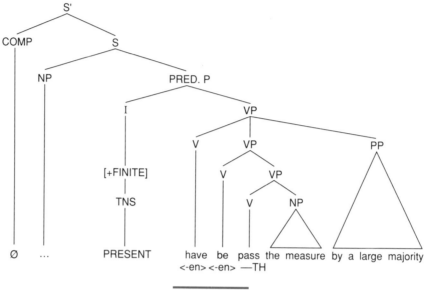

DIAGRAM 17.3

SUMMARY

Aspect describes the internal time structure of an event—it is used to signify certain ways in which an event is viewed or experienced. An event can be seen as a completed whole, as in progress, or as being repeated intermittently. Aspect deals with the "shape" or "time contour" of a situation, not with its time reference. English has two aspects, *perfect* and *progressive*. The forms these aspects take are easily recognizable. Perfect aspect *have* requires the verb following to be in its past participle (or *-en*) form, while progressive *be* requires the verb following to be in its present participle (or *-ing*) form.

$$\left\{ \begin{array}{c} \text{TNS} \\ \text{MODAL} \\ \text{to} \end{array} \right\} \quad \begin{array}{c} have \\ \text{<-en>} \end{array} \quad \begin{array}{c} \text{(be)} \\ \text{<-ing>} \end{array} \quad \begin{array}{c} \text{(be)} \\ \text{<-en>} \end{array} \quad \text{V ...}$$

The meanings the two aspects express do not all fall into neat categories. But an approximation of their most typical usages is both possible and useful. Perfect aspect characteristically presents an event as a completed activity, while progressive aspect presents it as an activity in progress. Perfect aspect indicates either a relation between two situations that occurred at different times or a single, stationary state of affairs that lasts from an earlier time to the time being focused on, typically the time of utterance. In both cases, two times are referred to. Perfect aspect can be viewed as having four major usages. The *past indefinite* (or "hot news") usage presents events recent enough to be new and relevant to the present, thereby connecting the present to these past events. The *state* usage portrays a stable state of affairs over a continuous period of time. The *change of state* usage presents a state of affairs that has changed from an earlier state as the result of a past event. Finally, the *recurrent event* usage portrays actions that are habitual or can be repeated more than once.

Perfect aspect is used in nonfinite clauses to indicate past time reference. In finite clauses, perfect aspect can indicate the relative time reference of events not presented in chronological order. In this respect, it resembles the time introducing words *before* and *after*.

Dynamic predicates take progressive aspect to present an event as in progress rather than being bounded by a starting point and an end point. A number of other functions arise from this basic one. For example, progressive aspect is used to indicate time overlap between two situations, the one with progressive aspect framing and including the time span of the other, which does not have progressive aspect. With present tense, progressive aspect is sometimes used to indicate an event scheduled to happen at some later time.

EXERCISE SET 17

1. Without correcting the sentences, explain what is wrong about the use or non-use of aspect in the following sentences:

  a. *She has visited Sacramento on June 6, 1987.*
  b. *I lived in Baltimore since 1979.*
  c. *Ignacio was knowing very well Spanish.*
  d. *Mark Twain has written* The Adventures of Huckleberry Finn, *a novel about the adventures of a white boy and an escaped slave on the Mississippi.*

2. If sentence 1d is wrong, how would you explain why this next sentence is perfectly acceptable?

  Mark Twain has been popular for many, many years.

3. Explain the differences in meaning between the sentences in each pair of examples:

  A 1. *She has gotten worse.*
      2. *She has been getting worse.*
  B 1. *We have experienced the problem of acid rain for eighteen years.*
      2. *We experienced the problem of acid rain for eighteen years.*
  C 1. *Marcus hadn't read that book.*
      2. *Marcus didn't read that book.*

4. Which of the four usages described for perfect aspect are illustrated in these sentences?

  a. *Bertrand has been a vegetarian since 1959.*
  b. *The company had denied any pollution violations at every state hearing for two decades.*
  c. *Alison Lurie has written a fascinating study of children's literature.*
  d. *Cyril has had at least five major operations in the past five years.*
  e. *Cyril has become a vegetarian.*

5. Draw D-structure trees for the following sentences:

  a. *Gabriel has been waiting for you.*
  b. *Hernando may be arrested by the secret police.*

6. Provide examples for each of the following guidelines for learners to tense and aspect use. Do you see any specific problems with these guidelines? What is your general opinion of them?

PAST TIME

  a. If events or states ended before now and have clear time boundaries or occurred repeatedly, use PAST TENSE.

b. If events occurred at some indefinite time in the past for which no time points can be specified, use PRESENT TENSE WITH PERFECT ASPECT.
c. If actions or processes continued over time without clear boundaries and/or served as background for other situations, use PAST TENSE WITH PROGRESSIVE ASPECT.

NOW
a. If actions or processes began in the past and continue now, use PRESENT TENSE WITH BOTH PERFECT AND PROGRESSIVE ASPECTS.
b. If states, relations, and attributes began in the past and continue now, use PRESENT TENSE WITH PERFECT ASPECT.
c. If states are in existence now, without reference to the past, use PRESENT TENSE.
d. If actions and processes are ongoing now, use PRESENT TENSE WITH PROGRESSIVE ASPECT.

GENERAL PHENOMENA
a. If habits or general truths and facts are specified, use PRESENT TENSE, or, if they refer to past situations, use PAST TENSE.

7. Describe the use of tense and aspect in the following extract. It is not necessary for you to correct any errors. Try to formulate generalizations about specific usages and/or suggest explanations.

I have been knowing many languages. When I am younger, my father was being alive and I was clever in to speak Panjabi because my father is from there, but now it has been forgetful to me. My father was being dead so I am not hearing the language. Naturally I am still speaking Gujerati because it is my first language. Gujerati is being a language so beautiful which many professors were writing books about it. Naturally it is being pride for me.

8. David Wallace has suggested the following examples to help students understand the differences in time reference between the past perfect and the ordinary past:

a. *Did we see the beginning of the film?*
    The film began when we arrived.
    The film had begun when we arrived.
b. *Was the baby asleep when I saw her?*
    When I last saw the baby, she was crying herself to sleep.
    When I last saw the baby, she had cried herself to sleep.[10]

Invent three more examples.

NOTES

1. A. Ota, *Tense and Aspect of Present Day American English* (Tokyo: Kenkyusha, 1963).

2. These examples are discussed within a formal semantic framework in Geoffrey Leech's insightful study, *Towards a Semantic Description of English* (London: Longman, 1969).

3. Christopher Ricks, "Diary," *London Review of Books* (January 1990): 21.

4. Interestingly, the subject constituent is the one that especially has to be a recent entity. So a sentence like *The Roman armies have invaded Britain* sounds a little strange, whereas its passive counterpart, *Britain has been invaded by the Roman armies,* is less strange. This must be because Britain still exists, whereas the Roman armies were disbanded many centuries ago.

5. See, for example, Jack Richards, "Introducing the perfect: an exercise in pedagogical grammar," *TESOL Quarterly* 13 (1979): 495-500.

6. Ernest Hemingway, *The Old Man and the Sea* (New York: Scribner Classic/Collier Edition, 1986), 96.

7. Ibid., 12-13.

8. In some dialects of English, however, forms like this actually do occur.

9. This account is roughly based on a more detailed and theoretically oriented account within a very different framework, in James D. McCawley, *The Syntactic Phenomena of English*, vol. 1 (Chicago: University of Chicago Press, 1988), 207-229.

10. David Wallace, "Introducing the Past Perfect" (ms., Department of ESL, University of Hawai'i, 1983).

18

Modals

The modal verbs are the hardest verb forms for non-native speakers to master. ESL and EFL teachers are familiar with sentences like the following (written by a German university student who had visited Washington with some friends):

> Last year we could have to visit the White House. I was very disappoint. Next time we will must to apply earlier for a pass.

Presumably the speaker and her friends applied too late for a pass. We might correct these sentences as follows:

> Last year we could have visited the White House. I was very disappointed. Next time we must (or will have to) apply earlier for a pass.

Indeed, we might even question whether words like *could* and *must* really are verbs. After all, negative forms like *not* or *n't* follow them instead of preceding them, as they normally do for verbs. Additionally, these modals don't take the *-ing* suffix, they don't take the singular *-s* suffix, and, as the following example shows, they don't occur as infinitives with *to*:

> *The lawyer advised him to must learn English.

In fact, as we'll see, there are yet more differences. To make matters worse, modals themselves don't form a single, uniform class. There are many irregularities in both form and interpretation.

MODALS AS DEFECTIVE VERBS

Many of the modals were originally ordinary verbs taking the full range of verb suffixes. Over time these verbs became increasingly specialized in their functions and so restricted as to their distribution that we might reasonably doubt whether they still belong to the category verb. In addition to true modals, or *core modals*, there are others that express the same kinds of notions as modals but are multiword forms and behave more like ordinary verbs. Since these often paraphrase modal meanings, they are called *periphrastic modals*. We'll look first at core modals and then at periphrastic modals.

The following are among the core modals, those least like other verbs: *may, might, must, can, could, will, would, shall, should, ought, need,* and *dare*. Now how can we explain the differences from other verbs? Here are the points of difference and a tentative explanation for each:

1. Core modals take no tense suffixes because, unlike other verbs, they are in the Inflection constituent of their clause and are therefore alternatives to tense.

2. Core modals cannot occur after *to* or in imperatives because core modals are *finite* forms, whereas infinitives and imperatives are nonfinite.

3. There cannot be more than one core modal in a sequence. The schema shown in Chapter 17 for the possible sequences of auxiliary and main verbs has only one slot for a tense or a modal. Thus there cannot be more than one core modal in a sequence.

4. We noted earlier that core modals never take tense suffixes. Although core modals occur with perfect and progressive aspects and passive voice, neither aspect nor the passive can convert a modal into an *-en* or *-ing* form. To do this, they would have to immediately *precede* the modal. But in fact they *follow* any core modal.

5. The negative forms *not* and *-n't* precede ordinary verbs but can only *follow* a core modal.

6. The core modals, with one exception, *ought,* can be followed only by bare infinitives, not by infinitives with *to*. A few other verbs, however, have this same restriction.[1]

CORE MODALS

Some core modals are more irregular than others. This is not surprising, since modals are one-time regular verbs that changed their function over time; historical change proceeds at a different pace for each form. Let's look at some of the more complex core modals.

Two core modals, *need* and *dare*, still have main verb counterparts. Compare the first pair of sentences, which use the modals, with the second pair, which use the main verb counterparts:[2]

> He need not reply to their letter.
> He dare not reply to their letter.

> He doesn't need to reply to their letter.
> He doesn't dare (to) reply to their letter.

Notice that the modal forms have no tense marking, are followed by their negative, and do not allow the *to*-infinitive. All this is as we would expect. But the modal *need* is exceptional in that it can occur only in negative clauses, as above, and in interrogative clauses:

> **Need** he reply?

In most dialects of English, the modal *need* is not common, especially in interrogatives, where it sounds very formal. The modal *dare* is even less common. In fact, some speakers even mark it occasionally for past tense, as though it were a main verb:

> He **dared** not reply.

Far more common than *need* and *dare* are the following somewhat irregular modals, each of which consists of two words:

ought to,   used to,[3]   had better,   would rather

Ought and *used* are so strongly connected to the following *to* that, in informal speech, the words merge:

> She **oughta** *have a celebration for them.*
> She **useta** *have lotsa (= lots of) parties.*

The *to* seems to be part of the modal rather than the infinitive marker *to*. In very informal use, these forms can have negative counterparts in which the modals behave like verbs in the verb phrase in using a negative with *do*:

> She **didn't oughta** *leave like that.*
> She **didn't useta** *leave like that.*

instead of these more prestigious forms:

> She **ought not** (or **oughtn't**) *to leave like that.*
> She **used not** *to leave like that.*

The core modal *ought*, although followed by *to*, is very close semantically to *should*. *Used to* is actually far closer in meaning to an aspect than to other modals in that it is used to mark a past situation as habitual if a dynamic predicate is used or as a longstanding situation if a stative predicate is used. *Had better* is a somewhat informal modal with a meaning between that of *should* and *must*. Although its *had* looks like the past tense of *have*, no other form of *have* can be used. Finally, *would rather* has the meaning "prefer to." The *would* and *rather* are separated in interrogatives but not in negatives:

> **Wouldn't** *you* **rather** *be driving a Buick?*
> *I* **would rather** *not, thank you.*

Some speakers substitute *had rather* for *would rather*. *Had rather* is a form that goes back at least to the fifteenth century. It is not used, however, in interrogatives in modern English:

> **Hadn't you rather be driving a Buick?*

Some Relationships Among the Core Modals

The core modals were once like other verbs in having present and past tense forms. The modals in the right-hand column were once the past tense forms of the modals in the left-hand column:

may	might
can	could
will	would
shall	should

Except in the case of *shall* and *should*, which today are quite distinct from each other, two major remnants of this relationship survive.

The first remnant is seen when direct quotations are replaced by reported speech. Reported speech often shows *tense shifting* in which, for example, present tense forms are replaced by past tense forms. As part of this tense shifting, the former present tense forms on the left may be replaced by the former past tense forms on the right. Compare these examples:

A

*"A solution to our disagreements **may** be imminent at this time," said Mr. Morita. "If the negotiators **can** work out a good compromise, I am sure the government **will** support it vigorously. I look forward to a better trading relationship."*

B

*Mr. Morita said that a solution to their disagreements **might** be imminent at that time. He commented that if the negotiators **could** work out a good compromise, he was sure the government **would** support it vigorously. He looked forward to a better trading relationship.*

When the quoted speech in (A) is converted into reported speech in (B), the modals *may, can,* and *will* are changed to *might, could,* and *would.* Notice that the present tense forms *am* and *look* have become *was* and *looked.* The change in the modal verb forms thus corresponds to the change in the tenses of the other verbs. In both cases, the shift marks a distancing from the immediacy of the direct quotation, an effect shown also by the change from first to third person pronouns and from *at this time* to *at that time.*[4]

The second remnant of the former past-present tense relationship between the modals comes in the use of past tense forms as more tentative, polite versions of present tense forms. As we saw in Chapter 16, a question like *Do you want to see me now?* can be replaced by *Did you want to see me now?* In the same way, sentences with the modals listed in the left-hand column can be replaced by sentences with the modals listed in the right-hand column:

Can *you finish them today?*
Could *you finish them today?*

Past Time Reference

Since modals don't have tense, there has to be some other way to refer to past time. The trouble is that any verb following right after a modal has to be a bare infinitive, so it too cannot take a past tense suffix. What happens then?

The following form refers to the utterance time:

There **may be** *some errors now in that computer program.*

Now, instead of referring to the utterance time, let's refer to an earlier time ("then"):

There **may have been** *some errors then in that computer program.*

What we did to make the clause refer to an earlier time was add after the modal the bare infinitive verb of perfect aspect, that is, *have.* This *have* converts the verb following it into the past participle (or *-en*) form, as we noted in Chapter 17. Thus the following sentence:

The delegates **should reject** *Yeltsin's proposals when they meet in Novosibirsk.*

can be changed to one referring to the past if perfect aspect *have* is used:

The delegates **should have rejected** *Yeltsin's proposals when they met in Novosibirsk.*

In the second sentence, *meet* was changed to past tense and perfect aspect was added after the modal.

PERIPHRASTIC MODALS

Periphrastic modals are multiword verb idioms used to express modal notions like possibility, probability, and necessity. With two exceptions, *have to* and *have got to*, their first word is always a form of *be*. These periphrastic modals play an important role in the system, but they hardly deserve the same label, *modal*, as words like *can* and *may*; as we shall see, they act much more like ordinary verbs. Each periphrastic modal corresponds approximately to one or more core modals. Compare these pairs of sentences in which the first sentence of each pair has a core modal, while the second contains a periphrastic modal:

1a. Chen-wen { **must** / **has to** } help us with this.

b. Chen-wen { **is obliged to** / **has got to**[5] } help us with this.

2a. Chen-wen { **can't/won't** / **is unable to** } help us with this.

b. Chen-wen is { **unable to** / **unwilling to** / **not able to** } help us with this.

3a. Chen-wen { **will** / **is going to** } help us with this.

b. Chen-wen is { **due to** / **about to** } help us with this.

The sentences with the periphrastic modals are not exact paraphrases of those with core modals, but their meanings are similar. Note that the negative *not* in *not able to* has as a counterpart the prefix *un-*, which is part of the periphrastic modal *be unable to*. The core modal *will* has periphrastic modal counterparts in addition to those given here; like *is due to*, they have narrower meanings than does *will*. They are the modals *be to* and *be supposed to*, referring specifically to prearranged future action. Yet other periphrastic modals include *be apt to* and *be likely to*, which correspond roughly to *may*; *be bound to*, which corresponds to *must*; and *be supposed to*, which corresponds to *should*.

These periphrastic modals differ from core modals in two significant respects. First, they can be marked for tense. Their verbs, *have* and *be*, have both past tense and third person present tense forms. Thus these modals don't belong in the Inflection constituent, but form part of the verb phrase. Second, they can be preceded by a core modal, a further indication that they don't belong in the Inflection constituent:

*Eunice Blenkinsop **may have to** take over that position.*

Although the *to* in a periphrastic modal is the *to* of the infinitive verb that follows, it has become part of the periphrastic modal. This incorporation is reflected in speech, where *have to* often becomes *hafta, supposed to* becomes *sposeta, got to* becomes *gotta,*[6] *going to* becomes *gonna,* and sometimes *is to* sounds like *izta.*

What kind of constituent structures can we assign to sentences with periphrastic modals? Grammarians have not come up with good answers to this question, even for S-structures. D-structures are yet more puzzling. There seems little point here in arbitrarily positing tree structures for such eccentric forms. We suggest using the abbreviation triangle, as in this next tree, for the sentence *Morgan was going to translate those documents:*

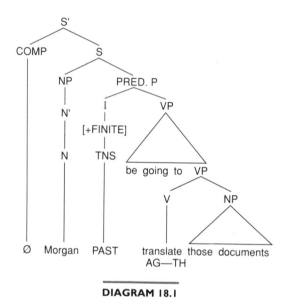

DIAGRAM 18.1

SUMMARY

Modals do not form a single, uniform class. Both their forms and their interpretations can present serious difficulties for learners of English. The core modals occur instead of past or present tense in the Inflection constituent of a finite clause. Only one core modal can occur in each clause; it takes no verb suffixes, never follows *to* as an infinitive, and, when it occurs with perfect and progressive aspects and passive voice, it is always the first item of the sequence following the subject. Any verb immediately following it must be a bare infinitive. The negatives *-n't* and *not* are inserted immediately after the modal. Forms like *may* and *might* are related historically as present and past tense forms respectively, and traces of this relationship survive in the optional tense shifting phenomenon of reported speech and in the use of the old past tense forms as more polite, less direct forms. More complex core modals such as *had better, would rather, ought to,* and *used to* consist of more than one word yet have the other characteristics of the core modals (if we consider the *to* on some of them as part of the modal rather than the infinitive marker *to*). The perfect aspect verb *have,* which converts a verb following it into a past participle, sometimes functions as a past tense marking for modals. Periphrastic modals are closer in many ways to ordinary verbs in that they form part of the verb phrase, allow verb suffixes, including tense markings, and can occur with other modals in the same clause.

EXERCISE SET 18

1. Explain in your own words the following terms:
   a. bare infinitive
   b. periphrastic modal
   c. tense shifting
   d. defective verbs
   e. utterance time
   f. core modal

2. Write five sentences using core modals. Then paraphrase each sentence, without using a core modal. Comment very briefly on any semantic differences you note.

3. Convert the following direct speech into reported speech using tense shifting wherever appropriate:

   "I can't understand why Jackie won't complain," Mr. O'Brien said. "This whole problem can only get worse if she doesn't go to the manager."

   "She doesn't have to complain publicly," Elsie pointed out, "but she must do something. We may all be in danger if we can't persuade her to talk to him about this."

4. Compare the first sentence of each pair with the second. Explain the meaning differences between them.
   1a. *They could have canceled their trip.*
   b. *They were able to cancel their trip.*
   2a. *They don't have to leave before dawn.*
   b. *They mustn't leave before dawn.*
   3a. *The dam may have collapsed.*
   b. *The dam must have collapsed.*
   4a. *The nurses should eat at five o'clock.*
   b. *The nurses should have eaten at five o'clock.*
   5a. *"She must read to them every night," the judge ordered.*
   b. *"She must read to them every night," the teacher said, "or they wouldn't be improving so rapidly."*

5. How do core modals differ grammatically from ordinary verbs?

6. Draw D-structure trees for the following sentences:

   a. *Cecilio should have destroyed those files.*
   b. *Garibaldi may be planning to withdraw from the island.*

   (Note that the container verb *plan* is like *try* in requiring that its embedded clause have an [e] subject whose referent is the same as that for the container clause subject.)

7. Here are two situations for role playing in which modals or their equivalents could be used:
   a. You are a travel agent. You have some flight schedules from three or four airlines for travel to London, Osaka, or some other city. A customer comes in wanting convenient flights to one of those cities, perhaps with one stopover.
   b. You have been shopping for groceries. When you get to the checkout stand with a full basket of purchases, including ice cream, you find that you have no money or checks with you. You live fairly close to the store.

1. Choose one of these and write a dialogue between the two participants. (This would not necessarily be for use by students.) Exchange papers with someone and comment on the use of modals or modal-like notions in their dialogue.

2. Invent a third situation for role play that could help students to learn and practice modal usage.[7]

NOTES

1. Compare *make* with *force* in the following examples:

> They **made** the Estonian leaders **leave**.
> They **forced** the Estonian leaders **to leave**.

Other such verbs are *see, hear,* and sometimes *help* and *dare*. In this respect, then, the core modals are no different from some irregular verbs. Note that in the passive counterparts of sentences containing *make, see, hear,* and *help,* the bare infinitives are replaced by *to* infinitives; for example, *The Estonian leaders were **made to** leave.* The verb *dare,* not to be confused with the modal *dare* to be discussed soon, has no passive counterpart.

2. Note the irregularity of the main verb *dare* in allowing a bare infinitive verb after it.

3. This is not the same verb as the main verb *use,* pronounced [yuz], which has a very different meaning.

4. This is an optional distancing. If Mr. Morita's comment was very recent, perhaps from the previous day, then the possibilities and predictions might still have been valid and the speaker could have preserved the immediacy by keeping the original modals and keeping the other verbs in present tense. Here is a third version:

> C. *Mr. Morita said that a solution to their disagreements may be imminent at this time. He commented that if the negotiators can work out a good compromise, he is sure the government will support it vigorously. He looks forward to a better trading relationship.*

Although the past tense has been retained on the utterance verbs *said* and *commented,* the present tense forms *is* and *looks* are there to show that the situation is ongoing. The modals have the same function.

5. The periphrastic modal *have got to* is much less common in American English than in Commonwealth English. Even less common is the past tense form *had got to.* In American English it usually occurs in its contracted forms: *Mason told me he**'d gotta** make up his mind pretty soon.*

6. In very colloquial use, *gotta* is often used without *have* or *'d* preceding it:

> *I told you, ya gotta go!*

This usage is considered substandard by many speakers.

7. For some useful ideas about such projects, see Sandra McKay, *Teaching Grammar: Form, Function and Technique* (New York: Pergamon Press, 1985), 70-77 and 132-143.

19

Modal Meaning and Use

In Chapter 18, we saw that the modals are an eccentric bunch of forms. Their interpretations may seem just as eccentric. Take the periphrastic modals. You can *be going to* eat without *going* anywhere. You can *be able to* leave at dawn, without being very *able*. The core modals, so different syntactically from the periphrastic modals, are no less semantically complex.

It's not too hard to explain the formal characteristics to students—that modals must be followed by bare infinitives, that only one modal can occur in a sequence, and so forth. However, the semantic explanations are more difficult. For example, *could have*, like *were able*, refers to past possibility, but the two forms differ significantly in their uses. Consider the following pair of sentences:

> Last year we **could have** visited the White House.
> Last year we **were able to** visit the White House.

Clearly, the sentences differ as to whether the past possibility was realized, that is, whether the visit actually took place.

Modals can be a problem even for native English-speaking children. Research carried out with British children has shown that twelve-year-olds have not yet mastered the full semantics of these strange verbs, though they have already acquired the ability to use them in grammatical utterances.[1]

But it is possible to find some system, some orderliness, in the apparent semantic chaos. After all, modals communicate a cluster of similar semantic notions in English. We are going to look at the core meanings of the various modals, examine how each differs semantically from the others and how the semantic differences affect grammatical structure, if they do, and work out what semantic properties modals share. As we will see, the semantics of the English modals is more systematic than it appears to be at first glance.

THE TWO MODALITIES: ACTION AND BELIEF

Modal verb meanings fall into two major semantic categories, one referred to as the *action modality* and the other as the *belief modality*.[2] Since most modals can be used in either modality, clauses containing them can be systematically ambiguous unless they are disambiguated by the linguistic or nonlinguistic context. Addressees must use contextual knowledge to determine whether in a sentence like the following the speaker is indicating belief (the belief modality) or giving permission for an action (the action modality):

> *The plumber* **may** *come this afternoon.*

Let's consider two contexts for this sentence:

> *"Elvira, maybe one of us should stay here. The plumber* **may** *come this afternoon."*
> *"Elvira, I've checked our bank account and we have a few thousand dollars left.*
> *The plumber* **may** *come this afternoon."*[3]

In the first context, the speaker is expressing the *belief* that it is possible that the plumber will come that afternoon. In the second context, the speaker is giving permission for the plumber to come. An *action* is being permitted. The ambiguity just described for *may* between action and belief modalities is characteristic of most modals.

Non-native speakers must learn to use contextual clues to disambiguate such sentences. The ambiguities present a challenge for teachers of English. The general consensus is that learners should first be presented with sentences that are as clear as possible and that there should be helpful contextual clues.

The action modality has to do with permitting, recommending, ordering, or prohibiting action (or with reporting such permission, recommendation, order, or prohibition). There is usually a choice of several modals for each of these functions. Note that there are differences in *strength*. Even though a number of modals signify recommendation, the strength of the recommendation may vary. And whether the recommendations are strong or weak, they are in any case stronger than permissions and weaker than orders and prohibitions. Strength is an important notion for modality.

The next two examples involve the action of going to the office of a military barracks:

> *You* **must** *now* **go** *to the barracks office.*
> *You* **may** *now* **go** *to the barracks office.*

The difference in strength between the two modals used is obvious. The first sentence imposes or reports an obligation to carry out the action; the second is weaker and appears to leave choice to the addressee.

The *belief modality,* on the other hand, has to do with the speaker's beliefs about the likelihood of a situation. Again, there are differences in strength. But strength here has to do with differences in the strength of the speaker's *belief.* For example, the modal *must* reflects a stronger belief than does *may* in these sentences:

> *The economic crisis* **must** *be getting worse in Peru.*
> *The economic crisis* **may** *be getting worse in Peru.*

Of course, the sentence could be uttered without a modal, in which case the situation is presented as a fact:

> *The economic crisis* **is** *getting worse in Peru.*

THE ACTION MODALITY[4]

Consider the difference between the A and B examples that follow:

A
The doctor leaves at noon.
Lily drives to Pittsburgh every day.
Clarissa studies economics at Florida State.

B

*The doctor **must** leave at noon.*
*Lily **must** drive to Pittsburgh every day.*
*Clarissa **must** study economics at Florida State.*

Each of the B sentences includes a meaning that is not part of the meaning of the corresponding A sentence. This meaning is essentially one of *obligation*. The speaker is either imposing or reporting an obligation with regard to the actions—the doctor's leaving at noon, Lily's driving to Pittsburgh, and Clarissa's studying economics at Florida State.

This obligation to act is also part of the meaning of sentences with *should* and *ought to*:

The doctor { **should** / **ought to** } *leave at noon.*

Lily { **should** / **ought to** } *drive to Pittsburgh every day.*

Clarissa { **should** / **ought to** } *study economics at Florida State.*

But, with *should* and *ought to*, the obligation imposed is less strong and therefore more easily disregarded. This weaker kind of obligation is a recommendation.

There is a further dimension of meaning, one related to the role of the speaker. An obligation is sometimes imposed not because the speaker has a reason, but rather because the speaker wants to exert authority. Let's contrast *must, should,* and *ought to* with another modal verb, *will*. Assume that both examples here are used to communicate an order. How do they differ?

*Clarissa **must/should/ought to** study economics at Florida State.*
*Clarissa **will** study economics at Florida State.*

The sentence with *will* sounds rather arrogant. The order is presented as an arbitrary one. In contrast, the *must, should,* and *ought to* sentences suggest that the speaker feels he or she has a reason for imposing this obligation, a reason going beyond an arbitrary "because that's what I want." Clauses with these three modals imply the existence of some other factor that *causes* the obligation to be imposed. The *will* sentence, however, implies that there is no justification for the obligation other than that it is the *will* of the speaker that Clarissa study economics at Florida State.

In fact, the modal *will* is often used to signify volition or intention. The senses of the two modals in the first of the two examples below are subtly different. The meaning of the first *will* is close to the meaning of *be willing to*, while the second *will* indicates *intention*. Intention is the imposition upon *oneself* of an obligation to take some action. In the second example, *won't* is equivalent to *not be willing to*.

*When you **will** take the garbage out, I **will** do the dishes.[5]*
*She **won't** pay unless you send her a more detailed statement.*

The periphrastic modal *be going to* is a near-paraphrase of *will*. The differences between the two are subtle: *be going to* is more likely to be used when the focus is on the speaker's intention at the utterance time, the time the obligation is imposed or the intention stated, rather than on the future situation. Consider the following examples:

> If Carol changes her mind, Arthur **will** meet with her.
> If Carol changes her mind, Arthur **is going to** meet with her.

For many speakers, the main clause of the first sentence can be understood either as a prediction or as a statement of intention about future action, possibly but not necessarily Arthur's intention. The main clause of the second sentence, however, is much more likely to be the statement of intention at the present moment and it is likely to be the *speaker's* intention. The speaker may, in fact, have *arranged* for Arthur to meet with her. Because *be going to* focuses on a time previous to the predicted event, it is often interpreted as a prior arrangement or plan:

> I am **going to** take the early morning train tomorrow.
> The car **is going to** be serviced this afternoon.

Now we'll look at *may* and *can*. Again compare the A and B examples:

A
> "Lily drives to Pittsburgh every day," her father told me.
> The teacher reported that Clarissa studies economics at Florida State.

B
> "Lily **may/can** drive to Pittsburgh every day," her father told me.
> The committee has decided that Clarissa **may/can** study economics at Florida State.

Here the additional meaning in the B sentences is that of *permission*. The granting of permission makes it possible for Lily or Clarissa to act, but they are not under an obligation to do so.

Sentences with these permission modals are also understood as if there is a cause or reason behind the permission. Sometimes the reason is stated; quite often it is implied. An important difference between *may* and *can* is in the reason behind the permission. *May* typically indicates that the reason is the authority of the speaker, that is, the speaker is authorizing the action. *Can* simply suggests that permission has been granted for some reason, without specifying the speaker as the authority. In short, whereas *may* locates authority in the speaker, *can* is more neutral. A schoolgirl speaking to her friends would probably use the *can* sentence below, not the *may* sentence. (Remember, both sentences have to be interpreted as indicating permission.)

> The class may leave at two o'clock.
> The class can leave at two o'clock.

Negation and the Action Modality

When we look at negation, it's not hard to understand the problems non-native speakers have with modals. A negative after a modal may include or exclude the part of the meaning signified by the modal. If it includes the modal notion, it is said to have a broader *scope* than if it excludes the modal. The part of the clause that a negative negates is the *scope* of that negative. The scope of *not* (or *n't*) in clauses with *must* is quite different from, for example, its scope in clauses with *may*.

When *must, ought to,* and *should* are used with *not* or *n't*, the scope is narrow—the negation does not include a denial of the obligation:

*"Lily **must not/ought not to/should not** drive to Pittsburgh every day," her father told me.*

The obligation is for Lily *not* to drive to Pittsburgh every day. So, while *must, should,* and *ought to* refer to an obligation to act in a specific way, the negatives *must not, ought not to,* and *should not* refer to an obligation *not* to act in that way. There is still an obligation; only the action is negated. The *not* has narrow scope.

The following is a near-paraphrase using the predicate *obligatory* instead of *must.* Note that for the sentence to be equivalent, the *not* has to be in the embedded clause, not the container clause:

*"It is **obligatory** for Lily **not** to drive to Pittsburgh every day," her father told me.*

Let's formulate a generalization about negation for these obligation modals:

FOR CLAUSES IN THE ACTION MODALITY:
A negative in an obligation modal clause has narrow scope, that is, it negates only the action, not the obligation.

May and *can* behave differently. For these modals, the scope of the *not* is wide, since it includes the modal notion of permission; *not* negates the permission sense indicated by the modal. While *may* and *can* mean that it is permissible to carry out the action specified, *may not* and *cannot* indicate that it is *not* permissible to carry out the action:

*Lily **may not** drive to Pittsburgh every day.*
*Lily **cannot** drive to Pittsburgh every day.*

This is different from it being permissible not to. The *not* after the modal has broad scope. If we check the counterpart sentence with *permissible* as the container predicate, we find the negative appears in the container clause before *permissible* instead of in the embedded clause:

*"It is **not** permissible for Lily to drive to Pittsburgh every day," her father told me.*

The linear order of the container predicate and the *not* is the opposite of that in the sentence with *obligatory.* We can now formulate a generalization about negation in clauses with permission modals. Let's show both generalizations together:

FOR CLAUSES IN THE ACTION MODALITY:
A negative in an obligation modal clause has narrow scope, that is, it negates only the action, not the obligation.
A negative in a permission modal clause has broad scope, that is, it negates the permission.

Along with this difference comes another apparent complication. The following two sentences with *permissible* and *obligatory* correspond to affirmative sentences with *may* and *must.* As we should expect, the two sentences are very different in meaning:

*"It is **permissible** for Lily to drive to Pittsburgh every day," her father told me.*
*"It is **obligatory** for Lily to drive to Pittsburgh every day," her father told me.*

However, the negative counterparts for these paraphrases of *may* and *must* are semantically close:

*"It is **not permissible** for Lily to drive to Pittsburgh every day," her father told me.*
*"It is **obligatory** for Lily **not** to drive to Pittsburgh every day," her father told me.*

Why are the negatives so close in meaning? Think about it. To deny someone permission to do something (as in the *not permissible to* sentence) is equivalent to asserting an obligation for that person *not* to do it (as in the *obligatory not to* sentence).

Now let's see how the same pattern holds for the permission modals *may* and *can* and the obligation modal *must*. Affirmative sentences with these two sets of modals are not at all equivalent, as you can see from these examples:

> *"You **may/can** go to that ball, Cinderella," her stepmother told her.*
> *"You **must** go to that ball, Cinderella," her stepmother told her.*

But the negative sentences are very close in meaning:

> *"You **may not/cannot** go to that ball, Cinderella," her stepmother told her.*
> *"You **must not** go to that ball, Cinderella," her stepmother told her.*

The affirmative sentence with *may* or *can* is very different in meaning from the one with *must*. In the first sentence, Cinderella hears that she is *permitted* to go to the ball; in the second, Cinderella hears that she is *obliged* to go to the ball. In contrast, the negative sentences are almost paraphrases of each other. Once again, to deny permission for someone to do something is logically equivalent to asserting an obligation for that person not to do it.

Suppose we needed to deny the obligation, that is, we wanted an action modality sentence equivalent not to this one:

> *"It is **obligatory** for you **not** to go to that ball, Cinderella," her stepmother told her.*

but rather to this one:

> *"It is **not obligatory** for you to go to that ball, Cinderella," her stepmother told her.*

in which the negative has broad scope. Is there a modal we could use to negate the obligation?

In fact, the modal *need* and the periphrastic modal *have to* are used for this purpose. Thus, to negate the obligation in *Cinderella must go to that ball*, we can use one of these alternatives:

> *Cinderella **need not** go to that ball.*[6]
> *Cinderella **doesn't have to** go to that ball.*

Relative Strengths in the Action Modality

We've seen that in the action modality the modals *may, can, must, will, need, ought to, should,* and *have to* signify either *permission to act* (or not act) in some way or *obligation to act* (or not act) in some way. One other modal, *shall,* can be used to indicate a strong obligation to act, so strong that the speaker seems to guarantee the action will be carried out. *Shall* is used infrequently in modern British English and has almost disappeared from American English, but even in American English it survives as an invitation or suggestion including the speaker in whatever action is specified:

> ***Shall** we dance, have a picnic, or just hang around the pool hall?*

This usage no longer carries any obvious notion of obligation, in contrast to more formal or ceremonial language in which the speaker or writer imposes on himself or herself or on others an obligation to act in such a way as to guarantee success:

> *We **shall** overcome.*
> *No nation **shall** seek to dominate others to serve selfish needs.*

Sentences with *shall* and the other modals can be arranged in order of their strength. The following list begins with the strongest:

> *Get married before the end of the year!*
> *(You **shall** get married before the end of the year.)*
> *You **will** get married before the end of the year.*
> *You're **gonna** get married before the end of the year.*
> *You **must** get married before the end of the year.*
> *You **have to** get married before the end of the year.*
> *You **had better** get married before the end of the year.*
> *You **should** get married before the end of the year.*
> *You **ought to** get married before the end of the year.*
> *You **may** get married before the end of the year.*
> *You **can** get married before the end of the year.*

The top sentence doesn't use a modal at all. But clearly the imperative is used to impose an obligation to act. So semantically it belongs here, and it is a very strong form. The sentence with *shall* is in parentheses because of the infrequent use of *shall* in such constructions.

The periphrastic modal *have to*, because it seems less strong than *must*, is more likely to be used in a situation in which the speaker is not asserting authority over the addressee, but rather, for example, reminding the addressee of an obligation. Think about the following two situations. In the first, a store manager is talking to a new employee, while, in the second, an employee is talking to a co-worker. Now here are two sentences, one spoken by the manager and one by the co-worker. Which sentence would you assign to which person?

> *You **must** be back from lunch by one o'clock.*
> *You **have to** be back from lunch by one o'clock.*

Native speakers almost invariably assign the first sentence to the manager and the second to the co-worker.

While the strength hierarchy we've specified for action modality modals is not wholly valid for all speakers and all occasions, it has worked well for teaching action modality forms to non-native speakers. The teacher works out a set of two-person situations in which an action modality modal could be appropriately used, such as a travel agent advising a customer, a doctor talking to a patient, an employee showing the boss how to use a word processor, and an army officer giving instructions to his or her troops about preparing their camp for a general's inspection. One technique is to present the class with alternative sentences, each with a different modal, and ask the class to discuss which were the most appropriate and why.

Action Modality and Time Reference

What about time reference? Although a predicate following an action modal is not, of course, marked for tense, time reference is nonetheless involved. The action modality has to do with ordering or recommending or forbidding. So it makes sense that the action this modality refers to wouldn't be at a time *previous* to the utterance time. After all, except in fantasy, it doesn't make much sense to order or recommend someone *now* to do something or not do something in the past. The action referred to usually occurs at a time later than the utterance time.

There are, however, two cases that appear to involve past time reference. In one, the speaker refers to a time that is past relative to some *future* time, as in the following example:

> *By Friday you* **must have/ought to have/should have** *completed two more assignments.*

In this example, the time referred to is not past relative to now but past relative to the following Friday, a future time.

The second case is one in which requirements as to past experience are imposed. Recall from Chapter 18 that perfect aspect is used after modals and in infinitive clauses to mark past time for the verb phrase following the modal, as in this example:

> *Applicants* **must have/ought to have/should have** *worked at least three years in a similar position.*

Here the perfect aspect is used, as it typically is used, to refer not to past action but to the state resulting from past action, that is, to the required status of being experienced in the same kind of work.

There is a third situation worth mentioning. Perfect aspect can in fact refer directly to time prior to utterance time with the modals *should* and *ought to:*

> *The electrician* **should have/ought to have** *installed the phone yesterday.*

Notice, however, that the past event of installing the phone *did not happen.* The sentence exemplifies what is known as the *counterfactual* usage, and the modals in such constructions are referred to as *counterfactual modals.* If you say, "he should have," you are also indicating that he didn't.

It is of course possible to refer to a past obligation or permission (or a future one), but a core modal cannot be used to do this. Periphrastic modals or main verbs can be used, since they allow tense marking and can occur after *will* or *be going to.* For *may* or *can,* the main verbs *be permitted* or *be allowed* are available:

> *She* **was permitted** *to leave early.*
> *Clark* **is going to be allowed** *to approve smaller construction projects.*

For *must* and for *will* in the obligation sense, the periphrastic modals *have to* and *be obliged to* are among the many options available. The following examples indicate past and future obligation respectively:

> *The Chief Justice* **was obliged to** *excuse herself from the Morton case.*
> *After that incident, they* **will have to** *fire him.*

For the action modality, the system is a complicated one, but the basic notions are the obligatoriness or permissibility of action. As we will see, these notions are also involved in the belief modality, but in relation to speakers' estimation of the obligatoriness or permissibility of inferences about situations.

Action Modality and Speech Acts

We have frequently referred to the functions of particular modals or classes of modals. We discussed prohibitions, orders, the granting or denial of permission, the stating of intentions. These are *speech acts,* acts we perform by uttering the language form. Assertions, promises, threats, requests, and invitations are other examples of speech acts. The following sentence is an ordinary declarative sentence, but it can be used to perform at least two distinct speech acts:

It's cold in here.

The sentence could be used just to make an assertion. It could also be used, especially by a supervisor to a subordinate, to communicate an order or a request that the window be shut, perhaps, or the heating turned on.

Languages vary in the ways particular kinds of constructions are used for particular speech acts. The Hindi counterparts of forms used in English to promise or to communicate an order, for example, may not be used for the same speech acts. So learning a language includes some learning of ways to perform particular speech acts in that language. This is a topic for a large and very different book,[7] but we'll give here some examples of speech act uses of modals in interrogatives.

Modals are used in interrogatives to make three major kinds of requests: requests for information, requests for some kind of action, and requests for permission. The first use is straightforward:

*Does Jeaves **have to** clean the glasses before she leaves?*
***Can** Aristotle lift 1500 pounds?*
***Should** she be in bed before eight?*

Requests for action typically use *will, would, can,* or *could,* sometimes together with *please*:

***Will** you stop hiding the truth from me?*
***Would** you (please) hold open that door for me?*
***Can** you see me at three o'clock?*
***Could** you (please) not make so much noise?*

An order is essentially a strong request for action. Interrogatives that express orders tend to be less strong than their corresponding declaratives. Thus, *Will you stop hiding the truth from me?* is considerably less strong than *You will stop hiding the truth from me.* As we've already noted, much depends on the relative status of the participants in the speech act. The sentence *Can you see me at three o'clock?* could be uttered as a polite request or even a plea, or if the addressee is subordinate to the speaker, it could be a polite order.

Requests for permission often have first person subjects and use the permission modals:

***Can** we (please) go home now?*
***May** I see you again?*
***Could** our group look after the vegetable garden?*

Notice in the last example that *can,* not *could,* would be used to grant permission.

This very brief discussion should suggest that using a language involves much more than using lexical forms in syntactically and semantically well-formed constructions. Language is not used in a vacuum. It is used in complex societies by speakers with many different kinds of personal, social, and political relations to one another and complex conventions for the appropriate use of language. Modals used in the action modality are sometimes referred to as "interactional" modals. The label is misleading in that the belief modality also involves interaction as speakers communicate or request estimates as to possibilities and impossibilities, likelihood, and truth. The modals are a powerful example of the interrelatedness of form, meaning, and social function. While we need to separate these three dimensions in order to determine the contribution each makes, it should not be forgotten that a grammatical description like this provides only a partial view of how a language works.

BELIEF MODALITY

Modals used in the belief modality express the speaker's belief about the likelihood of some situation, whether past, present, or future. Consider these examples with *must*:

> *I don't see Maude here. She **must have** left early.*
> *Look at all those reporters around Glenna. She **must** be very important.*
> *Jan's article didn't appear in this month's magazine. It **must be** appearing in next month's issue. (Compare: *It **must** appear in next month's issue.)*

The speaker is indicating obligation, but a different kind of obligation, the obligation to *believe* that something is or is not the case. In the first example, the speaker indicates his belief about a past situation. He believes now that she left early. Had he seen her leave, he would have been sure enough to say, *She left early*, but instead, his conclusion is based on *inference*. The fact that he doesn't see her obliges him to believe that she left early. The second example reports the speaker's belief about an ongoing situation, which, again, is inferred from evidence. The speaker doesn't *know* that Glenna is important or he would not have needed the modal. The third example involves an inference about a future situation. Notice that it is acceptable only when progressive aspect is used. The progressive aspect indicates what was described in Chapter 17 as "a present plan for future action." Apparently, *must* cannot refer to future time unless it is accompanied by progressive aspect. In the belief modality *must* requires progressive aspect to refer to future time. That is why the fourth example is asterisked. In the action modality the sentence is perfectly acceptable as an instruction or order.

Now see what happens to the examples if *may* is substituted for *must*:

> *I don't see Maude here. She **may have** left early.*
> *Look at all those reporters around Glenna. She **may** be very important.*
> *Jan's article didn't appear in this month's New Yorker. It **may be** appearing in next month's issue. (Or: It **may** appear in next month's issue.)*

With *must* the examples indicate what the speaker felt *obliged* to believe, but with *may* they indicate what the speaker felt it was *permissible* to believe. Again, the speaker's conclusions are based on inference from evidence, but the evidence isn't strong enough to *oblige* him to believe that Maude left early or that Glenna is very important or that Jan's article is going to appear in the next month's issue. It is strong enough to *permit* these inferences. Approximations to the *must* and *may* sentences in the first example of each set would be these:

> *Certain evidence **obliges** the speaker to believe that Maude left early.*
> *Certain evidence **permits** the speaker to believe that Maude left early.*[8]

The core modal *will*, as used in the belief modality, has often been described as a "future tense marker." As we've already seen, English has no true future tense, so we might amend the description to read "marker for future time reference." But is this description completely accurate? *Will* is certainly used to make clauses refer to future time and it frequently occurs with future time adverbs:

*The police **will** be at the airport **tomorrow**.*
*Sebastian **will** be reading his poetry in Istanbul **next week**.*

But we can cancel out this future time reference sense by substituting other forms for the future time adverbs:

*The police **will** be at the airport **right now**.*
*Sebastian **will** be reading his poetry in Istanbul **at this very moment**.*

What, then, is the real function of *will*? One way to determine this is to compare examples like the last set with sentences having no modal:

*The police **are** at the airport **right now**.*
*Sebastian **is** reading his poetry in Istanbul **at this very moment**.*[9]

While the present tense sentences assert their propositional content as facts, in the *will* sentences the speaker is a little more cautious and the content is presented as *inference*. The inference is about the situation now or, in the sentences with future time adverbs, about the future. Inferences about the future can be called *predictions*.[10]

Further evidence as to the basic function of *will* comes from a comparison with *must*:

*The police **will** be at the airport **right now**.*
*The police **must** be at the airport **right now**.*
*Sebastian **will** be reading his poetry in Istanbul **at this very moment**.*
*Sebastian **must** be reading his poetry in Istanbul **at this very moment**.*

The *will* sentences and the *must* sentences both represent inferences about the police's presence at the airport and Sebastian's poetry reading. In fact, they are essentially synonymous. Thus the basic function of *will* is similar to that of *must*. There are, however, subtle differences: The *must* sentences imply that the speaker has *reason* to believe in the truth of the propositional content; the *will* sentences do not carry such an implication. Because they therefore indicate that the speaker is acting in an authoritarian fashion, *will* comes across over as stronger than *must*.

As in the action modality, the periphrastic modal *be going to* is a near-paraphrase of *will*. But look at the following sentences:

*The police **are going to** be at the airport **right now**.*
*Sebastian **is going to** be reading his poetry in Istanbul **at this very moment**.*

While they are grammatical, it's hard to imagine the circumstances in which they would be uttered. Indeed, we would probably interpret the first example as expressing the action modality. The speaker has made sure that the police will be at the airport. The second is somewhat more easily interpreted as a belief modality utterance, but its likely context is still hard to determine. The reason is that *be going to* in its belief modality sense focuses on the present time if the *be* is in the present tense. The situation at the present time provides indications as to what will happen:

*Stuart has been making too many speeches. He **is going to** lose his voice if he doesn't rest it more.*
*The baby's temperature has dropped. She**'s going to** be all right.*

Other Obligation Modals in the Belief Modality

The periphrastic modal *have to* can be used in the belief modality, but this use is comparatively rare, being limited to situations in which speakers are asserting their belief very emphatically. The difference between the following two examples is clear:

> *Look over there! That **must** be Cyril Cusack.*
> *Look over there! That (just) **HAS to** be Cyril Cusack.*

Note that in such constructions, the *have* receives emphatic stress.

Compared to *must* and *have to*, which express a strong obligation for the speaker to believe that the propositional content of the clause is true, the modals *should* and *ought to* indicate a much weaker obligation. Suppose you and Albert were watching a slow-moving performance of the first act of Mozart's opera *Così Fan Tutte*. You might try to cheer him up by saying one of these two belief modality sentences:

> *The second act **should** be more exciting, Albert.*
> *The second act **ought to** be more exciting, Albert.*

You are indicating to Albert a weaker degree of belief as to the likelihood of a more exciting second act.

The implication that there is a cause for the belief expressed is present for *have to*, *should*, and *ought to*. In the last two examples, it is probably some experience as to what often happens in such performances or knowledge of the plot of the opera. To take one further example, if you had been waiting for your baggage at Washington National Airport and at long last saw a familiar-looking suitcase appear on the baggage carousel, you might say, *That **ought to** be my case*, if you weren't yet sure that it really was yours but the evidence pointed in that direction. Whatever the evidence is—the color of the case, the fact that everyone else's baggage has already arrived—it causes you to have that belief.

Now compare the last example with a sentence using *will*. Someone who says, *That **will** be my suitcase*, is talking as if she needs no evidence to support her belief.

Other Permission Modals in the Belief Modality

Although our examples of permissibility in the belief modality have used *may*, two other modals, *might* and *could*, are at least as frequently used to indicate beliefs the speaker feels are permissible for him or her. We'll repeat the examples, replacing *may* with the other two modals:

> *I don't see Maude here. She **might/could** have left early.*
> *Look at all those reporters around Glenna. She **might/could** be very important.*
> *Jan's article didn't appear in this month's magazine. It **might/could** be appearing in next month's issue. (Or: It **might/could** appear in next month's issue.)*

The three modals differ in strength, *might* being more tentative than *may*, and *could* more tentative than *might*.

The other permissibility modal, *can*, is not used for the belief modality in affirmative statements:

> *I don't see Maude here. *She **can** have left early.*

However, as we'll see, it is used in negatives and interrogatives.

Relative Strengths in the Belief Modality

Even more than in the action modality, the relative strengths of the different modals in the belief modality vary considerably with the linguistic and pragmatic context and the speaker's stress. Moreover, native speakers differ in the degrees of strength they assign to many modals.

Nevertheless, the following gradation from strong to weak seems reasonably accurate for many speakers. Again, we'll use sentence examples:

It **is** cold outside now.
It **will** be cold outside now.
It's **gonna** be cold outside now.
It **HAS to** be cold outside now.
It **would** be cold outside now.
It **must** be cold outside now.
It **should** be cold outside now.
It **ought to** be cold outside now.
It **could** be cold outside now.
It **may** be cold outside now.
It **might** be cold outside now.

Note that a finite clause without a modal is the strongest, because it presents the content as fact rather than inference or belief. In the action modality, remember, the strongest form listed was a nonfinite clause, an imperative. Other differences between the two modalities are that *shall* and *had better* occur only in the action modality, *might* and *could* occur only in the belief modality (except in reported speech), and contrastive stress on *have* in *have to* is obligatory in the belief modality but optional in the action modality. The stressed form is stronger than *must* in both modalities; the unstressed form, occurring only in the action modality, is slightly weaker than *must*. But keep in mind that there is considerable variation among speakers as to the relative strength of most modals.

Negatives and Interrogatives in the Belief Modality

Belief *must* and *may* occur in negative clauses:

She **must** not have liked that movie.
She **may** not have liked that movie.

However, speakers are more likely to use *can't* in such clauses:

She **can't** have liked that movie.

In conversation especially, speakers can avoid using any modals to communicate probability, using instead predicates like *be sure* and *believe*, or sentence adverbs like *perhaps* and *presumably*:

I'**m** not **sure** she enjoyed that movie.
I don't **believe** you like that man, do you?
Perhaps they don't like anchovies on their pizza.
Presumably they didn't meet him at the airport.

The subject of a predicate like *be sure* or *believe* has to be first person if the clause is to be a true counterpart to clauses with belief modals, since such clauses are used to communicate speaker beliefs.

This may be why *must* and *may* don't occur in interrogatives, since it seems strange to ask someone else what you, the speaker, believe about a situation. The following examples are not interpreted as being in the belief modality:

*Must she be tall?
*May she be tall?

although, of course, they can be given an action modality interpretation, for example, one in which a casting director is asking a playwright about a character in the play.

However, there are other core modals, notably *can, could,* and *might,* that can be used to ask about the *addressee's* belief concerning a situation. *Might* is now rare in interrogatives in spoken American English, and used only infrequently in British English. Here are examples in descending order of strength:

> **Can** *Charmay be too tired already?*
> **Could/couldn't** *Charmay be too tired already?*
> **Might/mightn't** *Charmay be too tired already?*

Notice that belief modality *can't* isn't used in negative questions.

There are other rather subtle differences among them, subtleties depending on the context in which the sentence is uttered. For instance, the example with *can* might be used to express the speaker's skepticism about Charmay's tiredness, just like its counterpart with *possible*:

> *Is it* **possible** *that Charmay is too tired already?*

Belief Modality and Time Reference

With modals, two time references are involved: the time of the speaker's belief about a situation and the time of the situation itself. So, in the sentence *The patient may undergo the operation next week,* the time of the possible operation is in the future, next week, but the time reference of the speaker's belief about the time of the operation is now, the present. Since the periphrastic modals can be marked for tense, it might seem easy to use them to refer to a past or present inference or belief. For instance, the periphrastic modals *be going to* and *be bound to* have the present tense forms *is/are going to* and *is/are bound to* and the past tense forms *was/were going to* and *was/were bound to.* But the past tense form in the belief modality does not necessarily refer to a past inference or belief.

Consider the following examples:

> *The 1957 book* **was** *going to be very successful. Already the bookstore chains had placed huge orders.*
> *The new policies* **were** *bound to be unpopular.*

These sentences are ambiguous between present belief and past belief, even though past situations, the book's success and the unpopularity of the new policies, are referred to. Insertion of the adverb *obviously* before *going to* and *bound to* makes the belief a past belief and not necessarily a belief of the speaker. If, instead, we insert *I see now that* at the beginning of each example, the reference is to a present belief.

In the belief modality, the core modals, which cannot be marked for past or present tense, always designate the speaker's belief at the time of the utterance. Unlike action modals, belief modals are used to make an inference now about something that was the case *prior to now.* This is done by using the perfect aspect form after the modal. Here are past time counterparts for most of the modal sentences we looked at earlier:

> *It* **HAD to have** *been cold outside then.*
> *It* **would have** *been cold outside then.*
> *It* **must have** *been cold outside then.*
> *It* **should have** *been cold outside then.*
> *It* **could have** *been cold outside then.*

*It **ought to have** been cold outside then.*
*It **may have** been cold outside then.*
*It **might have** been cold outside then.*

Note that the examples with *should* and *ought to* are normally *counterfactual* sentences, that is, they indicate that it was not in fact cold then. The combination *would have* is also counterfactual if it is part of a conditional construction, as in these sentences:

*(If we had known), we **would have** come to the airport.*
*Kennedy **would have** served another term if he had not been assassinated.*

SEMANTICS AND THE LOGIC OF THE MODALS

In Chapter 1 we referred to three major aspects of language study: syntax, the lexicon, and semantics. While we have been mostly concerned with syntax, this chapter has focused on semantics, because the semantics of the English modals needs to be unraveled for a proper understanding of these eccentric forms. The basic semantic notions used in this account of the English modals are a relatively small set: permissibility, obligation, negation, cause, act, and belief. We pointed out that, in combinations with the negative, permissibility sentences can be logically equivalent to obligation sentences. This equivalency was shown to explain why *may not* and *must not* sentences are essentially paraphrases in the action modality.

A more rigorous system explicating the logic underlying the modals would get rid of either permissibility or obligation by defining one in terms of the other.[11] But this would go far beyond our coverage of English syntax here.

SUMMARY

Modals fall into two major semantic categories: the *action modality* and the *belief modality*. Since most modals are used in either modality, clauses containing them may be systematically ambiguous unless the context disambiguates them. Both modalities deal with notions of permissibility and obligation.

In the action modality, some modals indicate the granting, or in the case of negatives, the denial, of permission to carry out some action, while others indicate the imposition of an obligation to carry out or not carry out the action. The strength of the obligation varies with the individual modal.

The belief modality involves the strength of the speaker's belief in the likelihood of some situation. Some modals indicate various degrees of obligation on the speaker to believe or disbelieve; others simply specify whether belief is permissible or not permissible.

A negative occurring immediately after a modal usually negates what follows but does not negate the modal. The part of the clause that a negative negates is the *scope* of that negative. In the action modality, the negative in a permission modal clause has wide scope, that is, negates the modal.

Two time references are involved for clauses with modals: the time at which the modal notion applies, typically the time of the utterance, and the time of the situation to which the modal applies, typically a time later than the time of utterance. For a modal to apply to a situation prior to the time reference of the modal, perfect aspect is used. In the action modality, the combinations *should have* and *could have* are often used as counterfactuals, that is, they imply that the action did not occur.

Since they are used to grant or deny permission or to impose an obligation, modals in the action modality play a significant role in speech acts. Declarative clauses with such modals are almost always stronger than their interrogative counterparts.

In the belief modality, *will* differs from *must, may,* and *can* in implying that there is nothing external causing the speaker to have a certain belief about a situation. In the action modality, *will* implies that the obligation is imposed arbitrarily by the speaker. *Will* also differs in that it can occur in interrogative sentences in either the action or belief modality, whereas *must, may,* and *can* are only understood in their action modality senses. *Could* and *might* in interrogatives are used in either modality.

Semantic notions such as permissibility and obligation are thus useful for providing an account of how meaning is organized within words such as the modals under discussion.

EXERCISE SET 19

1. Explain the ambiguity of each of these examples:

Joanne may not leave the house on Wednesdays.
Joanne must not leave the house on Wednesdays.

2. Draw a constituent structure tree for the following sentence:

The older delegates might have been boycotting the convention.

3. Explain the action and belief modality senses of the following sentences:

    a. *Shelley must have left that house by five o'clock.*
    b. *Could Jessica carry that chair?*
    c. *The governor can't be doing favors for those men.*

4. Make up two sentences in which modals are used counterfactually. Then explain briefly the situation in which each would be understood counterfactually and describe any other possible interpretations of your sentences.

5. The action modality modals can be arranged into two groups according to whether obligation or permissibility for action is involved. Think of four situations in which these modals could be used to advise, to warn, or to carry out some other speech act. The situations could occur, for example, in a public library, in a doctor's office, in a motor vehicle bureau office, or in a classroom. Write several sentences for each, using different modals from both groups.

6. The belief modality modals, whether core or periphrastic, can be arranged into two groups according to whether belief obligation or permissibility is involved. Think of four situations in which these modals could be used to advise, to warn, or to carry out some other speech act. The situations could occur, for example, in a court room, at a building site, at a local government meeting, or in a classroom. Write several sentences for each, using different modals from both groups.

7. After reading Mr. Ogata's story, discuss his use of modals. Some background is provided to clarify the situation.

Mr. Ogata is a clerical worker for a school of English in Osaka. He was given permission to take a four-day vacation last year, provided he returned to work an hour early on the fifth day. Unfortunately he was given the wrong amount of salary before he left that week. So Mr. Ogata, who already had some money problems, stayed only three days in the mountain resort of Karuizawa. What is the nature of the errors perpetrated by Mr. Ogata in telling his story and how might you help him avoid them in the future?

MR. OGATA'S STORY

Last year I asked my boss, Mr. Evans, if I may have taken a short vacation. He said that I could have stayed only four days. He said that I must have come early to working one hour at the fifth day. When I was receiving my salary I saw that the company must have made a mistake because they had given to me too little. My boss looked at it and said, "They may have given you Mr. Ogawa's salary." But Mr. Ogawa said, "They could not have, because that I have the amount which was right." So I could have stayed in Karuizawa only three days because the Pay Office could not have corrected their mistake on time. Mr. Evans is very sorry for me to have shortered my vacation and says that he writes when it is on time in March for arranging the vacations of the employees. Then I will ought to have a day extra.

NOTES

1. Jennifer Coates, "The acquisition of the meanings of modality in children aged eight and twelve," *Journal of Child Language* 15 (1988): 425-34. See also D. Major, *The Acquisition of Modal Auxiliaries in the Language of Children* (The Hague: Mouton, 1974).

2. The two modalities have a number of labels. Perhaps the most common are *root* for the action modality and *epistemic* for the belief modality. Another pair of labels, *social interaction* and *logical probability*, is used in Marianne Celse-Murcia and Diane Larsen-Freeman, *The Grammar Book* (Rowley, MA: Newbury House, 1983).

3. The use of *may* here is a very formal one, especially in spoken American English. The modal *can* is now much more common in the permission sense.

4. Our approach here and some of our analysis of the two modalities draws upon the very elegant semantic analysis of Domenico Parisi and Francesco Antinucci, *Essentials of Grammar* (New York: Academic Press, 1976). Their description, written within the now defunct framework of generative semantics, makes extensive use of logical formulae, relating both the permissibility and obligation senses of the modals to the notion BIND in various combinations with CAUSE, NOT, BELIEVE, DO, and other semantic predicates.

5. Note that when *will* is used in its pure volitional sense rather than its obligation or prediction senses, it can occur in *when* (and *if*) clauses.

6. Of course, *need* can be used as a main verb rather than a modal:

> *"You don't **need** to go to that ball, Cinderella," her stepmother told her.*

But this main verb *need* is generally used, as here, to signify need because of a lack of something rather than obligation.

7. See, for a beginning, Gillian Brown and George Yule, *Discourse Analysis* (Cambridge: Cambridge University Press, 1983), 231-234, and, for a more detailed and sometimes technical discussion, Chapter 9 of Robert M. Martin, *The Meaning of Language* (Cambridge, MA: M.I.T. Press, 1987).

8. The indicative mood of the embedded clause *that Maude left early* contrasts with the hypothetical mood of the embedded clauses in the action modality forms discussed earlier in this chapter:

> *"It is obligatory **for Lily to drive to Pittsburgh every day**," her father told me.*
> *"It is permissible **for Lily to drive to Pittsburgh every day**," her father told me.*

The action modality is used for actions which haven't yet happened. Action modality correlates with nonfinite clauses, while belief modality correlates with finite clauses.

9. If a future time adverb replaces *at this very moment* in this sentence, we have the prearranged present tense usage discussed in Chapter 16, one reserved for describing rigidly scheduled events.

10. This point is made very strongly by Parisi and Antinucci.

11. For a useful and important first step in this direction, see Geoffrey Leach, *Towards a Semantic Description of English* (London: Longman, 1969). George Miller and Philip Johnson-Laird's *Language and Perception* (Cambridge, MA: Harvard University Press, 1976) explores language in similar terms and is well worth the effort of reading (especially Chapter 7, "Some Meaning Patterns of English").

20

Prepositions, Particles, and Multiword Verbs

Like the modals and the article system, prepositions often present problems for language learners. English prepositions have a variety of functions and these can be very bewildering to the learner, who sees little logic in them. Moreover, there are words that look just like prepositions but function very differently. But first we must consider prepositions themselves.

Even when a single preposition is examined, it is difficult, sometimes impossible, to assign it a single clear interpretation. The preposition *by*, for instance, can indicate location:

> *Liliana waited for him **by** the canal.*

or time:

> *You must be at the station **by** five o'clock.*

or means:

> *Shirley won their votes **by** promising to revitalize the cities.*

or an agent:

> *Havel was nominated **by** the majority party.*

When it occurs without an object, it is usually considered an adverb, as in this example:

> *Since you'll be passing the office, Cecilia, would you stop **by** and give Robert these letters?*[1]

In this chapter we'll be considering major functions of prepositions and two other categories of words that look like prepositions yet don't behave like them. All three categories can combine with verbs to form special predications with some unexpected characteristics.

PREPOSITIONS AND THEMATIC ROLES

We saw in earlier chapters that predicates assign thematic roles to the arguments they require. Thus *denounce* assigns the agent role to its subject argument and the theme role to its object argument:

Sumukti denounced the incompetent engineers.
AGENT   THEME

Verbs in the passive voice can have an agent specified, but only if it occurs as the object of the preposition *by*. The preposition assigns it the agent role. The passive counterpart of *denounce, be denounced,* has no object argument in S-structure; the theme argument is subject:

The incompetent engineers were denounced by Sumukti.
THEME   AGENT

As we've already noted, *by* is also used to mark another role, that of *means.*

The preposition *with* is used to indicate two major thematic roles. The first is the role of *instrument*:

*Nina punctured the can **with** a sharpened screwdriver.*
INSTRUMENT

The second role is the *comitative* role, indicating someone accompanying another person:[2]

*Nina went to the ball **with** the handsome Prince Igor.*
COMITATIVE

The sentence with a comitative noun phrase has a near paraphrase with *and*:

Nina and the handsome Prince Igor went to the ball (together).

A related but somewhat different construction using *with* assigns the comitative role to a gerundive noun phrase signifying an accompanying event:

***With** Cyril strumming his ukulele, Emma began to dance.*

Three other roles can be indicated by prepositions. In the following example, the roles of goal, source, and benefactive are indicated by *to, from,* and *for,* respectively:

It was borrowed from Glen and given to Gretta for her baby.
SOURCE   GOAL   BENEFACTIVE

The benefactive role is semantically close to a more general notion of purpose, for which *for* can also be used, as in the following example:

He borrowed the money for a new car.

The car is not a true beneficiary. The *for* prepositional phrase means "in order to buy a new car." The purpose of his borrowing was the purchase of a new car. The same role can be assigned to a gerundive such as *for buying a new car.*

Most prepositional phrases are used as adjuncts, optional phrases which, like subordinate clauses, typically provide such perspectives as the purpose perspective just described, as well as location, time, manner, reason, and contrast. The location and time perspectives in the listing that follows are subdivided according to whether they refer to a position in space or time, or indicate movement of some kind:

LOCATION/TIME POSITION:	*in the garden, at the clinic, on the roof, on Friday, in 1967, at noon, before leaving*
LOCATION/TIME GOAL:	*to Bangkok, toward freedom, into bankruptcy, until evening, to the end of the day*
LOCATION/TIME SOURCE:	*from the wholesaler, from Yokohama, from March 1997*

LOCATION/TIME PATH:	*along the street, through the tunnel, across Manhattan, during the performance*
MANNER:	*with a flourish, in a persuasive tone*
CONTRAST:	*despite the rough terrain, in spite of her obstinacy*

Many of these categorizations can be broken down further. For example, the various location forms can be broken down according to whether they refer to motion along one dimension (*to, from*), motion or location in relation to a two-dimensional space (*on, onto, above, down, below, under(neath), beneath*), or motion or location in relation to a three-dimensional space (*in, into, within, inside, outside*). For teaching purposes, however, categorizing prepositions is not as useful as, for example, demonstrating the spatial relationships they express using teaching aids like a cardboard box and small toys.

PREPOSITIONS AND *WH* MOVEMENT

We are going to consider a phenomenon that will help us distinguish prepositions from look-alikes. This is more than a theoretical issue, since it is important for learners to be aware, at some level at least, of the distributional properties of these items. They need to understand the semantic distinctions corresponding to the distributions of the forms.

English has two major types of questions, *yes-no* questions like *Are you going to Hong Kong?* and *wh* questions like *When are you going to Hong Kong?* in which a *wh* word like *who, what, where, why, when,* or *how* is shifted to the beginning of the sentence.

When the *wh* word is inside a prepositional phrase, there are usually two choices as to the constituent to be moved—either the whole prepositional phrase or just the object of the preposition, the part containing the *wh* word. In the following examples, we will use [t] (for *trace*) to show the slot from which the constituent is moved. The [t] is useful for tracing the movement of constituents, especially since the same constituent can be shifted more than once. In these next examples, the whole prepositional phrase containing the *wh* word has been shifted to the beginning of the sentence:

> ***In what kind of car*** *are they traveling **[t]?***
> ***To whom*** *did you say that **[t]?***
> ***From which wholesaler*** *will you purchase the rugs **[t]?***
> ***Until when*** *can I keep this book **[t]?***

Usually, especially in the spoken language, the preposition is left behind:[3]

> ***What kind of car*** *are they traveling **in [t]?***
> ***Who*** *did you say that **to [t]?***
> ***Which wholesaler*** *will you purchase the rugs **from [t]?***

We are interested here, however, in sentences in which the preposition has been moved along with the *wh* word because, although other forms look like prepositions and may even appear to be in the same slot, only true prepositions can be moved via *wh* movement. We thus have a useful diagnostic test for prepositions.

PREPOSITIONAL VERBS

All verbs allow prepositional phrases as adjuncts; the kind of prepositional phrase varies depending on the verb. For example, *go* very often takes a prepositional phrase headed by *to; a from* phrase is possible but less likely, since *go* focuses on the goal, in this case the destination. *Come,* on the other hand, is more likely to have a prepositional phrase headed by *from,* although *to* or other prepositions are possible alternatives. A non-motion verb like *stay* is more likely to occur with prepositional phrases headed by *with, at, in,* or *on.* In all these cases, although the kind of verb determines the preposition heading its complement, the preposition has a consistent meaning, one independent of the verb meaning.

But certain verbs, which we will refer to as *prepositional verbs,* occur with prepositions whose meaning can be very closely tied in with that of the verb. For example, the verb *look* combines with the preposition *at* to signify "regard." The same verb can instead occur with *to* or *for,* but the meanings are quite different:

> *James looked at his sister.*
> *James looked to his sister for support.*
> *James looked for his sister.*

The first sentence means that James regarded his sister, the second that he sought support from his sister or relied on her for support, and the third that he tried to find his sister. The meanings are thus quite different when the prepositions are changed, but the differences could not be predicted from the meanings of the individual prepositions.

These prepositional verb combinations and others such as *listen to, long for, call on, decide on, cope with, talk about, approve of, dispose of, consist of, rely on,* and *wait for* appear to function as two-word verb units (actually, *multiword* units, as we'll see), many of which may correspond to single words in English as well as in other languages. With the exception of *consist of,*[4] most of these prepositional verbs have reasonably well-formed passive voice counterparts:

> *Roberta was always listened to.*
> *The radioactive waste has been disposed of.*
> *Jennifer was looked to for support.*

From the teaching point of view, it seems reasonable to treat these verbs (called *prepositional verbs*) and the prepositions they occur with as transitive verb units.

However, language professionals, especially teachers, who need to know more about English syntax than learners do, should be aware of evidence indicating that the word following the verb is in fact a preposition and that it forms a tightly knit grammatical unit not with the verb preceding it but with its object. The *wh* movement diagnostic test is useful here. We'll apply *wh* movement to sentences with the combinations *look to, look at, look for, rely on,* and *listen to.* The whole phrase after the verb has been fronted in each of these examples:

> **To whom** did James look for support *[t]?*
> **At/for whom** did James look *[t]?*
> **On whom** does James rely *[t]?*
> **To whom** does James listen *[t]?*

Since the *to, at, for,* and *on* in these sentences can all participate in *wh* movement, we conclude that they are prepositions functioning as heads of their prepositional phrases rather than special forms constituting part of a two word verb.

A further diagnostic test will be applied. True prepositions, like verbs, cannot be separated from their objects by intervening elements, as in **She went to rapidly the house.* This generalization is valid also for prepositional verb constructions:

> **James looked at anxiously his sister.*
> *James looked anxiously at his sister.*

James relied on heavily his sister.
James relied heavily on his sister.

The adverb *anxiously* can occur before (or after) the prepositional phrase, but not inside it.

Other evidence comes from prepositional verbs like *provide* (someone) *with* and *deprive* (someone) *of*, which take a direct object noun phrase as well as a prepositional phrase. Note that, in sentences with these prepositional verbs, the preposition is not adjacent to the verb but, rather, follows the direct object:

*They plied their Roman guests **with** food and drink.*
*The Italian troops provided the refugees **with** warm blankets.*
*The gossip robbed him **of** his reputation for integrity.*
*Those officials deprived the refugees **of** their privacy.*

Notice also that if the *wh* movement test is applied, the preposition can be fronted along with its object:

***With what refreshments** did they ply their Roman guests [t]?*

Except where *wh* movement fronts just the object, the preposition always immediately precedes its object. In short, although the verb determines what preposition is allowed, the preposition forms a unit with its object distinct from the verb. There are many other such verbs, including *accuse (someone) of, charge (someone) with, liberate (someone) from, blame (someone) for, attach (something) to, convict (someone) of,* and *tax (someone) with*.

The specific prepositions used with prepositional verbs are all "selected" by the verbs, but we know of no safe semantic guidelines for determining which prepositions go with which predicates. The particular selections made are generally arbitrary, determined by historical factors. What this means for the teacher is that, since the verb-preposition combinations are rarely predictable, the combinations must be learned item by item.

PREPOSITIONS AND DIRECTIONAL ADVERBS

Many verbs can be used transitively or intransitively. Verbs used intransitively don't take objects. Moreover, even verbs used transitively, such as *read* and *eat*, can occur without an object, though one is understood.

However, it is sometimes assumed that prepositions always require overt objects,[5] that there cannot be prepositions corresponding to verbs like *eat* and *read*. But consider the following sentences:

*We climbed **up** the slope toward him.*
*We climbed **up** toward him.*
*Jack and Jill fell **down** the hill.*
*Jack and Jill fell **down**.*
*Huggins passed the chocolate mousse **through** the hatch and we cheered.*
*Huggins passed the chocolate mousse **through** and we cheered.*
*Seagulls flapped lazily **above** us.*
*Seagulls flapped lazily **above**.*

When these forms occur without objects, they are called *directional adverbs*, although their meanings are clearly related to those of their ordinary prepositional counterparts. There is some justification for grouping these forms under the category *directional adverb:* They occur in the same slots as words like *ahead, away, back,* and *forward*, which are clearly directional adverbs that don't occur in preposition slots.

INTRANSITIVE PHRASAL VERBS

The word *up* is often used as a directional adverb, as in this example:

*The captain looked **up** and saw a huge albatross circling overhead.*

The word *up* indicates the direction of the captain's gaze. The captain might instead have looked *down* and seen dolphins swimming around her ship. She might have looked *across* at the giant blue icebergs moving toward her ship. She might have looked *away* when an old seaman stared at her. Although these forms follow *look,* the *up, down, across,* and *away* do not each form a multiword verb unit with *look.* They are simply verbs followed by directional adverbs.

Although the example below looks similar to those just cited, this time *up* combines with the verb and forms a multiword intransitive verb:

*Now that my application has been accepted, I think that things are really **looking up.***

The multiword verb *look up* is a verb idiom meaning "improve, get better." The meaning of *up* in the intransitive verb formed by this combination is very closely tied in with that of its verb and quite different from its normal meaning as either a preposition or a directional adverb. *Up* and other such words forming a semantic as well as syntactic unit with a verb are known as *particles.* They cannot have objects of their own, though the verb-particle *combination* can have an object. As we will see, unlike the prepositions that occur with prepositional verbs, they cannot be shifted with a following object to the front of their clause. Other such combinations are *throw up,* meaning "vomit," and *come through,* meaning "survive" and, as in this example, "do what I wanted or needed":

*Teresa really **came through** for me that time.*

In these examples, then, *up* and *through* are particles, and each verb plus particle forms a multiword verb. We'll call such combinations *phrasal verbs.* The examples in this section involve intransitive phrasal verbs; phrasal verbs may also be transitive.

SEPARABLE PHRASAL VERBS

Transitive phrasal verbs fall into two major groups, separable and nonseparable phrasal verbs, which differ in the number of slots in which the particle can appear. *Separable phrasal verbs* are verbs which allow, and sometimes require, the particle to occur in a slot that is not adjacent to its verb.[6]

Let's check another multiword sequence to see if it is a separable phrasal verb, that is, if it contains a particle and if that particle can be separated from the verb:

*Jerry Stoneham **looked up** the number in the directory and whistled in surprise, for it was the same number that he had found in the dead man's diary.*

Here *up* does not indicate direction or have any special meaning of its own. Rather, the combination of *look* and *up* has a special meaning, which is approximately "consult (a document) for."

Even though it is followed by the noun phrase *the number,* the *up* is not a preposition here. We'll apply the *wh* diagnostic test. This next example, in which the *up* has not been shifted with the *wh* noun phrase, is perfectly grammatical:

***What number** did Jerry Stoneham look up [t]?*

If we move the *up* along with the *wh* phrase, the result is ungrammatical:

> *****Up what number** did Jerry Stoneham look **[t]**?

So this *up* fails the *wh* diagnostic test for prepositions and is a particle. The verb *look* and the particle *up* combine as a transitive multiword verb. The following sentence shows that *look up* is a separable phrasal verb; *up* can be separated from *look*, and this separation is obligatory if the object is a pronoun:

> Jerry Stoneham **looked** it **up** in the directory.

Many transitive phrasal verbs, whether separable or inseparable, have single verb counterparts. These tend to be less common and are sometimes restricted to formal uses of language. The range of meanings a phrasal verb can have is likely to differ from that of its single word counterpart. For example, *make up* corresponds to both *invent* and *put makeup on*. One paraphrase for *blow up* is *inflate*, but the meaning "destroy by detonating an explosion" has no single word counterpart. The following matched pairs are close although not exact equivalents. All the phrasal verbs used are separable ones.

bring back	*return*	*drive out*	*expel*
bring up	*raise*[7]	*give up*	*surrender*
call off	*cancel*		*forsake*
call over	*summon*	*leave out*	*omit*
check out	*investigate*	*turn down*	*refuse*
do in	*kill*	*turn out*	*evict*

As a survey of our list would suggest, many separable phrasal verbs are idioms whose meanings differ from the meanings of the individual words.

NONSEPARABLE PHRASAL VERBS

The following sentences also contain transitive phrasal verbs:

> *Guess what! I **ran into** an old friend last night.*
> *Rita will **stand by** you, Jim. You know that.*
> *The minute he saw his rival, he **went for** him.*
> *I'd **jump at** the chance to play Queen Gertrude in that production.*
> *Roberto **came across** an old photograph of Laura in the desk drawer.*

Each of the multiword verbs is understood idiomatically. In the examples, *run into* means "meet by chance," *stand by* means "remain loyal to," *go for* means "attack," *jump at* means "accept enthusiastically," and *come across* means "find." The *wh* movement test confirms that the second word of each phrasal verb is not a preposition but a particle:

> *****Into which old friend** did you run **[t]** last night?*
> *****By whom** will Rita stand **[t]**?*
> *****For whom** did he go **[t]**?*
> *****At what** would you jump **[t]**?*
> *****Across what** did he come **[t]**?*

So *into, by, for, at,* and *across* in the examples are particles and form a phrasal verb unit with their verb. The fact that the units are all idioms supports this conclusion.

But these phrasal verbs differ from those discussed in the previous section in that they are *nonseparable phrasal verbs;* the particles must not be separated from the verbs:

I **ran an old friend **into** last night.*
Rita will **stand you **by** Jim.*
The minute he saw his rival, he **went him **for**.*
I'd **jump it **at**.*
Roberto **came it **across** in the desk drawer.*

Some phrasal verbs have three constituents: an ordinary verb followed by a directional adverb and a particle. These verbs are all nonseparable phrasal verbs. They include the following:

cut down on	*"reduce"*
drop in on	*"visit casually"*
get away with	*"violate a rule without punishment"*
go back on	*"violate an agreement"*
go through with	*"finish, complete"*
keep up with	*"stay level with"*
look down on	*"despise"*
make up for	*"compensate"*
put up with	*"tolerate"*
run out of	*"have no more"*
run up against	*"meet as an obstacle"*
stand up for	*"defend"*

Since none of the constituents of these verbs is a preposition, none can be fronted by *wh* movement. Here's one example of ungrammatical fronting:

****With what crime** did he get away [t]?*

D-STRUCTURES FOR MULTIWORD COMBINATIONS

How can we represent the structural properties of the combinations discussed in this chapter? Unfortunately, truly satisfactory analyses are lacking. What we show here are approximations which capture just some of the properties.

Prepositional verbs such as *wait for* would have the verb and its prepositional phrase as sisters under the V-bar:

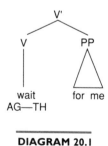

DIAGRAM 20.1

The verb selects the kind of prepositional phrase it requires. This is shown by the sister relation between the V and the PP. Prepositional verb combinations such as *congratulate NP on* have the object NP as an additional sister under the V-bar.

In much the same way, intransitive phrasal verbs, such as *throw up*, would have the V and the particle (PRT) as sisters:

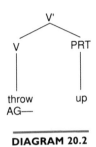

DIAGRAM 20.2

This approximation, however, fails to capture the fact that the verb and the particle constitute a single chunk expressing a single meaning. One possibility is for the verb-particle combination to be shown in D-structure as a single lexical unit like this:

throw
<up>

Of course, we would need to posit a process creating the actual particle as a separate item for S-structure. This analysis has the disadvantage of treating particles as if they were suffixes rather than separate words. For our purposes, the kind of representation shown in Diagram 20.2 is more convenient.

Transitive phrasal verbs, whether separable like *call up NP* or inseparable like *drop in on NP*, present a problem similar to the one discussed regarding *throw up*. For instance, it is the chunk *call up*, not just *call*, that selects the kind of object noun phrase allowed. It is *call up* that assigns the theme role to the object. You can call up a person or even a ghost, but not happiness or pepper. We will settle for the following approximation of D-structure in which the particle (or directional adverb plus particle) precedes the object:

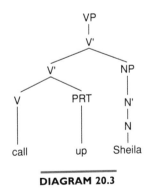

DIAGRAM 20.3

The verb and the particle form a V-bar, which in turn forms a higher V-bar with the object.

SUMMARY

This chapter has dealt with the ways prepositions, particles, and directional adverbs combine with verbs to form multiword predicates. Prepositions assign various thematic roles to their objects—agent, goal, source, beneficiary, instrument, and comitative are common roles. As an adjunct, a prepositional phrase can, like a subordinate clause, indicate a perspective such as time, location, manner, reason, purpose, and contrast.

Prepositional verbs are verbs requiring a particular kind of prepositional phrase to express a specific meaning. To express the meaning "try to find," the verb *look* has to have a *for* prepositional phrase, as in *look for the keys*. But the *for* is less closely attached grammatically to the verb preceding it than to the object following it. Some prepositional verbs require a direct object as well as a prepositional phrase. If there is a *wh* word in the prepositional phrase, the whole prepositional phrase can be fronted for a question, instead of just the noun phrase object of the preposition.

There are similar-looking constructions in which words like *up, on, down,* and *off* function as particles, not prepositions. If a *wh* noun phrase follows a particle, the particle, unlike a preposition, cannot be fronted by *wh* movement.

Phrasal verbs are verbs, transitive or intransitive, which combine with particles to form multiword verbs. There are two major types of transitive phrasal verbs. *Separable* phrasal verbs allow an object noun phrase to intervene between the verb and its particle; if the object is a pronoun, the particle *must* be separated from its verb. *Nonseparable* phrasal verbs never have their object right after the verb. Some nonseparable phrasal verbs consist of the sequence verb, directional adverb, and particle.

For the second-language learner, the constructions covered in this chapter are difficult because, except for Germanic languages, few languages have similar constructions, because apparently identical sequences are often structurally distinct and behave differently, and because the semantics of many of these forms is very idiosyncratic.

EXERCISE SET 20

1. Draw D-structure trees for the following sentences:
   a. *Students should take this matter up with the dean.*
   b. *Chester took that money out.*

2. Divide the items on this list of separable phrasal verbs among the members of your class. Each of you should check their meanings in a *large* dictionary and report on the meaning(s) each phrasal verb has. Some of the items (e.g., *turn over*) can also be used as intransitive phrasal verbs. Ignore the meanings of the intransitive usages.

blow up	give up	put away	track down
bring back	hand in	put off	turn out
bring up	lay down	send off	turn over
call off	lay off	set down	work in
check in	leave out	sound out	work out
do without	make up	take in	wrap up
fill up	melt down	take on	write down

3. Find the multiword verbs in the following passage and indicate whether they are intransitive phrasal verbs, separable transitive phrasal verbs, nonseparable transitive phrasal verbs, or prepositional verbs:

Jessica and Marvin came down to see the Watsons off. They had put up the Watsons for the past week at their summer cottage and had looked after them well. The plane was to take off at three o'clock. They parked in an ugly concrete structure and crossed over to the terminal where Jessica and Marvin helped the Watsons carry in their baggage. Marvin saw to it that they had plenty of reading material for the flight. The young man who checked in the Watsons asked them if they wanted to take out additional baggage insurance, but they turned down this offer. They had already looked into the advantages of extra insurance and had found out that they didn't need it. They didn't believe in excessive insurance.

4. Explain the different interpretations of *turn on* in the following sentences and note any grammatical differences associated with the different meanings:

   a. *James turned on the radio but the battery was dead.*
   b. *The pit bull turned on Janet and mauled her viciously.*
   c. *The silver limousine turned on Park Lane and parked in front of the museum.*

5. Describe the ambiguity in the following sentence:

   The taxi turned into a parking garage.

6. Use any appropriate tests to demonstrate whether the forms in bold print are prepositional verbs, phrasal verbs, or just ordinary verbs followed by prepositional phrases:

   a. *They should not **put off** a decision.*
   b. *An independent was **running for** president that year.*
   c. *The commissioner **turned in** his resignation.*

7. Wherever possible, replace the verbs in the following paragraph with multiword verbs:

   We investigated the story and discovered that Dr. Stanley had encountered an angry group of Kikuyu men who would not tolerate his patronizing manner. They rejected his offer of glass beads and advised him to return to his own country.

Read over the original and your revised paragraph and comment on the effect(s) of your revision.

8. Discuss the following sentences taken from compositions by non-native writers:

   a. *She criticized on her sister.*
   b. *I will discuss about cultural misunderstanding.*
   c. *They looked their grandchildren after.*
   d. *He would be exposed with battering.*

NOTES

1. Although this *by* has no object, it might, within the Principles-and-Parameters framework, be considered to have a covert object pronoun, since the occurrence of this *by* appears to be constrained by the same conditions constraining pronoun distribution described in Chapter 9. This kind of pronominal is sometimes referred to as "small pro" in technical discussion. While Italian and Spanish and a number of East Asian languages have such a pronominal—it occurs in the subject position of a finite clause, as in Spanish *Dijo que vendría* ["(He) said (he) would come"]—English is generally described as lacking such a form. The examples of other prepositions without objects in this chapter are, however, truly objectless and are not constrained in the same way.

2. There are also survivals of an older use of *with* meaning "against." This meaning is possible with verbs referring to combat such as *fight, strive,* and *struggle.* So the following sentence is ambiguous as to whether the warrior Wiglaf is Beowulf's companion or his opponent:

   *Beowulf fought **with** Wiglaf that day, as the poet has told us.*

It's not clear what the thematic role of Wiglaf should be. The comitative role could be broadly defined to include this oppositional role. Both are fighting together under either interpretation. This oppositional *with* also survives in the verb *withstand.*

3. This is sometimes referred to as *preposition stranding.* It was once common for prescriptive grammarians to condemn preposition stranding. Sentences, they said, should not end in a preposition. Occasionally one still hears this. Some sentences sound awkward if the preposition is moved with the *wh* phrase, while some are awkward if the preposition is stranded. Some time prepositions such as *before, after,* and *during* cannot be stranded; they must be moved along with the *wh* form.

4. *Consist of,* like *contain, weigh, measure,* and *equal,* is a copular-like verb that does not have a true object and, correspondingly, has no passive counterpart.

5. Of course, prepositions differ from verbs in not requiring subjects. This is true even when verb forms such as *regarding* and *considering* are converted into prepositions, as in *Regarding your damage claim, please send the valuation reports as soon as possible.*

6. But note that when there is the option to position the particle before or after the object, the two versions differ in their focus. When the particle is after the object, the sentence seems to focus more on the result of the action. So, while the sentence *The guests **turned on** the overhead lights* focuses on the action, *The guests **turned** the overhead lights **on*** focuses more on the result of the action: The lights were now on. This difference, having to do with information status and focus, can be strengthened or neutralized by the contexts in which the sentences are used.

7. This pair has two major senses, one as in *bring up a child,* the other as in *introduce a topic (for discussion).*

PART
VI

INTERROGATIVES
AND NEGATIVES

21

Operators, Interrogatives, and Negatives

"I should go to the housing office now?" asked one learner.

"Go you to school here?" inquired another.

Both questions are easily understood. Both can be answered with a *yes* or a *no*. These kinds of interrogative forms are known as *yes-no questions.* But neither form is right for an ordinary *yes-no* question. The first form is grammatical, but it is typically used when the speaker wants confirmation of information that has already been provided. The question form that best captures the speaker's intent in this case is this one:

Should I go to the housing office now?

For the second speaker, the form used should have been this:

Do you go to school here?

Instead of fronting the verb *go,* the speaker should have inserted the auxiliary verb *do* before the subject of the sentence. This *do* is also needed for negative clauses where no other auxiliary verb is available. Instead of saying, *I go not to school here,* we say, *I do not (or don't) go to school here.*

Assume that the two speakers quoted regularly form their *yes-no* questions as they did above. If so, the first learner has not acquired the rule shifting the appropriate verb (in this case, the modal *should*) around the subject. The second learner has overgeneralized the rule by incorrectly applying it to the main predicate. It is hard to predict how the first speaker would have formed a negative clause, but, if the second speaker were consistent, the *not* would incorrectly follow the main predicate. We will, in this chapter, be discussing the rules for forming both interrogatives and negatives, rules involving a new grammatical relation, that of *operator.*

THE OPERATOR AND ITS FUNCTIONS

The *operator* is a verb that has three main functions.[1] First, it precedes the negative and combines with it when the negative is contracted to *-n't,* as in these examples:

*O'Connor **will** not agree to this.*
*O'Connor **has** not agreed to this.*
*O'Connor **wouldn't** agree to this.*

Second, it is the verb that is moved around the subject to the initial position in *yes-no* questions, as in these examples, in which the slot from which the operator has been shifted is marked [t] for trace:

> **Will** O'Connor **[t]** *agree to this?*
> **Has** O'Connor **[t]** *agreed to this?*
> **Wouldn't** O'Connor **[t]** *agree to this?*

Apart from a difference in intonation, the occurrence of a verb (but not the main verb) before the subject is the major characteristic distinguishing *yes-no* questions from their declarative counterparts. Finally, the operator is the verb that also appears in the tag phrases of interrogative sentences like these:

> *O'Connor will not agree to this,* **will** *he?*
> *O'Connor has not agreed to this,* **has** *he?*
> *O'Connor would agree to this,* **wouldn't** *he?*

Such questions are known as *tag questions.*

The verb that is operator is always finite—it is always either a modal or a verb in the past or present tense. With just one exception in American English and two in British English, it is never the main predicate of its clause. This has not always been the case. In earlier forms of English, main verb predicates like *go* could function as operators, as in these examples:

> **Goes** *he [t] to Margate tonight?*
> *He* **goes** *not to Margate.*

How are *yes-no* questions and negatives formed when a clause contains no verb eligible to be the operator? In the following sentence, the only finite verb is the main predicate:

> *He goes to Margate tonight.*

Here are the corresponding *yes-no* question, negative, and tag question forms:

> **Does** *he go to Margate tonight?*
> *He* **doesn't** *go to Margate tonight.*
> *He goes to Margate tonight,* **doesn't** *he?*

When no other candidate for operator is available, *do* is introduced. It thus functions as a kind of emergency operator.

OPERATORS AND D-STRUCTURE

In D-structures, any operator is in the Inflection constituent, which must be finite. If the Inflection contains a modal, then that modal must be the operator. If the Inflection contains only past or present tense, then it has no verb eligible to be operator, and the tense is simply incorporated into the following verb. If, however, the verb phrase contains other verbs besides the main predicate, then the first of the verbs is recruited from the verb phrase and becomes the operator. Thus, if the verb phrase contains the perfective aspect verb *have* or progressive aspect verb *be* or passive voice verb *be*, then that verb, if it is the first verb in the verb phrase, must be shifted into the Inflection to combine with the tense.

In questions, once the operator verb has been marked for the tense, it moves around the subject to the front of the clause. In negative sentences, it simply moves from the verb phrase to the position in the Inflection *immediately* following the tense and thus to the left of the negative particle *not*. The following is a slightly simplified D-structure for *Has he visited Snodgrass?*:

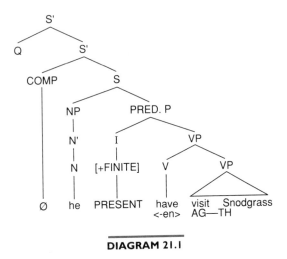

DIAGRAM 21.1

Since we need to distinguish interrogative sentences from ordinary declarative sentences, we have used a new node Q (for question) and have attached it to a higher S-bar.[2] As we will see, this new node is needed for other kinds of clauses, so we will now assume that all clauses have this new node, which will be left unlabeled except for questions.

Because there is no operator in the Inflection constituent for the sentence shown in Diagram 21.1, the auxiliary verb *have* is shifted into that constituent, becoming the operator, as in the following diagram:

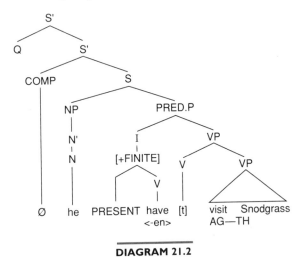

DIAGRAM 21.2

The *-en* must be combined with the main verb following, while the tense affix and the verb form combine in the Inflection. To make the sentence a grammatical question, the operator is moved into the complementizer slot; we call this shift *operator fronting*. Here is the resulting structure:

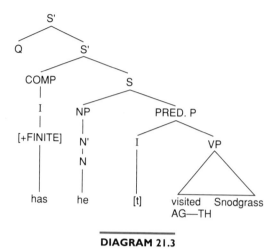

DIAGRAM 21.3

When a complementizer is in the slot, this fronting cannot take place. This is why *embedded yes-no* questions have no operator preceding their subject. The complementizer *whether,* which occurs with embedded *yes-no* questions, prevents the operator *could* from being fronted in the next example:

*The witness asked **whether** he **could** look at the drawing once more.*

This is why the following sentence is not grammatical:

The witness asked **whether could he look at the drawing once more.*[3]

although the sequence *Could he look at the drawing once more?* is fine if it is not embedded.

The negative sentence *They are not leaving for Glasgow* has the following simplified D-structure, with a new *negative* constituent as the first item in the verb phrase:

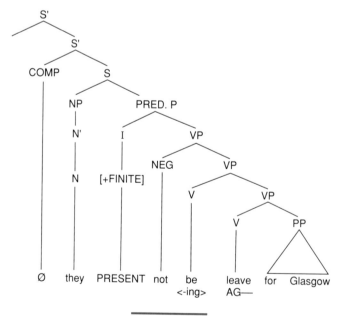

DIAGRAM 21.4

In the absence of an operator in the Inflection, the auxiliary verb *be* is shifted into the Inflection. The amalgamation of affixes with the verb forms takes place, combining present tense with *be* and *-ing* with *leave*, as in this structure:

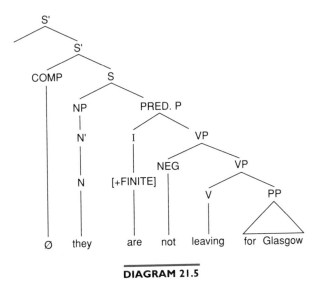

DIAGRAM 21.5

As mentioned earlier, when there is no eligible verb, not even a *have* or *be*, and an operator is needed, the emergency operator *do* must be used.

Now consider the following interrogative forms:

Was the world economy seriously affected by the new tariffs?
Were the economists honest?
Were the economists honest people?

The first example is straightforward. Since there is no modal, *be*, which came from the *be* plus past participle passive voice combination, is shifted from the verb phrase into the Inflection constituent and then fronted. But what about the second and third examples? In those sentences, the *be* form must originally have been followed by the adjective *honest* and the noun phrase *honest people*, respectively. *Be* is the only verb—hence, the main verb. Why is this *be* the operator then? The answer is that although *be* is the main *verb*, it is clearly not the main *predicate*, which is, in the second example, the adjective, and in the third the noun phrase. The major content of the verb phrase—the major predication—is expressed by the predicate adjective *honest* or the predicate noun phrase *honest people*. The point remains that it is the main predicate that cannot function as the operator.[4]

NEGATIVE QUESTIONS

A negative clause has *not* or *-n't* right after the tense or modal, that is, it follows the operator slot. If the contracted form *-n't* is employed, it is always attached to the end of the operator. That means the contracted form becomes part of the operator and is fronted with it if the clause is a negative question, as in the following sentence:

Hasn't Curtis been baking gooseberry pies?

which we'll show this way:

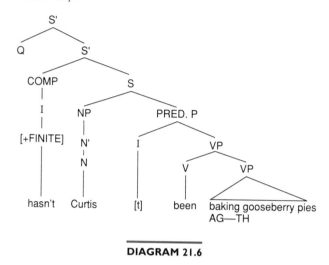

DIAGRAM 21.6

For most speakers, the negative has to be contracted so that it can be moved with the operator. If it is not contracted and the operator moves without it, the result is the extremely rare and, for most speakers, dubious question form:

> *Has Curtis not been baking gooseberry pies?*

Some speakers, especially speakers of British English, allow the uncontracted *not* to get attached to the operator constituent. This usage occurs primarily in ultraformal contexts, especially in formal oratory:

> *Has not Curtis been baking gooseberry pies?*

Such a question is more likely to be rhetorical rather than information seeking.[5] In general, the contraction *-n't* is used instead of *not* in negative questions.

TAG QUESTIONS

Tag questions consist of a declarative clause such as *Curtis has been baking gooseberry pies,* followed by a tagged-on *yes-no* question like *has he?* or *hasn't he?* As happens in declarative clauses, the *have* is shifted into the Inflection so as to combine with the tense. It is thus in the operator slot. The tag has a repetition of the operator in the declarative clause, *has,* and a pronoun referring to the subject. If a declarative clause has no verb eligible to be an operator, the tense has to be marked on the main verb. In the tag, there being no other operator, the emergency operator *do* is introduced:

> *Curtis baked a gooseberry pie, didn't he?*

One important fact about such tag questions is illustrated by the following pair:

> *Curtis has been baking a gooseberry pie, hasn't he?*
> *Curtis hasn't been baking a gooseberry pie, has he?*

If the declarative clause is affirmative, then the tag is normally negative. If the declarative clause is negative, then the tag question is affirmative. The negative in the tag is always the contracted form *n't*.[6] Following the analogy of positive and negative poles in electricity, the clauses and tags are sometimes said to have affirmative or negative *polarity*, a term that will come up again in this chapter. If the declarative clause has negative polarity, then the tag must have affirmative polarity, and vice versa. If this restriction is not observed, the sentence is likely to be interpreted not as a question but as a reflective statement to oneself, or perhaps as a sarcastic or threatening remark:

Curtis has been baking a gooseberry pie, has he?

Tag questions that are really questions are generally used less as simple information-seeking utterances than as requests for confirmation of what the speaker already suspects is or is not the case. If the declarative statement is affirmative, the speaker is expecting an affirmative answer; if it is negative, he or she is expecting a negative answer:

He studied for that exam, didn't he? (Of course he did!)
He didn't study for that exam, did he? (I know he didn't!)

Other languages have tag forms. For example, the Mandarin tag is *shì bu-shì* ("is not-is?"), while the French tag is *n'est-ce pas?* ("isn't it?"). These forms are less complex than the English ones, in that they don't vary with differences in the subject, verb, or the clause tense. Learners often "improve" English by using a simpler tag, for example, *You like foreign movies, yes?* In fact, native speakers often use simpler tags like *is that right?* or just *right?* as in this example:

Torik won't leave the palace, right?

ALTERNATIVE QUESTIONS

Alternative questions are questions that present options to choose from:

Will Mabel talk to me or will her brother go to the police?

Grammatically, these are simply clauses conjoined with *or*. Like other conjoined clauses they can undergo conjunction reduction, which omits all but the *contrasting* information from the second part. So this question:

Are you coming today or are you coming tomorrow?

can be reduced to this one:

Are you coming today or tomorrow?

The most obvious form of alternative question is simply a maximally explicit version of a *yes-no* question in which the affirmative question is followed by the negative:

Are you coming or aren't you coming?

This form is not common; the example above might be used if the speaker was impatient because the addressee was hesitating too long. Even so, a form that has undergone conjunction reduction would be more likely:

Are you coming or aren't you?

or even one with *not* in place of the second clause:

Are you coming or not?

THE PRAGMATIC DIMENSION OF QUESTIONS

We have been discussing questions as if their sole function is to elicit information, as in the following examples:

> *Is that the Vietnam Memorial?*
> *Where can I get a good vegetarian meal?*

But they can be used for other purposes. The following question is used to give an order:

> *Mr. Washington, will you come here for a moment?*

This next one is used to invite a friend to a political meeting:

> *Janet, do you have anything you have to do tonight? Joan Humphries is speaking at the Wilton Center.*

and the questions in the following dialogue function as stages of a marriage proposal:

> *"Elvira, do you really like me?"*
> *"I think I do. Yes, I do; I like you a lot!"*
> *"Elvira, what I want to say is, well, what I mean is…"*
> *"Yes, Jack?"*
> *"Then, why don't we get married?"*

The questions have the structure of an information-seeking request, but they are being used to perform a different function. When Jack utters the last question, he is obviously not seeking an explanation for their not getting married.

What we are discussing here is not the grammar of interrogatives but how they can be used to perform different speech acts. Orders, invitations, and threats (*Do you think you'll get away with this?*) are just some of the functions that interrogatives and other utterances can serve. As mentioned earlier, the study of speech acts is an important part of the field of *pragmatics*, which is concerned with how the context of an utterance affects the way the utterance is understood.[7]

POLARITY

The notions of negative and affirmative polarity are relevant to other related constructions. Compare the sentences in these groups of examples. The first and second sentences of each group are negative and are close paraphrases, the third is affirmative, and the fourth is an ungrammatical affirmative sentence:

> A 1. *She should bring **no** money with her.*
> A 2. *She shouldn't bring **any** money with her.*
> A 3. *She should bring **some** money with her.*
> A 4. **She should bring **any** money with her.*

> B 1. *He's talking to **nobody**.*
> B 2. *He's not talking to **anybody**.*
> B 3. *He's talking to **somebody**.*
> B 4. **He's talking to **anybody**.*

(The main stress in all the B sentences is on *talking* or *not*.)

C 1. *Pedro **no** longer buys antiques.*
C 2. *Pedro doesn't buy antiques **any** longer.*
C 3. *Pedro **still** buys antiques.*
C 4. **Pedro buys antiques **any** longer.*
D 1. *He has **never** talked to them.*
D 2. *He hasn't **ever** talked to them.*
D 3. *He has **already** talked to them.*
D 4. **He has **ever** talked to them.*

The first sentence of each group looks like an affirmative sentence, since it has no *not* or *-n't*. But they have a negative element: the quantifier *no*, the noun phrase *nobody*, and the adverb *never*. Other forms with a negative element are *no one, none, nothing,* and *nowhere*. The second sentence in each group is obviously a negative sentence, but the effect is less strongly negative than in the first. It seems that an ordinary negative sentence is weaker than one in which the negative marking is part of another word or phrase.

As the second sentence in each group shows, forms like *any* and its various compounds (*anyone, anybody, anything,* and *anywhere*) occur in negative clauses. The fourth sentence in each group, which contrasts in grammaticality with the third, shows that none of these forms go with *affirmative* statements. However, they are not really negative and should be distinguished from true negative forms like *no* and *never*. Most of these forms, which have been called nonassertive forms,[8] cannot occur in affirmative clauses unless heavily stressed. We refer to them as *negative polarity forms*.

However, even when unstressed, negative polarity forms occur in interrogative sentences:

> *Does she have **any** money?*
> *Has he **ever** talked to them?*
> *Will Pedro buy antiques **anymore**?*
> *Will **anyone** come to that meeting?*

in comparative constructions:

> *Clarence has more clothes than **anyone** else (has).*
> *She works harder than I **ever** did.*

in *if* condition clauses:

> *If De Gaulle **ever** felt humble, he did not show it.*

after quantifiers like *few* or somewhat negative adverbs like *rarely, seldom,* and *scarcely*:

> *Few of us have had **any** experience with children like these.*
> *They rarely allow **anyone** to inspect the original Ellesmere manuscript.*
> *Scarcely **anyone** was allowed to inspect the original Ellesmere manuscript.*

in clauses or gerunds embedded after negative predicates like *forbid, prevent, deny, unlikely, improbable,* and *impossible*:

> *Teresa denied that **any** money was missing.*
> *The court injunction prevented Ferreira from recruiting **anybody** for his organization.*
> *It is unlikely that Lewis **ever** visited the town again.*
> *It should be impossible for **anyone** ever again to treat innocent people like that.*

and in constructions embedded after certain negated container verbs, *think, believe,* and *regard* being the most common:

*I don't believe that **anyone** ever asked her.*
*She doesn't regard the contract as having **any** validity.*

What do interrogatives, negatives, *if* clauses, and these other structures have in common that allows these negative polarity forms? The answer is that they are all used to express thoughts about what is or may be unreal or untrue. If a speaker knew that someone had money, he would not ask if she had *any* money (unless, of course, he was being sarcastic or cunning). When an event *rarely* happens, most of the time it does *not* happen. When *few* people smoke nowadays, most people do *not* smoke. Questions and negatives deal with what the speaker believes is not true or real at some time or what might not be. The propositional content questioned or negated is not asserted to be true or real. We've already seen that there is a complex modal system to indicate various degrees of possibility, probability, obligation, and necessity. All of these notions have to do with the strength of the speaker's commitment to the truth of some proposition or the reality of some situation.

SUMMARY

This chapter has been about certain interrogatives, especially *yes-no* questions, and about negatives. Finite interrogative and negative clauses all need a verb functioning as an *operator* in the Inflection constituent. If the Inflection contains a modal verb like *will* or *should*, then that modal is the operator. If the clause is negative, the *not* must follow this operator and often gets attached to it in its contracted form *n't*. In questions which are not embedded, the operator undergoes *operator fronting*, being shifted around the subject into the complementizer slot. If Inflection contains past or present tense instead of a modal, then another verb must be found to serve as operator. If the verb phrase contains auxiliary verbs like perfect aspect *have*, progressive aspect *be*, passive voice *be*, main verb *be*, or, primarily in British English, main verb *have*, then whichever of these is leftmost in the verb phrase is moved into the Inflection constituent to become the operator. This operator combines with the tense in the Inflection. If there is no modal and the verb phrase has no eligible verb, then auxiliary verb *do* must be introduced into the operator slot; this "emergency operator" *do* gets the tense and, in negatives, precedes the *not* or its attached contraction *-n't*. When the question is a negative one, the *-n't* form is much more likely than *not* and it moves with the operator.

Tag questions consist of a declarative clause followed by a tagged-on *yes-no* question. The operator and its tense in the declarative clause are repeated in the interrogative tag. If the declarative clause has no operator, so that the tense has been marked on the main predicate, then *do* is used with the tense in the tag. In tag questions intended as questions, if the declarative clause is affirmative, then the tag is normally negative, and vice versa. The negative in the tag is always the contracted form *n't*. If the declarative clause is affirmative, the speaker expects an affirmative answer. If the declarative clause is negative, the speaker expects a negative answer. English is unusual in the complexity of its tag question structures.

Alternative questions are interrogative clauses linked by *or*. These can undergo conjunction reduction, which omits all but the *contrasting* information from the clause following the *or*.

Interrogative sentences have a range of pragmatic functions apart from seeking information. They are often used to perform such speech acts as ordering, inviting, and threatening.

Nonassertive forms such as *any, anyone, anywhere, ever,* and *even* can occur in either declarative or interrogative clauses. They are sometimes referred to as *negative polarity* forms, but they are not true negatives like *no, none, no one, nowhere,* and *never.* Therefore, in declarative clauses, they must normally be accompanied by *not.* They are allowed, however, in other constructions used to express thoughts about what is or may be unreal or untrue.

EXERCISE SET 21

1. Draw approximate D-structures for the sentences below and explain the processes that convert them into S-structures:

    a. *Can the child read?*
    b. *Have the women eaten their lunch?*
    c. *Does Jeremy like that painting?*

2. Explain in your own words the two statements below:

    a. The word that functions as the clause operator need not start off in the Inflection constituent.
    b. The category *main predicate* is more significant than that of *main verb* for understanding question formation.

3. Besides the negative polarity forms listed in the chapter, there are negative polarity idioms. Which of the idioms listed below are negative polarity forms? Find this out by trying them in (1) negative clauses, (2) *yes-no* questions, and (3) affirmative declarative clauses:

    a. *kick the bucket*   e. *budge an inch*
    b. *lift a finger*   f. *bat an eye*
    c. *raise the roof*   g. *blew his top*
    d. *hold the line*   h. *put his foot in his mouth*

4. It has been claimed that the following pair of sentences reflect slightly different speaker beliefs or expectations. Discuss this claim in no more than one paragraph. You should find it useful to imagine likely contexts for the sentences.

    a. *Is anyone there?*
    b. *Is someone there?*

5. Compare the ways in which the following two sentences might be used:

    a. *Do you have enough money to get home?*
    b. *You have enough money to get home?*

6. As discussed in this chapter, questions are not necessarily used to elicit information. Discuss a likely context and function for the following questions:

    a. *Don't you have any sense?*
    b. *You didn't bring the money, did you?*
    c. *You've brought the money, haven't you?*
    d. *What makes you think I'll help you?*

7. Discuss the nature of the problems with the following sentences based on utterances by non-native speakers:

    a. **Did Fujii can go to that exhibition?*
    b. **She has any chance to pass.*
    c. **The lady wanted to know if did we have Yami yogurt in Japan.*
    d. **That couldn't be imported here, couldn't it?*
    e. **Do those people who have such big houses be rich?*

NOTES

1. This account of the *operator* function is based primarily on that given in R. A. Close, *English as a Foreign Language: Its Constant Grammatical Problems,* 3rd ed. (London: Allen and Unwin, 1981), 111–112.

2. This corresponds to the specifier slot for the complementizer phrase in current X-bar Theory. It is the slot into which *wh* phrases are shifted both in *wh* questions and relative clauses.

3. Some spoken dialects of American English do, in fact, allow such sentences, but these are relatively few. Much work remains to be done on these dialects, which have a number of other interesting properties.

4. Many speakers of British English allow *have* to be an operator when it is the main verb. Examples are sentences like *Has she a pilot's licence?* and *They haven't a car for us to drive.* My personal experience as a speaker of British English suggests that sentences like these are increasingly rare and are associated with certain prestige dialects.

5. Those relatively few speakers who allow the uncontracted *not* to either precede or follow the clause subject in negative questions usually associate the different order with subtly different interpretations, the postsubject *not* negating only the following verb phrase.

6. In some nineteenth- and early twentieth-century fiction, most notably the Sherlock Holmes stories by Arthur Conan Doyle and, rarely now, in law courts, an uncontracted *not* is used in negative tags. In that case, the *not* always follows the subject:

> *Claudia has been baking a gooseberry pie, has she not?*

7. For a more detailed discussion of questions from this perspective, see E. Goody, ed., *Questions and Politeness* (Cambridge: Cambridge University Press, 1977).

8. For an insightful and thorough account of these phenomena, see R. Quirk, S. Greenbaum, G. Leech, and J. Svartvik, *A Comprehensive Grammar of the English Language* (London: Longman, 1985), 778-787.

22

Interrogatives and *Wh* Movement

Structurally there are two major question types: *yes-no* questions, discussed in Chapter 21, and *wh* questions. *Wh* questions are so named because they contain question words that, with the exception of *how*, begin with *wh*. The *wh* question word is normally at the beginning of the clause and may be part of a question phrase (e.g., *for what reason* and *whose apple*). In contrast to *yes-no* questions, which ask about an entire proposition, *wh* questions ask about a part of a proposition, requesting information about an argument of a predicate or about semantic domains like time, place, and manner.

The following list shows some of these semantic domains along with *wh* words and phrases used to ask for information about them:

TIME:	*when, at what time, on which day,* etc.
PLACE:	*where, at what place, in which town, to which country,* etc.
PERSON:	*who, by whom, with which friends, whose house,* etc.
NONHUMAN:	*what, which, with what,* etc.
MANNER:	*how, in what way, in which way, by what means,* etc.
REASON:	*why, for what/which reason,* etc.
QUANTITY:	*how much, how long, how many, how clever,* etc.

OPERATOR FRONTING AND *WH* MOVEMENT

To see how *wh* questions are formed, first consider the following declarative sentence:

> *Joseph will bring Stella's mother from Spain.*

Suppose a questioner did not know who Joseph will bring. The question would require a *wh* word. So we could replace *Stella's mother* in the original sentence with a *who* or *whom*:

> *Joseph will bring **who(m)** from Spain?*

As we saw in the last chapter, to form a question, an operator is needed. In this sentence, the modal verb *will* functions as the operator, so operator fronting shifts *will* around the subject:

Will Joseph [t] bring who(m) from Spain?

But this is not enough for an ordinary *wh* question. The next step is for the *wh* word to be moved to the position before the complementizer slot in an operation known as *wh movement.* The result is the following question:

Who(m) *will Joseph [t] bring **[t]** from Spain?*

In our constituent structure tree, we'll attach the *wh* word to the highest S-bar node like this:

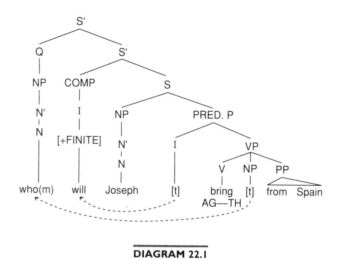

DIAGRAM 22.1

Other *wh* questions can be formed from this sentence in the same way. For example, suppose the speaker knew that Joseph was bringing someone's mother from Spain but didn't know the mother was Stella's mother. We could put the *wh* word, in its possessor form, into what is normally the determiner slot for the noun phrase. So, instead of *Stella's mother,* the noun phrase would be *whose mother:*

*Joseph will bring **whose mother** from Spain?*

Operator fronting shifts the operator into the slot before the subject:

Will *Joseph [t] bring whose mother from Spain?*

After the operator has been fronted, the *wh* word has to be moved out of its position. This time, since it is in the determiner slot of a noun phrase, the whole noun phrase has to be moved:

Whose mother *will Joseph [t] bring **[t]** from Spain?*

The operator fronting and *wh* movement operations are shown on this constituent structure tree:

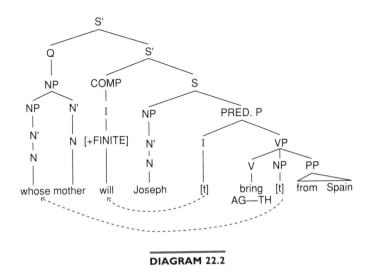

DIAGRAM 22.2

In the two examples above, the position emptied has been the object position. If location is questioned, the prepositional phrase is affected instead. In the D-structure of the location question there is a *wh* phrase that is the object of the preposition *from*:

*Joseph will bring Stella's mother **from where?***

The operator is fronted in the usual way:

***Will** Joseph [t] bring Stella's mother from where?*

Notice that here we have two options for *wh* movement. One option is to move just the *wh* noun phrase:

Where** will Joseph [t] bring Stella's mother **from [t]?

The second option is to move to the front the whole prepositional phrase containing the *wh* noun phrase:

***From where** will Joseph [t] bring Stella's mother [t]?*

More specific phrases such as *from which country* can be used instead:

***From which country** will Joseph [t] bring Stella's mother [t]?*

When the unknown item is the referent of the subject, the *wh* word doesn't have to move far. After operator fronting, the question *Who will bring Stella's mother from Spain?* looks like this:

***Will** who [t] bring Stella's mother from Spain?*

Then *wh* movement moves the *wh* word to the beginning of the sentence, leaving an additional [t] in the slot from which the word has been moved:

***Who** will [t] [t] bring Stella's mother from Spain?*

as in this diagram:

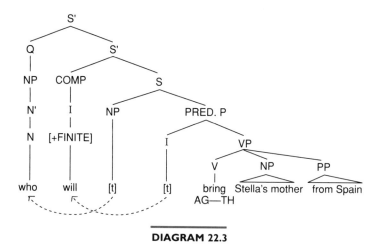

DIAGRAM 22.3

Note that, although the linear order of the constituents is exactly the same as if neither the operator or the *wh* word had moved, the hierarchical structure is now different.

DIFFERENCES IN ASSUMPTIONS

A speaker uttering the *wh* question *Who did Marlon meet?* assumes the major part of the proposition—that it is true that Marlon met someone—and just asks the addressee to identify that person. Similarly, a speaker uttering the question *Whose car did Louella wreck?* assumes that Louella has wrecked a car and wants to know just the detail represented by the *wh* word *whose*. *Wh* questions thus assume *(presuppose)* the general proposition to be true and ask only for information about one item, that represented by the *wh* word.

Yes-no questions are different. They do not normally presuppose the major proposition they contain but instead ask about its truth or falsity. Thus the sentence *Is it possible for those journalists to get visas?* does not assume either that the journalists will (or won't) get visas or that it is possible (or impossible) for them to get visas.

However, there are *yes-no* questions that function a little like *wh* questions semantically in seeking to elicit information not about the truth or falsity of the whole proposition but about time, place, and other domains for which there are *wh* words. This is done by specifying a possible answer to a *wh* question in a *yes-no* question. So instead of asking this *When will those elections take place?*, questioners who either want to make a special point about the time or think they know the time but want confirmation might ask this:

*Will those elections take place **this year**?*

with a heavier stress on *this year*. The *yes-no* question, like the *wh* question, assumes that elections will take place and simply asks when they'll take place. Typically in such *yes-no* questions, the information not presupposed comes at the end of the question, a position in which new information is most often placed.

Similarly, someone wanting to identify Lincoln's assassin might ask this *wh* question:

Who assassinated Abraham Lincoln?

But someone who suspected that John Wilkes Booth assassinated Lincoln could use a passive *yes-no* question mentioning the likely agent. This would ensure that *John Wilkes Booth* is in the important clause-final position for new information:

*Was Abraham Lincoln assassinated **by John Wilkes Booth**?*

INTERROGATIVES IN SOME OTHER LANGUAGES

Counterparts to both *yes-no* questions and *wh* questions in some other languages vary in interesting ways. French is less restrictive than English as to what constituents can serve as operators; it allows main predicates to be operators if they are verbs. Thus the following declarative sentence:

> *Elle veut   manger   votre   sandwich.*
> She wants   to-eat   your   sandwich.
> "She wants to eat your sandwich."

has a *yes-no* question counterpart in which the main verb, *veut*, is moved to the position in front of the subject:

> **Veut**-*elle [t]   manger   votre   sandwich?*
> wants she   to-eat   your   sandwich
> "Does she want to eat your sandwich?"

Chinese, Japanese, Korean, Thai, and many other languages do not have operators to be fronted. Although they have counterparts for *wh* words, these counterparts do not move to the front of their clause. In Japanese, for example, *yes-no* questions differ from their declarative counterparts only in intonation and the addition of *ka* at the end of the sentence. So if the declarative sentence is this:

> *Kore wa   zisyo   desu.*
> this TOPIC   dictionary   is
> "This is a dictionary."

the corresponding *yes-no* question, uttered with rising intonation, is this:

> *Kore wa   zisyo   desu   ka?*
> this TOPIC   dictionary   is   QUESTION
> "Is this a dictionary?"

If the word for dictionary, *zisyo*, is replaced with *nan*, "what," we have the counterpart of an English *wh* question:

> *Kore wa   nan   desu   ka?*
> this TOPIC   what   is   QUESTION
> "What is this?"

The word for "what" is in the same position before the predicate as was the word for "dictionary."

EMBEDDED INTERROGATIVES

Like other clauses, questions can be embedded inside container clauses. When they are embedded they are often called indirect questions, in contrast to unembedded questions, called direct questions. In Chapter 16 we discussed contrasts in tense and in the pronouns used in direct and indirect discourse. Now we see a further contrast regarding the use of the operator in finite interrogative clauses in direct and indirect discourse. The main difference in structure between direct and indirect questions is that in indirect questions operator fronting is not applied. Consider the following pairs of embedded and unembedded *wh* questions:

  a. *When could Dr. Hayden [t] go to Monroe Park [t]?*
  b. *Carlotta asked when Dr. Hayden could go to Monroe Park [t].*

a. *Why did they [t] choose Rochester [t]?*
b. *I was wondering why they chose Rochester [t].*

a. *What did Dante [t] want [t]?*
b. *Beatrice asked what Dante wanted [t].*

The *wh* question asked in the (a) sentence of each pair is embedded in the (b) sentence of the pair. But notice that operator fronting has not been applied to the embedded questions. Thus, in the first pair the *could* in the embedded question follows the subject and in the next two pairs the embedded questions need no operator, so *do* is not introduced into them.

Nevertheless, speakers of many dialects of American and Commonwealth English do in fact apply operator fronting in spoken English:

*Carlotta asked when **could** Dr. Hayden [t] go to Monroe Park.*

The embedded question is the same as it would be if it were not embedded. Speakers of such dialects are not necessarily quoting the direct question, since they may change person and tense (or the modal) to suit the situation:

Sheila: *What do you want, Sally-Ann?*
Natasha: *What did Sheila say?*
Sally-Ann: *She asked me what did I want.*

Now let's look at embedded *yes-no* questions. Consider the following example:

Paul: *Hey, Carl, have you read that report yet?*
Jean: *What did Paul say, Carl?*
Carl: *He asked me whether I had read that report yet.*

What distinguishes the embedded and unembedded sentences—apart from the shifts in pronoun and tense—is the appearance of *whether* in the embedded question.

Finally, let's look at embedded alternative questions. In Chapter 21 we discussed the following alternative question:

Will Mabel talk to me or will her brother go to the police?

The embedded counterpart is this:

The dean asked Mabel whether she would talk to him or whether her brother would go to the police.

The embedded alternative question, then, also uses *whether*. Here again, *if* can be substituted for *whether*, although the result is slightly less formal:

The dean asked Mabel if she would talk to him or if her brother would go to the police.

The use of *if* is more restricted than the use of *whether*. First, clauses with *whether* can be subjects of container clauses, while, for most native speakers checked, those with *if* cannot:

Whether Iliescu resigns or not is of no concern to me.
**If Iliescu resigns or not is of no concern to me.*

Second, only *whether* clauses can introduce nonfinite clauses:

*Caesar asked the soothsayer **whether to** go to the forum that day.*
Caesar asked the soothsayer **if to go to the forum that day.*

In Chapter 21 we discussed alternative questions in which the affirmative question was followed by the negative:

Are you coming or aren't you coming?
Are you coming or aren't you?
Are you coming or not?

Embedded alternative clauses with *whether* can have the negative alternative added as
or not:

He asked me whether I had read that report or not.
He asked me whether or not I had read that report.

If also allows *or not*, although less commonly than in *whether* clauses, and only at
the end of the clause:

*He asked me **if** I had read that report **or not.***
He asked me **if or not I had read that report.*

LONG *WH* MOVEMENT

English interrogative sentences can be very complicated, especially when related to
complicated declarative sentences like the following:

*Senator Corcoran proposed that Title II authorize the Federal Power Commission [e] to
integrate the operating companies into the Appalachian regional system.*

Let's replace the object of the prepositional phrase *into the Appalachian regional system*
with the *wh* phrase *which system*:

*Senator Corcoran proposed that Title II authorize the Federal Power Commission [e] to
integrate the operating companies into which system.*

Now we're ready to turn this declarative sentence into a *wh* interrogative. First, we
apply operator fronting:

***Did** Senator Corcoran [t] propose that Title II authorize the Federal Power Commission
[e] to integrate the operating companies into which system?*

Next, we apply *wh* movement. The whole *wh* phrase must be moved from its original position to the highest S-bar for each clause until it arrives at the S-bar node,
marked Q for question. The resulting question is this one, with the various slots in
which the *wh* phrase appeared on its journey upward indicated by [t]:

***Into which system** did Senator Corcoran propose [t] that Title II authorize the Federal
Power Commission [t] [e] to integrate the operating companies [t]?*

Alternatively, just the *wh* determiner *which* and its head noun *system* can be fronted to
produce this grammatical but very clumsy sentence:

***Which system** did Senator Corcoran propose [t] that Title II authorize the Federal Power
Commission [t] [e] to integrate the operating companies into [t]?*

Sentences like these do not occur in spoken English, except perhaps in law courts
or legislative hearings. But sentences only a little less complex are not too uncommon
in formal written English. Readers (or listeners) encountering a *wh* form at the beginning of a question do not know its thematic role, but must hold the form in memory
until they arrive at the original [t] position from which it was shifted. At this point the
reader can determine the thematic role of the moved *wh* item, whether it is, for example, an agent, a goal, or a theme. As we shall see, relative clause constructions, which
may also have *wh* words and phrases, can be complicated in much the same ways.

Such *wh* questions and relative clauses are interesting for research into the role of syntactic complexity in reading comprehension. Both structures require of readers closer attention to the syntax and retention of the *wh* phrase in memory.

SUMMARY

Wh questions ask about part of a proposition, perhaps about an argument of a predicate or about semantic domains like time, place, and manner. As with *yes-no* questions, operator fronting applies first; then *wh* movement shifts the *wh* noun phrase or prepositional phrase so that it ends up in the highest S-bar node of the sentence, a node marked Q if the sentence is a question.

Semantically, a *wh* question assumes (or presupposes) the truth of the major part of the proposition and seeks information about the *wh* phrase. *Yes-no* questions usually seek to determine the truth or falsity of the whole proposition, but sometimes just seek information about adjuncts of time, place, and other perspectives.

French, Spanish, and German are among those languages that have counterparts of operator fronting and *wh* movement. However, these languages also allow the main predicate to be the operator provided it is a verb. Other languages such as Japanese, Korean, and Chinese, have neither operator fronting nor *wh* movement.

Operator fronting is not permitted for embedded interrogatives (indirect questions) except in a few dialects. Embedded *yes-no* questions and alternative questions are introduced by *whether* or, with some restrictions, *if*. Long *wh* movement shifts the *wh* phrase from its original position to the highest S-bar for each clause until it arrives at the S-bar marked Q, usually the main clause.

EXERCISE SET 22

1. Compare the use of the two *do* forms in this sentence:

Do you do this often?

2. Turn the following into embedded questions:
  a. *What do the voters want?*
  b. *Will the more extreme nationalists agree to this proposal?*

3. Write one *wh* sentence for each of the seven semantic domains specified for *wh* words or phrases at the beginning of this chapter. Mark with a [t] the gap from which the *wh* form is moved.

4. Draw a D-structure tree for the following *wh* question and then explain how it becomes a surface structure:

What could the defendant have lied about?

5. State the two meanings of the following sentence:

When did Prince Charles announce that he would fly here?

Then explain the ambiguity of the sentence in terms of the *wh* movements that might have taken place and the positions from which the *wh* forms may have originated.

6. Describe how you might teach a low-level class about operator fronting and the use of *do*.

7. Evaluate the following questioning of a woman charged with inciting a public disturbance while making a speech at an outdoor meeting. Focus on the presuppositions exploited in the prosecutor's questions.

Prosecutor: *How did you come to participate in the riot at the Travco plant on Monday, February 15, 1993?*

Defendant: *I didn't participate in any riot. It was a meeting. I was speaking about promotion discrimination against female workers at the plant. Security attacked us. Colville wanted to make trouble.*

Prosecutor: *Why did you cause this disturbance?*

Defendant: *There was no disturbance until Colville told security to break up our meeting. Women have been working here for twenty years but only men are in supervisory positions. They're promoted over us even if they have less experience. And worse qualifications too.*

Prosecutor: *Answer my questions, please. We don't need speeches. You didn't get promoted. Was that why you wanted to disrupt the factory? Why did you assault the security guard who asked you to return to work?*

Defendant: *I didn't. He pulled me off the wall and I fell on him.*

Prosecutor: *You attacked him, didn't you?*

8. *Wh* questions, we pointed out, direct attention to particular parts of a sentence, unlike most *yes-no* questions. Ronald Scollon has shown how conversation with adults using *wh* questions can lead children to lengthen their utterances and add constituents corresponding to the *wh* forms in the questions.[1] Does this seem to be true of the following dialogue, which is part of a conversation between a child and her mother? Describe the child's language output and the mother's input to the child.

Child: *Fall down.*

Mother: *What fell down?*

Child: *Drop it.*

Mother: *What did you drop? Cashew?*

Child: *Yeah.*

(Five minutes later, the child tries again to report what happened.)

Child: *Cashew fall down.*[2]

NOTES

1. R. Scollon, "A real early stage: An unzipped condensation of a dissertation on child language," in E. Ochs and B. Schieffelin, eds., *Developmental Pragmatics* (New York: Academic Press, 1979), 215–227.

2. I owe this data and some discussion of it to Miki Loschky and her daughter.

PART
VII

COMPLEX SENTENCES

23

Embedded Clauses and Noun Phrase Movement

We would expect complex sentences—sentences with subordinate and embedded clauses—to be harder to understand than simple one-clause sentences. However, this is not always so. Subordinate clauses have in their complementizer slot semantic markers indicating perspective—time, reason, contrast, location, purpose, manner, and so forth. These markers link each clause semantically to its container clause and, along with such signposts as *however* and *therefore*, they alert addressees to the semantic organization of the discourse. The presence of such semantic markers is one reason it is possible for some complex sentences to be easier to understand than a sequence of short single-clause sentences. A sequence of such short sentences, lacking overt semantic markers, may require a heavier reliance upon contextual inference.

As for structure, subordinate clauses are structurally very similar to simple sentences. If the content is well organized and the vocabulary well chosen, complex sentences consisting of main and subordinate clauses need not present problems for either production or comprehension.

Embedded clauses are different. They function semantically as arguments of predicates. Since they themselves also contain predicates and arguments, problems can arise because the addressee must sort out which arguments go with which predicates. Furthermore, in many cases, the subject arguments may be covert ([e]) or they may have been shifted from their original slots ([t]). The same is true for objects. The goal argument of *order*, for example, as in *ordered the two hostages to ...*, is shifted into the subject slot of its clause if the verb is in the passive voice: *the two hostages were ordered to ....*

Look now at a more complex, yet still fairly straightforward, sentence:

It was alleged that someone had ordered two hostages to pick up the money.

The predicate ORDER requires an agent (the "orderer"), which is a role filled by *someone*, and two other arguments—the goal (the person to whom the order was addressed), expressed as *two hostages*, and the theme (the content of the order), which we would show in a D-structure as *[e] to pick up the money*.

Now we will change our sentence so as to have *two hostages* out of the slot following *ordered*:

It was alleged that two hostages had been ordered to pick up the money.

The propositional content (or core meaning) is unchanged, but because the verb is in the passive voice, *two hostages* cannot be in the usual object slot after the verb; it is now in the subject slot.

Yet even a more radical kind of movement is possible, one which moves *two hostages* right out of its clause:

Two hostages were alleged [t] to have been ordered [t] [e] to pick up the money.

The noun phrase *two hostages,* which belongs semantically with the verb *ordered,* now precedes the verb *were alleged,* which assigns no thematic role to its subject. It would not be surprising if such a sentence were harder for a non-native reader to process.[1]

The situation could be worse still if what is moved is an embedded sentence rather than a noun phrase. In the following sentence, the embedded clause *that the rapid deforestation was causing serious erosion* is assigned the theme role by the verb preceding it, *prove*:

It was hard to prove that the rapid deforestation was causing serious erosion.

But the embedded clause can be raised into the highest clause and become subject:

That the rapid deforestation was causing serious erosion *was not hard [e] to prove [t].*

Once again the moved argument is now a distance away from the verb that assigned it a semantic role.

Embedded clauses themselves can be hard to process; moving them away from the predicates they belong with can make comprehension more problematic for non-native readers. These embedded clauses are usually complements of a predicate; the predicate is actually the *head* and determines what kind of complement it will allow. Thus the verb *report* can have as its complement an ordinary noun phrase such as *a burglary* or an embedded clause such as *that his villa had been burglarized.* Complements, whether clauses or noun phrases, are said to complete the meaning of the head. They are shown on tree diagrams as sisters of their head.

So far in this chapter we have used examples in which the head for the complement has been a verb. But, as briefly mentioned in Chapter 6, other kinds of constituents can also be heads.

COMPLEMENT CLAUSE ARGUMENTS AND TYPES OF HEADS

A verb that functions as the head for a complement may allow only certain types of embedded clauses to be its complement. Heads are said to *select* their complements. Thus the head verb *want* requires that a clause embedded as its complement be a non-finite clause, as in *I want you to bring your sister.* German speakers sometimes produce sentences like *I want that you should bring your sister* because the German verb *wunschen* ("want") selects finite complement clauses.

We noted above that the head of a complement need not be a verb. Any of the other major categories—adjectives, nouns, and prepositions—can also be heads. Let's take a finite clause—*that Crenshawe had negotiated with the terrorists*—and make it the complement of each category of head. First, we'll make the clause a verb complement:

*The prosecutor **believed** that Crenshawe had negotiated with the terrorists.*

The head is the verb *believed,* the embedded clause is the complement of *believed,* and the two constituents together form a verb phrase. We can show the verb phrase like this:

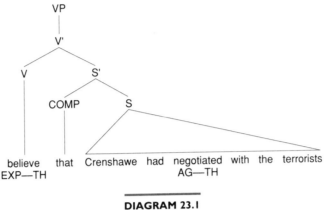

DIAGRAM 23.1

Now we'll make the clause a complement of the adjective *certain*:

*The prosecutor was **certain** that Crenshawe had negotiated with the terrorists.*

The head is the adjective *certain,* the embedded clause is the complement of *certain,* and the two constituents form an adjective phrase:

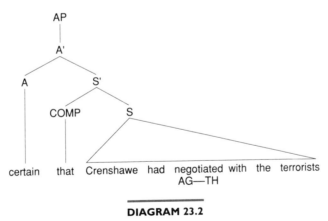

DIAGRAM 23.2

Prepositions don't take complements with *that,* except for the idiom *in that,* as in the following example:

*The administration had deceived them **in that** Crenshawe had negotiated with the terrorists.*

This structure could be analyzed in the same way; there is a prepositional phrase with *in* as the head and the embedded clause as its complement:

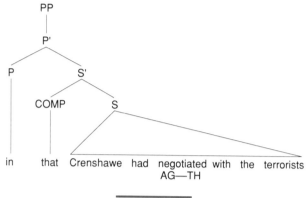

DIAGRAM 23.3

Finally, we'll make the embedded clause a complement of the noun *belief*:

*Dalgleish knew about the prosecutor's **belief** that Crenshawe had negotiated with the terrorists.*

Now we have a noun phrase with *belief* as the head and the embedded clause as its complement:

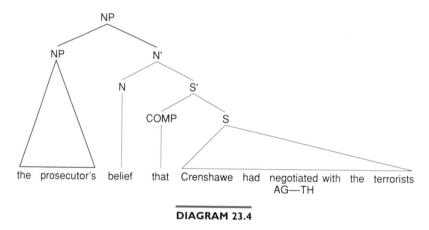

DIAGRAM 23.4

In these structures, the head has the semantic function of a predicate and the complement clause is an argument of that predicate. To see this, let's look at some noun heads with complements, for which this claim might seem less clear:

*the **fact** that Crenshawe had met the terrorists*
*that **rumor** that Crenshawe had met the terrorists*
*her **order** (for Crenshawe) to meet the terrorists*
*this **plea** (for Crenshawe) to meet the terrorists*
*your **refusal** [e] to meet the terrorists*
*this **attempt** [e] to meet the terrorists*

Semantically, the head noun is a kind of label characterizing the content of the complement clause. The propositional content of the clause is labeled as a fact, a rumor, an order, a plea, and so forth. Thus, the head is a predicate and the complement an argument of that predicate.

COVERT COMPLEMENTIZERS

The complementizers *that* and *for,* which function to introduce embedded clauses, can often be omitted. More precisely, a covert complementizer occurs instead.

>   *Sellars claims **(that)** Paramount will accept his offer.*
>   *Sellars needs **(for)** Paramount to offer him a sizable advance.*

However, the complementizer *for* cannot be replaced by a covert complementizer in contexts where it is needed to assign case. The absence of the overt complementizer *that* poses no such problems, since *that* does not assign case and the embedded clause subject *Paramount* gets nominative case from the finite Inflection in its clause. In the second example, the embedded clause has nonfinite inflection and *Paramount,* therefore, does not get nominative case. *Paramount* gets objective case, since *for,* unlike *that,* is a preposition and prepositions assign objective case. So what happens when *for* is not present? How can the sentence still be grammatical? The answer is that the container clause verb *needs* is also a case assigner.[2]

Nonfinite clauses that are complements of adjectives must be introduced by the complementizer *for* if they have an overt subject:

>   *It was important **for** a public hearing to be announced [t].*

Without *for,* the subject could not get case. If there is no overt subject, there is no overt complementizer; the complementizer is a covert one that we mark as *[e]*:

>   *It was important **[e] [e]** to announce the public hearing.*

The second *[e]* is the covert subject of the complement clause. In finite adjective complement clauses, the complementizer is often covert in informal discourse:

>   *She thought it ridiculous **(that)** no evidence was introduced.*

The subject noun phrase, *no evidence,* gets its case from the finite Inflection.

In contrast, noun complement clauses that are finite almost always have the complementizer *that,* even though case is assigned by the finite Inflection. Native speakers should check their intuitions about replacing *that* with a covert complementizer in the following noun complements:

>   *the fact **that** Crenshawe had met the terrorists*
>   *the news **that** Crenshawe had met the terrorists*
>   *that rumor **that** Crenshawe had met the terrorists*
>   *his allegation **that** Crenshawe had met the terrorists*

For nonfinite noun complements, the complementizer *for* only occurs when it is needed to assign case to an overt subject:

>   *the necessity **for** someone to announce the hearing*
>   *the necessity **[e]** to announce the hearing*

Note that when an embedded clause is in subject position, its complementizer must be overt:

>   ***For** Paramount to offer him a sizeable advance would please Sellars.*
>   ***That** Paramount will accept his offer pleases Sellars.*

The need for *for* in the first example could be explained by the need to assign case to *Paramount.* But what about the second example? If a covert complementizer replaced *that, Paramount* would still be assigned case. What seems to be operating here is a *pro-*

cessing constraint. Without the complementizer *that*, an addressee would be likely to identify the clause as an independent clause rather than an embedded clause. The occurrence of the finite verb *pleases* after *offer* would be the first clue that would force the addressee to reanalyze the structure. With *that*, this processing difficulty is avoided.

NONFINITE CLAUSES AND NOUN PHRASE MOVEMENT

With certain predicate adjectives, intransitive verbs, and passive verbs, the overt complementizer *for* is not needed, even when the complement clause has a subject. The reason is that these predicates allow the subject to move out of the complement clause into the subject slot of the container clause, where it can get case. With most predicates such movement is not possible. The most common predicates allowing this movement are the adjectives *likely, unlikely, sure,* and *certain,* the intransitive verbs *seem* and *appear,* and passive verbs like *be expected, be believed, be thought be reported,* and *be alleged,* all of which take nonfinite clauses as complements.

The following examples show the contrast between *likely,* which allows movement, and *unusual,* which doesn't (the complement clauses are shown in square brackets and the complementizers are all [e]):

    a. *... PRESENT be unusual [[e]* **refugees** *to behave like that].*
    b. ***Refugees** are unusual [[e] [t] to behave like that].*

    a. *... PRESENT be likely [[e]* **refugees** *to behave like that].*
    b. **Refugees** *are likely [[e] **[t]** to behave like that].*

When the subject is moved, and tense and agreement convert *be* into *are,* the sentence with *likely* is grammatical, but the sentence with *unusual* is not.

In the sentence with *likely, refugees* is in the subject slot and so gets nominative case. However, its thematic role of agent was acquired not from the container predicate *be likely,* but from the embedded clause predicate *behave.* It's not the refugees that are likely but rather the situation of their behaving like that. In this way we know that *refugees* must have started out in the embedded clause and been moved. The movement is shown on this constituent structure tree:

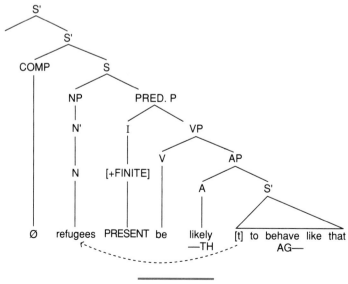

DIAGRAM 23.5

The embedded clause now has no overt subject. We've marked the empty subject slot with a [t]. When noun phrases have been moved like this, a [t] indicates one of two possibilities. The first is that the unfilled position marks the D-structure slot to which the noun phrase belongs semantically. If this is so, then the addressee can identify from the predicate of that clause the thematic role assigned to the moved noun phrase. The second possibility is that the slot marked with a [t] was just an intermediate stop through which the noun phrase passed on its way from a yet more deeply embedded clause. If this is so, then there must be at least one other slot marked with a [t] from which the same noun phrase was moved. There may even be three or more, if the sentence is very complicated:

These candidates are likely [[t] to be thought [[t] to seem [[t] to have betrayed the voters]]].

Notice the difference between the following sentences:

Rebecca Swensson is certain [that she will protest the decision].
Rebecca Swensson is certain [[t] to protest the decision].

In the first example, no noun phrase has been moved. Let's assume that the noun phrases *Rebecca Swensson* and *she* refer to the same person. Even so, each is assigned a separate thematic role by its predicate. Rebecca Swensson feels the certainty. In D-structure, the predicate adjective *certain* assigned the role of experiencer to *Rebecca Swensson*, while the predicate *protest* assigned an agent role to *she*.

In the second example, the noun phrase *Rebecca Swensson* has been moved. Back in D-structure, the container clause subject slot was empty and *Rebecca Swensson* was in the embedded clause, where it received its thematic role from the predicate *protest*. A moved noun phrase keeps the thematic role it was assigned in its D-structure position. So *Rebecca Swensson* and [t] together have just one thematic role, that of agent. The predicate *certain* assigned no thematic role to its empty subject slot. Check the sentence: The certainty is felt not by Rebecca Swensson, who is mentioned in the sentence, but by the speaker or writer of the sentence. Contrast this with the first example, the example in which no movement occurred. There we are not told whether the speaker feels any certainty. For these two examples, then, the different assignment of thematic roles at D-structure makes a crucial semantic difference.

Think now about the following sentence in which different thematic roles are assigned to the same referent:

*The officers forced **Juan** [[e] **[e]** to write a confession].*

Juan and the second [e], representing the covert subject, both occur in D-structure. Although they refer to the same person, they don't have the same thematic role. Juan is assigned the goal role by *forced*, while [e] is assigned the agent role by *write*. If there had been no [e] in D-structure, and the noun phrase *Juan* had then been shifted from the embedded clause to the container clause, leaving a trace ([t]), we would expect the *Juan* and [t] to have the same thematic role, that assigned in D-structure by the predicate *write*. But instead the same referent is represented twice in the sentence, once in the higher clause, whose predicate assigns *Juan* the goal role, and once in the embedded clause, where it appears as an [e] in D-structure and is assigned an agent role by the predicate *write*.

Sentences that look very similar at S-structure may thus look quite different at D-structure, a difference reflected in important semantic differences.

Tough Movement

For a still more limited group of predicates, another kind of noun phrase movement is possible when the complement clause is nonfinite. These predicates are sometimes called "tough" predicates after one member of the group, the adjective *tough*. They all refer to degrees of ease or comfort.[3] Other "tough" predicates are *difficult, hard, easy, fun, awkward, impossible, dangerous, good, convenient, nice, tricky, fascinating,* and *a pleasure.*

Look at the following two structures with "tough" predicates. In each, the subject slot in the container sentence is unfilled:

> ... PAST be hard [for the experts to evaluate the earthquake damage].
> ... PRESENT be fascinating [[e] to watch those dolphins].

Since the container clauses have finite Inflection, their subject slots must be filled in order to satisfy the subject constraint. There are several ways to do this. *It* can be inserted:

> It was hard [for the experts to evaluate the earthquake damage].
> It is fascinating [[e] to watch those dolphins].

The whole theme clause can be shifted into the subject slot:

> [For the experts to evaluate the earthquake damage] was hard [t].
> [[e] To watch those dolphins] is fascinating [t].

Alternatively, the subject constraint can be satisfied by applying *tough* movement, in which the *object* noun phrase of the embedded clause is shifted into the subject slot of the container clause.[4] The following sentences result:

> **The earthquake damage** was hard [for the experts to evaluate **[t]**].
> **Those dolphins** are fascinating [[e] to watch **[t]**].

The transitive verbs in the complement clauses no longer have object noun phrases following them, and the container clauses now have overt noun phrases in their subject slots.

But the new subjects of the container clauses still have the thematic roles assigned to them by the predicates in the complement clauses. It was not the earthquake damage that was hard but evaluating the earthquake damage. The dolphins may indeed be fascinating, but our example sentence really means that watching the dolphins is fascinating.

The object noun phrase that is shifted in *tough* movement isn't necessarily the object of a verb:

> **That doctor** is difficult for Tony to work with **[t]**.

In this example, *tough* movement has shifted the object of the preposition *with* into the container clause subject slot. Sometimes there are several noun phrases eligible for *tough* movement. For example, the following structure:

> ... PRESENT be easy [e] to play **folk songs** for **children** on **that guitar**.

can end up as any of these sentences:

> **Folk songs** are easy [[e]to play **[t]** for children on that guitar].
> **Children** are easy [[e] to play folk songs for **[t]** on that guitar].
> **That guitar** is easy [[e] to play folk songs for children on **[t]**].

Each of these reflects a slightly different focus. There is a strong tendency for the noun phrase chosen for *tough* movement to be either definite or generic. *Tough* movement typically results in the positioning of a topic noun phrase at the beginning of the sentence, the regular position for topics. *Tough* movement sentences thus have a more specific focus than the more general form with *it*:

> *It is easy [[e] to play folk songs for children on that guitar].*

The differences lie in the way the information is structured, rather than in the propositional content. Interestingly, speakers of topic-comment oriented languages like Japanese, Korean, and Chinese sometimes produce sentences like **That doctor will be possible for you to talk to* when they intend the subject of the sentence to be its topic. Initial position in a sentence is the right place for a topic.

SUMMARY

A text consisting of complex sentences is not necessarily more difficult for English language learners than one with simple sentences. Subordinate clauses have semantic markers indicating their function in the sentence, whereas simple sentences often lack markers indicating their function in a text. Embedded clauses, however, can present problems. Constituents that belong together semantically, such as a predicate and its arguments, are often not adjacent to each other. In this respect embedded clauses differ significantly from both simple and subordinate clauses. Case requirements and the subject constraint, for instance, may separate one of the noun phrase arguments from the clause in which its predicate occurs. This separation does not necessarily make comprehension more difficult for native speakers, since they know implicitly how many arguments are associated with each and can quickly determine which container clause argument is co-referential with an argument in the complement clause or was shifted from a now empty slot in the complement clause. For non-native speakers the comprehension task may be much harder.

Embedded sentences can be complements of the major lexical categories of English—verbs, nouns, adjectives, or prepositions. In tree structures, the embedded clause and its head are sisters at D-structure. The type of embedded clause—essentially whether it is finite or nonfinite, whether it has an overt subject, whether *tough* movement is permitted, and which of the complementizers may occur—is selected by its lexical head. Where alternate forms are allowed, they usually differ in focus (i.e., in their information structure). In *tough* movement, the *object* noun phrase of the embedded clause is shifted into the subject slot of the container clause.

Non-native speakers of topic-prominent languages may overgeneralize the *tough* movement pattern because it is a pattern which allows for the topic at the beginning of the sentence.

EXERCISE SET 23

1. Draw a constituent structure tree for the sentence *Maggie ordered Gerald to climb over the wall.*

2. The sentence *Josephine seems to like Napoleon* has had noun phrase movement applied to it. Which noun phrase has been moved and why?

3. Convert the following sentences into noun-headed complements. The first is done for you:

> a. *They demanded that Arkoff hand over the documents.*
>   ANSWER: their demand that Arkoff hand over the documents

   b. *I requested Josephine to take me to the Emperor.*
   c. *The interrogator claimed that Arkoff had lied.*
   d. *She was convinced that Leif was still alive.*
   e. *The ambassador decided to close the consulate.*
   f. *They conspired to destroy the printing presses.*

4. In terms of the grammatical description in this chapter, describe what is wrong with the following sentence:

   *That man is easy to build a cottage.

5. How might comprehension difficulties caused by complex *wh* questions be similar to those presented by *seem* sentences and sentences to which *tough* movement has been applied?

6. Burt and Kiparsky[5] note that non-native students make errors like the following:

   *Jeremy is unusual to drive a new auto.
   *The door is strange to be open.

   a. Draw what you think might be the D-structure trees for the two ungrammatical sentences above. They should correspond to the likely intentions of the speakers.
   b. In terms of the grammatical description in this chapter, describe the noun phrase movement that may have been applied and explain what has gone wrong and what should have happened instead.

7. Choose a complicated paragraph from a college-level textbook in the physical or social sciences and rewrite it to make it easier for non-native students to understand. Then compare the sentence structures in the two pieces and comment on what you observe.

NOTES

1. For an important discussion of the relevance of such issues to first language acquisition, see S. Pinker, *Language Learnability and Language Development* (Cambridge, MA: Harvard University Press, 1984), 209–242.

2. An alternative analysis is that the clause is introduced by a covert preposition with the same case-assigning properties as *for*. Covert prepositions could also be suggested for *the next day* in *He arrived late the next day*. Compare *He arrived late on the next day*.

3. This characterization is due to R. Quirk, S. Greenbaum, G. Leech, and J. Svartvik, *A Comprehensive Grammar of the English Language* (London: Longman, 1985), 1225.

4. This *tough*-movement analysis presents a problem for the version of Case Theory adopted in this book, since a noun phrase that already has objective case has also to become nominative in its new subject slot. Noun phrases cannot have two cases. Chomsky, in proposals for a major revision of linguistic theory ("A Minimalist Program for Linguistic Theory" [M.I.T. Working Paper, 1992]), has proposed a more abstract treatment of case, which would include such structures. His proposal is still too sketchy for adequate coverage here.

5. M. Burt and C. Kiparsky, *The Gooficon* (Rowley, MA: Newbury House, 1972), 91-92.

24

Predicates and Clause Arguments

In the preceding chapter we discussed the relationship between clause complements and their heads, which could belong to any of the four major word categories for English. We saw that constituents of an embedded clause are often shifted into the container clause, so that understanding the semantic relations among the various constituents might sometimes be difficult for non-native speakers. This chapter deals with a related area that can also puzzle non-native speakers, such as which kinds of embedded constructions go with which heads and what the semantic consequences might be of selecting one kind of embedded construction over another.

Our topic requires that we explore classifications of predicates, classifications that sometimes overlap, with predicates being classified in more than one way. The complicated relationships between predicates and their complements pose difficulties for many language learners. For English-speaking children, the acquisition of container predicates followed by a nonfinite clause comes quite late, the acquisition of predicates followed by a finite clause even later.[1] For non-native speakers, selection of the wrong complement type for a particular predicate is a fairly common error. Here are some examples:[2]

> *He wants that I go.
> *When he had finished to eat...
> *They refused helping their neighbors.
> *I'll never forget to see that accident.

Complement selection is often assumed to be arbitrary, and to a significant extent it is. But, as we shall see in this chapter, it is also influenced by semantics, especially the semantics of the container predicate.

A SEMANTIC CONTRAST

In Chapter 7 we noted some semantic differences among finite clauses, nonfinite clauses, and gerundives. As we pointed out then, where a particular container clause predicate allows a choice among these forms, differences in meaning come into play.[3] Let's look at this phenomenon in more detail. Here is a very clear example. The verb *try* allows either a nonfinite clause or a gerundive to be embedded after it; only finite complement clauses are prohibited:

Sylvia tried [[e] screaming].
Sylvia tried [[e] to scream].
**Sylvia tried [that she screamed].*

Notice that the sentence with the gerundive complement and the one with the nonfinite clause complement are not paraphrases. According to the sentence with the gerundive complement, Sylvia actually screamed. This sentence with the gerundive portrays Sylvia as using screaming to achieve some other goal. The goal is not specified but could be, for example, that of gaining someone's attention. However, in the sentence with the nonfinite clause, Sylvia did not succeed in screaming. The nonfinite clause sets up screaming as a goal, which Sylvia strove unsuccessfully to achieve.

The crucial difference is that in the nonfinite clause the activity is just a *potential* one, as yet unaccomplished, whereas with the gerundive it is real, already accomplished. The following examples make this contrast very clear:

Gunther forgot [[e] to lock the door].
Gunther forgot [[e] locking the door].

In the infinitive example, Gunther didn't actually lock the door. In the example with the gerundive, he did.

A second and very important semantic difference between the two sentences has to do with the location *in time* of the locking event. Both sentences report a locking event and a forgetting event. In the sentence with the gerundive, the forgetting occurs *after* the door was locked. *Forget* in this example "looks back" to a prior event. In the sentence with the nonfinite clause, however, at the time when Gunther should have remembered to lock the door, the locking had not yet happened and, of course, did not happen. When you are asked not to forget to carry out some action, the action, if it happens, takes place afterward. In this usage, *forget* with the nonfinite clause "looks forward." It is the combination of the nonfinite clause *to lock the door* with the container predicate *forget* that is forward oriented. The same predicate in combination with the gerundive is backward oriented. We'll refer to backward-oriented predicates as *reactive* predicates because they refer to reactions to a situation.

As we will see in the next sections, not all predicates are like *forget* (and *remember*) in occurring in both forward-oriented and reactive combinations.

Forward-Oriented Predicates

Predicates like *want, persuade,* and *eager* are themselves forward oriented. Clauses embedded after them refer to a *potential* situation rather than an existing one. Since nonfinite clauses are so often understood to refer to a potential situation, they are the forms normally selected by forward-oriented predicates.

Let's look at *want.* If you want something, presumably you don't have it yet. So, not surprisingly, *want* allows nonfinite clauses, but not finite clauses or gerundives. (For convenience in the examples following, we do not mark covert complementizers.)

Jeremiah wanted [[e] to leave].
**Jeremiah wanted [that he leaves].*
**Jeremiah wanted [[e] leaving].*

Note once again that the time reference of the container clause is previous to the time at which the situation represented in the complement clause might be realized. Jeremiah experiences the feeling of wanting to leave before the time that he would leave if his wishes were fulfilled.

Sentences with complement clauses embedded after forward-oriented predicates make no commitment, then, that the goal expressed as the nonfinite complement clause will ever be achieved. The event referred to in the embedded clause is a potential one:

*They advised Gladstone [[e] **to support the legislation**].*
*Gladstone was reluctant [[e] **to support the legislation**].*
*It will be impossible [for **Gladstone to support the legislation**].*

None of the sentences contain the assertion that Gladstone actually supported the legislation.

Here is a partial list of predicates which form forward-oriented constructions with *nonfinite* complement clauses:

VERBS

advise	*fail*	*remind*	*want*
agree	*force*	*request*	*wish*
ask	*hope*	*seek*	*yearn*
aspire	*learn*	*strive*	
beg	*long*	*struggle*	
command	*order*	*teach*	
compel	*persuade*	*tell*	
convince	*plan*	*try*	
decide	*refuse*	*urge*	

ADJECTIVES

anxious	*hard*	*reasonable*
crucial	*important*	*redundant*
desperate	*impossible*	*reluctant*
determined	*keen*	*ridiculous*
difficult	*necessary*	*safe*
eager	*possible*	*unwilling*
essential	*prepared*	*urgent*

These predicate adjectives behave very much like verbs taking nonfinite complements. Consider, for example, the following sentence with the predicate *eager* and its nonfinite complement:

*Caesar was eager [[e] **to leave before winter**].*

This sentence communicates Caesar's feeling about some potential as yet unrealized action. The time reference of the container clause precedes the time at which the action referred to in the complement might be realized. If you're eager or anxious or aspiring or hoping to do something, the eagerness, anxiety, aspiration, and hope must come before you actually do it. Similarly, if you are persuaded or urged or told to do something, the time of the persuasion, urging, or telling precedes the time when you might in fact do it.

Certain forward-oriented predicates, most notably *require, demand, recommend, prefer,* and *suggest,* allow and, in some cases, require a *that* clause with a verb unmarked for tense. The construction is a descendant of older subjunctive mood forms whose role has for most verbs been taken over either by finite clauses with modals like *might* and *should* or by nonfinite clauses. The first two pairs of examples following shows verbs that permit both kinds, while the third shows a verb permitting only tenseless *that* clauses:

a. *We required [that she leave at once].*
b. *We required her [[e] to leave at once].*
a. *We preferred [that you spend the holidays with Sheila].*
b. *We preferred [(for) you to spend the holidays with Sheila].*
a. *We suggested [that Sykes invest in tin].*
b. **We suggested Sykes [[e] to invest in tin].*

Certain container predicates, which can or must have *nonfinite* complement clauses, carry as part of their meaning the implication that the situation referred to by the complement clause *must have* occurred. Examples are *cause, compel, force,* and, to a lesser extent, *convince* and *persuade*:

The recession caused the government [[e] to abandon its free trade policies].
The new law compelled the surgeons [[e] to justify their high fees more adequately].

The situation designated by the complement clause must have occurred. When the government is caused to do something, it does it. When surgeons are compelled to do something, they do it. The truth of the complement is necessarily implied as part of the meaning of the container predicate. If these container predicates are negated, then the truth of the complement clause is left open. We will adopt the label *implicative verb* for these verbs.[4]

Reactive Predicates

Compare the following sentences. The first one uses the forward-oriented predicate *intend,* while the second uses the reactive predicate *regret*:

Gladstone intended [[e] to support the legislation].
Gladstone regretted [[e] supporting the legislation].

In the first example, there is no indication of whether in fact Gladstone ever supported the legislation. In the second example, the combination of a reactive verb and a gerundive complement indicates that the action described in the gerundive was realized—he did support the legislation. His support for the legislation was more than a potential action; it really happened. In fact, the sentence would have been committed to the belief that it really happened even if *not* were inserted into the container clause:

Gladstone did not regret [[e] supporting the legislation].

In both the affirmative and negative versions, the container clause with *regret* indicates Gladstone's *reaction* regarding his past support of the legislation. He was sorry or not sorry that he had supported it.

The time reference of the container clause is *after* that of the embedded clause—the opposite of what happens with forward-oriented predicates combined with nonfinite clauses. Reactive predicates, which usually take as complements either finite clauses or gerunds, have a later time reference than that of their complement. The following partial list of reactive predicates contains only verbs, since, apart from forward-oriented adjectives, all adjectives that take complements normally take either finite embedded clauses or prepositional phrases. Such prepositional phrases may contain gerundives, but these gerundives arise not from the reactive status of the container predicate but from the fact that they follow prepositions.

abhor	*discover*	*remember*	*resist*
appreciate	*dislike*	*renounce*	*resume*
avoid	*enjoy*	*repel*	*rethink*
consider	*forget*	*repent*	*ridicule*
deny	*regret*	*repudiate*	*scrutinize*
detest	*reject*	*resent*	*watch*

In general, these verbs have to do with realized experience, whether past or ongoing; all allow gerundive complements. In most cases, sentences with gerundives have finite counterparts that are synonymous or almost synonymous:

> *Myrtle regretted (it) [that she had left the party so early].*
> *Myrtle remembered [that she drove a Mercedes].*
> *Myrtle forgot [that Jenny went to bed early].*

One other special feature should be noted for reactive verbs. As we mentioned earlier concerning a *regret* sentence, the situation described in their complement clause is typically assumed to have happened or to be true, even when the main clause is negative:

> *Pat resented having chosen to study Italian rather than Spanish.*
> *Pat didn't resent having chosen to study Italian rather than Spanish.*

Whether or not Pat felt any resentment, she had still chosen to study Italian rather than Spanish.

Some Complexities of the Forward-Oriented Versus Reactive Distinction

As always in dealing with human language, grammatical formulations seem to be less neat and regular than we might like. For example, *forget, regret,* and *remember* are not always used as reactive predicates. Where they are not, the situation described in the container clause is assumed to have occurred *before*, not after, the forgetting, regretting, and remembering, and the meaning is likely to be somewhat different. Used in this nonreactive sense, these verbs take nonfinite clauses as complements. Compare these two sets of examples:

Reactive sense (container clause situation occurs *after* embedded clause situation):

> *Myrtle forgot [Jenny's going to bed early].*
> *Myrtle remembered [[e] driving a Mercedes].*
> *Myrtle regretted [[e] leaving the party so early].*

Nonreactive sense (container clause situation occurs *before* embedded clause situation):

> *Myrtle forgot [[e] to go to bed early].*
> *Myrtle remembered [[e] to drive a Mercedes].*
> *Myrtle regretted [[e] to leave the party so early].*

But these nonreactive uses of *forget, remember,* and *regret* with nonfinite embedded clauses don't have the semantic properties we would expect of forward-oriented predicates. The first two examples report Myrtle's forgetting or remembering an *instruction* or *recommendation* to go to bed early or to drive a Mercedes. The complement clause is essentially an embedded imperative—*Go to bed early! Drive a Mercedes!* Remember that, as main clauses, nonfinite clauses (without *to*, of course) are imperatives. The third example would typically be used to report a speech act. Myrtle is explaining, perhaps to her hosts, that she has to leave early. The sentence does not necessarily claim that Myrtle really felt regret. She is simply using a polite and very formal style.

Nonfinite clause complements following reactive adjective predicates like *happy, sad, horrified,* and *pleased* can refer to ongoing or past events, not just future or potential events:

Cromer was happy [[e] to have been chosen to represent her country].
Cromer was happy [[e] to be going to Verona next year].

In the first example, Cromer's happiness is clearly a reaction to something that had happened previously. Note that sentences with these predicates and their nonfinite complements all have paraphrases with finite complements, as in the following example:

Cromer was happy [that she had been chosen to represent her country].

This is not the case with forward-oriented constructions.

Some verbs used as either forward-oriented or reactive predicates have slightly different meanings depending on their use. The verb *like*, for instance, if it is preceded by *would* or *-'d*, is close in meaning to *want* with a nonfinite clause but is closer to *enjoy* with a gerundive:

Shelley would like [[e] to dance in the dark].
She would like/would have liked [[e] dancing in the dark].

When an experience is *enjoyed*, its time reference is open. The experience could be happening now, have happened in the past, or could happen later on. The enjoyment is experienced at the same time as the dancing, perhaps also being felt immediately after. But the enjoyment is not understood to precede the experience. *Enjoy* is a reactive verb. But *wanting* something to happen can only precede the happening. *Like* can be used in both senses. In its reactive use, it allows a gerund as its complement. In its forward-oriented use, it allows a nonfinite clause as its complement.

FINITE CLAUSES, SEMANTICS, AND TIME REFERENCE

Now let's look at some semantic properties of finite embedded clauses occurring as complements of verbs that also take nonfinite complements. We'll start with the container verb *hope*. The verb *hope* allows either a nonfinite or a finite clause as its complement, but notice the difference between the way the following sentences are understood:

O'Connor hopes [[e] to leave early].
O'Connor hopes [that he left/will leave early].

With the nonfinite clause, *hope* is similar in meaning to *plan*. The early departure is a *potential* event; it has not yet taken place. With the finite clause, *hope* expresses a more general feeling or desire, similar to wishing. It is not a plan. Moreover, as the example shows, the early departure could have happened previously or it might not have happened yet.

Finite complements allow for the greatest flexibility. They can refer to the past, present or future, or to some hypothetical situation. This is because they can have either modals or present or past tense verbs. Nonfinite clauses have infinitive verbs whose time reference is less obvious. They normally refer to hypothetical time or time subsequent to that of the container clause. Hoping *about* something in the past, present, or future is quite different from hoping to do something.

The verbs *persuade* and *convince* also can have either a nonfinite or a finite clause as complement clauses. With nonfinite complements, *persuade* and *convince* mean something like "cause someone to intend to take some action":

> Andromeda persuaded/convinced Perseus *[[e] to leave at once]*.

With finite complements, however, their meaning is "cause someone to believe something":

> Andromeda persuaded/convinced Perseus **that the ship was close by.**

A SPECIAL CLASS OF VERBS

There is another group of verbs—we might call them *believe*-class verbs—which take nonfinite clause complements that are paraphrases of finite complements. There is no difference at all in propositional content between these nonfinite complements and their finite counterparts. Unlike the other nonfinite clauses discussed so far, these never have the complementizer *for*. Their subjects always get objective case from their container clause verbs. Compare these two sentences:

> She believed *[that Caesar had betrayed them]*.
> She believed *[Caesar to have betrayed them]*.

While there may be a slight difference in emphasis—*Caesar* is more prominent in the nonfinite alternative—the sentences have exactly the same propositional content.[5] Other verbs like *believe* include *discover, think, prove, assume, fancy,* and *consider*.

One problem with sentences whose container predicates are *believe*-class verbs is that their surface structures look identical to those of very different structures, for example, those with container predicates like *advise* and *order*. Essentially the crucial difference arises from a difference in valency (the number of arguments a predicate requires). Look at the noun phrase following the container verb in these sentences:

> Dr. Fuentes advised **the congressman** *[[e] to study Korean]*.
> Dr. Fuentes believed *[**the congressman** to be a liar]*.

Native speakers of English know—though they might not be able to put it in words—that the noun phrase *the congressman* following *advised* is an argument of that verb, as our bracketing indicates. The verb *advise* has three arguments: the adviser (the agent), the advisee (the goal), and the actual advice (the theme). In other words, *advise* has a valency of three. Part of the meaning of the sentence is that Dr. Fuentes advised the congressman. So the subject of the embedded clause is a covert noun phrase ([e]) with the same reference as *the congressman*. However, part of the meaning of the second example is *not* that Dr. Fuentes believed the congressman. In fact, from the rest of the sentence, it's clear that she didn't believe him. The noun phrase *the congressman* is not an argument of *believe*; it is the subject argument of *be a liar*. The verb *believe* requires only two arguments: the believer and the belief.

ASPECTUAL PREDICATES

Aspectual predicates are predicates denoting beginning, continuing, and ending. They fall rather arbitrarily into two groups. Group A verbs, a very small group, can have as their complements *either* gerundives *or* nonfinite clauses, while Group B verbs, which include several phrasal and prepositional verbs, allow only gerundives:

Group A	**Group B**
begin, continue, cease, start	*finish, postpone, give up, stop, commence, go on, keep on, break off, put off, leave off, take up*

Consider the following examples with Group A verbs:

Humphrey began eating at 3 o'clock.
Humphrey began to eat at 3 o'clock.

Humphrey ceased eating rhubarb.
Humphrey ceased to eat rhubarb.

Humphrey continued reading.
Humphrey continued to read.

Humphrey started complaining.
Humphrey started to complain.

In the appropriate contexts there are very subtle semantic differences between the sentences with gerundives and those with nonfinite clauses. Take the last examples with *start*. The gerundive form suggests that the complaining is ongoing, while the nonfinite clause suggests that the complaining may not yet have begun. Contrast the following examples:

Humphrey started to complain but changed his mind when he saw the plum pudding and custard.

Humphrey started complaining but changed his mind when he saw the plum pudding and custard.

The first sentence allows for the interpretation that Humphrey had not yet uttered his complaint. In the sentence with the gerundive, the first syllable or more of the complaint had been uttered. The gerundive form thus represents a more fully realized activity. If we compare the two examples with *cease*, we note that the gerundive version is somewhat more likely to be used for a specific (i.e., real) rhubarb-eating incident, while the nonfinite version is much more likely than the gerundive to be used for a general habit of rhubarb-eating.

As for the Group B verbs, none allow nonfinite clauses, except for *stop* and *go on* in special cases such as when the clause is a purpose adjunct. In general, phrasal and prepositional verbs do not take nonfinite clauses as complements. Non-native speakers sometimes mistake Group B verbs, especially the single-word forms, for Group A verbs, producing sentences like these:

*When we had finished to eat, we cleaned all up and went back.
*My father stopped to smoke two years ago and now he is fat.

Note that the sequence *stopped to smoke* is in fact grammatical if the nonfinite clause *to smoke* is interpreted as a purpose clause like *in order to smoke*. Under this interpretation the clause is not a complement of the verb; it is an adjunct. The non-native speaker of the sentence, however, clearly intended it to be understood as a complement, the object argument of the verb.

The combination *go on* occurs with an infinitive in the following sentence:

*The judge **went on to denounce** the lawlessness of youth today.*

in which *went on* means something like "moved to the next stage (of his speech)" rather than just "continued," as in this next sentence with a gerundive:

*The judge **went on denouncing** the lawlessness of youth today.*

EMBEDDED CLAUSES AND GERUNDIVES IN SUBJECT POSITION

So far we've seen embedded clauses and gerundives as complements, that is, as part of the predicate phrase. But many predicates also allow embedded clauses and gerundives as subjects. Examples are verb phrases headed by *amuse, surprise, astonish, dismay, create (a sensation)*, adjective phrases headed by *significant, unfortunate, courageous, foolhardy*, prepositional phrases like *of great significance*, and noun phrases like *a sensational story* and *the last straw*. In most cases, gerundives, finite clauses, and nonfinite clauses are almost equally acceptable, as the following examples indicate:

For Myrtle to steal a new Mercedes ⎰ was foolhardy.
⎱ astonished the Jaguar salesmen.
⎰ was of great significance.
⎱ was the last straw.

That Myrtle stole a Mercedes ⎰ was foolhardy.
⎱ astonished the Jaguar salesmen.
⎰ was of great significance.
⎱ was the last straw.

Myrtle's stealing a Mercedes ⎰ was foolhardy.
⎱ astonished the Jaguar salesmen.
⎰ was of great significance.
⎱ was the last straw.

Predicates thus seem much more involved with their complements than with their subjects. Note that the nonfinite clause in the first example about Myrtle needn't itself indicate that Myrtle actually did steal a new Mercedes. What does tell us that she stole the car is the container predicate. The container predicate thus cancels out the hypothetical sense of the nonfinite clause.

SUMMARY

The semantics of predicates does not completely determine which forms can serve as their complements, but meaning clearly plays a significant role in complement selection. Nonfinite clauses are more suited to potential situations rather than realized situations. Gerundives, on the other hand, tend to fit better with realized situations. Consequently, container predicates that are forward oriented, looking forward to something that may not yet have happened, often select nonfinite clauses, while reactive predicates, looking back to prior situations, are more likely to select gerundive constructions. But some predicates can take either nonfinite or gerundive complements, though the alternation typically reflects a semantic difference, as we saw with *hope*. Finite clauses, which can use a modal or tense marking to indicate past, present, or hypothetical situations, fit with most container predicates, whether reactive or forward-looking, the major exceptions being very strongly forward-oriented verbs like *try, strive, want,* and *fail*, which have to do only with potential situations.

Clauses embedded under reactive predicates are assumed to refer to realized rather than potential situations. This is the case even when the reactive predicate is negated. Predicates that are normally reactive are sometimes used nonreactively, as we saw with *forget, regret,* and *remember.*

The choice is more open for embedded clauses and gerundives when they serve as subjects. Container predicates are more closely tied to their complements than to their subjects and are therefore more "permissive" as to what can function as their subject.

Unfortunately, as this chapter makes clear, the semantics of predicates is not an infallible guide to the kind of complements each predicate can take. In many cases, the kinds of complements allowed have to be learned predicate by predicate. Nevertheless, the semantics frequently does determine the choice of complement, so the generalizations made here should provide some useful guidelines for teaching and insights into errors.

EXERCISE SET 24

1. Here are three fill-in-the-blank items from an exercise designed to test whether learners have mastered the alternation between nonfinite complements and gerundive complements. Add two more items of the same type.

    a. *Nancy promised (come) to the meeting but avoided (say) whether she would speak.*
    b. *Jason and Marion enjoyed (talk) about their project but postponed (do) anything on it.*
    c. *The supervisor denied (gossip) about the project but agreed (appear) before the investigating panel.*

2. List the complement constructions in the following passage and specify for each (a) whether it is a gerundive, a finite clause, or a nonfinite clause, and (b) for which noun, verb, adjective, or preposition it is a complement:

> *Because of Johnson's granting the award to Katz, the commission felt that no further action was necessary. The commission was anxious for the courts to take up the matter. Katz regarded Johnson's permission for him to leave the country as a sign that the president trusted him.*

3. Draw a constituent structure tree for the sentence *Shelley was eager to visit Rome.*

4. List the kinds of complements (apart from ordinary noun phrase objects) that the following verbs allow:

    a. *forbid*   d. *neglect*
    b. *permit*   e. *condescend*
    c. *avoid*   f. *recollect*

5. Write an explanation for an inquiring student of the differences between the following pairs of sentences:

    a. *She heard him knocking on the door.* versus *She heard him knock on the door.*
    b. *I saw her swimming to the shore.* versus *I saw her swim to the shore.*

6. The following activity will test how you apply analytical techniques to structures not discussed in this chapter but relevant to the main topic. The complementizer *whether* introduces both finite and nonfinite clauses.

    a. List ten container predicates that allow *whether* clauses, and indicate whether the clauses can be nonfinite as well as finite.
    b. How do nonfinite *whether* clauses differ semantically from finite *whether* clauses?

7. How are the following verbs different from the forward-oriented predicates like *try* or *seek*, which were discussed in the chapter?

    a. *predict*   c. *imagine*

    b. *anticipate*   d. *foresee*

NOTES

1. See S. Pinker, *Language Learnability and Language Development* (Cambridge, MA: Harvard University Press, 1984), 209–242.

2. These examples are all taken from M. Swan and B. Smith, eds., *Learner English: A Teacher's Guide to Interference and Other Problems* (Cambridge: Cambridge University Press, 1987).

3. Differences like most of those discussed here are described in D. Bolinger, "Entailment and the Meaning of Structures," *Glossa* 2 (1968): 119-27.

4. For a detailed discussion, see L. Kartunnen, "Implicative verbs," *Language* 7 (1971): 157-82.

5. Indeed some past grammatical theories (as well as current frameworks with grammatical relations as a central focus) have claimed that the version with the finite complement is converted into the second version by means of a process that converts the complement clause subject into the container clause object. This putative process is usually called Subject-to-Object Raising.

25

Relative Clauses

Consider the following sentence spoken by a Chinese student of English:

She gave me the book is dog-eared.

One of the verb phrases, either *gave me the book* or *is dog-eared*, is intended as the main assertion and the other as identifying information. From the context, it became clear that the part of the sentence about the giver was information intended to identify the particular book. (It's unlikely that the giver of the book is being described as dog-eared.)

In Chinese, relative clauses and other modifiers come before their head. In English we can say any of the following:

The book that she gave me is dog-eared.
The book which she gave me is dog-eared.
The book she gave me is dog-eared.

In all of these the modifying clause follows the head noun *book*. But in Chinese, the relative clause meaning *she gave me* occurs before *book*. So this student needed to learn not only how relative clauses are formed in English but also where they occur with respect to their head noun.

Relative clauses are specialized constructions used to provide identifying information, but they are not the only means of providing such information. Ordinary sentences that communicate propositions can also be used to identify entities. Consider the following dialogue:

> Colette: *I met that lawyer again yesterday.*
> Suzanne: *The one working on the Oceanside case?*
> Colette: *No, the bald one. Don't you remember? You had an argument with him last month.*
> Suzanne: *Oh, him! He's an idiot. What did he say?*

Here the function of identification is fulfilled by the ordinary sentence *You had an argument with him last month.* This sentence has no special structure to mark its identifying function. But the same identifying function can be fulfilled more economically in a relative clause:

*I met the lawyer **that you had that argument with.***

Relative clauses (also called *adjective clauses*) are clauses linked to a noun in their container clause, frequently with a *wh* form like the relative pronouns *which* and *whom*. As we shall see, they typically differ from other embedded clauses in having one constituent missing or, if it includes a relative pronoun, out of its expected order. There are two major types of relative clauses in English. *Restrictive relative clauses* are embedded clauses used to identify a noun phrase referent by providing further information to narrow down the reference; *appositive* or *nonrestrictive relative clauses* also provide additional information about a noun phrase referent that has already been adequately identified, so the new information is not needed for identification. We will see that there is a structural difference too.

We'll begin with an account of restrictive clauses. A restrictive relative clause is embedded inside a noun phrase and follows its head. But there is one important difference from other clauses embedded inside noun phrases. As we will see, a relative clause is not a complement of the head noun. A constituent structure tree would therefore not show the embedded clause as a sister of the head noun.

Restrictive relative clauses come in quite varied forms. There are both finite and nonfinite relative clauses; the finite clauses can be relative clauses indicating place, time, and other perspectives. In addition, there are participial modifiers (*astonished by that news, containing hydrochloric acid*), which are essentially another type of relative clause. All will be discussed in this chapter. We will begin with the more basic types.

FINITE RESTRICTIVE RELATIVES AND GAPS

Look at the subject noun phrase in the sentence *The clarinetist who(m) they are sponsoring bought a new instrument*. The head noun is, of course, *clarinetist*. It is followed by the relative pronoun *who* (or *whom*). Then follows the actual finite clause, the embedded sequence *they are sponsoring*. But unlike the other kinds of finite embedded clauses studied so far, this clause cannot stand on its own as an independent sentence.

The problem is that the clause has something missing. The transitive verb *are sponsoring* has no object noun phrase following it. What has happened to the object? Clearly there is a connection between this gap—the absence of an object at the end of the clause—and the presence at the beginning of the clause of an additional element, *who*.

As in the interrogative clauses discussed in Chapter 22, the *wh* phrase starts off at D-structure in its logical slot, the object position following the verb. The same *wh* movement rule applies as the one that applied to *wh* questions in Chapter 22. The *wh* phrase is moved out of its original slot, leaving a gap we mark with a [t]. It is shifted to the S-bar slot that would be marked with a *Q* if the clause had been an interrogative instead of a relative, in other words to the highest S-bar following the head noun. The *wh* phrase is attached to a higher S-bar than is the complementizer for that clause, as shown in this diagram:

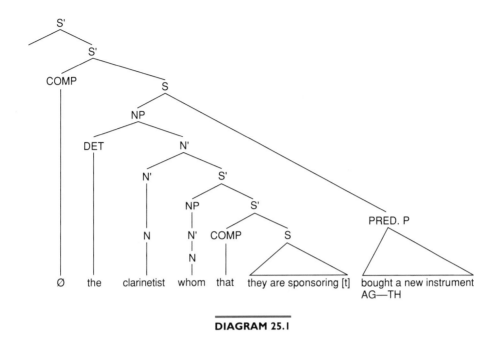

DIAGRAM 25.1

Note that the relative clause is attached to an N-bar on the tree but, unlike a complement of the head noun, it is not a sister of the head noun. Complement clauses need a certain type of head noun, an abstract head noun like *fact, belief,* or *order,* while relative clauses can follow any kind of common noun. The link between a head noun and its complement is much closer than that between a head noun and a relative clause. Relative clauses and their heads are thus less dependent, less tightly connected than complements and their heads. This difference is reflected in our constituent structure trees when we make a complement clause a sister of N, while a relative clause can only be a sister of N-bar. The difference in structure explains why relative clauses are normally placed further away in a noun phrase when a complement clause also occurs:

> *the announcement [that the Green Party had been elected] [which contained many typographical errors]*

> **the announcement [which contained many typographical errors] [that the Green Party had been elected]*

The unasterisked sentence has the complement clause *that the Green Party had been elected* immediately adjacent to the head noun. Note that this complement clause is actually the theme argument of the noun *announcement.* It's what someone announced. But the *which* relative clause is not an argument of *announcement.* It exists simply to identify more precisely the announcement. It identifies the announcement, while the complement clause states the content of the announcement.

There is one other difference that we have referred to already, the inability of the relative clause to function as an independent clause because it has a gap, a missing constituent.

When we read a clause with a fronted *wh* pronoun (known in this context as a *relative pronoun*), we have to wait until we get to the gap to find out how it fits into the clause. Relative clauses all have this gap, the slot that we mark in surface structure as [t].[1] This gap is the original site of the *wh* pronoun, the one the clause is identifying; the head noun of the whole noun phrase determines its reference.

But not all relative clauses have overt *wh* pronouns. Compare these three sentences:

The clarinetist who(m) they are sponsoring [t] bought a new instrument.
The clarinetist that they are sponsoring [t] bought a new instrument.
The clarinetist they are sponsoring [t] bought a new instrument.

The second sentence has no *wh* pronoun, although it does have the complementizer *that* before the subject *they*. The third sentence has no overt element at all between the head noun and the relative clause subject.

Assume that originally all three relative clauses had *that* in their complementizer slot. This is reasonable since they are finite embedded clauses and *that* is the likely complementizer for such clauses. The *wh* movement rule we've described shifts the *wh* pronoun into the slot before the complementizer. Here is how that part of the constituent structure should look at this stage:

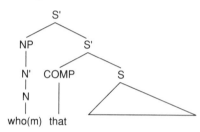

DIAGRAM 25.2

Of course, we do not say *who(m) that*. English does not allow the sequence of a *wh* phrase followed by the complementizer *that*. To get the first of our three sentences, the complementizer *that* must be deleted from the D-structure. It is deleted by the same optional rule that deletes it from complement clauses in sentences like this:

*Victoria knew **that** she was a great clarinetist.*

When we apply this complementizer deletion to the relative clause structure, we get this sentence:

*The clarinetist [who(m) **0** they are sponsoring [t]] bought a new instrument.*

The *0* indicates the now empty complementizer slot. The absence of the *that* makes no difference to the meaning of the sentence since *that* has no special semantic contribution of its own.

A second alternative is *wh* deletion, which removes the *wh* noun phrase *who(m)*. This *wh* deletion, much like complementizer deletion, removes an element whose semantic contribution is minute. Note that this *wh* deletion rule does not apply to interrogatives. In interrogatives the *wh* word makes a crucial semantic contribution. There is a general constraint, the *recoverability constraint*, which prevents deletion of material containing semantic content that cannot be inferred from the rest of the sentence.

But in our relative clause this problem does not arise. After *wh* deletion has been applied, we have this sentence (with brackets around the relative clause and with *0* to indicate the deletion):

*The clarinetist [**0** that they are sponsoring [t]] bought a new instrument.*

A third alternative is to apply both *wh* deletion and complementizer deletion. This yields our last form:

*The clarinetist [**0 0** they are sponsoring [t]] bought a new instrument.*

Let's look now at the following D-structure noun phrase:

the house [that they went to which]

The *wh* phrase is inside the prepositional phrase *to which*. *Wh* movement applies to this construction to move into the higher S-bar slot either the *wh* phrase (i.e., the relative pronoun *which*):

*the house [**which** that they went to [t]]*

or the whole prepositional phrase *to which*:

*the house [**to which** that they went [t]]*

Now we'll apply to the first example complementizer deletion, *wh* deletion, or both, yielding three paraphrases:

*the house [**which 0** they went to [t]]*
*the house [**0 that** they went to [t]]*
*the house [**0 0** they went to [t]]*

All three relative constructions are well formed.

But notice what happens if the same rules are applied to the second example, the one in which the fronted phrase includes the preposition *to*. We can apply complementizer deletion to yield the following well-formed relative construction:

*the house [to which **0** they went [t]]*

But if we apply *wh* deletion to delete the whole fronted phrase, the result is bad:

*the house [**0** that they went [t]]*

as it also is if both complementizer deletion and *wh* deletion are applied:

the house [0 0** they went [t]]*

The recoverability constraint blocks the deletion of the prepositional phrase containing the *wh* phrase because it also contains *to*, a significant meaning-bearing word.

The constraint applies in a similar way to relative clause constructions in which the *wh* phrase is in the determiner slot as in *whose computer*, in which *whose* fills the slot often occupied by determiners such as *the, a,* and *this*. Look at this D-structure:

*The man [that they borrowed **whose computer**] works at the bakery.*

When *wh* movement is applied, it must shift the whole noun phrase containing *whose*, yielding this:

*The man [**whose computer** that they borrowed [t]] works at the bakery.*

Now complementizer deletion can be applied, yielding a well-formed sentence:

*The man [whose computer **0** they borrowed [t]] works at the bakery.*

But we do not have the option of applying *wh* deletion to delete the *wh* phrase containing the noun *computer*, since *computer* is an important part of the meaning. The application of *wh* deletion to remove *whose computer* would result in another violation of the recoverability constraint:

*The man [**0** they borrowed [t]] works at the bakery.*

which has a quite different meaning.

In the examples we've seen so far, the [t], the trace of the shifted *wh* phrase, has been fairly close to the head noun. This isn't always the case. The trace could, for example, be inside another clause embedded inside the relative clause, as in this rather clumsy D-structure:

> *The man [that Jocelyn claimed [that Elizabeth said [that she wouldn't marry who(m)]]] is my nephew.*

which we'll show in abbreviated form this way:

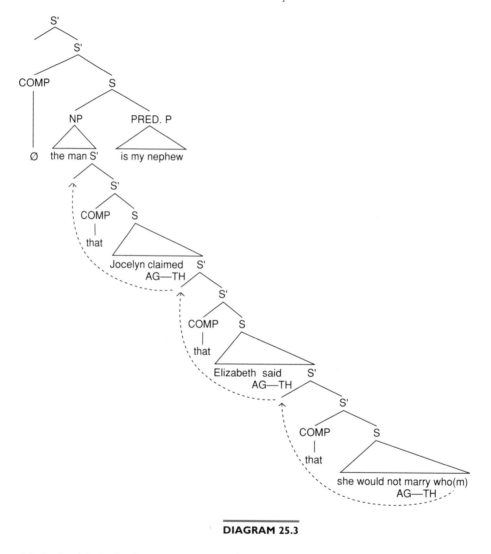

DIAGRAM 25.3

This is the kind of *wh* movement described in Chapter 22 as long *wh* movement. The whole *wh* phrase must be moved up from clause to clause until it reaches the front of the highest clause. So, the first *wh* movement applies to shift the *who(m)* into the highest S-bar slot for its clause:

> *The man [that Jocelyn claimed [that Elizabeth said [who(m)* that she wouldn't marry *[t]]]] is my nephew.*

Wh movement applies again, shifting the *wh* pronoun into the highest S-bar slot for the next clause up:

*The man [that Jocelyn claimed [**who(m)** that Elizabeth said [[t] that she wouldn't marry [t]]]] is my nephew.*

and finally into the highest S-bar slot for the next clause, where it follows the head noun:

*The man [**who(m)** that Jocelyn claimed [[t] that Elizabeth said [[t] that she wouldn't marry [t]]]] is my nephew.*

Now *wh* deletion, complementizer deletion, or both can apply:

*The man [**0** that Jocelyn claimed [t] that Elizabeth said [t] that she wouldn't marry [t]]]] is my nephew.*

*The man [**who(m) 0** Jocelyn claimed [[t] that Elizabeth said [[t] that she wouldn't marry [t]]]] is my nephew.*

*The man [**0 0** Jocelyn claimed [[t] that Elizabeth said [[t] that she wouldn't marry [t]]]] is my nephew.*

If a restrictive clause has no overt subject, either a *wh* word or the complementizer *that* is required:

I met the lawyer **0 [t] argued with you.*
*I met the lawyer **who** [t] argued with you.*
*I met the lawyer **that** [t] argued with you.*

Why is this? The reason is that if the *subject* of the clause is the *wh* phrase, then *wh* movement would move the *wh* phrase *out* of the subject slot, leaving a [t]. The finite clause would thus have no overt subject, a violation of the subject constraint.

Finite relative clauses are allowed to have a [t] in subject position, but only if the original subject is in the higher S-bar slot. If you just look at the linear sequence of such a sentence, and not at its hierarchical structure, the *that* in the complementizer slot looks as if it is an overt subject. The same is true of the *wh* pronoun if it is retained and the complementizer deleted. The first of the two sentences following has the *wh* phrase deleted, while the second has the complementizer deleted:

*The house [**0 that** [t] looked most comfortable] belonged to the Langdons.*
*The house [**which 0** [t] looked most comfortable] belonged to the Langdons.*

Speakers appear to be treating the forms as if they were in the subject slot. This may be why the subject constraint can be violated.

APPOSITIVE AND RESTRICTIVE RELATIVE CLAUSES

Appositive (or nonrestrictive) relative clauses look like restrictive relatives but they lack the identifying function. This chapter deals mainly with restrictive clauses for several reasons: They are crucial for identifying referents, they vary more in structure, and they can present some serious problems for learners, who might, for instance, have trouble identifying the thematic role of a shifted *wh* phrase unless they can determine the site from which it was shifted.

Yet the distinction between restrictive and appositive relative clauses is a crucial one for English. Compare the following sentences with restrictive and appositive clauses:

Restrictive: *The bankers who had cooperated with the drug lords were given heavy sentences.*

Appositive: *The bankers, who had cooperated with the drug lords, were given heavy sentences.*

We'll use these two examples to illustrate seven major differences between the two types of relative clause.

First is the key difference in function. Whereas the major function of restrictive clauses is to identify referents, that of appositive clauses is typically to add information about referents already thought to be adequately identified. Thus, the sentence above with the appositive clause is about bankers. The appositive clause *who had cooperated with the drug lords* is not used to identify the bankers; it does not pick out a particular subset of bankers; it merely provides additional information. Deletion of the appositive clause would not affect the interpretation of the main clause. In contrast, the restrictive relative clause specifies only those bankers who had cooperated, a subset of the class of bankers referred to in the sentence with the appositive clause. If it were deleted, the meaning of the main clause would be changed.

The second difference lies in the clause's position in constituent structure, as indicated by the pronunciation. In the sentence with the restrictive relative clause, the heavy stress falls on the first syllable of the compound noun *drug lords,* marking *drug lords* as the end of the noun phrase whose head is *bankers.* The restrictive clause is thus inside the noun phrase headed by *bankers:*

[the bankers [who had cooperated with the drug lords]]

In the sentence with the appositive, a heavy stress falls upon the first syllable of *bankers,* marking that noun as the end of its noun phrase. So the appositive clause is actually *not* part of the noun phrase whose head is *bankers:*[2]

[the bankers] [who had cooperated with the drug lords]

In written English, this difference is reflected in the punctuation: Commas enclose the appositive, separating it from the noun phrase preceding it and the rest of the sentence. Such commas are not used for restrictive relatives.[3]

This difference in constituent structure reflects a third difference—a difference in information structure. If we think of constructions as units of information, then a head noun and its restrictive modifier form a single information unit, while a noun phrase followed by an appositive form two distinct information units.

Sometimes the additional information unit provided by the appositive is added to continue the narrative line, as in the following example:

Hanson introduced Senator Obfusker to my mother, who promptly began to interrogate him about his support for tobacco subsidies.

The relative pronoun *who* in this last example could just as well be replaced by *and she.* This continuative usage of appositive clauses occurs most often in literary works and, less often, in more formal spoken narrative.

A fourth difference is that proper nouns can be followed by appositives but not by restrictives. Compare our example sentences when a proper noun is substituted for the head noun *bankers:*

Restrictive: **Carl Roberts who had cooperated with the drug lords was given a heavy sentence.*

Appositive: *Carl Roberts, who had cooperated with the drug lords, was given a heavy sentence.*

A fifth difference is that a certain kind of restrictive relative clause, an intransitive clause, which can be *extraposed,* that is, moved out of the noun phrase to the end of the container clause. This movement is not allowed for appositive clauses. So the relative clause in the following example can only be interpreted as a restrictive clause:

*The women arrived **who wanted to run for the Senate.***

There is no well-formed appositive counterpart:

The women arrived, **who wanted to run for the Senate.*

The sixth difference concerns the phrases permissible for the slots at the beginning of the relative clause. Restrictive relatives allow a *wh* phrase or the complementizer *that*. Appositive clauses only allow a *wh* phrase:[4]

Restrictive: *The bankers 0 that the police had arrested had cooperated with the drug lords.*

Appositive: **The bankers, 0 that the police had arrested, had cooperated with the drug lords.*

Seventh, whereas appositive clauses always have a *wh* word, if the restrictive clause has an overt subject, both of the slots preceding the subject can be empty. Grammarian Otto Jespersen used the label "contact clause" to describe clauses with no relative pronoun or complementizer.[5] Here are the examples:

Restrictive: *The bankers **0 0** the police had arrested had cooperated with the drug lords.*

Appositive: **The bankers, **0 0** the police had arrested, had cooperated with the drug lords.*

Yet another type can be noted. There is one type of appositive clause common in spoken English in which the clause is not about the noun phrase preceding it, but about one or more of the clauses immediately preceding it:

He did not seem to notice us, which was a great relief to me.[7]

The relative pronoun *which* has as its antecedent the whole clause preceding it. There is no similar phenomenon in restrictive clauses.

The contrast between restrictive and appositive relatives is not *always* as clear-cut as we've shown so far.[6] Restrictives with an indefinite noun head which is specific in reference rather than generic seem almost indistinguishable semantically from appositives. So, if *a tall tree* refers to a specific tall tree, then a restrictive relative clause following it is understood in much the same way as an appositive:

The hurricane blew down a tall tree that had stood at that corner for three centuries.

NONFINITE RELATIVE CLAUSES

Read through the following passage:

"I need a person to talk to," she said. "Albert's left me and the kids are driving me crazy. The forms for me to fill out are too complicated and I have only this money to pay my rent with." She showed me a twenty-dollar bill.
I guided her to Mr. Fitzroy's office.
"The lady to see you has arrived," I said.

This passage contains a number of relative constructions of a type we have not yet discussed:

a person to talk to
the forms for me to fill out
this money to pay my rent with
the lady to see you

These are all relative constructions with a nonfinite clause as the modifier. In each case, there is a head noun, the embedded clause restricts the reference of the head, the embedded clause has a gap, generally the object of either a verb or a preposition, and the missing object corresponds to the head noun.

Finite relative clauses all have the complementizer *that* in D-structure. We've seen in earlier chapters that nonfinite clauses do not need an overt subject. If the subject is covert, the *for* complementizer must be deleted, because the complementizer *for* is not needed to assign case to the subject, as in this next sentence with [e] as the covert subject of the relative clause:

> *The only suspect 0 [e][8] to see Lunyatin that night was Alberta Harrar.*

As we might expect, when they have an overt subject noun phrase to assign case to, nonfinite relative clauses must retain *for* as their complementizer, as in *for me to fill out*. However, it does not occur in D-structure when the subject is covert.

Here is a D-structure diagram for the first example, *a person to talk to:*

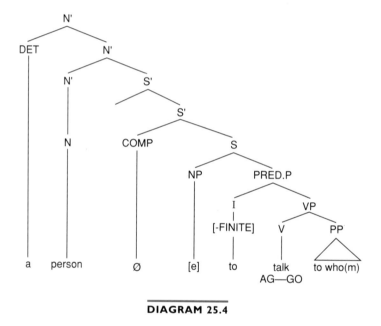

DIAGRAM 25.4

The relative clause has as its subject the covert noun phrase [e]. The *wh* phrase is still in the position in which it receives its thematic role. There are two options now. One is to have *wh* movement apply just to the relativized noun phrase, yielding this:

> *a person [**who(m)** 0 [e] to talk to [t]]*

Contrary to what happens in finite restrictives, the *wh* pronoun must be deleted,[9] and the result is the noun phrase we wanted:

> *a person [0 [e] to talk to [t]]*

The other option, which we also had for finite relative clauses, is to move the whole prepositional phrase containing the *wh* noun phrase:

> *a person [to who(m) 0 [e] to talk [t]]*

The result is grammatical if somewhat clumsy. The *wh* pronoun cannot be deleted this time because the preposition would have to be deleted too, and this would violate the recoverability constraint.

PARTICIPIAL MODIFIERS

A *participial modifier* is essentially a relative clause that has its main verb in either the present participle (*-ing*) form or the past participle (*-en*) form:

> *a man [0 claiming to be president of Iraq]*
> *the woman [0 suspected of embezzlement]*

The gap in these relative constructions is in the subject slot. It was thought earlier that these were simply reduced forms of finite relative clauses:

> *a man [who was claiming to be president of Iraq]*
> *the woman [who was suspected of embezzlement]*

In early transformational grammar it was thought that a deletion transformation removed the *wh* phrase plus the *be* verb. However, besides theoretical problems concerning the deletion process, that analysis could not easily account for constructions like *a bottle containing hydrochloric acid* because there is no finite relative clause with the *-ing* form of *contain*. We might speculate that participial modifiers lack an Inflection constituent, as do gerundives, or that their Inflection is nonfinite, but no clear answer is yet available.

Here are some sentences with participial modifiers:

> *A man [0 0 [t] claiming to be the president of Grenada] arrived at Kennedy last night.*
> *The bottle [0 0 [t] containing hydrochloric acid] had a green cork.*
> *The woman [0 0 [t] suspected of falsifying the petitions] will be arraigned Friday.*
> *The bottle [0 0 [t] opened by Dr. Darrigrand] had a red cork.*

The first *0* in each example is the higher S-bar slot into which the subject *wh* phrase is moved, the second *0* is the empty complementizer slot, while the [t] is the trace in the subject slot of the shifted subject *wh* phrase. As in the nonfinite clauses discussed in the previous section, the *wh* form has to be deleted.

Note the semantic difference between the present and past participle clauses. The difference is one of active versus passive voice. In the first sentence, for instance, the man does the claiming. In the third example, however, the woman isn't the one who suspects; she is the one who is suspected, that is, the [t] subject is the subject of a passive voice clause.

This construction, in which the modifier follows its head, is not to be confused with the participial construction briefly discussed in Chapter 6, which occurs as an *adjunct* expressing such perspectives as time and reason:

> *[e] visiting these factories, the inspectors always carried cameras.*
> *[e] irritated by these excuses, they insisted on a thorough inspection.*

These are not relative constructions; they are nonfinite *subordinate* clauses, as noted in Chapter 6. In some cases, a more explicit marking of perspective appears:

> *When [e] visiting these factories, the inspectors always carried cameras.*

PLACE AND TIME RELATIVE CONSTRUCTIONS

There are *wh* relative clauses in which the *wh* forms are *where* or *when*. These correspond to other relative clauses in which the *wh* is in a prepositional phrase. Compare the examples in the following set:

- a. *the town where I lived [t]*
- b. *the town in which I lived [t]*
- c. *the time when I made that decision [t]*
- d. *the time at which I made that decision [t]*

The *where* phrase in example (a) seems to be the equivalent of the prepositional phrase *in which* in example (b), and the *when* phrase in example (c) seems to be the equivalent of the prepositional phrase *at which* in example (d). This is not to say they are always exact paraphrases. Since *where* can occur instead of *in which, on which,* or *at which,* forms with significant meaning differences, it's clear that the semantics of *where* and *when* is more general.[10]

Relative clauses of place and time can also be appositive:

*Florence, **where I spent my childhood,** is famous for its art galleries.*
*That year, **when Giuliana studied with Carapetto,** changed her whole life.*

FREE RELATIVES

Many *wh* constructions can occur without an overt head noun. These forms are known as *free relatives.* Here is an example:

*I'll go **when it is time to go** and stay **where I am welcome**.*

which also has a near-paraphrase with *-ever*:

*I'll go **whenever it is time to go** and stay **wherever I am welcome**.*

One major semantic difference is that forms without *-ever* refer to a definite time, whereas *-ever* forms are indefinite. The difference, which is rather subtle for the preceding examples, is very clear with the following pair of free relative constructions:

Osborne will deny what they are saying about him.
Osborne will deny whatever they are saying about him.

In the first example, the speaker probably knows what they are saying about Osborne, while in the second the speaker seems not to know or to be making an emphatic statement in which *whatever* is close in meaning to *anything.* The forms without *-ever* look very much like embedded questions such as these:

She asked what they have been saying about me.
Maureen found out where the music was coming from.

However, in embedded questions, the indefinite *-ever* forms are not permitted.
Certain types of indefinite free relatives have no definite counterparts:

The bookstore has ordered whichever book they selected.
The doctor will prescribe whatever therapeutic treatments are needed.
She will find this difficult however clever she thinks she is.

These *-ever* forms occur in the determiner slot of a noun phrase in the first two examples, and the degree slot of an adjective in the third.

Free relative clauses are perhaps the ultimate example of clauses used to refer rather than to present propositional content. Grammatical analyses of them vary widely.[11] Those constructions starting with *what, whatever,* and *whichever* can be treated as noun phrases

in which there is no overt head noun and the *wh* phrase has been shifted to the slot
before the complementizer, as in the following constituent structure diagram:

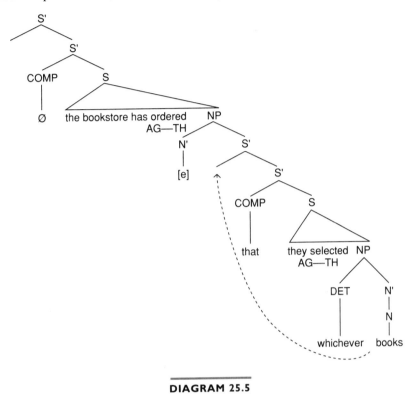

DIAGRAM 25.5

In the case of our third example, *wh* movement shifts the predicate adjective phrase
to the front of the clause:

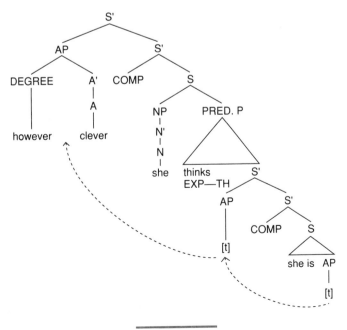

DIAGRAM 25.6

Free relatives with *when, whenever, where,* and *wherever* can behave like noun phrases in functioning as objects of prepositions:

> *We'll leave that* **to when your mother comes home.**
> *He can keep the car* **until whenever we need it.**

Free relatives also look suspiciously like the time and place subordinate clauses discussed in Chapter 6; the free relative analysis might be feasible for time and place subordinate clauses too.

LEARNING PROBLEMS WITH RELATIVE CONSTRUCTIONS

Relative clauses are less common in conversation than in writing, but they do occur in both, and when they occur they are important. Their key function, identification, is a crucial one that learners need to understand.

We'll look very briefly now at what happens in a few other languages to see what interference might occur from those languages. The languages referred to are not necessarily a representative sample, but the discussion should give you some idea of what factors are involved.

As noted in an earlier chapter, relative clauses in such languages as Chinese, Japanese, and Korean precede rather than follow the head noun they modify. Here is the Mandarin version of the example we gave at the beginning of this chapter:

```
[Ta  gei wo]   de           [na ben          shu     wo        e]
she  give me   MODIFIER that CLASSIFIER      book    dog-eared ASPECT
"The book she gave me is dog-eared."
```

The Chinese relative clause, marked as a modifier by the possessive marker *de* that follows it, is followed by the head noun *shu* (which has a determiner and classifier before it too).

Not surprisingly, speakers of these languages may position clause modifiers before their head noun and also link them to the head noun with the possessive marker *'s,* the counterpart to Chinese *de* and Japanese *no,* as in this next example:

> *Mariko is [like go dancing's woman].*
> "Mariko is a woman who likes to go dancing."

Additionally, although these languages have forms like our *wh* phrases, they are used in questions but not in relative constructions. Consequently, speakers of these languages tend to omit the English *wh* forms as well as the *that* complementizer:

> **I want to go out with girl is taking my biology class.*[12]

When speakers of Austronesian languages like Indonesian, Malaysian, and Javanese form relative clauses, they rarely have trouble with the position of the clause, perhaps because, in their languages also, relative clauses follow their head nouns. But these speakers tend to use only the modifier *that* and occasionally have trouble with relative clauses in which the *wh* phrase is not the subject. This is probably due to the fact that these constructions have no close counterparts in their languages.

BEYOND RELATIVE CLAUSES: A GENERAL NOTE ON LANGUAGE TEACHING

While it is helpful for teachers to know something about how their students' first languages work, the acquisition of such knowledge is not always practical, especially if students are from many different language communities. What is often more practical is for teachers to note any patterns in the errors made by their students so that they can try to determine what generalizations or rules the students appear to be following. Once teachers have that kind of information, they can use it to provide enough appropriate language input for students to reformulate, consciously or unconsciously, their generalizations and rules. The learners have to be at an appropriate stage for using this input, of course, and some will learn more rapidly than others. Their progress can be checked quite efficiently with drills that require them to answer well-formulated questions. For example, a teacher wanting to check progress with relative clauses might require students to answer questions about restaurants in town, eliciting answers such as, *This is the restaurant **that serves the freshest sashimi*** or *The fast food place **that we went to** was not clean.*

The major task for the language teacher is a difficult one—to make the language being taught a living thing for the learners, something they can use to achieve goals important to them, to gain knowledge for themselves, and to communicate their feelings, needs and experiences to others. Knowledge of the structures and processes of the language, both conscious and unconscious, is only one component of true language acquisition, but it is an indispensable component. The challenge for teachers and other language professionals is to stimulate learners so that learning about English and learning to use English forms becomes a way of growing into another world.

SUMMARY

Relative clauses fall into two major types, *restrictive* and *appositive* relative clauses. Restrictive relatives function to identify the referent of a noun phrase, while appositives provide supplementary information about the referent, information not needed for identification. However, especially when the container noun phrase is indefinite, the distinction between restrictives and appositive becomes hazy.

The Inflection in a relative clause—and hence the clauses themselves—can be finite or nonfinite. *Wh* relative clauses of place and time correspond to others in which the *wh* is in a prepositional phrase. These place and time clauses follow a head noun, and begin with the *wh* phrase, but the actual *wh* phrases are *where* and *when.*

Less familiar in discussions of relative constructions are participial modifiers and free relatives. Participial modifiers have predicates which are either present participles or past participles. Present participles indicate active voice in such clauses, while past participles indicate passive voice. Free relatives are constructions without an overt head noun. They begin with a *wh* word such as *what* or *whoever.*

Relative clauses contain a gap, actually a trace ([t]) of a *wh* phrase that has been shifted, via *wh* movement, to the empty slot at the beginning of the clause and may subsequently have been deleted. This trace is sometimes inside another clause embedded into the relative clause.

Relative clauses, like other embedded clauses, always follow their head, in this case their head noun. Like other kinds of clauses, they have a slot into which *wh* forms can be moved and also a complementizer slot, which can be used for complementizers like *that* and *for.* In constituent structures, relative clauses are under an N-bar but, unlike complement clauses, they are not sisters of the head noun. Any common noun can take a relative clause, while not every common noun allows a complement clause.

The sequence at the beginning of a relative clause of a *wh* phrase followed by a complementizer is not allowed in surface structure. Consequently, one or the other must be deleted. If the subject of the clause is an overt noun phrase, both may be deleted. But if the subject of a relative clause is a gap (i.e., the trace of a *wh* phrase), then either the *wh* phrase or the complementizer must be overtly present. This seems to be a way to avoid the subject constraint for finite clauses. *Wh* phrases cannot be deleted if part or all of their semantic content cannot be interpreted from the rest of the clause. This *recoverability constraint* blocks deletion of *wh* phrases in interrogatives and prepositional *wh* phrases in relative clauses.

Learners whose first language has modifiers preceding their heads may experience difficulty in positioning these modifier clauses. Many languages lack counterparts to English *wh* forms and complementizers in relatives, and their speakers may omit them. It may be practical and very helpful for teachers to try to determine what rules or principles underlie their students' error patterns. They can then tailor to provide students with data for more valid generalizations. Various kinds of exercises can be used to elicit valuable data concerning students' grasp of English structures.

EXERCISE SET 25

1. Draw D-structure trees for the following sentences.
   a. *The patient whom Sylvia examined hated hospitals.*
   b. *We visited the huge hall that Tasha had played in.*
   c. *I know a bank where the wild thyme grows.*
2. Explain how the D-structure for (c) above becomes a surface structure.
3. Explain the semantic difference between the following sentences:
   a. *She claimed to have seen the flying saucer, which had contained three chickens and a giraffe.*
   b. *She claimed to have seen the flying saucer which had contained three chickens and a giraffe.*
4. You have been explaining to an advanced class the distinction between restrictive and appositive clauses, and you have taught the class that proper nouns do not take restrictive relative clauses. A grammatically sophisticated student asks you, "What about *Are you the Stephen King that writes horror stories?*" How could you answer that student?
5. What do you notice about the meaning relationships in the following sentences?
   a. *Jane needs friends to talk to.*
   b. *Jane needs friends to talk to her.*

Paraphrase the two sentences converting *to talk to* and *to talk to her* into finite relative clauses.

6. Explain with your own examples the recoverability constraint.
7. Write two sentence-combining exercises, each requiring students to convert three pairs of sentences into three single sentences in which the original second sentences are relative clauses. In the first exercise, the gaps or traces should be the subjects of the relative clauses, though your students will not think of them as traces, of course. In the second exercise, the traces should be objects of verbs or prepositions. Give the answers, too.
8. How could you use the following items to help students master relative clause structures and other modifiers?
   a. a large photograph
   b. a mail order catalog
   c. one other item chosen by you

NOTES

1. There are some minor exceptions to this generalization, primarily in informal spoken English in situations in which a sentence is complicated and the speaker puts in a pronoun to help the addressee keep track:

> He's the kind of guy that, if you met him on the street and he was dressed like the Pope, you wouldn't recognize **him**.

Notice that if the *if* conditional clause inside the relative clause is omitted, the relative clause with the *him* no longer seems well formed.

2. It's not clear how best to represent appositive clauses on a constituent structure tree. One way would be to show an appositive clause as a separate branch connecting directly to the S-node as a sister of the noun phrase. A plausible alternative would be to connect the noun phrase and the appositive clause as daughters of a higher noun phrase.

3. Commas are used for *both* types in German, so that German students of English may sometimes identify appositive clauses in printed text as restrictive clauses.

4. However, in informal speech, *that* has been observed to occur, though rarely, in appositive clauses.

5. O. Jespersen, *A Modern English Grammar on Historical Principles [Part III: Syntax]*, 2nd vol. (London: Allen & Unwin, 1927).

6. For an important data-based criticism of the restrictive-appositive distinction, see R. Huddleston, *The Sentence in Written English: A Syntactic Study Based on an Analysis of Scientific Texts* (London: Cambridge University Press, 1971).

7. This example is taken from E. Kruisinga and P. Erades, *An English Grammar, Volume I: Accidence and Syntax, First Part*, 8th ed. (Jakarta: P. Noordhoff N.F., 1953), 137.

8. In a more technical discussion, this would be shown as PRO, the special covert element whose reference is sometimes indefinite and determined by the discourse context, sometimes controlled by a container predicate specifying either the container subject or a container object as its co-referent.

9. This *wh* deletion rule is obligatory for nonfinite clauses but optional for finite clauses. Of course, in either finite or nonfinite clauses, *wh* deletion can be blocked by the recoverability constraint, as happens when the *wh* form is preceded by a preposition. What is lacking in this account and all others that we know of is a reasonable explanation for the obligatoriness of the deletion in nonfinite clauses.

10. In earlier times, there was a place *wh* counterpart for other preposition phrases. So *whence* corresponded to *from which place* and *whither* to *to which place*.

11. Three rather different analyses of these forms are to be found in C. Baker, *English Syntax* (Cambridge, MA: M.I.T. Press, 1989), 163–181; J. Bresnan and J. Grimshaw, "The syntax of free relatives in English," *Linguistic Inquiry* 9 (1978): 331-91, and J. McCawley, *The Syntactic Phenomena of English*, vol. 2 (Chicago: University of Chicago Press, 1988), 431–432, 451–458.

12. For useful discussion of these and related issues, see T. Odlin, *Language Transfer: Crosslinguistic Influence in Language Learning* (Cambridge: Cambridge University Press, 1989).

ANSWER KEY

These are not definitive answers to the exercise set questions but rather suggestions and guidelines, many of which can be counterargued. I have not provided answers for some questions requiring individual responses such as the invention of examples and practice exercises for language learners. I have sometimes supplied more detailed answers than would or should be required of students because the answer brings up useful issues for consideration by English language professionals, especially those concerned with pedagogy.

EXERCISE SET I

1. a. descriptive
   b. prescriptive
   c. prescriptive
   d. descriptive

2. The knowledge of language possessed by native speakers is *implicit,* unconscious knowledge of the rules, as evidenced by the grammaticality of their utterances and their ability to distinguish between grammatical and ungrammatical structures (except, perhaps, for some borderline constructions). But native speakers cannot specify explicitly what the precise rules are. However, for example, a driver must be able to specify the traffic rules, that is, he must have an *explicit* conscious knowledge of those rules.

3. a. The child has unconsciously formulated an overgeneralized rule that the past tense of a verb is formed by adding to the base form the past tense suffix (spelled *-ed*).
   b. The adult is trying to correct the child's overgeneralization by modeling the correct form. The data from the dialogue suggest that acquisition of one's native language occurs in ordered stages and that it is futile to try to force acquisition of a rule when the child is not ready for it. The adult in the dialogue is focusing on the form, while the child is paying attention just to the content.

4. A number of reasonable answers are possible for this question. Here is one:
   Both groups of students need to know basic sentence structures in the language and the grammatical requirements imposed by lexical items; for example, the fact that *tell* can

take two objects, as in *tell Jack a story*. The prospective literature students may need to spend time on complex sentence formation, including many constructions that occur in novels, poems, and essays but are rare in conversation. The computer company students probably need more work on grammatical structures common in informal spoken English, especially Australian English, since they may be working with Australian supervisors. The grammar of imperatives, requests, prohibitions, and instructions is likely to be important for their English, both spoken and written.

EXERCISE SET 2

1. For each pair of verbs, the second verb includes the meaning of the first. The A2 and B2 verbs add the notion of causation and the sentences specify the causer. The C2 verb, however, adds the notion of accompaniment and the sentence specifies the accompanier.

2. The verb *accused* adds a judgment about the letter-writing: it was a bad thing to do.

3. The teacher was focusing on pairs of forms sharing a meaning, but differentiated by the presence or absence of the CAUSE notion. In fact, as we shall see in Chapter 5, more complicated grammatical and semantic facts are also involved.

4. x LEND y z
Arshad lent Dr. Jamali a computer diskette.

x KNOW y
Clancy knew that the meeting had been postponed.

x SMILE
The strange cat was smiling.

x FIND y
Ivan found a small radio transmitter.

x ELAPSE
A year had already elapsed.

x OFFER y z
The Wolverhampton team will offer Vachek a better contract.

5. a. x HUNGRY   valency = 1
  b. x SCIENTIST   valency = 1
  c. x EXAMINE y   valency = 2
  d. x TELL y z   valency = 3

6. a. ARG 1: Doctor Tam
    ARG 2: Leonard
    ARG 3: that he would prescribe erythromycin
  b. ARG 1: to make a false confession
  c. ARG 1: Captain Sullivan
    ARG 2: her daughter to be a liar
  d. ARG 1: whoever robbed that house

7. It is useful for teachers to be able to do the kind of propositional analysis described in the chapter, although learners would gain little benefit from it as compared to other learning tasks. Such analysis should help teachers see more precisely some of the semantic complexity of expository prose, especially academic prose. Teachers then will be more able to formulate questions to assist them in determining what learners have failed to comprehend in their reading. For example, the sentence *The president's denunciation shocked the nation* contains two propositions, *x SHOCK y* and *x DENOUNCE y*. While learners may be able to identify the two arguments of *SHOCK*, some may have trouble identifying the two arguments of *DENOUNCE*. The reference of the second argument of *denunciation* has to be determined from the context, and it can probably be determined from a preceding sentence. Some readers may even fail to identify *the president's denunciation* as a semantic proposition. A teacher can, therefore, check whether students are familiar with the pairing *denounce—denunciation* and can ask who is denouncing what or whom.

EXERCISE SET 3

1. a. The child was frightened by her behavior.
   b. That the matter was serious was agreed by the Council.

2. It was agreed by the Council that the matter was serious.

3. The two sentences are very close in meaning. *Teresita*, however, is the subject of the first sentence and the object of the second. But, in both sentences, the predicate assigns *Teresita* the same thematic role, that of experiencer. Thus the experiencer role can correspond to either a subject or an object. Since the grammatical relations do not correspond on a one-to-one basis to thematic roles, subjects and objects should not also be treated as thematic roles.

4. theme TALL
   theme IRRITATE experiencer
   experiencer BELIEVE theme
   theme ASTONISH experiencer
   experiencer ANXIOUS
   agent PERSUADE experiencer theme
   — BE PRAISED theme

5. 1. IRRITATE: It irritated Ramsour *that he had not been invited.*
   2. BELIEVE: Vygotsky believed *that language comes first from social encounters.*
   3. ASTONISH: It astonished the group t*hat Judith would agree to such a proposal.*
   4. ANXIOUS: Turpin was anxious *to demonstrate his sincerity.*
   5. PERSUADE: Gaffney has persuaded Evelyn *to act as mediator.*

6. a. theme
   b. experiencer
   c. agent
   d. theme
   e. theme

7. The predicates LOVE and LIKE require an experiencer and a theme in both German and English. But the German verb for LIKE requires the theme to be its subject, while the English verb requires the experiencer to be the subject. English speakers may, therefore, be confused by the German forms. Part of the problem arises from the assumption that English *liked* is the exact equivalent of *gefällt* in every respect. So some English speakers may expect the order of the thematic roles to be identical. Other English forms similar in meaning to *like* are similar to the German verb in having the theme as the subject rather than object:

> *Hans pleases Maria.*
> *Hans attracts Maria.*

Teachers could avoid tying the German verb so closely to English *like* by comparing it with English forms like *enchant, please, be popular with,* and *attract/be attractive to,* as well as *like.*

8. A computer translation program could not work on a linear word-by-word translation procedure but would need to have stored in its memory the number of arguments associated with each English and German form used as a predicate, the thematic roles borne by each argument, and, of course, their grammatical relation. When *liked* is replaced by *gefällt,* the arguments around the predicate would have to be reordered.

EXERCISE SET 4

1. b. *Ota Tanaka Kyoto-in saw.* OR *Ota Kyoto-in Tanaka saw.*
    c. *Brown suit-in man sushi ate.* OR *Sushi brown suit-in man ate.*
2. a. entered the hall
    b. climbed up the cliff
    c. had started smoking before age twelve
    d. failed to impress his family
    e. will take over the assignments
3. b, c, d, e

4.

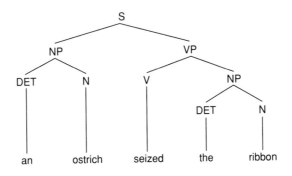

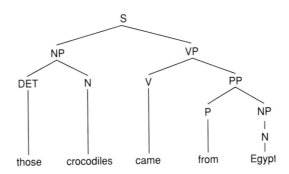

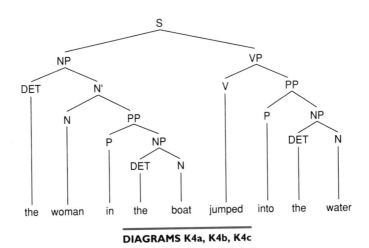

DIAGRAMS K4a, K4b, K4c

5. The determiner *those* and the noun *crocodiles* are sisters; they are daughters of NP. The verb *came* and the prepositional phrase *from Egypt* are sisters; they are daughters of VP. The preposition *from* and the NP *Egypt* are sisters. They are daughters of PP.

6. a. noun, verb   d. noun, adjective, verb
     b. noun, verb   e. adjective, verb
     c. adjective, verb   f. noun, verb

7. Either the lawyer had suspicious eyes or the judge had suspicious eyes. In the first case, the prepositional phrase *with suspicious eyes* is a sister constituent of both *looked at* and *the judge,* and a daughter of the verb phrase node. In the second case, *with suspi-*

cious eyes being a modifier of *judge,* it is a sister of *judge* under the noun node labeled N′, just as *from Thailand* was shown under N′ in Diagram 4.10.

Either Phil used a red flashlight to hit the man or Phil hit a man carrying a red flashlight. In the first case, the prepositional phrase *with a red flashlight* is a sister constituent of both *hit* and *the man* and a daughter of the verb phrase node. In the second case, *with a red flashlight* being a modifier of *man,* it is a sister of *man* under the noun node labeled N′.

8. In the Southern Slonal language, sentences are verb initial. The basic order is VSO. The language has postpositions instead of prepositions, and determiners (like *nyui,* "that") precede their head noun. Tense is marked as a prefix on the verb, *ata-* (indicating future) and *ila-* (indicating past or completed action). Objects are suffixed with *-i.*

EXERCISE SET 5

1.

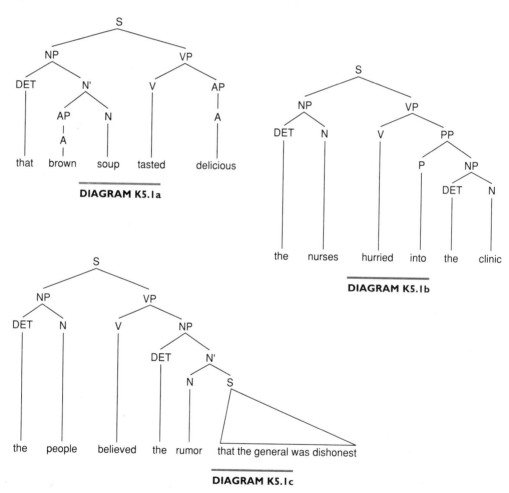

DIAGRAM K5.1a

DIAGRAM K5.1b

DIAGRAM K5.1c

2.   a. Adjective phrase; head: *tall*
     b. Verb phrase; head: *sings*
     c. Noun phrase; head: *child*
     d. Prepositional phrase; head: *beyond*

3. a. object complement
    b. subject complement
    c. object complement
    d. subject complement

4. In (a) *a masterpiece* is an argument of the ditransitive verb *lend* and has a referent distinct from that for *his mother*. It is assigned the theme role by the verb. In (b) *a masterpiece* is not an argument but a predicate stated about *that book* and it has no independent referent. It is a predicate noun phrase without a thematic role. The book **is**, according to Marcel, a masterpiece.

5. a. Marcel lent a masterpiece to his mother.
    b. *Marcel called a masterpiece to that book.
    c. *His mother is a masterpiece.
    d. That book is a masterpiece.

Superficially, the two sentences look as if they have the same structural characteristics, but only the sentence with *lend* has a paraphrase with *to*. Although both *lend* and *call* appear to take two arguments in their verb phrase, the second noun phrase after *call*, *a masterpiece*, functions as an object complement, making a predication about the book.

6. Sentence (a) can mean that he was described as being a taxi, that is, *a taxi* is an object complement making a predication about him. With this interpretation, *a taxi* is a predicate noun phrase. But the sentence is more likely to mean that I called a taxi for him, where *a taxi* is a separate argument with its own thematic role, theme. The same ambiguity and underlying structural difference is found in the (b) sentence.

7. Having heard ditransitive clauses with *give, make*, and similar verbs and also their counterparts with the prepositions *to* and *for*, the children appear to have overgeneralized the alternation between the ditransitives and the *to/for* counterparts to include clauses with other verbs that have an object followed by a *to* indirect object prepositional phrase or a *for* benefactive prepositional phrase.

EXERCISE SET 6

1.

TABLE AK.1

Subordinator	Clause	Perspective
as	Foulkes lay there	TIME
where	he had dropped it	LOCATION
O	to look for it	PURPOSE
although	the hounds had gone	CONTRAST
since	the men knew he was . . .	REASON
if	he stayed (where he was)	CONDITION
because	traces of . . . were obvious	REASON
although	Dorfman deplored the violence	CONTRAST
if	this government ignored the people	CONDITION

2.

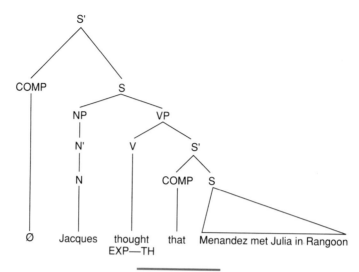

DIAGRAM K6.2a

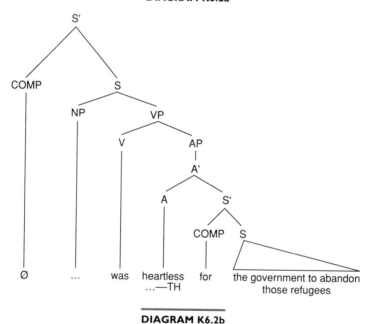

DIAGRAM K6.2b

3. The NP *Jacques* and the VP *thought that Menandez met Julia in Rangoon* are sisters and are daughters of the S. The V *thought* and the embedded S' *that Menandez met Julia in Rangoon* are sisters and are daughters of the VP.

4. The conjunction *but* can only link two clauses.

5. The events they refer to occurred sequentially and the order in which the clauses appear reflects their time order. If the order is reversed, the meaning is changed in that the supper eating occurs before the boy sat down instead of after.

6. Answers will vary according to the textbook chosen. Teachers can help their students recognize these devices and their functions by highlighting them and by asking questions requiring the learner to demonstrate understanding of the logical relationships. So, for the following sample:

Rosenblatt's later work concentrates on the reader's transaction with the text. This is a major factor contributing to her more recent neglect of the social function of literature. This has led to the dismissal of her more recent work by Marxist critics.

the teacher might ask not only how Rosenblatt's later work differs from her earlier work (it pays less attention to literature's social function), but also *why* there has been this change (one reason—but not the total explanation—is that she has been concentrating on the reader's encounter with the text). The further question *Why do Marxist critics dismiss her more recent work?* tests the students' understanding of the phrase *has led to.*

EXERCISE SET 7

1. (Note that we use M for the category *modal*.)

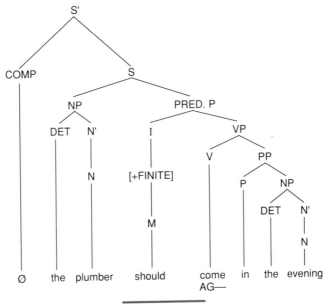

DIAGRAM K7.1a

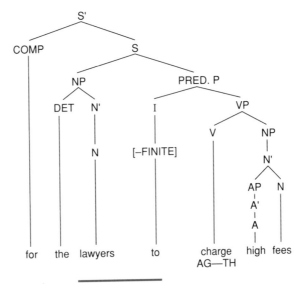

DIAGRAM K7.1b

2. The complementizer *for* and the S *the lawyers to charge high fees* are sisters; they are daughters of S'. The NP *the lawyers* is the sister of the PRED.P *to charge high fees* and both are daughters of S. The DET *the* is the sister of the N' *lawyers* and both are daughters of NP. The I *to* and the VP *charge high fees* are sisters, and they are daughters of PRED.P. The V *charge* and the NP *high fees* are sisters, and they are daughters of VP. Finally, the AP *high* and the N *fees* are sisters and they are daughters of N'.

3. a. 1. although Sebastian thought (that his sister must have drowned)
    Type: finite   Subject: Sebastian   Tensed V or M: thought

  2. that his sister must have drowned
    Type: finite   Subject: his sister   Tensed V or M: must

  3. he sailed to Salonica
    Type: finite   Subject: he   Tensed V or M: sailed

  4. [e] to search for her
    Type: nonfinite   Subject: [e]   Tensed V or M: (none)

3. b. 1. Elliot ordered his deputy ([e] to arrest the smugglers).
    Type: finite   Subject: Elliot   Tensed V or M: ordered

  2. [e] to arrest the smugglers
    Type: nonfinite   Subject: [e]   Tensed V or M: (none)

3. c. 1. Tell the doctors (that they *must* help the poorest patients).
    Type: nonfinite   Subject: [e]   Tensed V or M: (none)

  2. that they *must* help the poorest patients
    Type: finite   Subject: they   Tensed V or M: must

4. In 4a the [e] refers to *the girl*, the object of *begged*, while in 5b, since there is no object, the [e] refers to the subject of *begged*, *Alexander*. If we substituted *promised* for *begged*, the [e] would refer to the container clause subject *Alexander*, regardless of whether there was another noun phrase immediately preceding the [e].

5. The (a) sentence may not present any difficulty since the antecedent of [e] is the immediately preceding noun phrase. Sentence (b), however, is more difficult because *promise* is exceptional in that its subject, *they*, rather than the closest NP preceding [e], is the antecedent of [e]. Moreover the embedded clause has a transitive verb but contains no object noun phrase. This is because the object, the interrogative pronoun *who*, has been shifted to the beginning of the sentence. The embedded clause has no overt noun phrases, although the verb requires two argument noun phrases. The comprehension process is, therefore, likely to be more complex. In (c) the [e] has no antecedent in the sentence. The reference of the [e] must therefore be determined pragmatically. The [e] refers to anyone. Because all or almost all languages determine the reference of a covert noun phrase from the context, this may not present any problem.

6. None of the three sentences has an overt subject before the forms *working* and *enjoying*. The reference is determined pragmatically in sentence (a) and, in the absence of any context, must be understood to refer to anyone or everyone. The antecedent of the covert subject of *working in an orphanage and enjoying the work* in (b) is *Derek Croft*. Sentence (c) presents a problem since this kind of grammatical structure normally requires that the subject noun phrase of the main clause be understood as the antecedent. This would mean that the children were working in the orphanage and enjoying the work. However, in light of who we might expect to work in an orphanage, we might believe the speaker intended Derek to be understood as the worker. Here the pragmatics conflicts with the grammar. English teachers sometime refer to such participle constructions as *dangling participles,* since they are not clearly linked to an antecedent. All three sentences could have been written by native speakers. The third sentence is of a kind frequently written by native speaker students in writing courses and condemned by teachers as ungrammatical for the meaning intended.

EXERCISE SET 8

1.

TABLE AK.2

Determiner	Head Noun	Complement	Modifier
that	suitcase		heavy
several of those	batteries		
none of the	books	about space	that she had read
the	news	of her marriage	surprising
the	hatred	of hypocrisy	fierce, which you expressed

2. Here are five examples:
   1. two of the mayor's five sponsors
   2. the circuses
   3. these four coins
   4. several of the rebels
   5. little of her money

3. Examples:

   VERB: conclude that the rainforests are doomed
   VERB: decide to plant hardwood trees
   ADJ: afraid that the chief might collapse
   ADJ: aware that she might lose
   NOUN: the attempt to rent her apartment
   NOUN: the announcement that she would run for president

4. b. the Dutch BAN nuclear weapons
      AGENT   THEME

   c. they   RESENT the insult
      EXPERIENCER   THEME

   d. Ismail GIVE Abdul a stereo
      AGENT   GOAL THEME

   e. Laurence Olivier NARRATE the story
      AGENT   THEME

5. a. *the partners' purchase of a minicomputer*
         OR

> *the purchase of a minicomputer by the partners*
> b. *his suspension of the rules*
> c. *my impatience with his laziness*
> d. *the obstinacy of the young executive*

6. Answers will vary.

7. Students can become more familiar with the internal structure of structurally complex noun phrases, with the semantics (e.g., thematic roles) associated with such constructions, and with noun morphology and consequently with more vocabulary.

EXERCISE SET 9

1.   COUNT: *hill, recession, victory*
       NONCOUNT: *envy, optimism, turf, liquor, turbulence*
    BOTH COMMON: *culture*

2. a. We'll have two *coffees* and a hot chocolate with cream.
      They bought some Tanzanian coffee for her mother.
   b. Have a glass of mango juice.
      The glass they used for the windows is tinted.
   c. She cooked a small chicken for the family party.
      They ate lots of roast chicken and mashed potatoes.
   d. Durians are not a popular fruit outside Southeast Asia.
      Did you eat much fruit from their orchards?

3. For most speakers checked, the first question, with *some*, indicates the speaker's assumption that the addressee has some warm clothes, while the version with *any* indicates no such assumption. Variations in the intonation, however, may affect our interpretations.

4. Answers will vary.

5. 1. No article is used for noncount indefinite noun phrases.
   2. The definite article *the* is needed since there is only one period that can be referred to as *the last twenty-five years*.
   3. No article is needed for generic indefinite plural noun phrases.
   4. The indefinite article *an* is required since this is a singular indefinite count noun phrase.
   5. If there is only one Mojave reservation, then the definite article would be used. If there are several, then this would be an indefinite specific count noun phrase and the indefinite article is needed.
   6. The noun in this specific rather than generic noun phrase is followed by an identifying modifier, so the definite article is used.
   7. This is a generic predicate noun phrase, a special case of the indefinite generic count noun. So an indefinite article is used.
   8. This is an indefinite plural that needs no article but can take *some* if the reference is to specific textbooks.
   9. The definite article is required (for the most likely meaning); in the context of an elementary school, we can assume that specific children are involved.
   10. There is only one Bureau of Indian Affairs. Therefore, the definite article is used.
   11. The definite article is required; in the context of an elementary school, we can assume that there is just one principal.
   12. The definite article is required because the school has been previously identified to the addressee.

6. Here are two examples:

DIALOGUE ONE

A: Do you have some sugar you could lend me?
B: Of course. How much would you like?
A: Just a little. Maybe half a cup.
B: Here it is. Take as much as you need.
A: Thanks a lot. I'll pay you back this afternoon.
B: No need. I'm on a diet and I've given up sugar.

DIALOGUE TWO

A: Do you have some onions you could lend me?
B: Of course. How many would you like?
A: Just a few. Maybe three.
B: Here. Take as many as you want.
A: Thanks a lot. I'll pay you back this afternoon.
B: No hurry. I've got plenty.

7. We will go into more detail here than we expect of your answer because the piece brings up some useful issues.

The noun phrase *most of the peoples* includes what is probably a generic phrase referring to the majority of the class of human beings in Iran. But the plural count noun *peoples* is only used when more than one ethnic or national group is being referred to. The writer apparently doesn't know that the word *people* in its singular form is used as a plural for *person*. Thus we say *people are* rather than *people is*. The other plural form, *persons,* is used primarily in legal language. The indefinite noncount form *people,* without an article, should clearly have been used. The definite article is also possible (if preceded by *of*). The second occurrence is also in a generic noun phrase (*people who are very religious*—a class of people), which does not take an overt article. Other examples are *the religious peoples* and two noun phrases using *persons* with the definite article.

In her use of *the ghost* as a generic noun phrase, the writer seems to be drawing on an old-fashioned and slightly pompous usage of a singular definite noun phrase to represent a type of entity, as in *The elephant is an ungainly creature.* This form is rarely heard nowadays except in travelogues, botanical guides, and similar publications. Ghosts here are not being treated as types but as *both* any and all members of a class of beings. The indefinite plural *ghosts* or, better still, *spirits,* is thus the appropriate form. A similar error occurs in the later phrase *the man or woman* except that the focus is more individual rather than collective—on *any* man or woman. Hence, the indefinite generic *a man or woman* should have been used. The noun phrase *the dead* reflects a confusion of vocabulary. The phrase refers not to the state of death but to those in that state. The right form, of course, is the name of the state—*death,* a noncount abstract noun like *misery, happiness,* and *politics,* which takes no overt article.

Instead of the definite noun phrase *his soul,* Soraya uses the indefinite possessive *a soul of his,* which suggests to native speakers that individuals have more than one soul. This usage may be part of a broader bias against modifiers or specifiers before the head noun and in favor of *of* prepositional phrases, as in *soul of man* instead of *man's soul, meaning of religious* instead of *religious meaning,* and *two of different shapes and characters.* Two quantifiers—*most* and *two*—occur in the piece, both followed by an *of* phrase, one correctly, the other incorrectly. The difference has to do with the meaning of *most,* which specifies a subgroup of a more inclusive group (a relation sometimes called *par-*

titive), whereas the *two* shapes and characters are not a subgroup but constitute the whole group, thus making the *of* unnecessary.

As far as we can tell from the very limited data, Soraya has not mastered the forms appropriate for generic reference. She has overgeneralized *of* prepositional phrases to include structures which should have the corresponding constituent before the head noun. The one exception is *my country Iran*, which she may have acquired as a single idiom chunk. The one relative clause in the piece, *who are very religious*, is correctly formed, but we would want more data before we could conclude that she has mastered relative clauses.

EXERCISE SET 10

1. a. *their*: third person plural NP-internal possessive
    it: third person singular objective
    him: third person singular objective
    her: third person singular NP-internal possessive
    theirs: third person plural independent possessive

   b. *we*: first person plural nominative
    he: third person singular nominative
    yours: second person singular/plural independent possessive
    his: third person singular NP-internal possessive
    us: first person plural objective

2. An antecedent is the noun phrase to which a pronoun refers. The antecedent of *them* in the sentence given could be either *Bogart and Bacall* or *the reporters* since neither is in the same local domain as *them* and both are third person plural.

3. We should expect the (a) sentence with the indefinite noun phrase *a friend of his* to imply that Marion is just one of several friends, while the (b) sentence with the definite noun phrase *his friend* should suggest that Marion is his only friend. Although these expectations don't completely hold, the second sentence suggests a closer relationship than the first. The difference in closeness is clearly related to the difference in definiteness. To be *the* friend of someone is more special than to be just *a* friend, perhaps one of many.

4. The generalization is inadequate because it fails to explain such phenomena as the presence of the pronoun *him* and the possible antecedent *Addison* in the following clause:

   Addison resented Pope's description of him.

The pronoun and its antecedent are in the same clause, but while the local domain of the antecedent is that clause, the local domain of *him* is the noun phrase *Pope's description of him*. A more accurate generalization would cover both clauses and noun phrases as domains. A pronominal and its antecedent cannot occur together in whichever of these is the most deeply embedded.

5. a. *Jasmine* can be the antecedent of *she* since the two forms are not in the same local domain and, although the pronominal precedes its antecedent, it is in a lower ranked clause.
   b. *Ruggles* cannot be the antecedent of *him* because the two noun phrases are in the same local domain.
   c. *Ruggles* can be the antecedent of *him* because the two noun phrases are not in the same local domain.

d. *Ruggles* cannot be the antecedent of *him* because the two noun phrases are in the same local domain.

e. *Li* can be the antecedent of *him* because the two noun phrases are not in the same local domain.

f. *Heisenberg* can be the antecedent of *him* because the two noun phrases are not in the same local domain. *Heisenberg* is the subject of a noun phrase, while *he* is the subject of a clause embedded in that noun phrase.

6. Here is one plausible answer:

The author is presenting someone talking about her family. By starting with *she*, the author is indicating that we have come upon the speaker in the middle of her story about her family. The effect is dramatic. We are plunged into the world of the narrator and her family and treated as if we already familiar with the general situation. We are provided enough detail for us to make the pragmatic inference that the *she* is the narrator's mother. A similar kind of inference links the pronominal *I* with the noun phrase *the start of a baby*. The narrator assumes that we will figure out the likely antecedent of *they*, presumably some military or civilian authority. Similarly, the referent of *our* in *our back door* can be assumed to be the narrator and her mother. The lack of *grammatically determined* antecedents for the pronominals in this narrative requires us to make inferences, to participate more actively in the narrative by filling in crucial information. Of course, the text provides all the necessary clues for the correct inferences, but we are led to assume that we are contributing actively to the narration and our interest is aroused.

7. Answers will, of course, vary. Other such tasks could be to change the sentences so that they refer to the future or to change affirmatives to negatives. All of these tasks test students' knowledge of the relevant forms not as isolated forms, but in the context of full sentences. Moreover, such exercises could provide a useful lead-in to training students in the micro-editing of their English writing.

EXERCISE SET 11

1. The referent of the [e] in the (a) sentence is determined by the discourse context. It can be a general statement with the referent being anyone or perhaps someone either participating in the discourse, such as the speaker or addressee, or someone mentioned previously. In the (b) sentence, the [e] refers to the addressee. The grammar rather than the discourse context determines the reference.

2. Since imperatives always demand action of the *addressee*, the subject is always second person. The imperative sentence has a second person covert subject, which is the antecedent of the reflexive and is in the same local domain. If the subject is second person, then the reflexive has to be second person in order for there to be a reflexive-antecedent relation. This is what makes **Wash himself now!* not grammatical. None of the other reflexive forms can occur in this slot except for *yourselves*, which is also second person.

3. a. *Her* is free within its local domain, *her father*; it can, therefore, have *Susan* as its antecedent, since *Susan* is outside the local domain of the noun phrase, or it can refer to some other female referent.

b. *Her* can refer to any female referent except Susan because *Susan* is in the same local domain, the clause *Susan admired her*.

c. *Her* is free within its local domain, *her father*; it can, therefore, have *Susan* as its antecedent or it can refer to some other female referent.

d. *She* can refer to any female referent except Susan. It cannot have *Susan* as its antecedent because it precedes *Susan* and as the rule in Chapter 10 stated, *a pronominal can only precede its antecedent if the pronominal is in a lower ranked clause.* *She* is not in a lower ranked clause.

e. *Herself* must refer to Agnes.

f. *Herself* can only refer to George. In fact, its antecedent is [e], the covert subject of the embedded clause. The ditransitive verb *want* requires that the embedded clause subject have the container clause object as its antecedent. *George* must, therefore, be a name for a female.

g. *She* can refer to Susan or to some other female referent. *She* is free within its clause; it can have an antecedent in the container clause domain or it can refer outside the sentence.

4. The covert unit [e] stands for a referent that is a required part of the propositional content, one signified by the absence of a phonetically realized pronoun. Since the unit is thus psychologically (but not phonetically) real for native speakers, second language learners need also to become aware of its significance.

5.

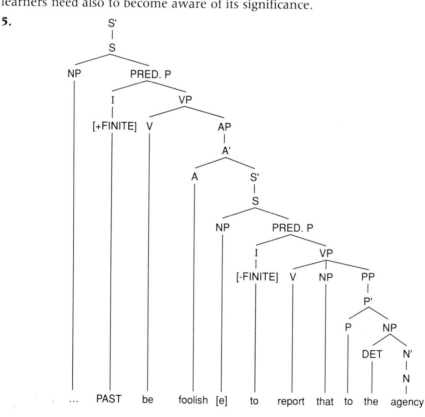

DIAGRAM K11.5

6. Answers will, of course, vary, but sentences like those given for question 3 should test students' ability to determine the antecedent of each pronominal and anaphor.

7. Answers will, of course, vary.

EXERCISE SET 12

1. a. The subject of the embedded sentence can only get nominative case from the clause's finite Inflection. Since *her* is the objective case form and there is no adjacent case assigner for objective case, Case Theory rules out the sentence.

b. The subject of the embedded sentence cannot get nominative case from the clause's nonfinite Inflection. It is, however, adjacent to *considered,* which assigns objective case. Since *she* is the nominative case form and there is no adjacent case assigner for nominative case, Case Theory rules out the sentence.

c. *He* is an object of the container clause. It is adjacent to *persuaded,* which assigns objective case. Since *he* is the nominative case form and there is no adjacent case assigner for nominative case, Case Theory rules out the sentence.

d. The noun phrase subject of the embedded clause, *his wife,* is not adjacent to a finite Inflection, so it cannot get nominative case. Neither is it adjacent to the verb *persuaded,* so it cannot get objective case. Since it has no case, Case Theory rules out the sentence.

e. *Olga* does not have a case assigner preceding it, so it cannot get objective case, nor does a finite Inflection follow it, so it cannot get nominative case. Since it has no case, Case Theory rules out the sentence.

f. *Tony* cannot get objective case, since it follows a passive voice verb. There is nothing else adjacent to assign case to it. Since it has no case, Case Theory rules out the sentence.

2.

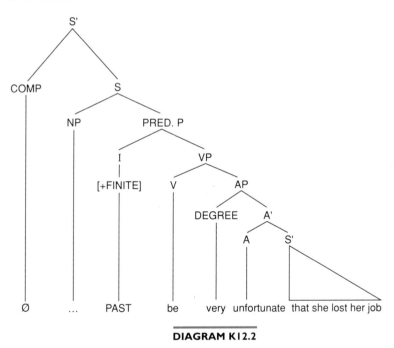

DIAGRAM K12.2

3. Unlike overt noun phrases, embedded clauses don't need case. So the clause *that she lost her job,* which is not assigned case by the adjective *unfortunate,* can, nonetheless, stay at the end of the sentence, as in (b), where the filler *it* satisfies the subject constraint by filling the subject slot (and getting assigned nominative case). But an ordinary noun phrase after *unfortunate* cannot get case. Therefore, it *must* move to the vacant subject slot, where it can get nominative case. Since this hasn't happened in 3d, Case Theory would rule out that sentence.

4. a. Inflection is the constituent of the predicate phrase that specifies the finiteness or nonfiniteness of its clause. Finite Inflection indicates either tense or a modal in D-structure.

   b. Inherent case is case assigned in D-structure to a noun phrase by virtue of its position in the second object slot for a ditransitive verb like *give* or in the determiner slot of a noun phrase. In the first situation, the inherent case is objective; in the second, the inherent case is possessive.

   c. The case filter is a constraint ruling out sentences in which a noun phrase has no case.

5. a. *Sarah was believed to have been a great actress.*
   b. In the asterisked version, *Sarah* cannot get case from either the passive voice *believed* that precedes it or the nonfinite Inflection that follows it.

   a. *I knew Kennedy was certain to run for the presidency.*
   b. In the asterisked version, *Kennedy* cannot get case from either the adjective *certain* or the nonfinite Inflection.

   a. *That dog will be captured.*
   b. In the asterisked version, *that dog* cannot get case from from the passive voice verb *captured.*

   a. *The situation seems to be serious.*
   b. In the asterisked version, *the situation* cannot get case from the verb *seems* or from the nonfinite Inflection of the embedded clause.

   a. *The public was unlikely to support that legislation.*
   b. In the asterisked version, *the public* cannot get case from from the adjective *unlikely* or the nonfinite Inflection of the embedded clause.

6. In English, a noun phrase is required to be immediately adjacent to its case assigner or the case filter will apply and the sentence is ruled out. From the data, we see that French, although possessing a case filter, allows at least some adverbs of time and manner to intervene between the case assigner and the case receiver. The adjacency requirement is thus less strict. There is not enough data in the sample sentences to justify broader generalizations.

7. One exercise might be to convert appropriate sentences whose subjects are either finite or nonfinite embedded clauses into the counterpart filler *it* sentences. Another exercise might require learners to go in the opposite direction, converting appropriate filler *it* sentences with finite or nonfinite embedded clauses into the counterparts without *it*. Examples would, of course, have to be provided. Such exercises will also make students more aware of the two types of embedded clauses.

EXERCISE SET 13

1.

TOPIC	COMMENT
our annual meeting	it seems that some stockholders wish to oppose our proposals
Gildenstern	he didn't have a chance
those expenses	Carmody won't pay them
your last letter	the president has authorized me to inform you that he will pay no attention to it
that dinner	I can't stand roast turkey
that rock	they cannot lift (it)

2. Counterparts:

he	SUBJECT
them	OBJECT
it	OBJECT OF PREPOSITION
	(in a more deeply embedded clause)

3. The sentence is different in that its topic noun phrase seems to have been extract-ed from the clause. The verb *lift* is a transitive verb requiring a noun phrase object. This is why **They cannot lift* is ungrammatical. Yet this incomplete structure can occur *if* preceded by a topic noun phrase, as in *That rock they cannot lift*. This suggests *that rock* was initially the object of *lift*. Note that the topic noun phrase must be of a type that could follow the verb. That is why the following sentence with an abstract noun phrase topic is bizarre:

> **Obedience they cannot lift.*

The verb *lift* normally requires a concrete noun phrase as its object. As further evi-dence, note also that the topic-comment sentence is understood as if the noun phrase did, in fact, follow the verb.

4.

they	OLD
Clarence	NEW
was drowned in a barrel	OLD
that garden	OLD
a stone fountain	NEW
happy	OLD
not for long	NEW
what surprised the investigators	OLD
was the incredibly fast growth of the microbes	NEW

5. a. Jeffrey is hard to argue with.
   b. Politics will not be discussed by us here.
   c. Victory seems to be impossible.
   d. ?A wolf Mildred saw on the roof.

Sentence (d) is strange because in its original version the noun phrase *a wolf* is under-stood as an indefinite *specific* noun phrase and thus is ineligible to be topic. It is inter-esting that a dialect of Yiddish English allows sentences like the answer given for (d). The speaker is communicating a sarcastic as well as skeptical attitude to Mildred's sup-posed experience.

6. If the grammatical forms are well sequenced, students should know or find out that, for example, *The president met with trade union leaders yesterday* would come earlier in a text than *the president's meeting*.

7. Answers will vary. Here is an example of a story that could be used for the purpose:
   It was *an autumn morning* and *a tall, very thin man* was walking along *a highway* toward *a small town*. At *the edge of the town* he saw *a sign* reading *Broxham: Population 2400*. *The information* on *the sign* was comforting. *The town* was just the right size. It was early in *the morning* and there was no one yet in *the streets*, not even in *the business dis-trict* that he came to. In *the business district* he saw *a small restaurant which had not yet opened*. On *the street corner nearby* was *a green wooden bench*. He went to *it* and sat down, *his body* aching from *the long walk*.

EXERCISE SET 14

1. Out of context, the sentence is ambiguous as to whether it refers to the state of frozenness or to an action of freezing the peas. In the structure corresponding to the first sense, *frozen* is just an adjective. It therefore allows a preceding degree specifier like *completely*:

> *The peas were completely frozen.*

The sentence would sound strange with an agent phrase:

> **The peas were completely frozen by the factory.*

In the passive sentence, *frozen* is a verb referring to an action and can be accompanied by a manner adverb as well as by the agent phrase:

> *The peas were frozen very thoroughly/efficiently by the factory.*

2. a. Each car was stopped on the freeway by the police.

> OR

Each car was stopped by the police on the freeway.
   b. This case will be considered by two justices.
   c. No passive!
   d. They were considered criminals by the prosecutor.
   e. Sugita was fined one hundred thousand yen by the judge.
   f. Calexco was sent detailed proposals by several companies.
   g. That tariff boundaries are harmful to international trade is believed by them.
   h. That she was guilty of any crime has been denied by people.

3. g. It is believed by them that tariff boundaries are harmful to international trade.
   h. It has been denied by people that she was guilty of any crime.

4. Activities will vary.

5. Conclusions will, of course, vary among the discussion groups. Here is a possible answer:

Clearly the paragraph reveals some major problems with the grammar, but her treatment of the content is excellent. The overall sequence is very competent and the presentation direct. It's important for a student writer to be told about her strengths in some detail.

The student has not mastered passive voice forms and may be strongly influenced by her first language. But part of the problem is more general in that, except for *-ing*, she uses no suffixes on either nouns or verbs. Since the passive requires use of the past participle form, combinations like *have been abuse* and *is cause*, instead of *have been abused* and *is caused*, are to be expected.

There are ten instances of what appear to be attempts at passive or passive-like verb constructions with a theme argument as their subject: *can hardly define, being asking, not consider, being take, reporting, have been abuse, may be become, is cause, be turn*. The first of these could alternatively have been intended as *is hard to define* and contains a lexical error, *hardly*, that is not our concern here. But, in the light of the systematicity of the passive errors, we group it with the other nine. The sequence *may be become* reveals a misgrouping of *become* with transitive rather than copular verbs. *Become*, of course, cannot be passivized.

6. Answers will vary here. The first exercise might be a more general one dealing with English verb forms, including the past participle. Of course, if she displays total ignorance, more exercises and instruction are needed. The second exercise might be a comprehension exercise with sentences like *Mercer was told by Janeway to register for a language course.* In this sentence, which noun phrase has the agent role and which has goal refer to people who could fill either role? Who told someone to register for the course—Mercer or Janeway? The third exercise might require her to replace active voice transitive sentences with passive voice sentences.

EXERCISE SET 15

1. Here are three revised versions for each sentence. You can probably think up others.
   a. It was the Ottawa police that were looking for a yellow Volvo.
   What the Ottawa police were doing was looking for a yellow Volvo.
   What the Ottawa police were looking for was a yellow Volvo.
   b. The one who held up the First National Bank was that woman.
   It was the First National Bank that that woman held up.
   It was that woman that held up the First National Bank.
   c. What the social workers believed was that unemployment would demoralize the youth of the nation.
   It was the social workers that believed that unemployment would demoralize the youth of the nation.
   The ones that believed that unemployment would demoralize the youth of the nation were the social workers.

2. a. Depending on the intonation, the speaker could be emphatically asserting that the plumber was the person who came to repair the sink or identifying someone as the particular plumber who came to repair the sink.
   b. Similarly, the speaker could be emphatically asserting that the conveyor belt is the machine that carries the screwtop lids or identifying a conveyor belt as the particular one that carries the screwtop lids.
   c. My ignorance is the thing that worries me, or I don't know what it is that is worrying me.

3. a. It was Leonardo who drew that sketch.
   b. It was his plan that failed.
   c. It was on that morning that she appeared at the castle gate.
You may think of several other possibilities for some of the sentences.

4. a. What Crashaw wanted to do was sell off all the agricultural land.
   b. Where George was born was (in) New Jersey.
   c. What the plant manufactured was automatic transmissions.
   d. What Darlene used to patch up her walls was mud.
Again, you may think of several other possibilities for some of the sentences.

5. One possibility suggested by Sandra McKay[1] is to show a simple drawing of a room and ask the students to describe the room. Students should produce sentences like *There is a long low table in front of the couch.* It might be interesting to use magazine pictures of, say, a typical U.S. or British living room and, if obtainable, of a Japanese living room, so that comparisons could be made.

6. The use of the noun *campaign* requires the reader to use pragmatic knowledge of the context to determine that a political campaign rather than, for example, a military campaign is being referred to. The pronominal *his* could refer either to Bush or to Perot. This is knowledge provided by the grammar. A reader with knowledge of the incident may know which meaning is intended, and the probability is that it refers to Bush since what is *distorted* is probably something not associated with the distorter, though this isn't always the case. Grammatical and lexical knowledge don't help the reader to choose between the two possibilities. On the other hand, grammatical knowledge requires that *himself* can only refer to Perot. Grammatically, *his children* could be those of Perot, Bush, or someone else, but pragmatically *his children* refers to Bush's children. We have enough information from the paragraph to make the reasonable inference that Bush was referring to his own children. By using the definite noun phrase *Perot's unscrupulous behavior* to characterize Perot's alleged actions, Bush presents Perot's allegedly unscrupulous behavior as old information, old since Bush provided details cited earlier in the passage. The insertion of the adjective *unscrupulous* used in the noun phrase presents this evaluation of the alleged actions as fact. This factual status arises from the grammatical form. The author achieves the same effect with the noun phrase *the wild accusations,* which the author or perhaps Clinton uses as a label for all the charges and accusations. The use of the definite noun phrase marks the content as old information familiar to addressees and thus assigns factual status to the claim that the accusations are wild. So both syntactic/semantic knowledge and knowledge about information structure are involved. The passage draws on various kinds of knowledge, interweaving and combining them to produce a plausible interpretation for readers.

7. Baldwin begins by using a filler *it* construction to postpone until the end of the first sentence the introduction of the overall topic of the paragraph, the common need felt by black men. This builds the sentence up to a climax at the end. Then Baldwin uses parallel *wh*-cleft clauses to focus the attention on the different aspects of what black men had in common until he summarizes them in the final sentence.

Baldwin uses active and passive voice contrastively in the long sentence beginning, *What they held in common was the necessity....* The actions the black men needed to take are represented by active voice verbs: *to remake the world, to impose this image,* while predicates referring to actions and perceptions of the non-black world are in the passive voice: *be controlled by, held by.* The effect is of a careful balancing of the two worlds and a contrast between the present, in which others are the agents or the perceivers, and the desired future in which black men assert their identity as men, men who act.

EXERCISE SET 16

1. b. PAST | have | be | live
         | | <-en> | <-ing> |

   c. Modal | have | be | comfort
            | | <-en> | <-en> |

   d. to | have | be | steal
         | | <-en> | <-ing> |

   e. Modal | have | be | avoid
            | | <-en> | <-ing> |

f. Modal | be | kidnap
         | <-en> |

g. TNS   define

2. b. Dr. Foster was examining Henry.
   c. Francisco is lying.
   d. Yeltsin has been greeting the new ambassador.
   e. They had been taking the horse to Shanghai.

3. Answers will vary. The activity can be used to contrast past tense or modal forms with and without perfect and progressive aspects. The time-line grid, McKay points out in her book, is a useful way to introduce the past perfect. She suggests reviewing past and present progressive usage by asking students to imagine that it is one particular year in the past, and then asking them to report on what they are doing at that time (*I'm attending kindergarten in Mexico City...*) or imagining that they are news reporters in, say, 1986, and describing one major event in the news. For a fuller discussion of such activities, the McKay book is strongly recommended.

4. One possibility: Students could write three short paragraphs about their lives, what they had achieved or failed to achieve so far, what they were doing now, and what they hope to do in the future.

   Another possibility: Students could describe a series of actions involved in making a dress, changing the oil in a car, making a cake, getting a job, or other suitable tasks from the perspective of doing it the following day, describing it as it is happening, and describing it as if it had been done the previous day.

5. Answers will vary.

6. The predicates *know, be tall,* and *contain* would be problem cases because they are stative predicates and use the simple present rather than the present tense progressive aspect combination to refer to present time.

7. The first sentence with the simple present tense verb *thinks* indicates that he has already formed his opinion, while the version with *is thinking* indicates that he hasn't yet made up his mind completely, although he is leaning toward the stated opinion. The thinking is an ongoing process. In the second pair, the first sentence presents the woman's attitude as a steady, unchanging state. She is not necessarily participating in a group session. In the second sentence, it seems likely that she is in such a group and that she is becoming increasingly hostile. However, the use of the progressive aspect also suggests a possible temporariness about her feeling: She's hating it now but her feelings may change. In the third pair, the first sentence presents the situation as a (relatively) permanent one. The second sentence shows an ongoing process, one which may have started recently. In the last pair, the first sentence treats the living situation as a long-lasting, perhaps permanent one, while the second suggests that, although this is an ongoing living situation, it is a recent one and may not be long lasting.

EXERCISE SET 17

1. a. This is the past indefinite usage of perfect aspect and cannot be accompanied by the point of time phrase *on June 6, 1987.*

b. The simple past tense, unlike the present perfect, does not cover time up to the present, which is the sense of the durative phrase *since 1979*.

c. *Know* is a stative verb that cannot be used with progressive aspect.

d. The use of perfect aspect suggests that the novel has only recently been written and that Mark Twain has joined Elvis Presley in still being alive. It is, in fact, possible to use the sentence appropriately in a suitable context, but describing such a context would be too complicated for our purposes.

2. This is acceptable because Mark Twain's name is being used to represent his writings, which are still being published.

3. The (A1) sentence with perfect aspect indicates a change of state and can be used if she is not continuing to get still worse. The (A2) sentence with combined perfect and progressive aspect indicates that the deterioration is continuing.

The (B1) sentence with perfect aspect indicates, unlike the (B2) sentence with a simple past tense, that the acid rain problem continues.

In the (C1) sentence, the past tense perfect aspect combination connects two past times, one at which he failed to read the book, the other at which this failure was noted. The (C2) sentence simply specifies the past failure to read the book.

4. a. state
     b. recurrent event
     c. past indefinite
     d. recurrent event
     e. change of state

5.

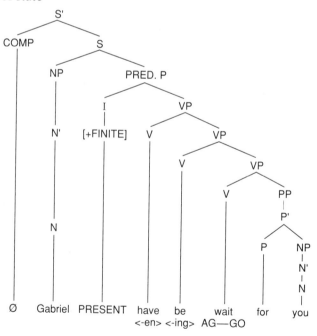

DIAGRAM K17.5a

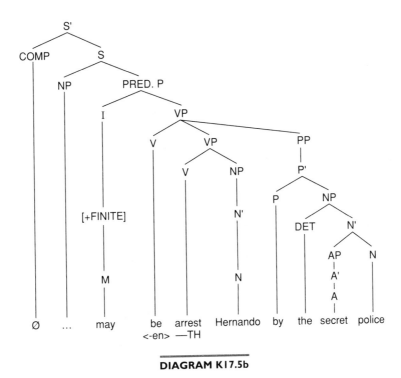

DIAGRAM K17.5b

6. Examples will vary. Some meanings of the various forms are not covered by the guidelines. Guideline (a) under PAST TIME specifies the use of past tense for events or states that occurred repeatedly. This overlooks the use of present or past tense with perfect aspect for recurrent events. The use of past tense with perfect aspect is not covered. Learners who view verbs like *think, believe,* and *feel* as designating processes may have trouble with guideline (d) in the NOW section. However, the guidelines overall provide the learner with a useful aid for tense and aspect usage. The approach is communicative, using the various time notions needed as the categories for organizing the grammatical forms. This is the opposite approach from the one used in the chapter, which starts with the forms and describes the meanings associated with them. While the approach in the chapter is a more comprehensive and concise way to brief language professionals, it seems less effective as a technique for presenting grammatical content to many language learners.

7. The writer's main problem is the overuse and misuse of progressive aspect. He uses progressive aspect with statives like *know, be alive, be dead,* and *be a language.* That problem, along with lexical problems, also occurs in *it is being pride for me.* He uses progressive aspect instead of perfect aspect in *many professors were writing.* He uses progressive aspect to express habitual experiences and actions as in *I am still speaking Gujerati* instead of *I still speak Gujerati.*

There is one use of present tense where past tense is the appropriate choice, but otherwise the other problems, which are many, do not have to do with tense or aspect.

8. Answers will vary.

EXERCISE SET 18

2. Answers will vary.

3. Mr. O'Brien said that he couldn't understand why Jackie wouldn't complain. He claimed that the whole problem could only get worse if she didn't go to the manager.

Elsie pointed out that Jackie didn't have to complain publicly but she had to do something. They might all be in danger if they couldn't persuade her to talk to him about that.

4. a. According to both sentences, they had the opportunity to cancel their trip. According to the second sentence, they did not cancel; according to the first sentence, they did.

b. Both sentences are about leaving before dawn, but the first states that there is no obligation on them to leave before dawn, while the second places an obligation on them not to leave before dawn.

c. The first sentence states that the speaker believes it to be possible that the dam has collapsed. The second sentence indicates that the speaker is fairly certain (on the basis of some unspecified information) that the dam has collapsed.

d. It is more likely that the sentences use the action modality rather than the belief modality. If so, the first sentence is a recommendation regarding eating at a time later than the utterance time. The second sentence would be used to report the speaker's opinion regarding an earlier event. In the belief modality, the first sentence would be a very unlikely form, while the second indicates the speaker's belief about what probably happened.

e. The first sentence reports an obligation placed on her to do something in the future. The second sentence reports the teacher's strong inference that she read to them every night, a belief based on their rapid improvement.

5. Negative forms like *not* or *n't* follow modals and precede ordinary verbs. Unlike other verbs, these modals don't occur in the past participle form, don't have past tense endings, don't take the *-ing* suffix or the singular *-s* suffix, and don't occur as infinitives with *to*.

6.

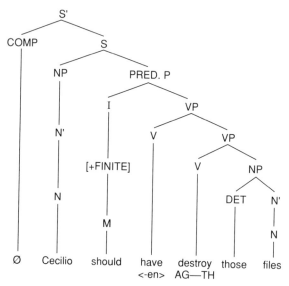

DIAGRAM K18.6a

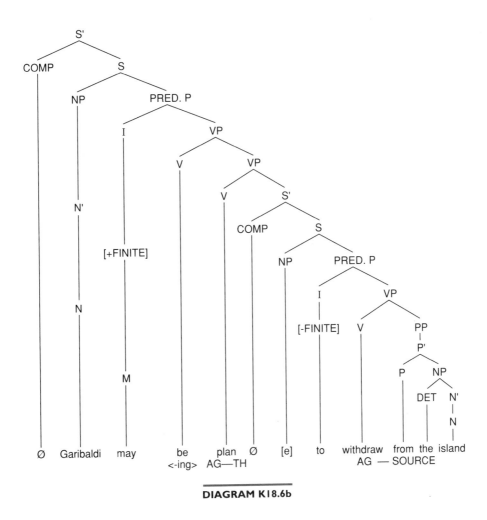

DIAGRAM K18.6b

7. Answers will vary.

EXERCISE SET 19

1. The *may* sentence can mean either that Joanne is forbidden to leave the house on Wednesdays—the action modality—or that it is possible that Joanne doesn't leave the house on Wednesdays—the belief modality.

   The *must* sentence also means that Joanne is forbidden to leave the house on Wednesdays—the action modality. It also has a belief modality meaning—the speaker strongly infers on the basis of information not specified in the sentence that Joanne does not leave the house on Wednesdays.

2.

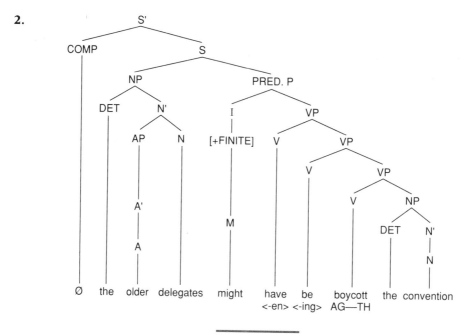

DIAGRAM KI9.2

3. a. In the action modality, the speaker is telling someone to see that Shelley leaves the house by five (in the future), while, in the belief modality sense, the speaker believes it to be possible that Shelley left that house by five (in the past).

b. In the action modality, the speaker is asking for permission for Jessica to carry that chair, while in the belief modality sense, the speaker is asking the addressee whether he believes Jessica able to carry that chair.

c. In the action modality, the speaker is telling someone that there is an obligation to ensure that the governor doesn't do favors for those men. In the belief modality sense, the speaker believes it is not possible that the governor is doing favors for those men.

4. Answers will vary.

5. Answers will vary.

6. Answers will vary.

7. Mr. Ogata's general problem with modals seems to be that he has accepted too whole-heartedly a generalization of limited applicability, the generalization that, to make modals refer to past time, perfect aspect *have* must be added. This generalization is reasonably valid for belief modals but works only sporadically for action modals. In fact, it isn't really the modality that is marked for past time reference but only the verb following.

Mr. Ogata uses the belief modality combinations *may have* and *could have* instead of action modality *could*, and belief modality *must have* instead of action modality *would have to*. There is another kind of error in *will ought to have*—the use of two core modals in sequence. Mr. Ogata has assumed that *will* is needed because future time reference is intended.

What might be done to help Mr. Ogata? He appears from this limited piece of data to be someone who wants to know and apply grammatical rules. So it should be helpful to provide him with some direct grammatical instruction in the modals, especially the two major modalities, with practice exercises and some examples of their use. But

Mr. Ogata might also benefit from help with alternative ways to express modal notions, for example, the use of adverbs like *probably, definitely,* and *perhaps.* Periphrastic modals like *be obliged to, be able to,* and *be unable to* might be easier for him to manage until he progresses further, as might predicates like *be forced to.*

EXERCISE SET 20

1. a.

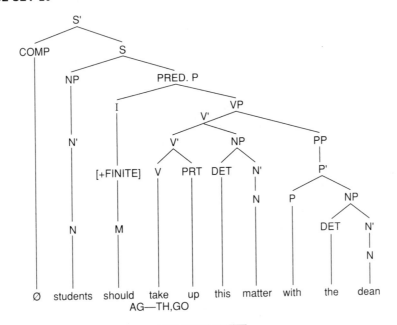

DIAGRAM K20.1a

b.

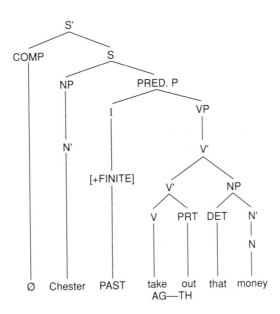

DIAGRAM K20.1b

3. Intransitive phrasal verbs: *come down, take off, cross over*

Separable transitive phrasal verbs: *see off, put up, carry in, check in, take out, turn down, find out*

Nonseparable transitive phrasal verbs: *see to, look after, look into*

Prepositional verbs: *believe in*

4.
  a. *Turn on* is a separable transitive phrasal verb meaning something like "push the button to activate the mechanism." The particle *on* can be moved to follow *the radio* (and has to be if *the radio* is replaced by *it*).
  b. *Turn on* here, meaning "attack," could at first glance be either a nonseparable transitive phrasal verb or a prepositional verb. But, through *wh* movement, we can form questions like *On whom did it turn?*, which seems well formed. So *turn on*, in its attack sense, must be a prepositional verb.
  c. In this sentence, *turn*, meaning "make a turn," has no special connection with *on*, a preposition heading its own prepositional phrase, an adjunct (i.e., an optional constituent).

5. The normal meaning is, of course, that the car made a turn into the garage; a possible but rather unlikely meaning is that the car was magically converted into a parking garage.

6.
  a. The *off* can be shifted to the position after the object and it cannot be fronted with *wh* movement, so *put off* must be a separable transitive phrasal verb.
  b. The verb and the *for* can be separated by an adverb like *energetically*, but the adverb cannot occur between the *for* and the following object noun phrase, suggesting that *for* is a preposition. *Wh* movement is possible: *For what position is he running?* and the core meaning is located in the verb rather than in a verb plus preposition, since *against* and other prepositions can occur or the verb can occur without a preposition, as in *She's going to run again.* We conclude that this is an ordinary verb followed by a prepositional phrase.
  c. The *in* can be shifted to the position after the object and it cannot be fronted with *wh* movement, so *turn in* must be a separable transitive phrasal verb.

7. *We looked into the story and found out that Dr. Stanley had met (up) with an angry group of Kikuyu men who would not put up with his patronizing manner. They turned down his offer of glass beads and advised him to go back to his own country.*

Opinions may vary as to the effects of the changes. Some readers claimed they made no difference, others that the revised paragraph was less formal, more direct, more emphatic.

8. The verbs in (a) and (b) are transitive verbs, which should be immediately followed by their noun phrase objects. The writers have miscategorized the verbs. Sentence (d) has the wrong preposition. The writer has not yet learned the lexical structure with *to: expose NP to something.* However, (c) is quite different, since the writer has treated a prepositional verb and its preposition *after* as a separable transitive phrasal verb and has incorrectly shifted the preposition so that it follows its object.

EXERCISE SET 21

1. a.

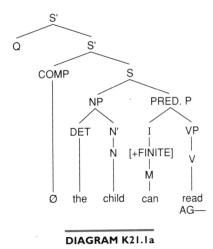

DIAGRAM K21.1a

The operator *can* is shifted by operator fronting into the complementizer slot.

b.

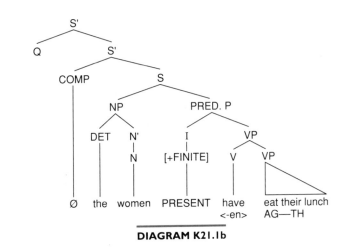

DIAGRAM K21.1b

Since the Inflection has no operator, the auxiliary verb *have* is shifted into the Inflection to become the operator. The tense amalgamates with the operator (since the subject is plural, the form resulting is still *have*) and the *-en* amalgamates with the main verb *eat*. Then operator fronting shifts the operator into the empty complementizer slot.

c.

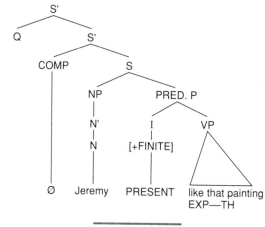

DIAGRAM K21.1c

The Inflection has no operator. It cannot recruit one from the verb phrase this time because the verb phrase contains no auxiliary verb. So the emergency operator *do* is inserted in the Inflection immediately after the tense. The two amalgamate, and then operator fronting shifts the operator into the complementizer slot.

2. a. Modals are the only operator verbs that start off in D-structure in the Inflection constituent. If the Inflection contains no operator verb, then one is recruited from the verb phrase or, if the verb phrase contains no auxiliaries, *do* is inserted.

    b. The verbs *be* and *have* can function as main verbs when the main predicate is an adjective or a noun phrase. But unlike other main verbs that have more semantic content and therefore can function as main *predicates,* they can in British English be shifted into the Inflection. In American English, main verb *have* is also treated as a main predicate, although main verb *be* is not and can be shifted. The generalization is that main *predicates* rather than main verbs cannot be shifted into the Inflection.

3. (b), (e), (f).

4. The (b) sentence is the more likely form if the speaker thinks that someone probably is there.

5. The (b) sentence is the more likely form if the speaker thinks that the addressee probably has the money.

6. Some variation is to be expected in the interpretation of the context and function of these sentences. A discussion of class responses can be very interesting. Here is one plausible set of responses:

    a. No answer is expected. The speaker is expressing outrage at some supposedly stupid behavior by the addressee.

    b. The speaker suspects that the addressee hasn't brought the money.

    c. The speaker may be seeking reassurance that the addressee has brought the money.

    d. The speaker may be irritated that the addressee takes for granted help from the speaker.

7. a. The speaker may have assumed that the *do* operator is used for all *yes-no* questions.
   b. The speaker isn't aware that *any* is a negative polarity item and thus occurs only in negatives and *yes-no* questions. The corresponding positive polarity form is *some*, but the indefinite article *a* would do.
   c. The speaker has applied operator fronting to an embedded question. The complementizer slot to which an operator is moved is filled by *if* in this example.
   d. When a negative occurs in either the main clause or the tag, the other verb must be affirmative.
   e. Since the *be* in *be rich* is not the main predicate, it is the verb that must function as the operator.

EXERCISE SET 22

1. The first *do* is of course the operator, while the second is the main predicate. As the main predicate, this *do* must be in the D-structure.

2. a. The candidate asked what the voters wanted.
   b. We wondered whether the extreme nationalists would agree to that proposal.

3. Answers will vary.

4.

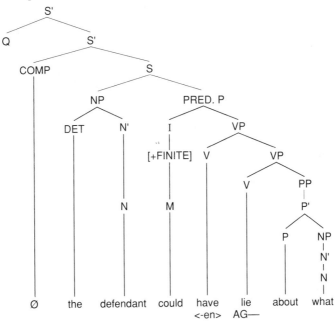

DIAGRAM K22.4

The perfect aspect *have* causes the verb following to be in its past participle form *lied*. The modal verb *could* functions as the operator. Operator fronting shifts *could* around the subject into the complementizer slot: *Could the defendant [t] have lied about what?* Next, the *wh* word is moved to the Q slot, yielding *What could the defendant [t] have lied about [t]?* A clumsier alternative would be to shift the whole prepositional phrase containing the *wh* noun phrase. The resulting sentence is *About what could the defendant [t] have lied [t]?*

5. The sentence is ambiguous as to whether the questioner wants to know when Prince Charles made the announcement or when the flight was supposed to take place. The *when* originated either in the predicate phrase in the container clause or in the predicate phrase in the embedded clause.

6. Answers will vary. Virginia French Allen calls operators *green words* (using a traffic light metaphor) because they are the words that *go* (move) when questions are formed.[2] They are also words that allow negatives to follow them. Students can make false affirmative statements about something serious or humorous they pretend they can do (knit, fly a helicopter, etc.), then convert them into negatives while telling the truth, and finally form them into questions addressed to other students. *Do* is an emergency green word when no other is available.

7. The prosecutor's questions are all heavily loaded to presume the defendant's guilt rather than determine the facts. The first *wh* question (*How did you ...*) is couched so as to presuppose that the defendant participated in a riot. The defendant challenges the prosecutor's characterization of what happened, claiming that she was participating in a *meeting*, not a riot, and that the meeting was disrupted by the security force. The prosecutor's next question changes the characterization to *disturbance*, but the question is also phrased so as to presuppose that the defendant caused the disturbance, inquiring only as to her motive. The prosecutor's next two questions contain the presuppositions that the defendant wanted to disrupt the factory and that she assaulted a security guard. In all the questions so far, the prosecutor has used *wh* questions that take for granted the defendant's guilt and simply ask about her motives. Only in the last question in the extract does he make a direct charge, one that she could answer *yes* or *no* to without assenting to more hidden assumptions. Even that question, a tag question, is slanted toward the affirmative (compare *You didn't attack him, did you?*).

8. The child simply provides the predicate *fall down* in first reporting the incident. Since *fall down* is intransitive, the mother uses a *wh* question directed at the subject of *fall down*. However, the child changes to a subjectless transitive verb with *it* as its object, thereby not providing any additional information except that the child must have been holding the thing that dropped. The mother then shifts to a *wh* question directed at the object of *drop*, providing immediately after the question a candidate, *cashew*, for the object. The child assents. Five minutes later the child's second report uses the intransitive verb preceded by a filled subject slot. The child has thus made the connection between the subject position for *fall down* and the object position for *drop*.

EXERCISE SET 23

1.

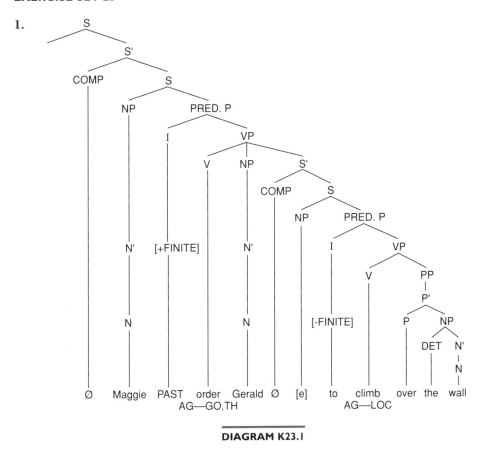

DIAGRAM K23.1

2. The noun phrase *Josephine* has been moved from the subject slot of the embedded clause *Josephine to like Napoleon* because it would not get case in its original slot but would get nominative case in the empty subject slot of the container clause as well as satisfying the subject constraint for that clause.

3. b. *my request to Josephine to take me to the Emperor*
   c. *the interrogator's claim that Arkoff had lied*
   d. *her conviction that Leif was still alive*
   e. *the ambassador's decision to close the consulate*
   f. *their conspiracy to destroy the printing presses*

4. The noun phrase *that man* has been shifted from the subject slot of the embedded clause *that man to build a cottage. Easy* is one of the class of predicates we described as *tough* predicates. These predicates allow *tough* movement, the movement of the object noun phrase of a verb or preposition in an embedded clause into an empty subject slot in the container clause. The original embedded clause subject *that man* cannot get case in its embedded clause slot; presumably, that is why it was shifted. But the *tough* predicate allows only the object to be moved. The sentence needs the complementizer *for*

to be placed before *that man*, allowing it to receive objective case. Grammatical S-structures can now be formed by using filler *it* in the container clause, as in *It is easy for that
man to build a cottage,* or alternatively by using *tough* movement of the embedded clause
object, as in *A cottage is easy for that man to build,* or even by shifting the whole embedded clause *for that man to build a cottage* into the container subject slot.

5. All three involve removal of arguments from slots adjacent to the predicates that
assign them their thematic roles, so the comprehension difficulties they pose should be
very similar.

6.   a.

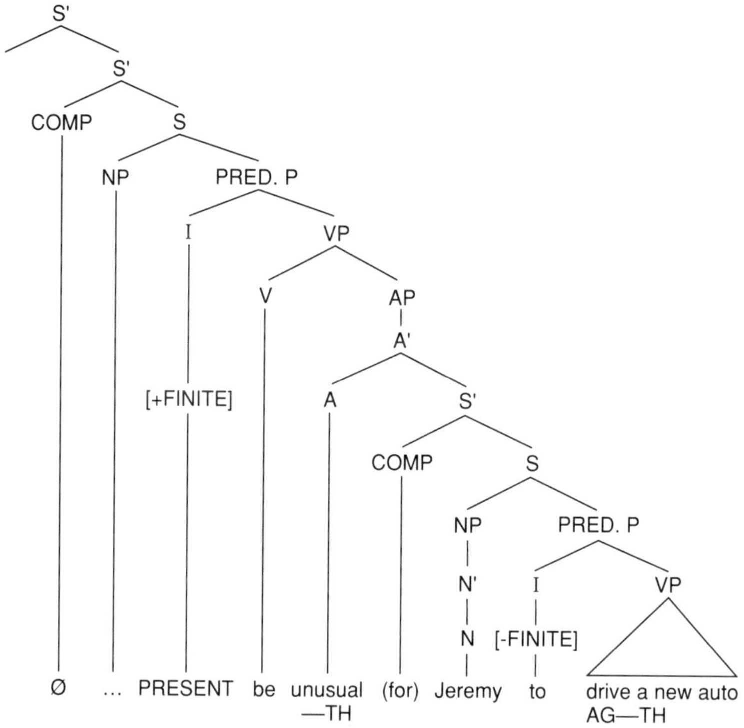

DIAGRAM K23.6a

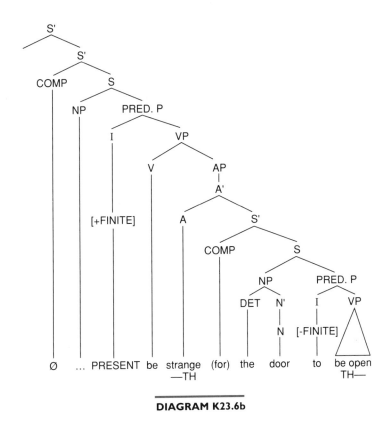

DIAGRAM K23.6b

b. In both sentences the noun phrase subject of the embedded clause has been incorrectly moved to the subject slot of the container clause. For the noun phrase to be assigned objective case, unless the complementizer *for* must be inserted. Grammatical S-structures can now be formed by using filler *it* in the container clause, as in *It is unusual for Jeremy to have a new auto* and *It is strange for the door to be open. Unusual* and *strange* are not *tough* predicates and thus *tough* movement of the embedded clause object is not allowed. As an alternative to inserting *it,* the whole embedded clause could have been moved into the container subject slot.

7. Answers will vary.

EXERCISE SET 24

1. Here are two further sample items:
    d. The committee suggested (stop) the project but the situation seemed (get) worse.
    e. They refused (admit) the inspectors because they hadn't finished (destroy) the evidence.
2. *Johnson's granting the award to Katz*
    a. gerundive   b. *of* (preposition)
    that no further action was necessary
    a. finite clause   b. *felt* (verb)

for the courts to take up the matter
    a. nonfinite clause   b. *anxious* (adjective)
for him to leave the country
    a. nonfinite clause   b. *permission* (noun)
that the President trusted him
    a. finite clause   b. *sign* (noun)

3.

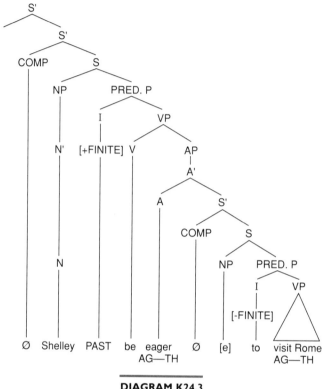

DIAGRAM K24.3

4.   a. nonfinite clause, gerundive
     b. nonfinite clause, gerundive
     c. gerundive
     d. nonfinite clause, gerundive
     e. nonfinite clause
     f. finite clause, gerundive

5. Essentially the first sentence of (a) indicates that she heard him knock a number of times, while the second can be used when referring to a single knock. In the first sentence of (b), the speaker presents the situation as an ongoing activity of some duration; the speaker may not have seen her start the swim and may even have not seen her arrive at the shore. In the second sentence, however, the focus is less on witnessing of the ongoing activity and more seeing the totality of her swim to the shore from its start to its completion.

6.   a. *ask, determine, establish, find out, inquire, know, show, state, tell, test, doubt, see, sure, unsure, clear, doubt.* Some of these sound better with nonfinite *whether* clauses if they are negated, and a few do not allow nonfinite *whether* clauses. Speakers have been found to vary considerably in their judgments of some sentences containing predicates with nonfinite *whether* clauses. For me, the predicates in the list that don't allow nonfinite *whether* clauses are *state, test,* and *doubt.*

b. As indicated by the examples below, nonfinite *whether* clauses refer exclusively to requests for permission for specified actions to be carried out, while the finite clauses may also include other kinds of situations. Both are embedded interrogatives.

*She wanted to know **whether she was a good combat pilot**.*
(Compare *Am I a good combat pilot?*, the unembedded question.)
*She wanted to know **whether to fly with the squadron**.*
(Compare *Should I fly with the squadron?*, the unembedded question.)
*?She wanted to know **whether to be a good combat pilot**.*

7. Although these predicates appear forward oriented, all permit gerundive complements, while none of them allow nonfinite complements. It's difficult to think of a good semantic explanation for this. The predicates *anticipate, imagine,* and *foresee* refer to the experiencing of an event before it happens, while *predict* refers to the reporting of an event before it happens. Thus, in all cases, the future or possible experience is viewed as having happened or in progress, as if it were an already realized event, the kind that gerundive complements typically designate.

EXERCISE SET 25

1. a.

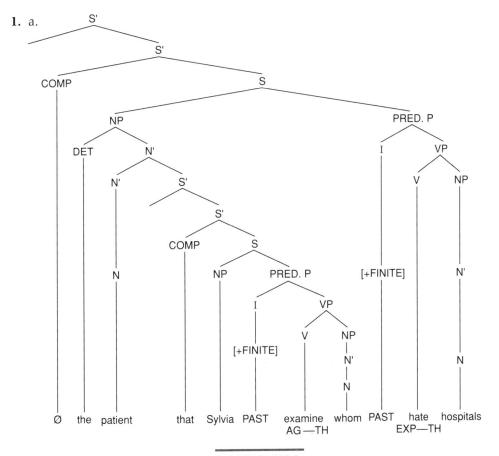

DIAGRAM K25.1a

b.

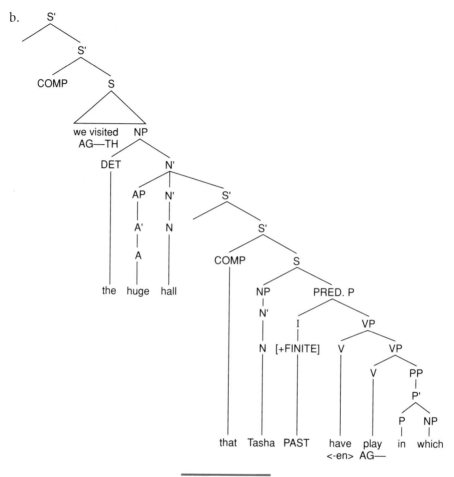

DIAGRAM K25.1b

c.

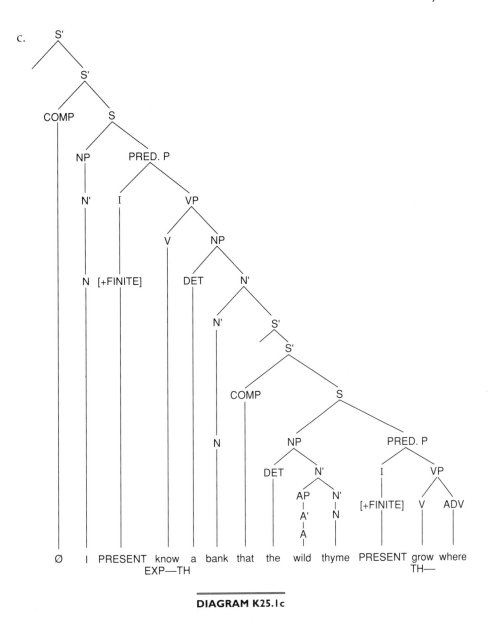

DIAGRAM K25.1c

2. The relative pronoun *where* is shifted into the vacant S-bar slot before *that,* and then *that* is deleted.

3. The first sentence, which contains an appositive, refers to a single flying saucer and then adds some additional details about its passengers. The second sentence, with a restrictive relative, distinguishes this particular flying saucer from others, for which the passenger description is not valid. The restrictive relative clause helps identify the flying saucer.

4. The normal function of a proper noun phrase like *Stephen King* is to refer to a single, unique individual. But the student's counterexample assumes that there are many individuals named *Stephen King* and asks for a more precise identification. In that sentence the proper noun phrase has been converted into a common noun phrase with a restrictive relative. When this happens, a determiner is needed. Note that such noun phrases can be plural: *There are three Stephen Kings in the phone book.*

5. In the (a) sentence, Jane is the one to do the talking while the friends are the listeners. But in the (b) sentence, the friends are the ones to do the talking while Jane is the listener. Here are two paraphrases with relative clauses:

    a. *Jane needs friends who she can talk to.*
    b. *Jane needs friends who will talk to her.*

6. Answers will vary.

7. Answers will vary. Here are two examples:

    a. *They met the woman. She recommended me for the position.*
    Subject: *They met the woman who [t] recommended me for the position.*

    b. *She was the doctor. I went to her about my skin rash.*
    Object of preposition: *She was the doctor that I went to [t] about my skin rash.*

8. Answers will vary. A large photograph of, say, a class of ten-year-olds provides opportunities to have students question each other as to the identity of a child that one is thinking of:

    A: *I am thinking of a boy in the second row.*
    B: *Is it the boy who is wearing a green jacket?*
       Is it the boy with a missing tooth?

A catalogue could serve as a stock list for younger learners to "shop" with. They would have to specify to a learner (or teacher) acting as shopkeeper which goods they want to buy. The catalogue might be available only for the shopkeeper's use. Such an exercise would draw on both production and comprehension skills.

NOTES

1. Sandra L. McKay, *Teaching Grammar: Form, Function and Technique* (New York: Pergamon Press, 1985), 62-63.

2. Virginia French Allen, *Inside English* (New York: Regents, 1983), 23.

GLOSSARY

adjunct: an optional constituent of a sentence such as a *because* clause or an adverb like *rapidly.*

anaphor: one of the two types of noun phrase, the other being *pronominal,* that refer to an antecedent. Anaphors must have their antecedent in the same minimal clause or noun phrase, that is, in the same local domain. Examples are reflexive forms like *herself* and reciprocal forms like *each other.*

antecedent: the usually more fully specified noun phrase to which a pronominal or an anaphor refers.

argument: a grammatical unit such as a noun phrase or clause required by a grammatical predicate; also a semantic unit (often shown as an x or y) required by a semantic predicate.

aspect: a grammatical marking usually used to indicate time contour of a situation—momentary, in progress, completed, iterative—and having a variety of discourse functions; English has perfect and progressive aspects.

aspectual predicates: predicates denoting beginning, continuing, and ending.

assertion: both what is declared to be the case and the act of declaring it. Assertions express information presumed new.

case: a property assigned after D-structure to noun phrases by case-assigning forms like verbs, prepositions, and Inflection, sometimes covert, sometimes overtly shown, as on possessives and pronouns. In certain constructions, case is not assigned by any assigner but instead is already present at D-structure and is known as *inherent case.* Case encodes the noun phrase's grammatical relations within its clause or container noun phrase. The cases assigned in English are nominative, objective, and possessive.

categoriality: the property enabling us to assign constituents to categories on the basis of shared grammatical characteristics.

classifier: the general term across languages for a word or suffix which specifies the class of a noun and typically occurs with a number word.

clause: the basic sentence unit consisting of a predicate and one or more argument noun phrases or clauses.

complement: in English a normally required phrase (or clause) following a head word such as a verb or preposition. In constituent D-structure trees, complements are always sisters of N, V, A, or P.

complementizer: an element such as *that, for,* or sometimes a covert category that introduces a clause.

conjoined: used of two or more constituents of the same rank or type that are linked together, usually with *and*.

constituent: a word or group of words functioning as a unit in a larger construction.

container clause: clause containing a dependent clause; container clauses are sometimes referred to as matrix clauses.

coordination: the linking of two constituents of equal rank.

copula: a verb such as *be* and *become* that is followed by a complement—an adjective phrase, a noun phrase, or a prepositional phrase—having a predicate function, e.g., a predicate noun phrase.

counter: a noun such as *slice, drop,* or *chunk,* typically used in English to convert a non-count noun phrase into a count noun phrase.

counterfactual: used to indicate what is contrary to fact.

covert noun phrase: a noun phrase that is psychologically and semantically real, but which is not phonetically represented; usually marked with an [e] in this book; a [t] is used to mark a slot from which a constituent has been moved.

D-structure (*also* **deep structure**): the level at which the basic semantic relations (thematic roles) are established within the Principles-and-Parameters model of grammar.

deep structure: see *D-structure*.

dependent clause: a clause other than the main clause of a sentence.

descriptive grammar (*also* **scientific grammar**): a description of the actual language forms used by native speakers of a language or dialect.

determiner: the broad category including the articles *a* and *the,* demonstratives like *that* and *these,* and quantifiers such as *all* and *three*.

direct object: the noun phrase or clause functioning as the object of a transitive verb or the second object of a ditransitive verb.

distribution: the set of positions in which a particular category can occur.

ditransitive: a subclass of transitive verbs having two objects; also a clause containing such a verb.

dynamic predicate: a predicate signifying an action or process; can occur as an imperative or with progressive aspect.

embedded clause: a dependent clause functioning as the argument of a predicate.

extraposition: the movement of a constituent to the end of its clause.

finite: a finite clause in English with either a tense (past or present) or a modal. Verbs in the present or past tense are also said to be finite.

gerundive: the term used in this grammar for a nonfinite clause-like construction functioning as an argument of a predicate and/or object of a preposition. The verb always has the *-ing* suffix. The term *gerund* is also used for this construction. Some traditional grammars differentiate between *gerunds,* which are defined as verbal nouns, and *gerundives,* defined as verbal adjectives.

grammatical relations: grammatically defined relations within a construction; these include *subject, object, head, modifier,* and *adjunct.*

head: the required lexical constituent of a phrase that gives the phrase its identity as a noun phrase, verb phrase, and so forth. The nonlexical constituent *tense* is sometimes defined as head of the predicate phrase.

hierarchy: the property contituents have of belonging alone or with other constituents to higher level constituents, which may in turn form yet higher level constituents.

imperative clause: a kind of nonfinite clause used to express orders, requests, and exhortations.

indicative mood: the mood used to express what is real or true, expressed as finite verbs in English.

indirect discourse: speech or thought reported rather than directly quoted.

indirect object: the first object of a ditransitive verb like *give* or *tell.*

Inflection (abbreviated as I): the sentence constituent that marks a sentence for finiteness; it typically contains present or past tense, a modal, or the infinitive marker *to.*

inherent case (*also* **structural case**): an exceptional kind of case not assigned to a noun phrase by an adjacent constituent but already marked on the noun phrase by virtue of its position in D-structure. English examples are the possessive case for possessor noun phrases preceding a noun head and objective case for direct objects in a ditransitive clause.

intransitive: a term for verbs not taking an object.

lexical category: a class of words, prefixes, or suffixes distinguished by shared grammatical characteristics.

lexicon: the set of words, word stems, and affixes of a language.

linearity: the property constituents have of occurring in linear sequences, one constituent following another.

local domain: a term for the smallest constituent containing a pronominal or anaphor and its antecedent; used in discussions of pronominals and anaphors.

main clause (*also* **independent clause**): the highest level clause, one which can often stand on its own as an independent sentence.

markedness: the degree of exceptionality, a continuum ranging from *unmarked* (very typical, predictable) to *highly marked* (very exceptional). The word *marked* is also used to indicate a marking of, for example, tense, number, or agreement.

modal: a type of verb, such as *may, can,* and *would,* occurring with other verbs in finite clauses in which no verb has past or present tense.

modality: a class of meanings signified by modals (and also by other forms such as *perhaps).*

modifier: a phrase inside a larger phrase that provides further information, but which is not required by the head word of the container phrase. On constituent structure trees, modifier phrases are sisters of N-bar, V-bar, or A-bar.

morphology: the study of word forms and affixes.

new information: the part of the propositional content a speaker assumes (or pretends to assume) is new to the addressee.

nonfinite: a verb or clause in English without tense or a modal, typically with *to* before the verb.

old information (*also* **given information**): the part of the propositional content a speaker assumes is already familiar to the addressee.

operator: the modal or other non-main verb that precedes the subject in questions, and, in negative clauses, precedes *not* or *-n't*.

parameter: a range of options from which a language may select a setting; for example, on the verb-object parameter, Japanese selects the object before verb setting, while English selects the object after verb setting.

passive construction: a construction in which the verb is in its past participle form and is preceded by *be* or another copula; the argument, typically the agent, that would have served as subject of its non-passive, i.e., *active* counterpart, is in an optional *by* phrase. The construction and the copula-verb combination are both said to be in the passive voice.

pedagogical grammar: a grammar organized for learning and teaching about the structures of a language.

periphrastic modal: in contrast to *core* modals which have no tense marking, periphrastic modals, e.g., *have to*, can show tense.

phrasal category: the higher order type of constituent to which a lexical category belongs.

polarity: a two-way parameter, e.g., affirmative and negative.

pragmatics: the study of the ways in which knowledge of the broader context of an utterance affects the ways in which an utterance is understood.

predicate: the central semantic unit of a proposition, requiring one or more arguments; also the relation that the central grammatical unit of a construction, typically a verb or adjective, has to the construction.

prescriptive grammar: a set of rules requiring certain ways of speaking and writing and rejecting other ways as incorrect even when in common use by native speakers.

processing constraint: a limitation on possible forms and combinations reflecting human mental or physical limitations.

pronominal: one of the two types of noun phrase, the other being *anaphor,* that refer to an antecedent.

proposition: a semantic unit consisting of a predicate, its arguments (or "participants"), and any optional participants.

propositional content: the meaning, expressed as one or more propositions, resulting from the combination of the meanings of the parts of a clause or other complex form. This meaning may be modified or replaced by meanings due to pragmatic factors.

quantifier: a word such as *all, many, five,* and *few,* which occurs most often in the determiner slot.

reference: the relation between a linguistic element (such as a noun phrase) and the entity it designates. For example, the noun phrase *John Keats* designates a 19th-century English poet. This poet is the *referent* of the noun phrase *John Keats.* Anaphors and pronominals refer to more fully specified noun phrases with nonlinguistic referents.

relative clause (*also* **adjective clause**): a clause embedded in a noun phrase and usually modifying the head noun. It narrows down the reference of the whole noun phrase or provides additional information about the referent.

role: see *thematic role.*

S-bar (or S′): the constituent made up of the complementizer plus the clause the complementizer introduces. There is also a higher level S-bar to which *wh* forms can be shifted.

S-structure (*also* **surface structure**): the level in the Principles-and-Parameters model (or Government-and-Binding model) at which sentences undergo no further transformations and are ready for conversion into phonetic sequences and for the application of semantic interpretation processes.

semantics: the meanings associated with the forms of the language.

specifier: a relation within a phrase borne by forms such as articles (for noun phrases) and intensifiers such as *very* (for adjectives and adverbs).

speech act: an act performed by uttering a specific language form such as *I promise to tell the truth,* which, when uttered, is also an act of promising.

stative predicate: a predicate signifying a state; does not occur as an imperative.

subject constraint: a constraint in English requiring that finite clauses have overt subjects at S-structure.

subjunctive mood: the mood, expressed with uninflected verbs in English finite clauses, used to indicate that the situation is hypothetical or that it is dependent on some other situation or that action is recommended.

subordinate clause: a dependent clause functioning as an adjunct—grammatically, an optional clause.

subordinator: a clause introducer that marks its clause as dependent in relation to another clause and also indicates the relevance of the clause content to the content of the clause on which it depends.

surface structure: see *S-structure.*

syntax: the grammatical principles, units, and relations involved in sentence structure.

tense: a syntactic constituent marking a clause as finite; English has two tenses, past and present. Tense is often but not always used to mark time reference, either absolute, i.e., relative to the time of utterance, or relative, i.e., relative to the time of some other situation.

thematic role (*also* **theta role**): the semantic role such as agent or theme assigned to a noun phrase or clause by a verb, adjective, or other predicate, or (sometimes) by a preposition. For a listing and definition of thematic roles, see Chapter 3.

topic: the part of the information that tells what the sentence is about; in English, always definite or generic.

topic-prominent language: a language in which sentences tend to be organized around two major constituents, one representing the topic, the other the comment; such sentences are called Topic-Comment structures.

transformation: a process as formulated within the Principles-and-Parameters model, shifting constituents from their D-structure slots into other positions.

transitive: a term for verbs having an object; also used for the clauses containing such verbs.

utterance: a speech form spoken or written.

valency: the property possessed by a predicate of requiring a certain number of argument noun phrases or clauses.

INDEX

A

a, 98, 108–10

A-bar, 74

Absolute time reference, 194

Abstract nouns, 112

Acquisition of language, 33, 36–37

Action modality, 225–33, 241*n8*
  and negatives, 228–30
  relative strengths in, 230–31
  and speech acts, 232–33
  and time reference, 231–32

Active voice, 159
  and copular verbs, 56
  and participial modifiers, 313
  vs. passive voice, 160, 168–71
  and thematic roles, 21, 27–28
  and transitive and intransitive clauses, 55

Adjective clauses, *see* Relative clauses

Adjective phrases:
  embedded clauses in, 74–76
  as modifiers, 101
  predicate adjective phrases, 56, 59–60
  in *wh* clefts, 178

Adjectives:
  arguments of, 74–75
  and case, 139–40
  and complements, 99, 283
  and objects, 74–76
  vs. past participles with *get*, 167
  and propositional content, 13

in sentence structure, 42
and thematic roles, 74–76
and verbs, 75
see also Adjective phrases;
  Predicate adjectives

Adjuncts, 55, 68–69, 160, 244, 298, 313

Adverbial clauses, 67
see also Subordinate clauses

Adverbs:
  directional adverbs, 247
  frequency adverbials, 204
  and subordinate clauses, 67
  and time reference, 203, 234

Adversative passive, 168

after, 67, 92*n4*, 205

Agent role, 20, 23, 26–27
  and *by*, 244
  and passive voice, 21, 160, 167, 170

all, 111

a lot of, 112

Alternative questions, 263, 274

although, 68, 71–72

Ambiguity, 38–40, 102–3, 226

an, 98, 108–9

Anaphora, 133*n2*

Anaphoric, 133*n2*

Anaphors, 127, 128–32, 133*n2*
  see also Reciprocals; Reflexives

Antecedents, 117
  and anaphors, 128–32, 130–32
  of covert noun phrases, 127–28

and pronominals, 120–24, 130–31

any, 112, 265

anyone, 128

Appositive relative clauses, 304, 309–11, 319*n2*

Arguments, 13, 14–16
  of adjectives, 74–75
  of *believe*-class verbs, 297
  clauses as, 14–15, 21
    of adjectives, 74
    embedded, 66, 68–69, 82
  and predicates, 291–301
  in complex sentences, 281–84
  in ditransitive clauses, 57–58
  in D-structure, 76–77
  noun phrases as, 27–28, 74–75
  of prepositions, 25–26
  semantic roles of, 15–16
  and valency, 10, 12–14, 17, 297

Aristotle, 187

Articles, 97

as...as, 68

as if, 68

Aspect, 187, 199–215
  and core modals, 218
  in sentence structure, 199–200, 210–12
  uses of, 201–10

Aspectual predicates, 297–98

assassinate, 9–10

Assertion, 149

as though, 68

Austronesian languages, 316